THE
AFRICANS

THE AFRICANS

▲

How do you explain a continent where hundreds of thousands of people have been killed for no other reason than that they belonged to the wrong tribe? How do you explain a continent whose heads of state applauded Idi Amin when he walked into a summit wearing his Stetson and six-shooters, having just presided over the massacre of several thousand Ugandans, including the Anglican archibishop? What do you say about the president of Tanzania, who translated Shakespeare into Swahili in his spare time and held more political prisoners than South Africa? For every Amin, however, there is a Leopold Sedar Senghor, the former Senegalese president, an erudite man who was a strong contender for the 1962 Nobel Prize for Literature. For every corrupt and callous African president stashing millions of dollars in his Swiss bank account there is an African teacher earning $60 a month, proud that his students are Africa's hope for tomorrow.

This is a book about Africa today: the story of people who won their freedom on battlefields and at negotiating tables, only to discover that their white colonial masters had been replaced by black neocolonial leaders more concerned with personal power and wealth than national consensus or development.

Many readers will find this an unsettling book because the Africa of the 1980s is neither a happy nor hopeful place. Across the whole continent economies are collapsing, cities are deteriorating, food production is declining, populations are growing like weed-seeds turned loose in a garden. Governments fall at the whim of illiterate sergeants and disgruntled despots, prisons are as overcrowded as the farmlands are empty, and at last count the number of refugees in Africa had reached the incredible figure of five million.

But, troubled as these early years of nationhood have been, Africa need not dwell forever in the uncertain twilight zone. Its dreams have been only mislaid, not lost.

ALSO BY DAVID LAMB

The Arabs

T H E
AFRICANS

▲

DAVID LAMB

With a New Preface and Epilogue

VINTAGE BOOKS
A Division of Random House
New York

Vintage Books Edition, June 1987

Preface and Epilogue Copyright © 1987 by David Lamb
Copyright © 1983 by David Lamb
Map Copyright © 1983 by Anita Karl and J. Kemp

Library of Congress Cataloging in Publication Data
Lamb, David.
The Africans.
Reprint. Originally published: New York: Random
House, c 1982. With new preface and epilogue.
Bibliography: p.
Includes index.
1. Africa, Sub-Saharan—History—1960–
I. Title
[DT352.8.L28 1987] 967 86-40461
ISBN 0-394-75308-9

Manufactured in the United States of America
79B8

FOR SANDY, WHO WENT THE EXTRA MILE WITH ME

What does Africa . . . stand for?

—HENRY DAVID THOREAU, c. 1850

To build a nation, to erect a new civilization which can lay claim to existence because it is humane, we shall try to employ not only enlightened reason but also dynamic imagination.

—PRESIDENT LEOPOLD SENGHOR
of Senegal, c. 1960

Do you realize what wealth Africa has? People are cutting each other's throats for it, and it's only the tip of the iceberg. What Africans are doing to Africans is unbelievable.

—JOE KADHI, *Kenyan journalist,* 1976

We can't go on blaming the colonialists eternally for all our problems. Yes, they set up the system, but it is us who have been unable to change it.

—JOSEPH MAITHA, *University of Nairobi economics professor,* 1979

I dare to hope for the future of my Africa, though sometimes it is not easy.

—GODFREY AMACHREE, *a Nigerian chief and millionaire businessman,* 1980

CONTENTS

▲

INTRODUCTION

▲

Our ancient continent . . . is now on the brink of disaster, hurtling towards the abyss of confrontation,
caught in the grip of violence, sinking into the dark
night of bloodshed and death.

—EDEM KODJO, *secretary-general of the
Organization of African Unity*

WE ARRIVED IN AFRICA during the drought of 1976. The plains had
turned brown and had cracked. The cattle were dying and children's
bellies swelling. Thick black clouds engulfed Mount Kenya, where
powerful spirits are believed to dwell, influencing all that is evil and
good in the cycles of life. For nearly a year the gods had been angry
and not a drop of rain had fallen. An impoverished people waited
for better times, their lives controlled by forces they could neither
understand nor alter.

My wife, Sandy, and I stayed in Africa until 1980, she working as
a free-lance filmmaker, I as a correspondent for the *Los Angeles
Times*. Two new countries were born and eleven governments overthrown during these four years. The droughts came and went many
times. The refugee population grew into the millions, the wars
spread like brushfires. And through it all the Africans maintained a
resilience and stoicism unknown in the West. They simply carried
on, accepting both good fortune and misfortune with a single
thought: The Fates are powerful.

From our base in Nairobi, Kenya, I traveled through forty-eight
African countries, logging more than 300,000 miles by air, road and
rail. Sometimes, for months on end, I bounced from wars to coups
d'état thousands of miles apart, catching midnight flights to little-
known countries where very nice people were doing very terrible
things to one another. But the madcap moments of ferment were
not the real exhilaration of Africa. That came in the brief respites

when Africa was at peace with itself, and there was time to explore the cities and villages, to talk and question, to feel the exuberance and despair of a newly independent people caught between past and present.

I interviewed presidents and witch doctors, university professors and guerrilla leaders, merchants and peasants. I spent a few fearsome hours in one of Idi Amin's Ugandan jails, accused of being a mercenary or a CIA agent, and many wonderful days on the starlit African plains, where the stillness and solitude seem eternal. Over glasses of whiskey and cups of coffee, in stately mansions and homes made of cattle dung and mud, from the desert wastelands of Djibouti to the oil fields of Nigeria, I talked with hundreds of Africans about their countries, their lives, their dreams. This book, part political travelogue, part contemporary history and wholly personal, is a result of those travels and tries to answer two questions that perplex even the Africans themselves: What is Africa and who are the Africans?

I have limited the book to the area I know best—sub-Sahara Africa, which comprises the forty-six countries south of a line drawn from Morocco to Egypt. The five Moslem countries to the north share little politically or economically with the rest of contemporary Africa. But sub-Sahara Africa—or black Africa, as it is commonly called—contains cohesive elements enabling it to be considered as an entity. Even white-ruled South Africa, as peculiar a country as there is in the world today, can be explained within the context of its hostile black neighbors.

No continent has been more mistreated, misunderstood and misreported over the years than Africa. Ask an American to mention four things he associates with Africa and the answer is likely to be "pygmies, jungle, heat and lions." Yet pygmies have been all but extinct for decades, jungle is now as uncommon as snow in Southern California, the heat is no more intolerable than that in Washington, D.C., on a summer's day, and lions are so few in number that most Africans have never seen one.

If you had read Ernest Hemingway, you knew that Africa was an enchanting, spectacularly beautiful land; if you had read Robert Ruark, you knew that Africans were usually unsophisticated and occasionally savage. Not much else seemed worth knowing. Africa was a mere footnote to history, an appendage that one American journalist in World War II dismissed as "just a bunch of real estate." But the Africa of the 1980s can no longer be brushed aside so glibly. Africa today is influencing events and policies in foreign capitals from Moscow to Washington. Extraordinary changes are propelling it toward a destiny its presidents cannot comprehend or control. Where these changes take Africa will influence, and perhaps determine, the world's direction in the twenty-first century—*if* Africa can harness its natural and human resources. And if it can, Africa is the grand prize of the Third World.

When John Gunther published his book *Inside Africa*, in 1953, not a single black nation had gained its independence from the imperial powers of Europe. Today there are fifty-one independent countries in Africa, and every one except South Africa is ruled by the majority. The Africa that Gunther wrote about was the last frontier of white colonialism, an orderly, uneventful place where the pulse of nationalism beat only faintly. The Africa I encountered two decades later was the first outpost of black nationhood, volatile, unpredictable, truculent. Gunther's perspective was fashioned largely through interviews with white administrators and a handful of conservative Africans such as Emperor Haile Selassie of Ethiopia. But that Africa no longer exists. Today a journalist deals with Africans on their own terms, in their own territory—and finds that a new breed of radicals has replaced the old conservatives. The circumstances that shaped this change—and are still shaping it—were nothing short of cataclysmic.

If Africa is much discussed and little understood these days, it is hardly surprising, for the continent is as diverse and complex as it is huge. Africa is four times larger than the United States and has twice as many people. It spans seven time zones, and to fly from Nairobi in the east to Dakar, Senegal, in the west takes longer than to fly from New York to London. It is inhabited by 2,000 tribes or ethnic groups, most of which have a specific language or dialect. In many capitals you can have lunch with an Oxford-educated businessman who wears three-piece Western suits and asks you about last year's Superbowl game, then drive a few hours and dine on a recently slaughtered goat with illiterate herdsmen who hunt with bows and arrows, live on a barter economy and think all white men are missionaries or doctors.

To many Westerners, Africa simply makes no sense at all, primarily because they apply Western values to a land that is not comparable with any on earth. Punctuality, for instance, is an alien concept—noon can fall anywhere between 11 A.M. and 2 P.M. on the African clock—and although African airlines publish schedules, no one pays them much heed, least of all the airline companies themselves. Speaking concisely is not a regional trait, either, for most Africans will tell you what they think you want to hear. Ask an African to accomplish the impossible—"I'd like the sun to rise in the south tomorrow morning"—and he will smile, nod and say, "No problem." He knows perfectly well that there is a problem, but it's just his way of being accommodating.

How do you explain a continent where hundreds of thousands of people have been killed for no other reason than that they belonged to the wrong tribe? How do you explain a continent whose heads of state applauded Idi Amin when he walked into a summit wearing his Stetson and six-shooters, having just presided over the massacre of several thousand Ugandans, including the Anglican archbishop? What do you say about the president of Tanzania, who translated Shakespeare into Swahili in his spare time and held more political prisoners than South Africa? Or the pint-sized president of Gabon, who wears platform shoes, bans the word "pygmy" from his country's vocabulary, and while his countrymen are destitute, spends $2 million on a house in Beverly Hills, California, for his daughter and zips around Libreville in a gold-plated Cadillac followed by a silver-plated Cadillac ambulance?

For every Amin, however, there is a Léopold Sédar Senghor, the former Senegalese president, an erudite man who was a strong contender for the 1962 Nobel Prize for Literature. For every corrupt and callous African president stashing millions of dollars in his Swiss bank account, there is an African teacher earning $60 a month, proud that his students are Africa's hope for tomorrow. And for every reason there is to ignore sub-Sahara Africa as an inconsequential member of the international community, there are a dozen to treat it seriously. Among them:

First, Africa has one-third the votes in the United Nations, far more than any other region. Second, it has the largest reserves of untapped natural resources in the world, minerals essential to both the East and the West in times of war and peace. Third, its empty farmlands could feed itself and all of Western Europe. Even if another acre was never cleared, its fertile soil is capable of producing 130 times what it yields today.* Fourth, it is a potential battleground for the superpowers, who may well be as obsessed with Africa twenty years from now as they are with the Middle East

* This figure comes from a study made in 1979 by the U.S. Agency for International Development.

today. Fifth, it has human resources that are as undeveloped as its sunken treasures—455 million people, half of them no older than fifteen, who yearn for, and eventually will demand, lives free from disease, poverty and repression.

This is a book about those people and the events that shape their lives. It is not a survey of African art, culture, history or religion. It is only a book about Africa today, the story of people who won their freedom on battlefields and at negotiating tables, only to discover that their white colonial masters had been replaced by black neocolonial leaders more concerned with personal power and wealth than national consensus or development.

Many readers will find this an unsettling book because the Africa of the 1980s is neither a happy nor a hopeful place. The colonialists designed the scenario for disaster, and the Africans seem to be trying their best to fulfill it. Calamity waits within arms' reach, oblivious of Africa's potential strength. Across the whole continent, economies are collapsing, cities are deteriorating, food production is declining, populations are growing like weed-seeds turned loose in a garden. Governments fall at the whim of illiterate sergeants and disgruntled despots, prisons are as overcrowded as the farmlands are empty, and at last count the number of refugees in Africa had reached the incredible figure of five million—people driven from their homelands by wars, tyrants and poverty.

"Africa is dying," Edem Kodjo, secretary-general of the Organization of African Unity, told a group of African leaders in 1978. "If things continue as they are, only eight or nine of the present countries will survive the next few years. All other things being equal, absolute poverty, instead of declining, is likely to gain ground. It is clear that the economy of our continent is lying in ruins."

Events, no doubt, will overtake some sections of this book. Presidents I have interviewed and written about will be killed, imprisoned or exiled, political allegiances will waver, countries may even change their names. In Africa nothing political stays unchanged very long. But the people and happenings described here will, I believe, continue to be representative of Africa's third decade of independence.

As troubled as these early years of nationhood have been, Africa needs not dwell forever in the uncertain twilight zone. Its dreams have been only mislaid, not lost. The morass has escape routes. Africa is a continent of surprises: nothing is ever quite as it seems and nothing ever happens quite as it is supposed to.

PREFACE TO THE NEW EDITION

▲

ANYONE WHO HAS lived in Africa knows how tough it is to shake that wondrous continent from one's spirit and, after a year in the United States, Sandy and I returned in 1982. Based in Cairo, we stayed for another four years and went back often to visit the people and the places I had written about earlier.

The Africa I encountered on my second assignment remained an uneasy blend of hope and tragedy. Its economic health was growing more desperate by the month, yet a handful of countries had managed to achieve some genuine progress and many African leaders were engaged in an agonizing reappraisal of their priorities. What has become clear is that Africa alone cannot undo the damage of the past thirty years. It needs a massive global rescue effort, and it needs it now, before a disaster of wartime dimension befalls the continent.

Assigning blame for Africa's failures has become irrelevant, particularly because there is ample blame for all to share. But if Africa remains a sickly place into the 1990s, all the world suffers, and its economies and stability will be threatened. Just as surely as South Africa's system of apartheid is in its death throes, so must a new system of social justice, economic incentives and agricultural reform be born in black Africa. Perhaps then, from the ashes of what is past, Africa can get the fresh start it so desperately needs.

DAVID LAMB
Los Angeles
September 1986

THE
AFRICANS

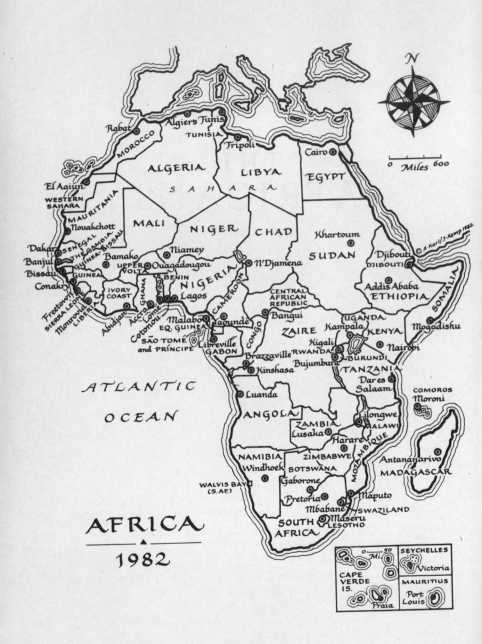

AFRICA
▲
1982

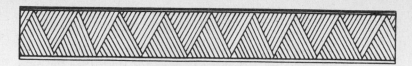

PORTRAIT
OF A CONTINENT

▲

We got caught up in the conflict of culture, of trying to graft the so-called sophistication of the European society to our African society. The result so far has been an abysmal failure. We are betwixt and between.

—LIEUTENANT GENERAL OLUSEGUN OBASANJO,
former Nigerian head of state

CARLOS MIRANDA, former guerrilla fighter and one-time prisoner of war, sat with his friends in the barren little café, idling away the Saturday afternoon over a bottle of Portuguese wine and a few memories. There really wasn't much else to do, anyway. Cacheu, in Guinea-Bissau, is a small quiet town and the day was hot. So the men sat at their rickety wooden table, just talking quietly or doing nothing at all, expending little energy except that needed to brush away the flies. The walls of the bar were bare save for a faded photograph of the president, Luis de Almeida Cabral,* and the stock of refreshments had dwindled to a dust-covered jug of rum, a case of Coca-Cola and an odd assortment of white wines, served lukewarm because the refrigerator, like the electricity in Cacheu, had long since broken down. The near-sighted bartender was propped like a broom against the refrigerator, squinting and sweating, and when a bottle slipped from his hands and shattered at his feet, he kicked the glass under the counter without a word and wiped his damp hands across his T-shirt. His family—a wife and seven young children— was sprawled out on the concrete floor nearby, fast asleep.

"Francisco broke another bottle," Miranda said. "No wonder there's nothing left to drink." Francisco had indeed been dropping too many precious bottles of Coke lately, and his carelessness had become a source of much annoyance.

---

* Cabral was overthrown in November 1980 by his prime minister and accused, among other crimes, of murder and torture. He was later allowed to take up exile residence in Cape Verde.

Outside the bar, along the one sandy road that leads away, to Bissau, once the capital of Portuguese Guinea and since 1974 the capital of the independent West African state of Guinea-Bissau, the town was very still. Dogs lay panting in the shade of drooping palms; a solitary woman sat in the square with a dozen turnips spread out in the dirt before her. The ancient rusted cannon atop the fort at the edge of town pointed toward the Cacheu River estuary; downstream, a hundred yards from the fort, three abandoned patrol boats swayed to and fro in the lazy currents. Lingering there between the fort and the boats were three centuries of history, a history that spoke of the birth and death of the Portuguese empire in Africa and the dawn of Africa's own troubled independence.

The stone fort, built in 1647, had been the symbol of Portugal's might when its colonial rule stretched from Africa to South America to Asia. And the Soviet-made patrol boats, left to rot and sink in the muddy waters of the river, were the discarded tools of the longest and militarily most successful liberation war ever waged in black Africa against colonial authority.

Carlos Miranda had been a soldier, and later a prisoner of the Portuguese, in that war, which lasted from 1961 to 1974. His guerrilla movement, with significant help from the Soviet Union and Cuba, had fielded a 10,000-man army and eventually forced the 35,-000 Portuguese and African government troops to abandon the countryside and withdraw into fortified urban areas. Their victory directly influenced the coup d'état that brought down the Lisbon dictatorship on April 25, 1974.

"You ask what the difference between colonialism and independence means to me," the thirty-six-year-old Miranda said, filling my glass with wine. "Well, I will tell you. The difference is great. Now I go to bed at night and I sleep comfortably. I do not worry about the secret police. And I do not tip my hat to the *Tuga* [Portuguese].

"Now I speak to a white man without fear. Before, white and black did not talk. But now at this moment I have the pleasure of sitting with you, a white, and I speak to you like a man. That is all we fought for, the right to respect. We did not hate the Portuguese people, only the Portuguese government. Even if you were Portuguese, I would still be happy to sit with you, because now we are equals."

It was, I thought, an eloquent response. Miranda—a customs clerk with nine children and a salary of $50 a month—had not been a leader in the liberation war, only one of the foot soldiers. But it was for people like him that the war had been fought, and independence had given him a priceless reward: self-respect. For Guinea-Bissau as a whole, though, things had not gone particularly well since the first unfurling of the country's yellow and green flag with a black star on a red field. Only one person in twenty could read, life expectancy at birth was only thirty-five years, and 45 percent of the children died before the age of five. Shortages of everything from rice to soap were epidemic, and when a merchant in the capital put four hundred pairs of just imported shoes on display one day during my visit, such a mob showed up that the police had to be called to restore order. The country had a small peanut crop and some animal hides to export and bauxite reserves worth exploiting, but not much else to build an economic foundation on. In all of Guinea-Bissau (population 800,000) there were only 24,000 jobs, 82 percent of them in the public sector.

Unlike two other former Portuguese colonies, Mozambique and Angola, Guinea-Bissau had not been a white-settler colony. The Portuguese came only to administer and to save enough money to retire on back home. Within a few weeks of independence, all but 350 of the 2,500 Portuguese in Guinea-Bissau hurried home. Most departed with no sorrows. And what they left as a legacy of three hundred years of colonial rule was pitifully little: fourteen university graduates, an illiteracy rate of 97 percent and only 265 miles of paved roads in an area twice the size of New Jersey. There was only one modern plant in Guinea-Bissau in 1974—it produced beer for the Portuguese troops—and as a final gesture before leaving, the Portuguese destroyed the national archives.

In many ways Guinea-Bissau is a microcosm of a continent where events have conspired against progress, where the future remains a hostage of the past, and the victims are the Carlos Mirandas of Africa. As setback followed setback and each modest step forward was no more effective than running in place, black Africa became uncertain of its own identity and purpose, divided by ideology and self-interests, perplexed by the demands of nationhood—and as dependent militarily and economically on foreign powers as it was during the colonial era. It moves through the 1980s as a continent in crisis, explosive and vulnerable, a continent where the romance of revolution cannot hide the frustration and despair that tears at the fiber of African society.

To many outsiders, Africa seems an intimidating and foreboding place. But remember, the changes that have swept Africa in less than a generation—forty-three new countries were born south of the Sahara between 1956 and 1980—have been as traumatic as those endured by any people anywhere in peacetime. Before we move on to examine these changes in detail, let's strip away a few mysteries and put the continent in a contemporary perspective.

Africa—its name may have come from the Latin word *aprica* ("sunny") or the Greek word *aphrike* ("without cold")—was once part of Gondwanaland, the hypothetical supercontinent that also included South America, Asia, India, Australia and Antarctica. Africa occupies 20 percent of the earth's land surface, or 11.7 million square miles. Only Asia is larger. Africa is 5,000 miles long, reaching from the God-forsaken deserts of the north to the lush wine country in the south, and 4,600 miles wide. Its coastline measures 18,950 miles—shorter than Europe's because of the absence of inlets and bays—and the equator cuts Africa just about in half. Africa's climate varies wildly, from temperate in the high plateaus, to tropical along the coastal plains to just plain intolerable in the sizzling deserts.

The coastal strip around Africa is narrow, and the interior plateaus are characterized by wide belts of tropical rain forest, wooded savannah and grassland plains. In the far north is the Sahara, the world's largest desert. It covers one quarter of the continent, an area as large as the United States mainland. In the far south is the Kalahari Desert, the world's seventh largest. The highest point in Africa is Mount Kilimanjaro in Tanzania, 19,340 feet tall and snow-capped the year round, but with the exception of Antarctica, Africa is, in proportion to its size, the flattest continent in the world, something like the Great Plains of North America without corn, an endless champaign that flows from country to country, through the cities and back into the dusty look-alike villages, yielding just enough food to provide millions of subsistence farmers with the meagerest of existences.

Wandering through those empty spaces, you realize that ten thousand American farmers turned loose on African soil could transform the face—and the future—of the continent as surely as they did their own land. It seems so easy. Yet farming in black Africa is still a hoe-and-sickle enterprise, more primitive than any in the world. For example, there are but 7 tractors for every 25,000 farmed acres (compared to 45 in Asia, 57 in South America and 240 in the United States) and Africa uses only 4 pounds of fertilizer for every acre. (Asia and South America each use about ten times more; the United States, twenty times more.) Just as distressing, each year Africans are working less and less land as the desert advances like a plundering army, taking as its booty the lean hopes of helpless people and leaving in its wake barren wasteland.

The Sahara alone is growing at the rate of 250,000 acres a year, and in Northern Africa, once the grassy breadbasket of the Roman Empire, the process known as desertization is actually a visible phenomenon. Only a generation ago the capital of Mauritania (Nouakchott, meaning "the Place of the Winds") was many days' walk from the Sahara. Now it is *in* the Sahara. Vast, dead expanses of shifting, rolling sand dunes stretch as far as the eye can see and beyond. Blowing sand piles up against walls and fences like snowdrifts, and the city streets dead-end at the desert's doorstep a few hundred yards away. No longer able to support their livestock, thousands of Berbers have poured into Nouakchott, buying homes that they use for storage while living under tents in their backyards. A way of life—and the spirit of a people—has changed forever.

Scientists point out that desertization is not unique to Africa, for deserts are growing on all six inhabited continents. Some blame nature for climatic changes and drought. Others cite man's abuse of the environment, particularly overgrazing and the destruction of forests that hasten the erosion of topsoil. Still others believe the phenomenon is cyclic because ages-old deserts have always grown and shrunk and shifted at the mercy of nature's many forces. Whatever the reason, the ecological metamorphosis is a frightening one for Africa, where weather satellites have detected a constant cloud of fine, reddish particles blowing toward India. The particles have been identified as topsoil, and it takes up to a thousand years to replace a layer of topsoil.

The irony of Africa's misfortunes is that this is the place where mankind originated—and this was a center of culture and sophistication long before the Europeans arrived. Fossils nearly 3 million years old found by the anthropologists Mary Leakey and her late husband, Louis, have shown that the evolution of man from his apelike ancestors probably took place in East Africa. And American and French scientists working in Ethiopia have discovered simple stone tools 2.5 million years old. The razor-sharp cutters and the fist-sized rock choppers, the oldest tools ever found, were used, they believe, to slice through animal skins and butcher carcasses.

As far back as 500 B.C., when the Nok culture flourished in Nigeria, furnaces were being used to smelt iron. The Nigerian state of Benin exchanged ambassadors with Portugal in 1486. At that time Timbuktu in Mali was a major trading center of international fame. The splendors of the Songhai Empire, which stretched from Mali to Kano, Nigeria, in the fifteenth and sixteenth centuries, were compared by early travelers with those of contemporary Europe. "As you enter it, the town appears very great," a Dutch visitor wrote about 1600 of Edo city in Benin. "You go into a great broad street, not paved, which seems to be seven or eight times broader than the Warmoes Street in Amsterdam . . . The houses in this town stand in good order, one close and even with the other, as the houses in Holland stand . . ." Now-priceless bronze busts were being cast in Nigeria's Ife state before Columbus set sail for America. Iron-age Africans started building stone structures in the area we call Zimbabwe as early as A.D. 1100, and sixteenth-century Portuguese maritime traders found that some West African textiles were superior to anything then being made in Europe.

Because the history of ancient Africa was passed from generation to generation by the spoken, not written, word, the origins, and sometimes the fate, of the old civilizations remain clouded in mystery. (One exception is Ethiopia, which did have a written language.) It was, though, intra-African warfare and not the arrival of the European that ensured the disintegration of Africa's early civilizations: the Ghana Empire was destroyed in the thirteenth century by Almoravid warriors from Senegal; the Mali Empire began to crumble in 1430 under pressure from the nomadic Tuaregs; the Songhai Empire was broken up in 1591 when its troops were defeated by an invading Moroccan army. With no written language, no way to store and exchange information, Africa lacked the building blocks a civilization needs; it was defenseless against a new enemy from the north—the white man.

The Portuguese, in the fifteenth century, were the first Europeans to undertake systemic voyages of discovery southward along the African coast. Thus began six centuries of contact between African and European in which the African—until recently, when he learned how to turn the white man's feelings of guilt into a gold mine of international aid—always ended up second best. The Portuguese explorers opened the door for the slave traders, who in turn ushered in the missionaries, who were, in their own right, agents of colonialism. Each invader—slaver, missionary, colonialist—sought to exploit and convert. Each came to serve himself or his God, not the African. With Europe looking for new markets and materials during the industrial revolution of the nineteenth century, the European powers scrambled for domination in Africa, Balkanizing the continent into colonies with artificial boundaries that ignored traditional ethnic groupings. By 1920 every square inch of Africa except Ethiopia, Liberia and the Union of South Africa was under European rule or protection or was claimed by a European country.

The manner in which colonial administrations governed virtually ensured the failure of Africa's transition into independence. Their practice of "divide and rule"—favoring some tribes to the exclusion of others—served to accentuate the ethnic divisiveness that had been pulling Africa in different directions for centuries. Before independence, the colonialist was the common enemy. When he left, the major tribal groups in each country had to confront one another for leadership roles, and on a continent where tribal loyalty usually surpasses any allegiance to the nation, the African's new antagonist became the African.

Tribalism is one of the most difficult African concepts to grasp, and one of the most essential in understanding Africa. Publicly, modern African politicians deplore it. Kenya's President Daniel arap Moi (*arap* means "the son of") calls it the "cancer that threatens to eat out the very fabric of our nation." Yet almost every African politician practices it—most African presidents are more tribal chief than national statesman—and it remains perhaps the most potent force in day-to-day African life. It is a factor in wars and power struggles. It often determines who gets jobs, who gets promoted, who gets accepted to a university, because by its very definition tribalism implies sharing among members of the extended family, making sure that your own are looked after first:

To give a job to a fellow tribesman is not nepotism, it is an obligation. For a politician or military leader to choose his closest advisers and his bodyguards from the ranks of his own tribe is not patronage, it is good common sense. It ensures security, continuity, authority.

The family tree of William R. Tolbert, Jr., the assassinated Liberian president, provides an illuminating example of how African politicians take care of their own. Tolbert's brother Frank was president pro tempore of the senate; his brother Stephen was minister of finance; his sister Lucia was mayor of Bentol City; his son A.B. was an ambassador at large; his daughter Wilhelmina was the presidential physician; his daughter Christine was deputy minister of education; his niece Tula was the presidential dietician; his three nephews were assistant minister of presidential affairs, agricultural attaché to Rome and vice governor of the National Bank; his four sons-in-law held positions as minister of defense, deputy minister of public works, commissioner for immigration and board member of Air Liberia; one brother-in-law was ambassador to Guinea, another was in the Liberian senate, a third was mayor of Monrovia.

In its simplest form, one could compare tribalism to the situation in a city like Boston, where one finds a series of ethnic neighborhoods, with the blacks in Roxbury, the Italians in the North End, the Irish in South Boston, the Jews in the neighboring town of Brookline, the WASPs in the Wellesley suburbs. Each group is protective of its own turf, each shares a cultural affinity and each, in its own way, feels superior to the other. Africa has 2,000 such "neighborhoods," some of which cover thousands of square miles, and each of those tribes has its own language or dialect—usually unintelligible to another tribe that may be located just over the next hill—as well as its own culture, traditions and, in most cases, physical features that make one of its members immediately recognizable to an individual from another tribe.

In Lusaka, Zambia, a university student I knew applied for a job and was told to report to the personnel manager. My friend leaned over the receptionist's desk and asked, "What tribe is he?" Told that the manager was a Mashona, my friend, who belonged to another ethnic group, replied, "Then I'll never get the job." He didn't.

A live-in cook in Africa earns about $75 a month—a luxury most expatriates can easily afford—and shortly after arriving in Nairobi, I hired a cook from the Kikuyu tribe, a gardener and an *askari* (night watchman) from the Luo tribe. For the next three months our house was in turmoil as they fought and cussed and argued with one another for hours on end. We fired the watchman after he accused us of trying to poison him—he said we were prejudiced against the Luos—and we put Dishun, the gardener, on indefinite sick leave when he accused the cook of bewitching him with evil spirits. We took Dishun to our British doctor, but the prescribed pills didn't help his stomach cramps. He returned to his village, where the witch doctor, using herbs and chants, quickly cured him. In the meantime we had hired a Kikuyu gardener and *askari*. They struck up an immediate friendship with the Kikuyu cook. Tranquillity returned to our home.

One day in Uganda I was talking with a U.S. diplomat at the embassy. His secretary entered the office and said a man was waiting to see him. "Is he Ugandan?" the diplomat asked. "No, he's Acholi," she answered. Her implication was clear: in Uganda, there were Acholis and other tribalists, but no Ugandans. One's identity was tribal, not national.

Only three countries in black Africa—Somalia, Lesotho and Swaziland—are blessed with ethnic uniformity. The result is that those countries are among the few to have a sense of national identity. But in most, such as Zaire, which has 200 tribes, the governments have failed to provide an alternative to tribalism because central authority is weak and often illegitimate and based on the perpetuation of power, not a sharing of power.

The significance of tribalism has not diminished with the end of colonialism, for several reasons. First, there is little intermarriage between various ethnic groups; second, in rural areas, where transportation and communication remain primitive, there is little movement in or out of tribal regions that have existed for generations; third, the family, clan and tribe are the essential elements of African society, the American equivalent of welfare, social security, police protection and Saturday night at the VFW; fourth, since most Africans' identity revolves around the tribe, taking away that identity would be like telling a devout Catholic that he has been excommunicated; fifth, nationalism is a new concept in Africa, not much more than three decades old, and its implications are not broadly understood; and sixth, African leaders have done little to convince their people that nationhood offers more benefits than tribalism.

To see the results of tribalism in its most extreme and ugly form, consider Burundi, landlocked and resourceless. A Christian nation of over 4 million inhabitants, Burundi is an East African land whose grassy, forested plateaus roll to the slopes of craggy, tortured hills. Despite its high population density—372 persons per square mile, or about ten times the density in the United States—Burundi has virtually no villages or cities. People live instead in family compounds known as *rugos*, and the only urban concentrations are at a few former colonial and commercial centers such as Bujumbura and Gitega.

There are three major ethnic groups: the Hutus, the Tutsi (Watusi) and the Twa. The short, stocky Hutus (comprising 85 percent of the population) are mostly farmers of Bantu stock, with dark, Negroid features. The Watusi (14 percent), who migrated to Burundi in the sixteenth and seventeenth centuries from the north, probably Ethiopia, are cattle people; they are tall, sometimes well over six feet, with long, narrow facial features, and their skin is slightly lighter than that of most other Africans. The Twa (1 percent) are pygmies who were driven into the bush and marginal grasslands by the Watusi generations ago.

Over the years the small group of Watusi immigrants subjugated the masses of aboriginal Hutus into a kind of feudal system. Much as in medieval Europe, a pyramid developed with Watusi lords giving their loyalty to more important Watusi nobility in exchange for protection. A *mwami*, or Watusi king, ruled at the top of each pyramid. Gradually the great majority of Hutus mortgaged their services and relinquished their land to the nobility, receiving in return cattle—the symbol of status and wealth in Burundi.

Centuries of tradition made the Watusi feel like a privileged, superior people, and the Hutus like an inferior class held in serfdom. The Watusi considered themselves an intelligent people capable of leadership and looked on the Hutus as no more than hard-working, dumb peasants. The Hutus had been conditioned not to disagree. When Belgium granted Burundi independence in 1962, challenges were raised to the concept of the Watusi's innate superiority, and the Watusi began to worry about the possibility that their power might be transferred to the majority, as had happened elsewhere in black Africa.

The minority Watusi government came up with a simple solution: it set out, in 1972, to massacre every Hutu with education, a government job or money. In a three-month period, upwards of 200,000 Hutus were slain. Their homes and schools were destroyed. Stan Meisler, then the *Los Angeles Times'* African correspondent, traveled to Bujumbura, the Burundi capital, a few months after the massacre and was shocked to see no more than a handful of Hutus. "It is a little like entering Warsaw after World War II, and finding few Jews there," Meisler wrote.

Many Hutus were taken from their homes at night. Others received summonses to report to the police station. So obedient and subservient had the Hutus become to their Watusi masters that they answered the summonses, which even the most unlearned soul knew was really an execution notice. Sometimes, when the death quotas at the prisons and police stations had been filled for the day, the queued-up Hutus were told to return the next day. They dutifully complied. The few Hutus who tried to escape the executioners seemed to make only token attempts. It was a pathetic sight. They would walk down the main road toward the border. If the Watusi gendarme stopped them, they would turn quietly back.

There were many grisly stories about the methods of execution, all difficult to verify, but Western diplomats who were serving in Bujumbura at the time said one thing was clear: the Watusi did not use many bullets. The Hutus' bodies were then thrown onto military trucks, a pile of bodies and tangled limbs filling the uncovered cargo hold of each vehicle. For several days they rumbled through Bujumbura in broad daylight on their way from the city to a field near the airport. Then the government decided to be more subtle and shifted the death convoys to night runs. Bulldozers worked under spotlights, digging long narrow rows of graves.

In neighboring Rwanda, another former Belgian colony that gained its independence in 1962, a similar tribal imbalance existed. There the Watusi made up 10 percent of the population, the Hutus 89 percent. In 1959 the Hutus overthrew their Watusi masters, killing an estimated 100,000 and winning majority rule. Persecution of the Watusi continued through 1964, at which time the English philosopher Bertrand Russell called the killings "the most horrible and systematic human massacre we have had occasion to witness since the extermination of the Jews by the Nazis."

But except for a few voices like that of Russell, the general reaction of Africa and the world was silence. A representative of the Organization of African Unity flew into Bujumbura at the height of the killings and congratulated President Michel Micombero, a thirty-two-year-old alcoholic who was later overthrown, for the orderly way he was running his national affairs.* The Western missionaries in Burundi and the Christian church continued their work on God's behalf without a word of protest. As far as I know, no country cut its diplomatic relations with the Micombero government. And at the very moment an investigator from the International Commission of Jurists was being officially received in Bujumbura at an elabo-

* Micombero died in 1983, at the age of 42, in Somalia, where he had lived in exile as a non-person.

rate reception, twenty-two Hutus were being beaten to death in the police chamber a few blocks away.

If the white South African government had conducted similar atrocities against black Africans, the rage would have rocked the continent like the explosion of a volcano. But that would have been different: the whites' injustice toward blacks is considered racist; the blacks' mistreatment of blacks is just part of national growing pains and is somehow acceptable to both Africa and the world beyond.

Sadly, not a great deal has changed in Burundi since the nightmare of the 1970s. Fear still rules the land, and in all except their strength in numbers, the Hutus are a destroyed, powerless people. More than 150,000 have fled to Zaire, Tanzania and Rwanda, and those who remain still work the fields for their Watusi masters, hold menial jobs and carry cards identifying their tribal origins. On my last visit to Burundi there was not a single Hutu private in the 7,-000-man national army, and the military government remained suspicious of—and occasionally vetoed—any international aid that might eventually breed opposition by educating or enriching the Hutus. All the power remained in the hands of the Watusi minority. And that, in a word, is what tribalism is about—power.

The ethnic diversity of Africa also creates an immense language problem, making Africa the most linguistically complex continent in the world. Canada's national unity is fractured by the presence of just two languages. Belgium is splintered by French and Flemish. But Africa, in addition to half a dozen imported European languages, speaks 750 tribal tongues, fifty of which are spoken by one million or more people. Both Swahili in East Africa and Hausa in West Africa are spoken by more than 25 million people. In Zaire alone, there are seventy-five different languages. In South Africa the whites speak Afrikaans, a colloquial form of seventeenth-century Dutch heard nowhere else in the world. The tribal babble intellectually cripples whole countries and leaves Africa in the unenviable position of not being able to understand itself.

The people of Djibouti, a pint-sized East African country, speak French; the closest other French-speaking Africans are nearly seven hundred miles away. The nomadic Masai of Kenya and Tanzania speak Masai, which has little similarity to any other tongue used in those countries. The Equatorial Guineans are the only people in black Africa whose national language is Spanish. In the rural areas of many countries the language barrier makes it impossible for people in neighboring villages to communicate. When President Daniel arap Moi makes one of his infrequent trips to northern Kenya he speaks Swahili, a language introduced by Arab traders, but the people there do not understand much Swahili and Moi does not understand their tribal tongues. Just the same, people gather obediently to hear his speeches and sit nodding their heads in agreement.

Imagine what would happen if the United States had a similar problem. If you were a manufacturer in Milwaukee and spoke only English, you could not communicate with your suppliers in Chicago; if you were a state senator from Los Angeles, you could not understand a legislative debate in Sacramento; if you were a long-distance truck driver crossing Montana, you would have trouble ordering a meal in Butte, Great Falls and Helena. What would happen? You would do exactly what the rural African does: you would stay within the security of your linguistic boundaries.

Only one country, Cameroon, officially uses two European languages, French and English. But the people who come from the old British part of Cameroon speak little or no French, while the people from the old French region speak little or no English. Meetings between Cameroon officials often bog down on the language problem. The government, though, seldom supplies interpreters for such meetings because the country is meant to be bilingual. As a result, few people understand one another until everyone drops French and English and begins speaking pidgin English, a language that developed in the slave depots of West Africa for the same reason that Swahili developed in East Africa: the slave traders needed a language to give orders to the slaves, and the slaves, representing many different tribes, needed a language to communicate with one another. Today pidgin is a written language that combines many English words with African grammar and syntax.

The Reverend M. G. M. Cole, an African who spent several years in Britain, once delivered an eloquent Sunday sermon against the imposition of a single-party system in Sierra Leone: "Teday the country happ. Make dis thing go as ee de go, en den de go. Nor cause any trouble. Nor gee the president headache ... Oona nor amborgin am ... nor forget two party. We nor want one party."

Cole spoke the Queen's English impeccably, but in this case he was just doing what he had to do to communicate—speak Krio, a language that grew out of pidgin English and is understood by 80 percent of the Sierra Leoneans. What he said translates as: "Today the country is happy. Let's continue things as it is, as they are. Don't cause any trouble. Don't give the president a headache . . . Don't you humbug him . . . Don't forget the two-party system. We don't want a one-party state."

The colonization of Africa brought languages (English, French, Portuguese, Spanish, German, Italian) that enabled Africans to communicate with the outside world and with one another. But the hodgepodge pattern that emerged when the European powers divided Africa did little to unify the land linguistically. Kenya, where about four dozen languages are spoken, is a fairly typical example of how an African country copes with the language barrier.

Swahili (properly known as Kiswahili) is the most widely spoken language in Kenya and, like English, is an "official" language. In 1975 President Jomo Kenyatta remarked casually one day that henceforth Swahili would be the only language used in parliament, as the constitution required. A mild panic ensued, and lawmakers rushed out to buy Swahili dictionaries. Some of them made no headway at all and therefore did not utter another word in parliamentary debate for months. Before long the constitution was amended; English returned as the main language of parliament.

Most Kenyans living in the city speak three languages—English and Swahili, neither of which they may command firmly, and a tribal tongue. Business and the affairs of state are conducted in English. Young children learn Swahili in school with English taught as a second language, but the language of Nairobi University is English. The government runs two radio stations, one in English and one in Swahili, and the six hours of daily television are about evenly divided between the two languages. In the deep countryside, peasant farmers and herders generally speak only their tribal language.

The language barrier is one of the biggest obstacles preventing Kenya and other countries from developing a true sense of national unity. How can Kenyans think of themselves as a national people if they don't even have a single language unifying them? Language is one of the most important instruments of nation-building, a potentially powerful unifying force.

Demographically, Africa is a young continent: half the population is no more than fifteen years old. And the babies keep coming—one city hospital alone, Mama Yemo in Kinshasa, Zaire, delivers more than 50,000 babies a year. Kenya has the highest population growth rate in the world (4 percent), and Rwanda is one of the world's most densely populated countries (444 people per square mile). The rugged, spectacularly beautiful hills and mountains of Rwanda are tiered like giant staircases. On each level, hundreds of feet above the valley floors, a family clan lives and farms. The dirt roads that wind through the valleys and across the hills are as busy as the sidewalks of New York's Fifth Avenue during lunch hour, a shoulder-to-shoulder procession of pedestrians—most of them barefoot and many of them drunk on homemade banana beer—in constant, seemingly undirected motion.

But Africa's problem isn't that it's densely populated; the problem is that it's unevenly populated. Zambia, twice as big as California, has only 5.3 million people, Rwanda, the size of Maryland, has 4.5 million. There are 30 persons per square mile in Africa, about the same as in the Soviet Union and North America, and far less than the 170 per square mile squeezed into Europe and Asia. The comparison is deceptive, though. About one third of Africa—or an area twice the size of India—is virtually uninhabitable, and some countries (like Kenya) are already using every inch of cultivatable land. No government except South Africa's has the resources to feed and provide adequate services for its people.

Population control remains a sensitive issue in black Africa, and few sensible politicians dare speak firmly in its favor. To do so would be to challenge the growth of an individual's tribe, to deprive parents of the hands needed to till the fields today and care for the elderly tomorrow, to denounce religious and traditional beliefs that have belonged to Africa for generations. Some governments consider birth control morally decadent. Others view it as an imperialistic plot to depopulate the Third World. But every argument ignores the unsettling fact that Africa's growth rate is more rapid than any continent's and represents the gravest threat facing Africa today.

If you look ahead and double Africa's population—which the United Nations predicts will happen by the year 2000—while halving the governmental services, a frightening scenario becomes quite plausible: governments grow weaker and crumble under waves of civil unrest; populations shift across borders as people migrate in search of food, land, goods and jobs; conflict and chaos erupt with too many people competing for too few commodities; foreign powers step into the vacuum, creating conditions of confrontation that pit the continent against itself, one bloc favoring the West, the other the East.*

Many demographers argue that Africans will not have fewer children until they perceive that to do so is in their economic interest and until they are assured that the children they do have will reach adulthood. This will happen, the argument goes, only after the family's standard of living improves, along with its security and health. In the developed world it has been well established that population control follows—rather than leads to—improved economic conditions.

Africa as yet shows no signs of following that trend. Kenya, for example, has made as much economic progress as any non–oil-producing black nation since independence. But its population growth rate is four times that of the United States—and growing. In 1960, just before independence, the average Kenyan female had 6.2 children; in 1970, she had 7.2; by 1980, 8.3. There are two possible conclusions: first, that Africa does not fit into the established pattern; second and more likely, that the standard of living has not improved sufficiently, and Africans feel even more threatened economically than they did during the colonial era.

Thirty African countries have growth rates of over 2 percent a year; ten others have over 3 percent. Only Gabon, in West Africa, has managed to achieve population stability—largely because 30 percent of the women have venereal disease. The government's response has been to build a $10 million fertility center to see how its people can produce more and keep pace with the rest of Africa.

Indeed, few concepts are as deeply ingrained in the African psyche as the need and the desire to produce. In many cultures an infertile man is an outcast; a barren woman is shunned and scorned. "If I cannot give my women children, I might as well be dead," a Masai cattle herder told me. The late king of Swaziland, Sobhuza II, Master of the Spears (1899–1982), fathered more than five hundred children by his hundred or so wives. In Moslem countries such as Niger and Upper Volta, it is common for men to have four wives and twenty or twenty-five children. Even in capitals that are predominantly Christian, men often have a city wife and a country

---

* Throughout, I have been using the terms "West" and "East" politically rather than geographically, i.e., "the West" is Western, industrialized countries and the United States; "the East" pro-Russian countries and the Soviet Union.

wife. The country wife of a Kenyan government minister, for instance, is probably illiterate and plump; she remains on the *shamba* (farm, or garden) to take care of the crops, and he visits her perhaps once a week. The city wife, stylish if not articulate, accompanies her husband to the various social functions he must attend.

In March 1977 Jean-Bédel Bokassa, leader of what was then the Central African Empire (now the Central African Republic), declared a national holiday for the birth of his thirtieth child and heir-apparent, Saint Jean de Bokassa de Berengo de Bouyangui de Centrafrique. The first cable of congratulations came from Idi Amin, then Uganda's president, who noted that he himself had thirty-two children. Said Amin: "May God bless you and give you more children."

The social and economic implications of Africa's preoccupation with virility, particularly when combined with its rampant urbanization, are disruptive and ominous. Unable to support his large family, the able-bodied male leaves the farm to find a salaried job. His wife remains behind to tend the crops and raise the children, debilitating, perhaps permanently, the extended family unit that is ordinarily a source of such strength in Africa.* In the city the new arrival soon learns that he has no employable skills. He joins the growing legions of urbanized Africans whose aimless existence is spent on street corners and in coffee houses. Because of increased demands on city services, they tend to disintegrate; public transportation breaks down; hospital beds are shared by two and three patients; electrical blackouts occur often; crime becomes a major social problem.† (In no Christian country today are city streets safe, for African or European, after dark. Interestingly, this is not true of the Moslem countries where people follow their religious teachings more faithfully. You can walk the streets of Zanzibar, Tanzania, or Mogadishu, Somalia, or a dozen other Islamic cities at any hour without the faintest worry of being robbed.)

As the cities become more crowded, African governments are forced to devote an increasingly larger share of their budgets to

* Large companies and governmental agencies in many African countries are required to provide housing for their city employees. The housing usually consists only of bachelor quarters because it is too expensive to build accommodations for families with fifteen or sixteen members. This practice also encourages the division of households and accounts for the fact that 60 percent of Nairobi's population is male.

† The colonialists had no problem with African urbanization, because "natives" needed special passes to enter white areas of most capitals. In South Africa they still do, and more than 300,000 blacks are arrested each year there for violating the "pass laws."

urban services and development, to the detriment of the rural areas, where 80 percent of Africa's people still live. That, too, gives impetus to the urbanization. In Nairobi, for example, there are 452 doctors at Kenyatta Hospital, the city's largest, but there is only one doctor in Kenya's desolate northern quarter, a region about the size of Iowa. In the Central African Republic, the country's only banks are in Bangui, the capital. In Chad, a country twice the size of Texas, there are no paved roads 120 miles outside the capital, N'Djamena.

Seeing the decay of the cities, many Western visitors are startled to learn how potentially prosperous Africa is. Like a closet millionaire, it hides the riches that future generations on distant continents will need to prosper, produce, even survive. It has 40 percent of the world's potential hydroelectric power supply, the bulk of the world's diamonds and chromium, 30 percent of the uranium in the non-Communist world, and 50 percent of the world's gold, 90 percent of its cobalt, 50 percent of its phosphates, 40 percent of its platinum, 7.5 percent of its coal, 8 percent of its known petroleum reserves, 12 percent of its natural gas, 3 percent of its iron ores, and millions upon millions of acres of untilled farmland. There is not another continent blessed with such abundance and diversity.

But youth and wealth have not provided the foundation or momentum for development and progress. I would be hard pressed to name more than four non–oil-exporting countries—Kenya, Cameroon, the Ivory Coast and Malawi—where there has been meaningful economic development, political stability and an emerging middle class. Elsewhere the portrait of Africa is a bleak one of chilling consequences, for the continent is not catching up with the rest of the world, it is falling further behind. Africa is no longer part of the Third World. It is the Fourth World.

▶ According to the United Nations Council on Africa, the economics of thirty of sub-Sahara Africa's forty-six countries have actually gone backward since independence. The real per capita income of the non–oil producers has increased less than 1 percent over the past decade, and 60 percent of the 370 million people in sub-Sahara Africa are malnourished. Seventeen black states and 150 million people entered 1980 facing what the United Nations Food and Agricultural Organization called "catastrophic" food shortages.

▶ The per capita income in Africa is $365 a year, the lowest in the world. In real terms that income—and the standard of living in

Africa—is falling, with peasant farmers at the mercy of price fluctuations on the world market for their crops. A decade ago a Zambian farmer needed to produce one bag of maize to buy three cotton shirts; today that bag of maize buys only one shirt. A Tanzanian farmer could buy a Timex watch with the proceeds from 7.7 pounds of coffee; today he needs to produce 15 pounds of coffee to buy the same watch.

▶ The infant mortality rate in black Africa, 137 deaths per 1,000 live births, is the highest in the world. In Upper Volta, where life expectancy is thirty-three years, the mortality rate is 189 deaths per 1,000 births. (By comparison, the rate is 12 per 1,000 in the United States.) Europe has one doctor for every 580 persons; Kenya, one of Africa's most developed countries, has one for every 25,600 persons.

▶ Only 11 percent of the age-eligible children in Africa are in school, compared to 35 percent in Asia and 45 percent in South America. In the twenty- to twenty-four-year-old age group, 1.4 percent of Africans are studying at a university. In Asia the figure is 5.7 percent, in Latin America 6.7 percent and in the United States 48 percent.

▶ The illiteracy rate in Africa is about 75 percent. That rate should continue to drop as more children attend school, but if Africa's population doubles by the year 2000, as expected, 60 percent of the continent will be illiterate. It will be the highest concentration of illiterate people in the world.

▶ When the independence era began in 1960, Africa produced nearly 95 percent of its own food. Today every country except South Africa is an importer, and by the year 2000 one of every two Africans will be eating food imported from other continents. When we arrived in Kenya in 1976, the stores were amply filled with both basic and luxury foods. By the time we left in 1980, there were long lines for everything from milk and flour to maize and butter.

Despite the awesome problems facing the continent, African leaders spend little time examining their own conduct and shortcomings and a great deal looking for a scapegoat. Usually every problem is laid on the doorstep of colonialism, for to criticize Africa as an African is considered treasonous. Perhaps Africa's reluctance to impose self-criticism is merely a defense mechanism for the humiliation it suffers so often when reminded that its armies are not very tough, its governments not very efficient, its ability to back words with deeds not very effective.

In Somalia the average government ministry has eight hundred civil servants. On any given day, a senior government official told me, only sixty of them show up for work. In Zaire a $1.8 million international grant to repair Kinshasa's broken-down city buses is swindled down to $200,000 by the time it reaches the transportation ministry, and ends up accomplishing nothing at all. In Nairobi a man calling the police station to report that his house is under attack by a band of bandits with machetes is told he will have to drive to the station to pick up some officers; the department has no cars on duty that night. In Zambia hundreds of government cars sit rusting in a huge parking lot outside Lusaka. Many need nothing more than a new carburetor or fuel pump. But with no mechanics around, and not much initiative to spare even if there were, it is easier to junk them and buy new ones with an international grant.

Stormed Zambia's President Kenneth David Kaunda at one moment of particular frustration: "If by next year all the five million Zambians choose to be lazy as they are now, I would willingly step down as president because I don't want to lead people with lazy bones."

Kaunda's comment underscores the fine line between racism and criticism that Western journalists must deal with in Africa. If a white person had made the same remark, it would be considered racist; but a black can say it and be accused of nothing more than honest criticism. This duality operates on all official levels of African government and its effect is to make Africa immune to censure. A government, for instance, might execute a dozen dissidents or persecute an entire tribe and label its actions "social reconstruction." If a Western diplomat or journalist calls it barbarism, the African dismisses him as a racist. The result is that Westerners, particularly scholars, often write timidly, even romantically, about Africa, and African governments go on doing pretty much what they want to their own people.

The Zambians, incidentally, did not suddenly spring alive, and Kaunda, who has been president since 1964, did not step down.

With Africa floundering economically and meandering politically, the continent remains as ripe for exploitation today as it was a hundred years ago. Both the East and West have stepped into the void, pouring military and developmental assistance into country after country in the hopes of creating new satellites. As a consequence, outside influence in Africa has increased and Africa's control over its own affairs, military and economic, has decreased.

"I think the time has come to leave Africa to the Africans," says President Étienne Eyadéma of Togo. "We can find solutions for African problems. The East and West must stop interfering in our internal affairs."

The demand is a commonly expressed one in Africa—and an empty one. If the East and West were to cut off their flow of guns, money and technology to black Africa, almost every government would collapse in a matter of months. Never has Africa been as dependent on foreign powers as it is today. With the exception of Nigeria, whose oil revenues reached $60 million a day in 1980, black Africa lives on the international dole. When national security is threatened, the first thing Africa does is call for help from non-African countries because few countries are capable of defending themselves. Only Angola and Ethiopia—two Marxist states armed by the Soviet Union—can assemble five hundred or more pieces of heavy artillery, tanks and rocket launchers.

Although black Africa has 750,000 men under arms, most armies are badly trained and poorly disciplined and serve little function other than internal security. As a guerrilla, the African is an effective fighter because his unit is small and loosely structured and his cause—liberation—is one he can understand. But as a member of a large organized army, his military capabilities are greatly reduced: now he is fighting for a nation that he does not really feel part of; he may be taking orders from an officer of a tribe hostile to his own; he is expected to operate sophisticated weapons even though he may never have driven a car or seen a pocket calculator. Even when elite units go into battle, they often end up putting down their guns and fleeing. More often the army has been the main instrument for terrorizing and exploiting the population.

The end of colonialism has not brought genuine freedom to Africa. With an external debt exceeding $35 billion, black Africa has become a cluster of welfare states, surviving at the whim of foreign donors and aid agencies. As President Moi of Kenya put it on a begging trip to West Germany, apparently without realizing the irony of his words: "No country can remain economically independent without outside assistance."

Some of Africa's problems—especially those caused by forces other than man—are so enormous, so constant, that a people of lesser spirit long since would have succumbed. The inescapable heat numbs the mind and drains vitality. Tsetse flies and a score of other insects carry terrible diseases that incapacitate entire villages. Simple disorders like diarrhea are fatal to tens of thousands of African children each year. Swarms of locusts—twenty or thirty million slim, shiny creatures that weigh an ounce each and eat their own weight daily—can cut through a nation's entire grain harvest in a matter of days, leaving not a living plant in their wake. The droughts stay too long and the rains fall too heavily. Nature, like man, is a cabal, disenfranchising a people from its own land.

Maybe sub-Sahara Africa can continue to stumble through the 1980s and into the 1990s, hoping, dreaming, talking, ignoring the life-death issues it must confront, accepting adversity and misadventure as the work of forces beyond its control. Or maybe there will be an awakening, a realization that with good fortune and sensible planning Africa can control its own destiny—or, at the very least, can maneuver its way through some of the storms.

But whatever, two decades of African independence has provided one invaluable lesson: progress is not inevitable.

COLLISION OF
PAST AND PRESENT

▲

There is no turning back. The old people in the villages just have to accept that things are changing and the traditions they grew up with are dying.

—OLIVER LITONDO,
a Kenyan television commentator

THE MUD is ankle-deep in Mathare Valley during Kenya's long, cold rainy season from March to June, and from a distance the area looks like a huge junkyard, its sides and floor cluttered with stacks of wood and cardboard and all manner of discarded oddities. Stretching out for more than a mile north of Nairobi, the valley is filled with a strange silence, leaving you with no more sense of motion or color than a one-dimensional black-and-white photograph would. At night you could drive right by it without realizing there was a living soul anywhere around.

Yet this valley is home to more than 100,000 people, a makeshift city as large as South Bend, Indiana. Like so many other Africans, the inhabitants had deserted their villages for the promises of the city. But the city had neither jobs nor homes for them, so they squeezed into the slums outside Nairobi, and places like Mathare Valley—with no running water or electric light—became the grave-yards of hope for Africa's shifting populations.

I remember walking through the valley one day, picking my way along the muddy paths that meander among the shanties, and being struck by how still everything was. It was like a movie without sound. I stopped at a lean-to whose roof was made of paper bags. A pot of maize porridge was cooking outside, and Mary Ngei leaned over the charcoal embers to protect her family's meal from the soft rain. Was she willing to talk for a while? Yes, she said. Was I willing to give her a few shillings for her time? Sure, I said. She pulled from her pocket a piece of paper that was worn and held together by tape. She unfolded it carefully, smoothing each wrinkle, and held it out for me to examine.

"There," she said, "you see. All A's. Hannah always got all A's."

Mrs. Ngei, forty years old and the mother of thirteen children, folded her daughter's report card in tidy little squares and tucked it under a loose board in her wooden bed where she kept a few other treasures. No, she said, Hannah was no longer in school. In fact, she wasn't quite sure where her fifteen-year-old daughter was. All her children had dropped out of school because the Ngeis were unable to pay the annual enrollment fee of 30 shillings ($3.70). The younger ones had become street urchins, begging and scraping for survival in the Nairobi streets, and the older ones, she feared, had turned to prostitution and thievery. Her husband walked to Nairobi almost every morning, looking for work as a casual laborer, but he had found no more than five or six days' employment in the year that they had been in the city, and she had no particular hope that he would return home that evening with either money or good news.

"Really," she said, "I don't know what we will do. This is no way to live. People get sick here, they just die. They don't get to see a doctor. We could go back to the *shamba* but there's no doctor there either. And no jobs and no money. What we need is to get Hannah back in school so she can be smart and get a job and help support us."

The Nairobi City Council views the valley dwellers as illegal squatters and periodically dispatches several bulldozers to level their jerry-built world. Knowing that they must often flee on short notice, the people disassemble their homes every morning, piling the cardboard and chunks of wood neatly on the ground. Every evening they rebuild them. The entire process takes only a few minutes, but it enables the squatters simply to pick up their homes and move if they hear the rumble of bulldozers approaching over the hill that separates Mathare Valley from the old colonial mansions now occupied by ambassadors and millionaire Kenyans. For two or three days after the bulldozers have cut through the hollow, the place remains empty. Then suddenly, mysteriously, one night the inhabitants return and by morning it once more is a tangle of shanties and filth, of people going through the dreary routine of life as though nothing had ever happened.

I wrote a story for the *Los Angeles Times* about the Ngeis and a few weeks later received a letter from a California reader saying she would like to pay for Hannah's education, perhaps even sponsor her at a school in the United States. Could I get in touch with the Ngeis? the writer asked. I returned to Mathare Valley. But in the time between my two visits the bulldozers had come and the Ngeis had gone. Someone said they were still in the valley and had set up their shack in a different place. Trying to find Mrs. Ngei was like picking a single face out of a sell-out crowd at Dodger Stadium. Two hours later, having failed, I went back to my office. Even good fortune had mocked the promises of the city.

Millions of Africans today, from Kenya to the Ivory Coast, from Niger to Botswana, are following the same path as the Ngeis, lured off the farms and into the cities by the dream of a better life. The result of the rural exodus is an urban nightmare: slums, crime, psychological trauma and economies that simply cannot expand fast enough to provide jobs or social services for the world's youngest and fastest-growing continental population. Here are some capital statistics: The population of Lagos, Nigeria, has grown from 300,-000 in 1970 to 3 million today. Nouakchott, Mauritania, had 5,000 residents twenty years ago; today it has 225,000. Nairobi, a city designed for 250,000, will have 7 million residents by 2050 if current growth rates continue. In 1960 only one black African city, Kinshara, Zaire, had a population of more than 500,000; now there are ten.

In Kenya the minimum monthly wage is $43, but the jobless rate runs about 45 percent, and as in other African countries, there is no such thing as unemployment compensation. Thirteen percent of Nairobi University's 1,800 graduates will be unable to find work for at least three years. According to the International Labor Organization, 60 million Africans—half the adult population—cannot find work, and if Africa is to meet the ILO's goal of full employment by the year 2000, it will have to create 150 million jobs, a target that is clearly unattainable. Upper Volta's major export is people, with 600,000 laborers doing seasonal work in neighboring countries. Unemployment in Djibouti can be as high as 85 percent, and the closest real job market is on another continent, in the Persian Gulf states.

More than half of Cape Verde's fisherman population has left the island republic for want of work, and today there are more Cape Verdians living in Massachusetts and Rhode Island than in Cape Verde. In Ethiopia and Tanzania city jobs are so scarce that the governments truck people, sometimes at gunpoint, back to the rural areas. Botswana, Malawi, Lesotho, Swaziland, Zimbabwe and Mozambique send tens of thousands of their unemployed young men to the South African mines.

Just a mile or two from Mathare Valley, in the heart of downtown Nairobi, Francis Thuo can look out of his window in the International House at the sprawling city below and can see, far off in the distance, the African plains where giraffes and zebras and antelope still roam in great numbers. Thuo, a prosperous businessman in his mid-forties who is chairman of the Nairobi Stock Exchange, wears a three-piece business suit with a Lions Club emblem in the lapel. He sends his five children to private schools and his office is tastefully and expensively decorated, with wall-to-wall carpeting and mahogany furniture.

A long time ago, shortly after he had dropped out of school, Thuo remembers walking across a bridge in Nairobi with his father, a meatcutter who could not afford the fees to educate his eight children. They stopped to watch a dozen men, bare-chested and sweating, labor with pick and shovel along the roadside.

"Look at them," his father said. "If you do not take your studies seriously, you will end up like them. There will be nothing for you to do in life but dig ditches."

Thuo never forgot the advice. He went to work in a gas station, then for an accounting firm. He taught himself to read and write. He studied economics at night and took correspondence courses in history, and in 1964, the year after independence, opened the first African brokerage house in East Africa. He is proud that he bucked the odds and won, particularly when he recalls that in his youth the colonialists gave the Africans virtually no opportunity "to prove our worth" except as common laborers.

"What concerns me these days is that our children are having it much too easy," he mused. "Unless we push, they just don't seem to be pulling their own weight. They want life handed to them on a silver platter."

His anxieties aren't much different than those you might hear in Middle America. That's not surprising, for Africans like Thuo—members of a new, emerging middle class—have dreams and goals and values with a distinctly Western flavor. They are educated, economically ambitious and dedicated to making their children's lives better than their own. They sacrifice for their children, complain about inflation, worry about the unruly behavior of today's youth and are greatly concerned with increasing their own wealth and security.

Thuo escaped from his past through sheer hard work and tenacity. Others moved up in class more through circumstance than design, being the benefactors rather than the creators of a system inherited from the colonialists. They simply stepped into the void left by the departing colonialists and expatriates, and as often as not, stayed there more because of tribal nepotism than merit. But Africa's new middle and upper classes, as minuscule as they may be, are an encouraging portent for the future. If they can grow and become a majority class, as happened in the United States, they could become the foundation of economic and political stability in Africa because more people will have a stake in their country's well-being. The Nairobi Stock Exchange that Thuo chairs represents a noteworthy step in that direction.

The exchange surely must be the world's smallest and most informal. It has no trading floor, no permanent home and no assessment for a seat. The five members of the exchange meet every morning over coffee to examine the status of Kenya's health. For about twenty minutes they scribble notes, bicker and barter, accomplishing their ritual with the good-natured kidding of old friends. International events have little influence on the market; it is local conditions that matter.

Prices are established during the morning "call-over," with the five members meeting in a different colleague's office each day. Actual trading is done over the phone or through the mails by Nairobi's five brokerage firms, which offer their clients seventy stocks valued from a few cents to a few dollars a share. (Blue-chip stocks in 1982 included City Brewery at 40 cents a share, Nation Printers and Publishers at 70 cents and Brooke Bond tea, $2.65.)

Thuo says "an educated witch doctor's guess" would be that about 1 percent of Kenya's 16 million people are stockholders. That is a significant figure, considering that Africans in the colonial era had virtually no money and usually reckoned their wealth by the size of their family or herd.

"Capitalism has been part of the African life since time immemorial," Thuo says. "Measuring your wealth in cattle or the size of your family was a sort of capitalism. This is a new world we live in

now and what we're dealing with is just another form of capitalism—money instead of cows."

With powerful binoculars you could very nearly see the village of
Meto—and another face of Africa—from Thuo's fourteenth-floor
office window. Meto, tucked in thorn-bush-covered plains south of
Nairobi, is populated by several hundred Masai, tall nomadic tribesmen who wander with their cattle in an endless search for grass and
water.

On the surface, Meto appears stationary in time. The people still
live in clusters of one-room huts known as *bomas* that are made of
mud, sticks and cattle dung. Small and comfortably cool even in the
heat of summer, separate *bomas* are reserved for each of the owner's
wives, and inside there is one section for the humans, another for
the calves and goats.

The Masai calculate their wealth in cattle—a man with, say, a
hundred head would be considered a millionaire—and each cow has
an almost mystical significance. The cows are seldom sold or
slaughtered. They are merely collected, much as a Westerner builds
his assets in a savings account. The cattle provide all the Masai's
needs: milk and blood to drink, meat to eat during special celebrations, bones to make jewelry and plates, skins to lie on, manure to
build homes, urine to brew into beer.

Circumcision rites last for several days and are a cause for great
celebration in Meto. The girls of the village are circumcised at pu-
berty, the boys when they are sixteen or seventeen years old. The
boys are now considered adults and allowed to lay with women for
the first time. Thus begins their seven-year apprenticeship as
morani, warriors charged with protecting Meto and its cattle. They
carry spears and wear only red clothes, which are tossed loosely
around one shoulder and fall to their knees. Strutting like peacocks,
the *morani* sport braided shoulder-length hair, are smeared with red
ochre and adorned with ostrich feathers, and they call after the
young women who walk by with shaven heads and ankle bracelets
tinkling with each step.

The problem is that there really isn't much for the *morani* to do
these days except to preen and look dashing. Tribal warfare no
longer exists in the traditional sense and the government has forbidden cattle raids by neighboring villages. There aren't even many
lions around Meto anymore, so the warriors no longer have to stalk

and kill one of the beasts as part of their initiation into manhood, a practice that continued until just a few years ago. Suddenly understanding math is more important than handling a spear.

"I was going to school in Nairobi but my father told me, when I was seventeen, to come home, to become a *moran* like my brothers had done," said Gideon Mardadi. He returned to his small dusty village, and he was circumcised in a ritual that lasted three days. He killed a lion with his spear and then for three years he idled about. "I soon came to realize that it was not good work," said Mardadi, now twenty-seven years old. "It was boring. I left and went back to school. I do not like to show disrespect to my father but there are other things that are important besides herding cattle."

Mardadi runs the farm-supply store in Meto, an unlit one-room shop that sells fertilizer and grain and various medicines for cows, all further evidence of the twentieth century's encroachment on rural Africa. He wears slacks and a red sweater and has a trim mustache. Except for the silver-dollar-sized hole in his left ear lobe, from which once hung beads and bones, he looks just like a man who has spent his life in Nairobi or New York.

The store Mardadi operates is part of the Kenyan government's attempt to settle the nomadic Masai and teach them modern management methods for their cattle. The program, if successful, would lead the Masai into the mainstream of Kenyan society. Says one Kenyan legislator: "It's time the Masai put on pants." Still, the government does not want to do too much for the Masai; they might become a threat to Kikuyu domination. In Meto, it has gone so far as to give them title to land, install water taps and build a health clinic and school. But the Masai will not be able to have both modernity and tradition. They will have to choose, as Mardadi already has done.

The three faces of Africa we have seen—Mary Ngei, trapped slum dweller; Francis Thuo, self-made entrepreneur; and Gideon Mardadi, warrior-turned-shopkeeper—reflect the vicissitudes of a continent where every life and every way of life are in transition. All three are Kenyans, living within a hundred miles of one another, but their lives are not unique to Kenya. For all across Africa, new pressures are reshaping old values, and old traditions are facing new challenges. The African's spiritual identity remains entwined with the heritage of village life, but his eyes are cast on—and increasingly his feet are planted in—the cities, for it is there that he can, with good luck, hard work or a combination of both, escape the bondage of poverty and ignorance that have enslaved an entire continent. Every young African coming to the city knows exactly what he wants: a Mercedes-Benz, the most singularly important symbol of wealth and status in Africa. The goal is so widespread that in East Africa wealthy members of the new upper class are referred to as Wabenzi (*wa* indicating the plural in Swahili).

Partly because the African was slow or unwilling to adopt Western ways, the colonialists branded him stupid and lazy. The myth was a cruel one that lingered far too long, for the African is neither. Given education and exposure to the outside world, he can be as articulate and alert, as sophisticated and intelligent as anyone you would meet in London or Chicago. Given an economic incentive and an obtainable goal, he is a tireless worker willing to accept great hardships. But the vast majority have neither education nor incentive, and in many cases these are the people who are running governments and armies. Thirty years ago only the black elite, less than 1 percent of the population, made it through the colonial system to positions of authority. Today anyone with the right connections can make it. The result is that Africa simply doesn't function very smoothly or efficiently.

And what does the future hold? That answer rests with the African child, whose days are as harsh—and yet as full of love—as that of any child on earth. His life is one of toil, not toys, and he endures burdens unknown to children in the developed world. What is taken for granted in the West—health, education, a reasonable standard of living, even survival itself—is still in the prayers of the world's poorest, least developed continent.

▶ According to the United Nations, 40 percent of African children under the age of five go through a period of malnutrition severe enough to cause mental or physical damage affecting their growth.

▶ The sub-teen African child-labor force numbers an estimated 16 million. The World Bank says that 27 children per 1,000 are in the African labor force, compared to 14 in Asia, 6 in South America and 1 in Europe and the United States.

▶ One child in eight dies before the age of two, usually from preventable illnesses, and in nineteen African countries the average child will not live to the age of forty. Two million of Africa's children are classified by the United Nations as refugees.

But practically nowhere in the world is the family as cohesive as in Africa. The young, the old, the infirm are never without care, food, shelter or love as long as there is a relative or tribal brother with anything at all to share. Individual interests are considered self-indulgent in rural Africa; what matters is the well-being of the collective unit. Elders are treated with deference and no child would dare question his word or authority. A child does as he is told, never forgetting that there is nothing more important than the family.

From his earliest days an African child in, say, Kenya, is strapped with cloths to his mother's back, accompanying her while she tills the fields, gathers firewood and collects water. The child is coddled and fed on demand, not on a schedule, and it is very rare indeed to hear an African infant cry.

By the time the child is four or five he has assumed the responsibility of tending the herd or caring for younger brothers and sisters. He is seldom balky and never disrespectful to his parents. His freedom is great and largely undirected. He may cut off the top of a banana tree and use it like a rubber tire to float in a stream. He may entwine palm leaves to make a soccer ball or build a little cart with wooden wheels, greasing the "bearings" with fresh cow dung. But almost certainly he has never had a store-bought toy, and if he lives in a small rural village, he may never have seen an electric light, a telephone, a flush toilet or a comic book.

"In the first year the physical development of children in rural Africa is precocious compared to Western norms," says Nina Darnton, an American child psychologist who spent three years working in Africa.

"There is tremendous stimulation and love between mother and child. Then, by the second year, the mother usually has had another baby and the first child is taken off her back and left pretty much alone, unstimulated. It's like a sudden fall from grace.

"The precocity levels out then with Western norms. By the third year it has declined. This is when, in the Western world, mothers are giving their children toys and sitting down to explain the way things work. But a mother in Africa doesn't have time for that.

"The children are left to their own devices. You have the feeling they're crying out for stimulation and direction. They have all this wonderful energy, a lot of it very creative, and nowhere to direct it."

If African parents share a single dream today, it is that their children get an education, the end result of which is a government job and the security that goes with it. This is the African equivalent of a social security system, because Africa's sons and daughters care for their aged parents as they would their own children. Education is pursued as an end to itself; the quest for knowledge is decidedly secondary.

The Njumbi primary school, not far from the town of Karai in Kenya, is typical of what rural Africa offers. You leave the paved highway and bounce along a rutted dirt road for fifteen or twenty minutes, through parched hills and past mud-walled, straw-roofed homes until you come to a cluster of low, weather-darkened buildings built with cement blocks during the colonial era. The headmaster, Michael Mathini, an energetic and amiable man of thirty who rides a bicycle to work, greeted us at the door. He led us into his office and pointed with great pride to a wall graph showing that his students scored above the national average in the annual state-administered examination.

The school had 620 students, four outdoor latrine pits, one dictionary, a few broken windows Mathini hoped to fix when he had some money to buy glass with, and seventeen teachers who earned from $80 to $135 a month. There were no amenities such as a library or classrooms with heat and electricity. The frayed books the children used were printed in London and contained illustrations of white children and Western-world fairy tales such as *Jack and the Beanstalk* and *Snow White and the Seven Dwarfs.* Hardly the type of exercise that would reinforce the identity of a black child who came to school barefoot.

I asked the headmaster who the children's heroes were, "Heroes?" Mathini repeated. "That is a Western idea. We don't have heroes or idols in Africa." Then, speaking of Kenya's first two presidents, he added, "But we do tell the children that we want another Kenyatta or Moi. We tell them, 'These people were born poor and naked like you, so you can advance without coming from a rich family.' "

The statement, though, was not entirely true. The children were being educated for jobs that were not available and taught the value of farmland they could probably never afford to buy. A city-bound African youth who has learned to read and write, even moderately well, does not want to work with his hands; he wants to be a clerk and wear a white shirt and a necktie and sit at a desk. That is status.

In the first-grade class room across from Mathini's office, thirty or forty boys and girls were learning to count with the aid of little twigs. They applauded with gusto each time one of them gave the teacher the right answer. The teacher spoke to them in Swahili, a language they had difficulty understanding because their native tongue was Kikuyu. In the tenth-grade room nearby, an ancient wooden radio sat on another teacher's desk and the dozen or so teen-agers there strained through the heavy static to hear the "creative writing" lesson being broadcast in English from Nairobi. The nursery school, a cement-floored room with bare blue walls located at the far side of the yard, had only a handful of children and fifty empty seats. The parents of the missing youngsters had been unable to pay the $1.85 semiannual school fee due the previous month and had been forced by the headmaster to withdraw their children from school until they came up with the money.

"These children know that without education there can be no employment," said the first-grade teacher, Francis Waruiru. "They are desperate to learn. Their parents put great pressure on them to learn so they can go to Nairobi and get a job with a good salary.

"Even William here tries hard, but William's a funny little boy. He writes everything upside down. See"—and the teacher, who had had no training in special education, held up William's paper for us to examine—"you cannot read what he writes."

"I don't know why he does that. I sit down with him and show him slowly and then he writes the right way. Then he goes back to his desk and writes upside down again. The whole trouble is that William is forgetful. I have told him he must just practice harder. He's really quite a mystery."

The school has no facilities or money to serve lunch, so at noontime we drove with the headmaster a mile or two over the hills to the Happiness Café in Kurai. Ours was the only vehicle in sight and it drew stares from the people along the road who wore, like African villagers everywhere, a bewildering array of Western clothing: ski caps with tassels, broken straw hats, tattered suits with wide lapels, winter overcoats with holes and patches—clothing that had once hung in the closets of American families, had been collected by charity organizations, sold by the ton to junk dealers in New York and, finally, shipped at a profit for sale in the marketplaces of a thousand African villages.

To an outsider, Karai had the make-believe aura of a frontier town on a Hollywood set. A donkey dozed outside the First and

Last Starlight Bar. The market, known as Oliver Njoroge's Popular Store, was empty. Except for a woman hunkered by a pile of potatoes, the wide dirt path leading through the town was deserted and the only stirring was that of the wind, which had turned everything dust-brown. Karai was a time capsule, exuding neither ennui nor energy. It was just there.

Eight peasant farmers sat at the long benches in the Happiness Café, eating the daily special, a thirty-six-cent bowl of beef stew. A sign on the wall said: "No credit Sunday through Sunday." The farmers ate in silence and paid no heed to the village idiot, who moved from table to table in a series of froglike jumps, holding out his palm for chunks of beef and grabbing crumbs of bread from the floor.

"I would be the first to admit that we don't have very advanced people here," said the subchief of Karai, James Kamau, as we finished our stew. "But the problem is that all the young men, anyone with an education, go to Nairobi now to find jobs as casual laborers, or to be servants and *askaris*.*

"Now, before long we will have water taps in Karai. The pipeline the government is building has already reached the hills by the primary school. Then we will have development and maybe the people will come back from the city. But if they do, how are we going to support them? Our farmland is not good here and all the land is taken. This is the very poorest part of Kikuyuland.

"What we need are more educated ladies, people who will come to understand family planning and the need for smaller families, many less children. Our children face a very hard life ahead and it will be even harder if there is no family planning. Pills are sent to the clinic but no one uses them."

As common as large families are, premarital sex is taboo in much of rural Africa and is punished severely, even by death in a few cultures. Removal of the clitoris—a brief, bloody operation that is performed without anesthetics—reduces the woman's potential for

---

* *Askari* means "guard" or "watchman" in Swahili. Armed with clubs, stones, whistles and sometimes spears, they guard private residences of anyone wealthy enough to own, say, a television set, as well as banks, hotels and most commercial enterprises with an inventory worth stealing. The majority are employed by large African-owned security companies that charge a client $180 a month for an *askari*'s services. An *askari* works twelve-hour shifts, usually seven days a week, and earns about $40 a month.

arousal during intercourse, making sex a female activity of procreation, not pleasure. Marriages are arranged soon after the circumcision ceremonies, when the boys are about seventeen, the girl fifteen. The purpose of the union has little to do with companionship or sharing as we know it in the West. Rather, it is solely to produce a bountiful crop of children, who can help in the fields and can eventually take care of their parents in old age.

In the cities, sexual morals are much looser, but affection between men and women is only rarely displayed or expressed. You will never see a young couple in East Africa exchanging touches or simply sitting quietly in a restaurant, looking at each other. Africans skip the preliminaries known in the West; where a European couple might kiss, Africans copulate.

It is also curious by Western standards that homosexuality in Africa is virtually unknown. True, in the cities you will often see men holding hands, but it is a sign of friendship, not homosexuality. Africa's tradition is rigidly heterosexual. Sexual roles—because of the emphasis placed on producing large families—are clearly defined, and parents never allow their children to play roles that would confuse their sexual identity. Any African having a homosexual relationship is quickly ostracized and in Kenya, for example, is guilty of a felony, punishable by five years in prison and up to a hundred lashes.

Perhaps more for economic than sexual reasons, male African prostitutes have appeared in recent years in areas where foreign influence is strong, such as touristy Mombasa on the Kenya coast, and Lagos, the boom capital of Nigeria. In 1978 a Swiss tourist spending Christmas in Mombasa was caught having an affair with a Kenyan male and sentenced to nine months in prison. But such incidents are rare, for the guilt of homosexuality is great. During Kenya's Mau Mau war in the 1950s, the Kikuyu guerrillas recruited new supporters by sending teen-age boys into the prisons to tempt inmates into performing sodomy with them. The disgrace was so painful that the inmates, fearing the act would be revealed, were beholden to the guerrillas and became, as ordered, part of the Mau Mau movement.

The one constant amid the changes that are transforming the character of a continent is the role of the African woman, a person whose physical and spiritual strength is nothing short of remarkable.

More often than not she is uneducated, barefoot, stoop-shouldered and beefy. Her comforts are few, her burdens many. But if liberation means the freedom *to* work, rather than *from* work, she is the world's most liberated woman.

The African woman produces 70 percent of the food grown on the continent, according to the United Nations. She works longer and harder and has more responsibilities than her husband. She is the economic backbone of the rural community, the maker of family decisions, the initiator of social change, the harvester of crops. She is the hub around which the spokes of society turn.

Drive down almost any country road in East Africa and you will see a procession of women padding along the shoulder, their backs parallel to the ground under the weight of huge piles of firewood or jars of water. The outdoor marketplaces—the most important source of economic activity in any village—are run and staffed exclusively by women. In the fields it is only women you see with hoes and sickles. And the men? The elderly ones are apt to be sitting in the shade of the trees, smoking their pipes, drinking homemade beer, discussing their cattle—or saying nothing at all. The younger ones are either in school, in the city or in the local beer hall.

"Our daughters are more important to us than the sons now," a woman with thirteen children told me in one Tanzanian town. "They have not forgotten how to work. But the sons are no good. They go off and get drunk, and when you find them, they have been knifed and killed."

Hyperbole aside, her statement reflects the frustration the African women feel, knowing that they remain second-class citizens despite their contributions to family and community. The Africa of the 1980s is still a man's society, as chauvinistic as the pubs of Australia, and it is an unusual woman who can rise above the positions of secretary, nurse or teacher.

In Kenya, women represent only 10 percent of the university enrollment, 16 percent of the labor force and 6 percent of the jobholders earning more than $375 a year. Their illiteracy rate—70 percent—is double that for men.

With few exceptions, women in Africa inherit nothing from their fathers and can be divorced by their husbands without any settlement. They are expected to remain sexually faithful, while their spouses are permitted, even expected, to have as many wives and girl friends as they can support. Every cent a woman earns goes to the family; a man's salary is spent on whatever he pleases, often himself. For the most part a woman is viewed as a baby machine, and with abortion being illegal in Africa except for medical reasons, and illegitimacy not being a stigma, they are productive machines indeed.

"You see all these men running around the city, saying they are looking for work," said Margaret Mugo, the only woman on Nairobi's forty-four-member city council. "What they really mean is that they're trying to get some money to pursue their own pleasures. The money they make doesn't get back to their wives and children in the village. They spend it on themselves."

In 1979 the Kenyan parliament (168 men and 4 women) considered a bill to legalize polygamy—a common practice which many Africans consider a sign of wealth and prestige—and to codify marriage standards. The intent of the bill was sensible enough: the attorney general merely wanted to safeguard the interests of wives and children, who often lose their inheritance when a husband dies, his possessions and property being divided among other spouses.

Many members of parliament didn't see it exactly that way, though. One of them, Kimunai Soi, argued that the corporal punishment section of the bill would deny a man his traditional right to beat his wife. "It is very African to teach women manners by beating them," Soi said on the floor of parliament. "If this legislation is passed, even slapping your wife is ruled out."

Another lawmaker, Oloo Aringo, contested a clause requiring a man to get permission from his first wife before marrying another. This, he said, was putting the horse before the cart. What was needed instead was to educate women so they would understand the necessity of polygamy. The majority agreed and the bill was scrapped.

"We are the people in the middle and we, the women, suffer most and we suffer quietly," said Felicita Olchurie, a college professor whose father had received three cows for approving her marriage.

"When you get married," she continued, "you belong to your husband. As simple as that. He treats you any way he chooses, usually disrespectfully, but as long as he doesn't beat you, you stay with him. Our problem is that we're not aggressive enough yet. We're too inhibited by our society, by our families. We'd rather suffer silently inside.

"I don't think our daughters will tolerate it. Their rights are bound to be broader than ours and their society will be much more open. In the end, though, the African man will still be the African man, and his main preoccupation will still be proving his virility."

Traditionally the male role in Africa was waging war, hunting, clearing land and building huts. Women were responsible for gathering wood, fetching water, raising children and harvesting crops. If there was extra food to sell, the woman kept the profits. She was the resource of Africa's rural development, and her role was largely autonomous, seldom subservient.

In the Fur society of western Sudan, men and women operated separately, each group cultivating its own plots. In parts of Ghana it was the "Queen Mother" of a village, not the chief, who determined the line of descent. In the Ivory Coast it is the women who still run the market economy, and in Kenya it is the women who own and operate the most successful farming cooperatives. But as Africa strives for modernity, complex social forces have upset the male-female relationship and handed the greater share of educational and economic opportunities to men.

The first vehicle for upsetting the balance was the missionary, who tried to convince Africans that their sexual mores were unhealthy, immoral and barbaric. Next came the colonialists. They built no schools for girls until after World War II on the premise that African women did not need education, and they introduced male-controlled cash crops such as coffee and cocoa that undercut the economic power of women, who traditionally grew the subsistence crops. Gradually the male's warrior-hunter role began to disappear and the young men drifted into the cities. They became the focus of the newly independent nations' rush into the twentieth century.

The universities changed their emphasis from the arts to math and science, subjects that customarily are male-oriented. The girls who managed to graduate from high school—65 percent of high school enrollment in Kenya and Ghana is male—found few places in college available and even fewer responsible positions in an already tight job market.

"I know of no inherent reason why social change, industrialization and modernization has to negatively affect the status of women, but we are seeing it happen in Africa," said Audrey Smock, an American sociologist working with the Kenyan government. "The African woman increasingly is falling backward to a position similar to that of the Western woman in the early stages of the industrial revolution."

Kenya has moved cautiously in the area of women's rights. In 1977 it gave working mothers entitlement to two months' paid maternity leave and discarded the law making it illegal to employ women between 6:30 P.M. and 6:30 A.M. The new law, however, grouped women and minors together, implying that the former were still something less than responsible adults.

Somalia, a Moslem country where some girls' vaginas are stitched together to ensure purity until marriage, was less subtle in its attempts to improve the women's lot. President Mohamed Siad Barré declared in 1975 that henceforth men and women were equal. Many Moslem scholars in Somalia protested, contending that the Koran held women inferior. Barré settled the argument by executing ten of the scholars and sentencing twenty-three others to prison for up to thirty years. The executions didn't provide any new opportunities for women, but no one debates the merits of sexual equality in Somalia anymore.

Only two hours by air from the green pastures of Kenya, Somalia is a foreboding land of desert and furnace heat. The people are nomads, lean and tough, and during the *tangambili* (the long, hot months between monsoons) the entire country slips into slumber, and nothing, nothing at all, carries the vaguest hint of urgency.

Great herds of camels plod along the sandy, sun-blanched streets of Mogadishu, the capital, headed for the waterfront and export to Saudi Arabia. Donkeys amble by, ignoring their masters' whips, and they move wearily past the mosques and beaches where old ladies sit sweltering in black *chadors* that cover everything but their eyes. The donkeys haul carts, loaded with bricks and cement blocks and sometimes grain, and from the rear of each beast hangs a canvas bag to catch its droppings. In the bone-dry fields outside Mogadishu, women stand eight-hour shifts as human scarecrows, perched on rock piles that elevate them above the maize, motionless except for their flapping arms that scare away the birds.

One day I met an old man named Abdullah in a Somali village. He had a wispy beard and watery eyes and, he said, a great loneliness. Two of his three wives had died, and nine of his eleven children had gone off to the city. All but three of his camels had succumbed to drought or the Somali-Ethiopian war that has dragged on for a thousand years. "There is little to do now but wait for death," he said.

Abdullah had not followed his children into the city because in Africa the cities are for the young and the able-bodied. They do not absorb the elderly, and if you walk the streets of an African capital, you see virtually no old people. To be poor and old in an African city is not a happy fate, so the aged remain in the rural communities, where the changes are less threatening and the extended family concept makes sure that a helping hand is always near.

Each Sunday, Abdullah's eldest son, Ahmed, who is a primary-school teacher, drives from Mogadishu to visit his father. Ahmed always brings a few shillings, several cigarettes and a cup or two of maize. Abdullah appreciates the visits but he is puzzled by his son's life—the Renault car he prefers to a camel, the slacks and sweater instead of flowing robes, the clean-shaven face. And Ahmed's two young sons are just as puzzled by their grandfather's customs. After visiting for an hour or so, they always start fidgeting. "When are we going home?" they ask their father, not meaning to be impolite.

Abdullah's wife prepared some potatoes one Sunday when Ahmed and his children visited. Everyone sat on the ground, outside Abdullah's mud-and-stick hut, eating the potatoes with their hands from a tin pot. Several chickens and two goats wandered among them. Abdullah seemed not to notice the flies but the children swatted at them constantly.

"Grandfather," the ten-year-old boy said, "how can you live like this? Why don't you get a table? You don't even have the sweet kind of potatoes like we get in the city."

The old man looked up, hurt, but said nothing. In a moment he dropped his gaze and went back to eating.

THE MEN
AT THE TOP

▲

We spoke and acted as if, given the opportunity for self-government, we would quickly create utopias. Instead injustice, even tyranny, is rampant.

—PRESIDENT JULIUS NYERERE OF TANZANIA

THE TELEVISION SCREEN fills with an image of heavenly clouds. A choir of voices swells in the background. The music grows louder, and as the clouds drift apart there emerges the face of a man, dark and handsome, a leopard-skin cap perched jauntily on his head. His gaze is steady and the faintest trace of a smile crosses his lips. The camera zooms in and holds for what seems like a very long time on the face. It speaks of strength, compassion, wisdom, though no words are uttered. What the viewer knows immediately is that this is no mere mortal. No indeed. It is Mobutu Sese Seko, a political survivor whose name translates roughly as "the all-powerful warrior who, by his endurance and will to win, goes from contest to contest, leaving fire in his wake." And this is the start of the eight o'clock TV news in Kinshasa.

Mobutu became president of Zaire in 1965, and though lurching from crisis to crisis, has managed to hold together his huge country with its 200 tribes and bloody history of instability. Like most African presidents, he rules as half-god, half-chieftain, combining the techniques of twentieth-century communication with ancient tribal symbolism. By his own decree he has become the embodiment of a homespun philosophy and a national symbol above criticism. He has caused his people great suffering, but at his command they turn out by the tens of thousands to line the parade routes and fill the stadiums and sing his praises. In short, Mobutu is more than a president. He is a cult.

His teachings—called Mobutism—have, by his order, become

the national philosophy. His portrait is the only picture allowed in public places; it even hangs in hotel elevators. His people wear Mobutu badges, pinned over their hearts, and T-shirts bearing his likeness, and Mao-style attire known as a Mobutu shirt. They sing his name in popular songs and recite his sayings ("It is better to die of hunger than to be rich and a slave to colonialism") in schools and factories. None of this, though, means that Mobutu's 26 million people have any great fondness for him. They are only doing what they are told to do and paying homage to their chief as they are expected to do. One day, when Mobutu is overthrown, they will tear down his statues, burn his pictures, curse his name and pay allegiance to a new chief.

Although Mobutu's excesses are extravagant even by African standards, the man himself is not an aberration among his presidential peers. He is but one in a fraternity whose members command respect by words, not deeds. These men represent a curious mixture of European influence and African tradition, and their power is absolute. Their overseas bank accounts are stuffed with pilfered funds, and their loyalties and concerns are distinctly self-centered, often having little to do with national advancement.

Mobutu is, in fact, more a creation of Western capitalism than he is of African custom. Like Africa's other second-generation presidents, he is the symbol of his country's sickness, not the sole cause of it. After independence the inherited European systems soon ceased to work and the substitute African systems broke down. Men like Mobutu were left to rule by experiment. They became, in effect, neocolonial governors, operating and living much in the style of their former white masters. The welfare of the African people is generally not much more important to them than it was to the colonial governors.

When Mobutu came to power, Zaire (formerly the Belgian Congo) was a country on the move. Rich copper mines stood ready for exploring, fertile fields for tilling. By the early 1970s, with copper bringing record prices on the world market, Mobutu, a former journalist and one-time army sergeant, found himself presiding over an unprecedented economic boom. His response was to go on a spending orgy that made economists' heads whirl. But his priorities were sadly confused; what he sought was not national development, but personal prestige and national grandeur.

He built palaces, eleven in all, and linked some of them to the capital with four-lane highways. He dedicated monuments to himself and constructed stadiums in which to address his people. He visited New York, admired the World Trade Center and had a small-scale duplication of the buildings constructed in Kinshasa. He bought off his enemies and turned his friends—most of them from his own Gbande tribe—into overnight millionaires. He redesigned the main street of Kinshasa and cut down the lovely old trees in the center divider so the boulevard could accommodate more military vehicles for a parade. He spent $15 million sponsoring the Muhammad Ali–George Foreman world championship fight in 1974. Said Ali: "Zaire's gotta be great. I never seen so many Mercedes." And as for himself—well, Mobutu was hardly the penniless army sergeant of a decade ago. He was now one of the world's wealthiest men, with assets conservatively estimated by Western intelligence sources at more than $3 billion. Mobutu, incidentally, did not have enough faith in his country's economic future to invest at home; like other African presidents, his fortune was in European banks and European real estate.

Of every dollar coming into Zaire, whether it was in the form of a foreign aid grant or a business contract, Zairian officials took twenty cents off the top for their personal cut. In 1977 Zaire's coffee crop was valued at $400 million. Because of smuggling and underinvoicing, only $120 million was returned to Zaire's treasury. The rest ended up in foreign bank accounts held by Mobutu and his Gbande colleagues. Everyone was on the take, and in Zaire you needed to know only two things to survive or prosper: Whom do I see and how much will it cost?

Not surprisingly, from the very beginning Mobutu and his pals were about the only ones excited over the course of developments in Zaire. So, trying to drum up some national spirit, Mobutu launched what he called an African "authenticity" program. "We are resorting to this authenticity," he said, "in order to rediscover our soul, which colonization had almost erased from our memories and which we are seeking in the tradition of our ancestors."

He ordered all Zairians to replace their Christian names with African ones, and set the example himself by dropping his first and middle names (Joseph Desiré) in favor of Sese Seko. He changed the Congo's name to Zaire (meaning "river"), forbade the wearing of Western attire, designed a national uniform that looks like a Mao suit, canceled Christmas and put up his portrait in the churches.

Carrying his zeal a step further, he expropriated $500 million in foreign enterprises and expelled the Asian merchants who had kept the economy running. Most of the Belgian plantation owners, technicians and businessmen were forced out, too. Mobutu awarded the confiscated businesses to his friends. In many cases the new operators merely sold the merchandise still in stock and closed up shop.

The Zairian people whispered about Mobutu's misdeeds, but only quietly because his secret police had permeated every level of society. In the U.S. Congress there were debates about Washington's cozy alliance with the Kinshasa government, but the official line was that Zaire was economically and strategically important, that it was a counterbalance to growing Soviet influence in central Africa and that Mobutu, a staunch anti-Communist, should be supported regardless of his shortcomings. As a result, Zaire in the late 1970s was receiving nearly half of all the aid money the Carter Administration allocated for black Africa. But Washington wasn't helping a country develop; it was merely buying the loyalty of a chieftain, much in the same way Europe did during the colonial era. It was encouraging the very conditions that could lead to revolution and expanded Soviet influence.

Zaire paid a heavy price for Mobutu's short-sightedness. Copper prices plunged and the boom of the seventies quickly became the bust of the eighties. Zaire became an economic cripple and a social misfit, and by 1980 Mobutu was experiencing the ultimate humiliation for a black African leader: he turned the running of his country over to foreigners. He invited back the Belgian businessmen whose firms he had expropriated in the 1970s. He brought in Moroccan guards to provide his security. The International Monetary Fund was running the central bank, and Belgian specialists were operating the customs department. Other Europeans were moving into the finance ministry, the taxation office and the transportation system. Mobutu called this new experiment for economic recovery the Mobutu Plan. It was well named because it was an attempt to save Mobutu, not Zaire.

By the time I made my last visit to Zaire—the country V. S. Naipaul described so vividly in A Bend in the River—it seemed to be rapidly disintegrating in spite of the Mobutu Plan. At Mama Yemo General Hospital (named for Mobutu's mother) unattended patients were dying because there were no bandages, no sterilization equipment, no oxygen, no film for x-ray machines. The dead often remained for hours in the intensive care unit before being removed because there was no room for extra bodies in the morgue.

The health clinics at the university campuses in Kinshasa and Lubumbashi had shut down because the medicines intended for use there had been diverted to the black market. The university cafeterias were closed for the simple reason that there was no food. With inflation running at over 100 percent, a bag of cornmeal needed to feed a family of six for a month cost $130, twice a laborer's monthly salary. In the rural areas people were reverting from cash-crop to subsistence farming because the transportation system had broken down and the food they had intended to sell at market lay rotting on the ground. (Zaire had 31,000 miles of main roads at independence in 1960; twenty years later only 3,700 miles of usable roads remained.)

Zaire's debt to foreign banks and governments soared to $4 billion in 1980, and shortages of food and spare parts became critical. The government's news agency closed down for lack of paper, 360 abandoned buses stood rusting near the airport, and the national airline, Air Zaire, could afford only enough fuel to operate one of every four domestic flights each day. Its Boeing 747 and Douglas DC-10 were repossessed. Through it all, Mobutu kept insisting that Zaire and its people were doing fine; the problems Western journalists wrote about, he said, were illusionary ones that merely underscored the media's bias against Africa.

President cultism is hardly unique to Africa. In the United States, after all, John F. Kennedy became a cult figure, in death perhaps more than in life. But what African leaders have managed to do is mold cultism into a fine art. They have bestowed upon themselves godlike qualities and the unquestioned authority of the most powerful chieftain. Most, however, are not leaders in the true sense; they are images, the creations of a sort of African-style public relations campaign. As peculiar as the phenomenon may seem to a Westerner, it makes sense in Africa, where the uneducated masses respond to strong central authority. They do not want to be bullied by their governments but they do expect their presidents to exercise the same kind of authoritarian control that tribal chiefs and colonial governors used. Anything less is considered a sign of weakness.

Mobutu may have carried cultism to the extreme, but almost every black African president is, in varying degrees, a cult figure who has adopted a nickname to convey a desired image. Mobutu and President Etienne Eyadéma of Togo both like to be referred to as "the Guide." Jomo Kenyatta, the late Kenyan president, was known as Mzee, the Swahili word for "Wise Old Man." Julius Nyerere of Tanzania is known as "the Teacher"; Hastings Kamuzu Banda of Malawi as "the Chief of Chiefs"; Félix Houphouët-Boigny of the

Ivory Coast as "the No. 1 Peasant"; and the late Macias Nguema Biyogo of Equatorial Guinea as "the National Miracle." Uganda's former president Idi Amin Dada used to refer to himself, only half in jest, as "the Conquerer of the British Empire."

Togo's Eyadéma has a presidential cheering section consisting of a thousand women and he wouldn't think of making a public appearance without it. The women's prime responsibility is to perform traditional dances and lavish their president with songs of praise—a ritual that Eyadéma says helps build a national spirit and identity. For $20, Togolese can buy wristwatches on whose face the illuminated portrait of Eyadéma fades and reappears every fifteen seconds. Eyadéma also has built a huge bronze statue of himself in the downtown square of Lomé, and commissioned an Eyadéma comic book in which he plays a Superman-type character.

In Malawi, everything from university dormitories to highways is named for President Banda, and women wear dresses embroidered with Banda's portrait. The mildest criticism of Banda guarantees a stretch in jail. "They say my people love me," observes President-for-Life Banda, "and I would be naïve to deny it."

The lead item on most radio newscasts in black Africa seldom covers the major news story of the day; instead it deals with what the country's president said or did that day, however routine or mundane. "President Daniel arap Moi said today that Kenya is a friend to all people of the world," reports the Voice of Kenya. Or: "President Daniel arap Moi has called on leaders in the country to refrain from spreading malicious rumors among *wananchi* [the masses]." In Jomo Kenyatta's final days, when he was a senile and largely incapacitated man of eighty-six years withering away in State House, the Voice of Kenya reported daily that he was on "a busy working tour of the coast provinces." The two daily newspapers were required to run the usual page-one photograph of Kenyatta conducting that day's affairs of state—even though they had to dig old pictures out of their files. The premise was that the people wouldn't know the difference. But they did, of course, and no one was surprised when the Voice of Kenya suddenly started playing funeral music without any announcement one day in August 1978. Kenyatta had gone on his last "busy working tour."

Moi, Kenyatta's vice president, allowed only a respectful period before he started taking down Kenyatta's pictures and putting up his own. Moi's words soon became the headline item on each newscast and the *wananchi* were soon urged to turn out and cheer their president each time he left State House. One cult—a legitimate one, given Kenyatta's great charisma and early influence in the anticolonialist movements—had ended and another one of questionable authenticity had begun. (Quite deservedly, Kenyatta remains a legendary figure in Africa.)

The honeymoon for Moi did not last long. In short order he turned Kenya into a one-party state and started arresting dissidents and journalists. As Kenya's economy deteriorated in the world-wide recession, Moi, a former schoolteacher, and his band of ruling elite grew richer by the day through various business deals. The inevitable happened early one morning in August 1982: a group of air force men seized the radio station and announced that they had overthrown the government. Before forces loyal to Moi could put down the attempted coup, more than 120 people had died and soldiers had gone on a rampage in Nairobi, looting, raping and shooting. The attempted coup coincided with a rash of worsening social problems in Kenya: widespread official corruption, rampant urban crime that included the murder of an occasional tourist, a stagnant economy and a government that would brook no criticism. Moi had a rare opportunity at that moment to exert his leadership and address himself to the root causes of the unrest. Instead he went for the jugular. He closed down the university for nine months and disbanded the air force. He turned Kenya into a one-party state, bought an independent daily newspaper and made it a mouthpiece of the party, ordered the arrest of several leading journalists and critics and went on a witch hunt for "traitors" in his cabinet. It was a distressingly familiar scenario in Africa, and it would solve nothing. The cancer had already started to spread, and Moi, a small man in the shadow of Jomo Kenyatta, was now fighting a delaying action.

Like Moi, few African presidents would consider taking a trip without summoning the full diplomatic corps to the airport or ordering the masses to line the route from State House to the terminal. I always found it a rather sad spectacle to watch thousands of Africans waving banners that they could not read and obediently applauding some man who demanded—but had not necessarily earned—their allegiance, respect and love. True, they didn't have many other opportunities to show they really did belong to a nation, but the prime purpose of the exercise was designed to pamper the egos of insecure men needing acceptance and authenticity.

Let's go to the banks of the Bangui River, deep in the heart of Africa, to see how one man dealt with that insecurity.

To an outsider, Jean-Bédel Bokassa seemed to have everything: a huge fortune and immense power, so many decorations that he needed a specially made jacket to display them all, and a fine family numbering nine wives and thirty legitimate children.

Since independence in 1960 he had been honoring himself with monuments and palaces and countless titles, including that of president-for-life of the Central African Republic. He was entertained abroad—for the trip to Peking he took his Rumanian wife as first lady—and even if he was considered a bit unorthodox, ambassadors listened to him, journalists quoted him and his countrymen paid him homage.

But what the former army sergeant didn't have—and what he craved—was respect, a sense of legitimacy. Except for the fear he engendered, people just didn't take him very seriously. His occasional savagery and frequent eccentricities did receive a lot of attention in the foreign press, but in the long run he was one of Africa's most forgettable presidents, a tragicomical figure who was never able to come to grips with the problems facing his hapless country. He fretted over his inadequacies a great deal and lost himself for hours at a time reading about the one man he idolized, Napoleon Bonaparte, who, in a moment of supreme arrogance, snatched his crown from the Pope's hands and crowned himself emperor in Paris' Notre Dame Cathedral in 1804.

Then it dawned on Bokassa. If Napoleon could do it, why couldn't he? Surely no one would take him lightly if he was emperor. And to the amazement of everyone, including his two million subjects, Bokassa declared one day that his republic was now an empire and he was no longer a mere life-president; he was Emperor Bokassa I. Bokassa invited the Pope (who respectfully declined) to the coronation and offered international television rights to the highest bidder. He waived the edict that foreign journalists entering his country had to post a $400 bond at the airport, and hired the French firm of Guiselin, which had embroidered Napoleon's uniforms, to design a coronation robe with two million pearls and crystal beads for $145,000. He drew up a list of earls and dukes, imported white horses from Belgium to pull his coach to the cathedral and spent $2 million for a crown topped by a 138-carat diamond.

All this seemed a bit lavish for a Texas-sized country with only 170 miles of paved roads and a per capita annual income of $250. The final tab was to reach more than $20 million, but French President Valéry Giscard d'Estaing, anxious to maintain political and economic control in France's former colony, quietly passed the word that Paris would arrange compensation for all unpaid bills. As Bokassa himself once put it, "Everything around here is financed by the French government. We ask the French for money, get it and waste it."

On December 4, 1977, Bangui, a dusty river town of 250,000 souls, was packed with several thousand guests—but not a single head of state. The temperature climbed past 100 degrees and the dignitaries sat sweating in their morning coats and Parisian gowns, waiting for Bokassa to fulfill his lifelong quest for Napoleonic glory. Finally a voice boomed over the loudspeaker, "Sa majesté impériale, l'empereur Bokassa sa premier," and everyone struggled to attention.

Bokassa entered the Bokassa Sports Stadium—which was next to Bokassa University on Bokassa Avenue, a stone's throw from the Bokassa statue—wearing a golden wreath on his balding head. He ascended the eagle-shaped golden throne, placed the crown on his head, just as Napoleon had done, and took an oath to defend the constitution, which he had suspended a decade earlier. His two-year-old son, Jean-Bédel Georges, dressed in a crisp white military uniform, fell fast asleep at his side. There was polite applause. Africa had its first emperor since Ethiopia's Haile Selassie was overthrown in 1974, presumed murdered and buried in an unmarked grave. But this was too much, even for Africa. Editorialized Senegal's weekly *Afrique Nouvelle:* "The event is worth examining because it stresses . . . in a tragic way an image of an Africa still stumbling in search of itself."

It also underscored the shallowness and sparseness of leadership in Africa and the silent obedience so many Africans will pay their rulers, no matter how despotic or unrealistic their ways. Publicly African heads of state scoffed at Bokassa's contention that the coronation was an attempt to develop "African authenticity" and promote a national pride. What they may have thought in private was another matter, for Bokassa had had the gall to do what a score of African presidents would have loved to do had they not been more sensitive to international reaction. Most were already imperial presidents in everything but title; Bokassa had merely made his role official. "They were jealous of me because I had an empire and they didn't," he later told an interviewer.

Jean-Bédel Bokassa was born in 1921, one of twelve children of a prominent Mbaka chief in what was then the French colony of Ubangi-Shari. His father, a village chief, was assassinated in 1927, and shortly thereafter his grief-stricken mother committed suicide.

It was a trauma from which the young Bokassa never fully recovered.

Bokassa, a short, trim man with a wide, Alfred E. Neuman grin, was educated at mission schools, enlisted in the French army in 1939 and fought gallantly in World War II. He survived the debacle at Dien Bien Phu and rose to the rank of captain, an unusual honor for an African in a European army. At the time of independence, in 1960, Bokassa became the Central African Republic's commander of the army, and Bokassa's uncle, Barthélémy Boganda, president. Boganda died five years later in a plane crash—sabotage was suspected—and Bokassa's cousin, David Dacko, became president. Bokassa overthrew his cousin on New Year's Day 1966, and after "rehabilitating" him in prison eventually elevated Dacko to the position of presidential adviser.

Bokassa's policies can be characterized as nothing more than unpredictable and during his reign the country slid steadily downhill economically, the people became poorer, the infrastructure and institutions fell apart chunk by chunk. The worse things got, the more bizarre Bokassa became.

He celebrated Mother's Day in 1971 by releasing all women from prison and ordering the execution of prisoners accused of matricide. Two were killed. The next year, in an attempt to curtail crime, he decreed that thieves would have an ear cut off for the first two offenses and a hand for the third. That failed to accomplish its intended results, so Bokassa personally supervised a ten-minute beating with clubs and rifle butts of imprisoned thieves. Three died, forty-three were maimed. Bokassa put the survivors on public display for six hours in the scorching sun.

"It's tough," he remarked to a horrified bystander, "but it's life."

Kurt Waldheim, the UN secretary-general, protested the beating, to which Bokassa had invited the press and other special guests. Bokassa responded by calling Waldheim "a pimp" and a "colonialist."

This would have seemed an appropriate time for some response from the outside world. But did Africa dissociate itself from Bokassa? Did Western governments curtail Bokassa's financial assistance or cut diplomatic ties? Did the church voice any protests? Not at all. No one said much of anything. African presidents are a clubby group not given to self-criticism; the West generally will support any African who is anti-Communist; and Christian missionaries expect Africans to behave in an uncivilized manner anyway. So Bokassa endured.

"It really gets my goat when people write that Bokassa is the Idi

Amin of Francophone [French-speaking] Africa," said the wife of an American missionary who had spent twenty-three years in the country, and who, like many missionaries, thought most Africans were still savages. "He's not that bad at all. This place is a lot saner and safer than some of the other African countries, where these people are killing each other like flies. Besides, there's complete religious freedom here. As far as Bokassa goes, he's still living with that one incident when he cut off some ears. But they did that in medieval England, too, you know."

Bokassa's religious tolerance was understandable because at least twice he converted from Christianity to Islam and back again. When Libya's strong man, Colonel Muammar Qaddafy, visited Bangui in 1976, Bokassa announced that he was adopting the Islamic faith and the name Salah Eddine Ammed. He pocketed Libya's gift of $2 million, but no sooner had Qaddafy gotten on his plane for the flight back to Tripoli than Ammed the Moslem said he had again become Bokassa the Christian.

To celebrate his birthday in 1973, Bokassa opened the nation's first television station (with his image filling the screen a good part of the time), although there were only forty TV sets in the republic. For his fifty-fifth birthday he ordered each of his countrymen to give him a present of 500 local francs (about $2.50), and when he told his people they would have to help pay for his coronation, he offered a simple explanation: "One cannot create a great history without sacrifices, and this sacrifice is accepted by the population."

Bokassa was to learn, though, that even emperors can err. In 1979 he decreed that schoolchildren buy and wear new uniforms bearing his portrait. Not coincidentally, he owned the factory that made the uniforms and the store that sold them. A mild protest followed. Students were rounded up, packed like sardines into the prison and clubbed by Bokassa and his policemen. More than eighty died. Amnesty International revealed the massacre, and France—which had kept Bokassa afloat by underwriting half his annual budget of $76 million—decided that enough was enough. Bokassa was now a liability. With hardly a shot being fired, France flew paratroopers into Bangui one night and restored Dacko to power.* The calendar had been turned back thirteen years; the Central African Republic was starting all over again.

* Dacko lasted less than two years in his second stint as president. He was overthrown in a bloodless coup in September 1981 by his own soldiers, who complained that Dacko was incapable of managing the economy. Dacko was allowed to stay in the country. Bokassa slipped out of France in 1986, returned to Bangui, and was promptly arrested at the airport.

Bokassa had been in Libya the night of the coup, trying to shake down Qaddafy for more money. When he learned he had been overthrown, Bokassa and his twenty-six associates flew straight to France, where he had extensive real estate holdings. But French authorities wouldn't even let him disembark. For fifty-six hours Bokassa waited in his plane at the air base in Evreau, west of Paris, while France looked for a country that would take him. The Ivory Coast, another former French colony, finally agreed, on the condition that Bokassa give no interviews, engage in no political activities and make no public appearances. Having been sentenced to death in absentia by a Bangui court, the fugitive emperor was now, in effect, a nonperson. You can drive by his house in the Ivory Coast capital of Abidjan, a stately mansion overlooking the lagoon, and on sunny afternoons see him walking his dogs in the yard. He will wave if he knows you are looking. But the gates to the wrought-iron fence surrounding the estate are locked, and most people pass by quickly, not bothering to return his greeting.*

Though Bkoassa's regime was as nonsensical as any in Africa, it should not be viewed in isolation. Its absurdity was the tragedy of all Africa, a continent that suffers so much at the hands of misguided leadership. Never has Africa been more in need of men with reasoned voices and clear visions, and never has the honor roll of leadership been so barren. The Old Guard—the first generation of presidents who took their people from colonialism to nationhood and governed through the sheer strength of their personalities—is largely gone now, the victims of old age or coups d'état. Authority has passed to a new group of leaders, younger, less educated, less sophisticated, less nationalistic than the Jomo Kenyattas of Kenya and Agostinho Netos of Angola. The Richard Nixons have replaced the George Washingtons. The new leaders have mastered power politics but little else. They have silenced all voices but those of the party line, and like their predecessors, they have failed to groom successors on the theory that any heir apparent is a potential threat. The result is a leadership vacuum into which unqualified men with a power base but no popular support can step and govern by whimsy.

At independence the Old Guard presidents were generally elected by popular vote, having been handpicked by the colonial powers as statesmen acceptable to London or Paris. They were soldiers or civil servants or those who had been at the forefront of the independence

---

*Bokassa was expelled from the Ivory Coast in December, 1983, after trying to rally political support back home. He took up residency in his chateau outside Paris while the French government tried unsuccessfully to find any African government that would offer him refuge.

movements. There were among them genuine leaders such as Ghana's Kwame Nkrumah, distinguished statesmen such as Angola's Neto, respected intellects such as Senegal's Léopold Sédar Senghor. The presidency, though, gave them their first real taste of affluence and influence. The multiparty democratic systems were dismantled one by one, presidential power was consolidated, the roots of cultism were planted. Soon it became as difficult for Africans to get rid of a black president as it had been to replace a white governor.

The practice of one man, one vote became, in reality, one man, one vote, one time. The president you got at independence was the one you would have until he died or was overthrown. Presidents don't retire to become their country's elder statesmen, because to be an ex-president in Africa is to be a nonentity. And the longer they stay in power, the more disdainful they become of their own people, and the greater become their own powers. One of the secrets of their longevity is to share enough of the spoils to create an elite, monied class of loyalists.

During Amin's rule, a Uganda Airlines Boeing 707 piloted by a free-lance American crew took off from Entebbe Airport each Tuesday for the eight-hour trip to Stansted Airport in England. There it took on a curious cargo: tailored clothes, expensive whiskey, cigarettes, gourmet foods, fine wristwatches, stylish sunglasses. It was an odd assortment of luxury items, considering that Uganda was then in the throes of economic collapse and there were long lines in Kampala for even the most basic goods such as milk and sugar.

But these were the rewards for Amin's loyalists, the officers in his 21,000-man army. While the civilian population remained imprisoned in poverty, the officers moved into rent-free, well-appointed houses in Kampala's lovely hillside suburbs of Lubiri and Kololo Hill. They drove Peugeots and Fiats, often taken at gunpoint from their civilian owners, and they owned the businesses Amin had confiscated from Asian merchants. They controlled the lucrative coffee-smuggling racket and the currency black market. It was a cozy trade-off: Amin was their meal ticket to the good life, and they were his to political survival.

Other presidents may have done it more subtly, but almost everyone—except, interestingly, those truly committed to socialism or Marxism—created a similar elite class, usually of people from their own ethnic group. It was the style of patronage politics that Boston's James Michael Curley or Chicago's Richard Daley would have appreciated: Take care of your own first, and they will get the others to fall into line.

The creation of neocolonial elite societies has been the subject of both controversy and criticism in Africa and has greatly retarded the development of nations and peoples. The former vice chancellor of Nairobi University, J. N. Karanja, observes: "If Africa is to develop, the elite must re-examine their consciences and understand and accept the unique history and circumstances of the African people.

"They must be honest and should realize that the African people did not fight for their independence so that they could become less free instead of freer, poorer instead of better off. It's time that the African people had the right to choose."

Elections, though, remain largely in the realm of fantasyland throughout Africa. In Gabon, President El Hadj Omar Bongo (his first name used to be Albert-Bernard until, having made the pilgrimage to Mecca, he decided El Hadj Omar was a more appropriate blend of Islam and Africa) celebrates his birthdays by holding elections and running unopposed; every seven years since 1967 his re-election has been nearly unanimous. In Somalia a single-party list of 171 candidates is presented to the electorate, who can check one of two boxes: Yes or No. In Burundi, where head of state Colonel Jean-Baptiste Bagaza sometimes travels about in an armored car followed overhead by an armed helicopter,* the country's sole party endorsed Bagaza's re-election in 1979 by a vote of 631–2; he was the only candidate. In Sierra Leone, elections resemble mini–civil wars with candidates being waylaid, kidnapped and forced to withdraw; the death toll during President Siaka P. Stevens' re-election campaign in 1978 topped a hundred. Everyone said it was an unusually quiet campaign.

When Milton Obote ruled Uganda from 1962 to 1971, he was responsible for abolishing parliament, nationalizing the economy, rewriting the constitution to make himself de facto life-president, jailing thousands of opponents, destroying the Buganda monarchy, terminating national elections, establishing a one-party state and creating a strong-armed enforcer named Idi Amin. In 1980 Obote returned to Uganda from exile in Tanzania to run for president again with these words: "Never again shall we allow an individual to suppress the will of the country and to destroy our democratic institutions." Obote regained the presidency in a rigged election, and

* Quoted from the *New York Times* (June 8, 1980).

within a few months the suppression of individual rights and the dismemberment of democratic institutions were well under way.

Because of the high degree of illiteracy in black Africa, candidates are usually identified on the ballot by a symbol rather than by a printed name, and in some rural villages, like those in Mozambique, voting is accomplished by a show of hands. In Zambia's 1979 presidential election, Dr. Kenneth David Kaunda chose for his ruling party the symbol of a magnificent eagle, proud and defiant, wings raised in flight. The opposition was assigned a snake. Needless to say, Kaunda won handily—just as he had every other election since 1964—although his policemen probably deserved more credit than the eagle; they kept the leading opposition candidates in jail until after the election.

In the face of such electoral obstacles, Africans have found alternative ways to express popular dissent and effect reform. In 1977, for instance, a peaceful revolt by women who operate the marketplace stalls in Guinea threatened to bring down the twenty-year rule of President Ahmed Sékou Touré. In Ghana the next year, a strike by middle-class professionals forced the government to abandon its plans for continued military rule. And riots in Liberia over an announced increase in the price of rice made President William Tolbert relent on his economic stabilization program and indirectly led to his overthrow a year later.

There were other signs as well in 1983 that democracy still stirred in Africa. The soldiers in Nigeria had handed over power to a duly elected civilian government and returned to the barracks while the country held national elections in 1979 and 1983. Kenya and Angola each had seen a smooth, constitutional transfer of leadership upon the deaths of their founding presidents. And in Tanzania and Kenya, the electorate had voted about half the members of parliament out of office. Africa took pride in these marks of maturity, but an important question still lingers: Is a Western-style democracy pertinent to the needs of Africa?

I don't think so. Not now, anyway. The splintered, struggling Africa of today cannot afford the luxury of multiparties and independent presses and honest debate. In countries where national goals are not clearly defined, such freedoms enable the various factions to fight for self-interests at the expense of majority concerns. National institutions are not strong enough to withstand these pressures. And governments are not cohesive enough to endure forces motivated by anything less than nationalistic concerns.

At this stage most African countries are best served by benign dictators. Democracy can come later, if it is to come at all. But for now democracy is no more a panacea for Africa's ills than is Communism. What Africa needs to develop is an *African* political system, imported from neither East nor West, that combines elements of capitalism and socialism, both of which are inherent to the African character. It should include two concepts that Africans today mistakenly view as contradictory—economic incentive and social justice.

The pity of contemporary Africa is that few presidents are secure enough to pursue policies or experiment with systems that might diminish their own power. And fewer still have displayed benevolence or wisdom in carrying out the affairs of state. The result is that many countries are run by men who are little more than clerks with guns.

It is, of course, easy to deride the Bokassas and the Amins and the other second-generation leaders whose competence has no more depth than a drop of blood. Their misdeeds, however, obscure the fact that Africa has produced some remarkable presidents who helped change the course of not just their continent, but the world. Among those figures, none was more memorable than Jomo Kenyatta, who a British colonial governor once predicted would lead his country "to darkness and death."

Gray-bearded and misty-eyed, Kenyatta would stand before the gathered masses in Nairobi's Uhuru (Freedom) Park, his bulky frame swaying from side to side, his right hand clutching a silver-handled fly whisk with white wildebeest hairs. His voice was forceful, his oratory almost magical. Finally he would raise the whisk over his head and call out a single word, *"Harambee!"*—his voice stretching and amplifying each syllable until the final "bay" sound came like a clap of thunder. The rapt crowd would lean forward and respond in unison, *"Harambee!"*

The Swahili word translates roughly as "Let's all pull together." For more than half a century—until his death in 1978—this was Kenyatta's rallying cry. As much as any single man, he showed the world that the pursuit of human dignity and prosperity, the desire for unity and racial harmony were not alien concepts to Africa.

"We do not want to oust the Europeans from this country," he said early in the struggle for independence. "But what we demand is to be treated like the white races. If we are to live here in peace and happiness, racial discrimination must be abolished."

Kenyatta did not live to see the fulfillment of many of his dreams. The East African Community, consisting of Kenya, Tanzania and Uganda, to which he attached much significance, collapsed in 1977; his vision of African unity remained imperiled by demagogues, ideological differences and wars; ignorance, poverty and disease continued to bedevil much of the continent; and his own country was divided by tribal factions and the emergence of a black elite whose accumulation of wealth and power had the distinct overtones of neocolonialism. His own family and confidants became little more than white-collar thieves, overseeing everything from the poaching of elephants to the smuggling of coffee. But Kenyatta left Kenya a better place than he found it. His legacy was a country in which a generation grew up accepting stability, relative prosperity and good racial relations as a normal part of life.

Jomo Kenyatta, who once referred to himself as a "rebuilder of destroyed shrines," was born about 1892—he was never sure of the precise year—in the fertile highlands north of Nairobi. He was then named Kamau wa Ngengi, the son of a peasant farmer. His grandfather was a sorcerer. As a herdboy, the youngster tended his father's sheep near the sacred *mugumo-wa-njathi* tree around which fellow Kikuyu tribesmen gathered to lament their eviction by white settlers from the lands they had owned for centuries. "The Kikuyu are no longer where they used to be," the people grieved in one song.

At the age of ten, young Kamau ran away to a nearby Church of Scotland mission, where doctors saved his life by operating to cure a spinal disease. Kamau learned to read and write at the mission and was baptized there with a new name—Johnstone. One of his chores each Sunday was to drape clean cloths over the pews when the Africans had left their service and the Europeans were about to arrive for theirs. Not surprisingly, Kenyatta later became critical of the church for perpetuating colonialism, once remarking, "When the missionaries arrived, the Africans had the land and the missionaries had the Bible. They taught us to pray with our eyes closed. When we opened them, they had the land and we had the Bible."

In 1921 Kenyatta, then twenty-nine years old, drifted to Nairobi, where he worked as a court interpreter and a water-meter reader. He was fond of dancing and he charmed women easily, employing, he said, a love potion his grandfather had taught him. While in Nairobi, he assumed the name Kenyatta, a Masai word referring to the beaded belt he wore. Later, feeling that his Christian name was not African enough, he took the name Jomo, which means "burning spear." The making—and the selling—of the chieftain image had begun.

Racial barriers where high in Nairobi in the 1920s. Young men like Kenyatta were barred from hotels, restaurants and all but menial jobs. Kenyatta, though, blessed with a magnetic personality, natural inquisitiveness and skillful oratory, learned how to circumvent the obstacles and soon grew into a local political force. He became propaganda secretary of the East African Association, which advocated the use of constitutional means for land reform, better wages, education and medical care for the Africans. It also campaigned against forced labor and for abolition of the metal identification tags each African was required to carry.

In 1928 Kenyatta joined as secretary-general a new and more outspoken group, the Kikuyu Central Association, whose main concern was the return of the highlands to the Kikuyus, the largest and most financially aggressive of Kenya's forty or so tribes. Kenyatta quit his government job as a water-meter reader and began a struggle that would not end until independence was achieved thirty-five years later. It is worth noting that at this point Kenyatta was concerned with the betterment of his tribe, not the broader issue of nationalism.

A group of Indians with Communist connections provided money and legal help in 1929, and Kenyatta went off to London to plead the Kikuyu case with Britain's colonial-secretary. He never got to see the secretary. Instead, he fell in with a Communist group known as the League Against Imperialism. He made a quick trip to Moscow, visited Berlin and played a minor role at the Communist-sponsored international Negro Workers' Congress in Hamburg. After eighteen months Kenyatta's Indian backers tired of supporting him and he returned to Nairobi.

His stay in Nairobi was brief. He was back in London the next year, 1931, and this time he would remain away from home for fifteen years. Living on the generosity of friends, he besieged the Colonial Office with petitions, fired off letters to newspapers, and dressed in African leopard-skin garb he wore for its eye-catching appeal, addressed his grievances to anyone in Trafalgar Square who would listen. He was learning the art of public relations, something that would serve him well throughout his career, and he was searching for a political system applicable to Africa.

In 1933 he spent four months in Moscow studying the tactics of revolution. Later he visited Denmark, Sweden and Norway to learn about cooperative farming. (Much later, after independence, he repudiated Communism and became one of Africa's most staunchly pro-Western leaders. "Don't be fooled into looking to Communism for food," he would say.)

Meanwhile, what had taken Kenyatta to England in the first place—the reinstatement of Kikuyu rights—had grown into the issue of rights for all Africans. In London he joined forces with two other African exiles, Hastings Banda, the future president of Malawi, and Kwame Nkrumah, the future president of Ghana, to form the Pan-African Federation, which demanded equal rights for all Africans. By the time Kenyatta returned to Kenya in 1946 with an English wife and son, he was a recognized leader of the African liberation movement.

But Kenyatta found that little had changed at home. The colonial government was making no concessions. And while Kenyatta was talking about constitutional change, many of his Kikuyu colleagues were taking fearful secret oaths to kill and drive the white man from Kenya. The movement became known as Mau Mau—(the origin and meaning of the word remain secret and undefined)—and before the British could defeat it in 1956 with the help of troops and dive bombers, four years after its inception, about 13,500 Africans and 95 Europeans had died.

Most of the whites killed were in the security forces; the rest, thirty-seven, were civilian settlers whose gruesome mutilation made world news, obscuring the fact that, as always, the Africans suffered far more than the Europeans, but the Europeans got the headlines. Thousands of Africans were killed by the Mau Mau guerrillas for refusing to take the oath of loyalty or for refusing to turn against their white masters. The Mau Mau were almost exclusively Kikuyus, and their purpose, initially at least, was tribally, not nationally, inspired. The Mau Mau Emergency, as the British called it, was the first black African war of liberation against the colonial powers and the only one the Europeans were to win anywhere in Africa during the next two decades. But even though the Africans lost militarily, they received an important psychological boost. They had stood up to the white man and all across the continent one could feel the first stirrings of the wind of change.

Inevitably, Kenyatta had been singled out as the Mau Mau leader—a charge he denied—and in the predawn hours of October

20, 1952, a day that is now a national holiday in Kenya, black and white government security men swept down on his home, hoping to surprise him in his sleep. Instead they found Kenyatta fully dressed, awaiting his arrest. His trial lasted five months.

"Our activities have been against the injustices that have been suffered by the African people," he said in court, "and if in trying to establish the rights of the African people we have turned out to be what you say, Mau Mau, we are very sorry that you have been misled in that direction.

"What we have done, and what we will continue to do, is to demand the rights of the African people as human beings that they may enjoy the facilities and privileges in the same way as other people."

Kenyatta was convicted and sentenced to seven years at hard labor in a remote prison in the northern Kenyan desert. His trial was a setup and the evidence against him was unsubstantial at best; he may have been his people's spiritual leader, but he was never a guerrilla and it is unlikely that he exerted any military influence over the Mau Mau. In 1959 Kenyatta was released from prison, only to be sent under house arrest to the isolated outpost of Lodwar, where he lived with a third wife.* The independence movement meanwhile was gaining momentum—seventeen African countries were born in 1960 alone—and the British were forced, by political pressure from Kenyans, to allow Kenyatta to re-enter politics.

"Where there has been racial hatred, it must be ended," Kenyatta said. "Where there has been tribal animosity, it will be finished. Let us not dwell upon the bitterness of the past. I would rather look to the future, to the good new Kenya, not to the bad old days. If we can create this sense of national direction and identity, we shall have gone a long way toward solving our economic problems."

Kenyatta became prime minister at independence on December 12, 1963, and at his swearing-in ceremony he and his aides forsook the native dress and monkey-skin robes they had worn during the campaign in favor of Western business suits. On Kenyatta's head was a cap widely worn by the Luo, another prominent Kenyan tribe. The symbol was a significant one of national unity. A year later Kenyatta was named president, and at his death he was, in effect, a

* Kenyatta's English wife, Edna Grace Clarke, and son did not remain long in Kenya and returned to England. He also had three African wives, at different times, spending his final years with a dashing spouse named Ngina. He never divorced his previous wives.

life-president, a saintlike figure whose authority was unchallenged, whose personal fortune was immense, whose country had truly lifted the dignity of the black man and accommodated the white man.

Kenyatta had two great failings: he failed to achieve a real national consensus because, in the final analysis, he cared more about his clan and tribe than about his nation, and he failed to listen to honest voices of opposition. Not long after his inauguration he stopped wearing the Luo cap, and the government and the economy remained in the hands of the Kikuyus, often to the social and financial detriment of other ethnic groups. Corruption grew to scandalous proportions. Kenyatta turned a blind eye.

Kenyatta's image was further tarnished when, in 1969, he jailed his Luo vice president, Oginga Odinga, on nebulous charges, and a popular young Luo politician who did not toe the Kenyatta party line, Tom Mboya, was killed in Nairobi by a Kikuyu gunman. Mboya was a responsible and intelligent leader with experience in labor and political affairs; he was, in fact, the very type of man many people—in both Africa and the West—were looking toward to provide Africa's second-generation leadership. In 1975 J. M. Kariuki, another immensely popular Kikuyu parliamentarian who had spoken out against the new "colonial" black elite, and who had once been jailed by the British as a suspected Mau Mau, was assassinated. Just before his death Kariuki was seen in the company of a senior police officer who reported directly to the president. Between 1975 and 1977, five parliamentarians who at least mildly opposed some aspect of Kenyatta's one-party rule were jailed without trial under the Public Security Act.

Such excesses, though, were minor by African standards and after Kenyatta died in his sleep, royalty, presidents and dignitaries from more than sixty lands poured into Nairobi for the funeral of the former herdboy who had become a symbol of an oppressed people's dreams. His silk-lined casket was borne through the streets on a British gun carriage pulled by forty-six soldiers. Kenyans by the hundreds of thousands lined the route and heard a twenty-one-gun artillery salute echo across Uhuru Park. Flags throughout Africa flew at half-staff. And the Very Rev. Charles M. Kareri warned the mourners in his sermon that Kenya must avoid the political and tribal infighting that usually marks the death of a president in Africa.

Daniel arap Moi, the man who succeeded Kenyatta, was a member of the small Tugen tribe. The tribal confrontation—even civil war—that many observers believed would follow Kenyatta's death never happened. Enough Kenyans had a stake in their country's continued progress to make violence and instability unappealing. Even though the real power remained in Kikuyu hands—Moi was chosen by the Kikuyu as a nationally acceptable front man for Kikuyu interests—the country's economic pie was big enough for the majority to share. The standard of living had improved for the average Kenyan, government services had extended beyond the cities and into the rural areas, a middle class had emerged that at least gave the less privileged a visible goal to aim for. That was Kenyatta's greatest gift to Kenya. Under him a generation grew up accepting peace and possible economic gain as a normal part of life. Its members had only to look across Kenya's borders to know what the alternatives were. Ethiopia and Uganda were wracked by bloody chaos, socialistic Tanzania was stagnating, Marxist Somalia was slipping backward. Only Kenya had come close to fulfilling the promises of independence.

What had Kenyatta done differently than other African presidents? Almost everything.

While Zaire's Mobutu was chasing away the whites, expropriating their plantations and businesses, Kenyatta had been encouraging Kenya's whites to stay because they had the technical and managerial skills that Africans had not yet learned. The result was that Kenya operates far more efficiently than most African countries, and foreign investment and tourists from the West have poured into the country, providing great economic stimulus. While Zambia's Kuanda was exploiting his mineral wealth (copper) and forgetting about other sectors of the economy, Kenyatta knew that Africa's future was on the farms and gave top priority to agricultural development. While Uganda's Amin was spending 50 percent of his budget on the military—not a single school or hospital was built in Uganda during Amin's eight years in power—Kenyatta devoted less than 7 percent of his financial resources to defense, leaving sufficient funds to construct scores of classrooms and health clinics. While Tanzania's Nyerere pursued socialistic ideals, nationalizing the economy and curtailing all individual economic incentives, Kenyatta followed a capitalistic course in which those with initiative received monetary rewards. Tanzania's production decreased; Kenya's increased.

The interesting aspect of all this is that Kenya is not a rich country. It has no significant mineral reserves, and less than 20 percent of its land is suitable for farming. But Kenyatta evaluated what assets Kenya had and then set out to make the most of them. Almost any country in Africa could have done at least as well as Kenya if it had had a Jomo Kenyatta.

Perhaps nowhere in the world do individual countries mirror the character of their presidents as much as in Africa. What a country is often depends solely on who the president is. A new man takes over and the country may move in an entirely different direction. Although heads of state still impose their view of the world on their people, presidential ideologies are less in fashion these days, having been moved aside by men of more pragmatic persuasions. The theorists proved themselves unable to adapt to unexpected pressures when their ideals of what Africa should be were challenged by the realities of what it had become. Tanzania, on Kenya's southern border, offers a striking illustration.*

In foreign capitals they call President Julius Nyerere "the conscience of black Africa." At home in Dar es Salaam he is known simply as Mwalimu, the Swahili word for "teacher." Scholars and statesmen from both East and West seek his advice; Moscow and Washington analyze his every word. For more than twenty years Nyerere has commanded a position of respect unique among African heads of state. His blueprint for socialism is a textbook model of Third World development. His salary as president is only $6,000 a year and on state visits he often travels in the economy section of commercial airlines. He was educated at Makerere University in Uganda and Edinburgh University in Scotland, and has translated *Julius Caesar* and *The Merchant of Venice* into Swahili. He gives no special favors to members of his own tribe, the Zanaki,† and his socialist dreams are tempered by the harsh realities of leading one of the world's twelve poorest countries.

"Let others go to the moon," he has said. "We must work to feed ourselves."

Certainly no one could fault the society Nyerere wanted to create. Tanzania, he said, would be a country without an army. Foreign

* A German colony from 1891 until the end of World War I, Tanzania was originally known as Tanganyika. It gained its independence from Britain in 1961. Three years later Tanganyika and Zanzibar, a small island republic twenty miles off the coast, merged into a single country called Tanzania.

† Zanaki translates as "Those who came with what?"

policy would be based on neutrality in the Cold War and on promoting African unity, particularly among neighbors. The economy would be founded on agriculture, and domestic affairs would center on fighting "the three enemies: poverty, ignorance and disease." The gap between rich and poor would be narrowed, and to prove his point in 1966, he slashed all middle- and high-level government salaries, including his own. As his foreign partners, he brought in the Chinese and they built a gleaming $400-million railroad from the Dar es Salaam port to the copper fields of Zambia. Over and over, he told his people they must be self-reliant; begging missions abroad, he said, would lessen Tanzania's respect in the world community. Tanzania would be a country where every man walked proud, where no man rose too far above the crowd.

At his modest beach front home, built with the help of a bank loan, he entertains guests on the veranda without the slightest touch of pomp. Flies buzz about and servants in shabby jackets serve warm orange soda. Nyerere kicks off his sandals and begins his discourse on Africa. His tone is teasing and his conversation is broken with frequent giggles and jokes. He makes his point gently, directly, in flawless English. Few visitors leave his presence without being spellbound.

"The way in which President Nyerere has dominated African affairs by the sheer power of his intellect and leadership is nothing short of miraculous," the former U.S. ambassador to the United Nations, Andrew Young, once said. "His domination is something you would expect from the leader of a nation of great wealth or military strength. Tanzania has neither."

Nyerere was born in 1920, the son of a Zanaki chief and his eighteenth wife, Mugaya. He was an inquisitive, bright youngster, one of the few in his village of Butiama to attend school. He scored high grades and at the Government Secondary School in Tabora was appointed a prefect. He soon discovered that a prefect's privileges included double rations. He agitated against such inequalities and they were dropped.

After receiving a degree in education at Makerere University in Uganda, he taught history and biology in Tanganyika until 1949; then, with the help of missionary Catholic priests, he obtained a scholarship to Edinburgh, where he studied British history, English, moral philosophy, political economy, social anthropology, constitutional law and economic history. There, he has said, his political philosophy evolved.

Back in Tanganyika in 1952 with a master's degree, he resumed teaching. He also became active in political affairs, remodeling an African social organization into a political association known as the Tanganyika African National Union (TANU) and laying the foundation for independence, which came peacefully on December 9, 1961. One month later he startled everyone by resigning as premier to concentrate on rebuilding TANU for the postcolonial struggle. He also wanted to prepare for the 1962 elections—which were to earn him 97 percent of the votes and the presidency of Tanganyika.

As impeccable as his credentials were, as graced with charm, intellect and humor as he is, Nyerere has one glaring weakness: he does not always practice what he preaches. And what he does practice has brought Tanzania few visible benefits. His 17 million people have adhered to his socialistic doctrine for two decades and at the end of the rainbow have found only an empty pot. Though Nyerere's image has remained remarkably untarnished, there now seems sufficient reason to question the wisdom of his motives. Consider:

► No other African president has ever overthrown a neighboring country's government. Nyerere has helped topple three: the Comoros in 1975, the Seychelles in 1977 and Uganda in 1979. He used 60,000 troops to rid Africa of Uganda's Amin, but his army of liberation quickly turned into an army of occupation, looting and killing. Nyerere, in an attempt to make sure that the puppet government in Kampala adopted a socialist course, became the de facto president of Uganda. When Amin's two successors began to act independently, Nyerere arranged for their removal from office and had them put under lock and key.

► Although Nyerere has been quick to condemn tyranny in black- as well as white-ruled Africa—he refused, for instance, to attend an African summit in Uganda in 1975 because Idi Amin was its host— Nyerere held until 1979 more political prisoners than South Africa. (He granted amnesty to 6,400 prisoners that year, and freed another 4,436 in 1980.) Nyerere tolerates no dissent and long ago brought the newspapers under government control and closed all avenues of opposition and free expression. His own re-election every few years is something of a sham: he won 99 percent of the "yes" votes in 1970, 93 percent in both 1975 and 1980. The electorate can only vote for or against Nyerere, who is the only presidential candidate.

► Nyerere complains (quite correctly) that the West uses foreign aid as a lever for influence, but he accepts more of it than any president in black Africa. In 1980 alone, Tanzania received $600 million in grants and low-interest loans from the West and because Nyerere and Tanzania are what Western liberals think Africa should be all about—nonaligned, socialistic, poor, idealistic—donors from Australia to Geneva and Washington beat a path to Dar es Salaam with fistfuls of money.

▶ Despite the injection of aid, few countries in Africa have made such modest progress in the independence era. Agricultural production is dropping, factories are limping along at 40 percent capacity, Dar es Salaam grows shabbier by the day, a listlessness engulfs the land and the people are perhaps the most dispirited and unmotivated on the entire continent.

In overstaffed government offices, drowsy secretaries rouse themselves only long enough to mumble, "Gone out," when a visitor enters, meaning that the boss has already come and gone for the day, even if it is not yet 10:30 A.M. In the Israeli-built Kilimanjaro Hotel the phone may ring twenty or thirty times before the operator bothers to answer it, and the last time I bought a plane ticket at the airport in Dar es Salaam, the clerk behind the desk asked me to fill in the coupon myself. He would return after his tea break, he said, to collect my money.

One Tanzanian student tells about attending an all-African party at a university in the United States. The room was packed with laughing students, dancing, drinking beer and trading stories from home. The Tanzanian looked around the room for a moment and headed directly for two young men, sitting morosely and alone in a corner. "As soon as I saw them there with those long faces I knew they were Tanzanians," he said.

At independence in 1961 Nyerere, to be sure, did inherit a country that was going nowhere in a hurry. Unlike neighboring Kenya, it had not been a "favored" British colony, and London had devoted little attention to its development. There were no significant resources and only one major export crop, sisal. University graduates numbered 120. Nyerere's eventual response, in January 1967, was to issue the Arusha Declaration, a Chinese-style masterplan for socialism. The economy was nationalized, as was all rental property valued at more than $14,000. Taxes were increased to redistribute individual wealth. Hundreds of *ujamaa* (the Swahili word for "familyhood") communal villages were established, populated in many cases by people who had been trucked by soldiers out of cities in military convoys. And Nyerere began spreading his gospel: work hard, forget personal gain, grow more. Then there will be a Tanzania for all Tanzanians.

Many critics contend that Nyerere's albatross is his own country, that he is an eloquent expostulator (though not a deep thinker) who simply deserved a better country to experiment with. Today all but the die-hard romantics agree that Nyerere's experiment is a failed one, that China's revolution has no more relevance to Africa of the 1980s than a glass of salt water has for a thirsty man. Mass mobilization is only possible when a homogeneous people believe that a shared goal is both worthy and obtainable: Nyerere's people are no longer believers—if indeed they ever were in the first place.

What Nyerere primarily has accomplished is to eliminate all incentives in Tanzania (anyone earning more than $30,000 a year is in the 95 percent tax bracket) and as a result nothing happens at all. The railroad to Zambia breaks down due to lack of maintenance and the theft of cargo, and the Chinese are called back to run it, having to replace the Africans in virtually every job from switchman to locomotive engineer. Day by day the country grows poorer, more lethargic, surviving as an international ward, the people clinging to little other than Nyerere's promise of a better life. On the nearby island of Zanzibar, once the most prosperous place in black Africa, there is no electricity most of the time and the shelves of stores are almost empty. Zanzibar's treasury, stuffed until the late 1970s with a hefty income from cloves, is barren, drained to support Nyerere's government on the mainland.

Nevertheless, Nyerere insists that his is the only path for his people. His leadership has spanned three decades and his doctrine has remained inflexible. The rest of Africa has changed during that time, yielding to new pressures, trying new systems, adjusting to new realities. Nyerere and Tanzania, though, are not much different than they were in 1961. They are anachronisms.

"People who think Tanzania will change her cherished policy of *ujamaa* and self-reliance because of the economic difficulties are wasting their time," Nyerere says. "We shall never change."

And that is precisely Tanzania's problem.

Revolution is a popular—and an overworked—word in Africa. Almost every president likes to think he is either the product or the producer of one. Even Idi Amin, as he went about Uganda killing his countrymen, once said, "As a revolutionary leader, I am too busy to rest." But carrying a gun does not make a revolutionary. Nor does repeating rhetoric. Nor does overthrowing a government. To be a revolutionary one must at least have a vision of the future and a plan to effect fundamental changes. Few African presidents have.

One legitimate revolutionary, though, deserves mention: President Samora Moisés Machel of Mozambique. As much as any head of state in Africa he is the creation of the struggle against colonialism. He is a man who is easy to hate or to love but impossible to ignore. To the Eastern bloc, he is the golden boy of Africa. To the West, he is a tough and uncompromising Marxist ideologue. To white-ruled South Africa, Mozambique's next-door neighbor, he is the symbol of radicalized arrogance. But regardless of from what perspective he is viewed, Machel's scorecard is consistent and uncontestable: his political personality was forged during the ten-year war of liberation against the Portuguese (1964–1974) and to him, the ongoing revolution is everything and all energies must be devoted to it.

Machel, who was born in 1933 to peasant parents, trained in Algeria and Tanzania for the war against Portugal. He was among the first 250 combatants to cross the Tanzanian border into Mozambique, launching an attack on September 25, 1964, against a colonial outpost to begin the war of independence. Before long he was commander in chief of the guerrillas, then president of the liberation movement. Whether on the battlefield or in the president's office, Machel remained an austere and disciplined man who demanded as much of himself as he did of others.

Just after the war, in a treaty that brought victory to Machel's guerrillas, the young president-to-be decided to take the first vacation of his life. He chose Tanzania, hardly a garden spot for tourists, because his guerrilla movement, called Frelimo, had been headquartered there and numerous liberation leaders still congregated there. On the first morning of his vacation, he was up at five-thirty, marching through the corridors of the shabby hotel like an army general, pounding on the doors of his small entourage. His colleagues stumbled out wearily and Machel directed them to the beach, where he led them on a ten-mile run. Then there was a protracted self-criticism session and each night there were lengthy meetings with various liberation leaders to discuss the futures of Rhodesia and South Africa. "Machel never slowed down," said one of his staffers. "We all went back to Mozambique exhausted."

Unlike most African leaders, Machel leads his 10 million people by deed, not just words. He eschews ostentatious living and personality cults, is honest beyond temptation—indeed, Mozambique is a country with virtually no corruption—and often travels around the nation, visiting factories, farms, hospitals and prisons, jotting down notes as he listens to the people's grievances. "It is necessary to know the temperature inside," he once said, "and the people are the thermometer."

A bearded, fiery orator who will deliver speeches that last four or five hours, Machel neither smokes nor drinks and frowns on his people engaging in wasteful activities such as dancing and partying, which, he says, drain energy that should be devoted to the revolution. In one angry May Day speech he ordered "popular vigilance groups" to shave bald the heads of long-haired young men, banned women from wearing tight jeans and shirts ("They only cause temptation," he said) and attacked the Christian church as an imperialistic institution "recruiting people against us, using its cassocks as disguise." One day his father, a Baptist preacher, took issue with his son's remarks and Machel stormed out of the family dining room, slamming the door behind him. It was a display of disrespect toward an elder almost unheard of in an African family.

Though his single-minded dedication to create black Africa's first authentic Marxist state does make Machel frequently belligerent and insensitive, he cuts an impressive figure and, once separated from the rhetoric delivered in packed stadiums, he speaks in articulate, measured tones, commanding both attention and respect.

The carpeted reception room to his office is barren except for a sofa, an easy chair and two large wall photographs: one of a teen-age Mozambican boy in an army uniform, the other of a small child, perhaps six years old, holding a rocket launcher. Machel is a short, almost elfin man, wiry and muscular. He enters his office with a flourish, dressed in neatly pressed jungle fatigues, a visored field cap and expensive European boots.

In a moment he is talking about the revolution, as if mesmerized, eyes closed, his voice singsong as he rocks back and forth in his chair. When he comes to a point that particularly excites him he will jump up, prance across the room and slap his visitor's knee to make a point.

"There is a song we sing here about the communal village," he says, "about the village where hunger is defeated, where there is no intrigue, where there is no crime, where disease is fought and conquered, where life is collective and productive, where schools end ignorance, superstition and illiteracy, where the New Man is born, where there is real unity among men of all races . . . "

Machel is a dreamer and his dream is a big one: he wants to liberate the Third World and he supports virtually every liberation movement known to man. Whether it is the Katanga rebels in Angola or the advocates for independence in Puerto Rico, Machel stands squarely on the underdog's side. His is a dream buoyed by the success of his own liberation struggle. He won a war and inherited an economically crippled country that was $640 million in debt at independence. He set out to create the New African Man and to bring education, health services and a political awareness to a long-oppressed people, and has had some successes. Whether Mozambique's socialist dream can be realized and the pitfalls of other African revolutions avoided probably depends on just one element—Machel himself, who, like his peers, has learned it is a great deal easier to run a guerrilla movement than a government.

There was, I thought, much to admire in Machel's style. Unlike Libya's Muammar Qaddafy, he was not an exporter of revolution and he had set sensible priorities at home. School enrollment had tripled since independence, half the population had been inoculated against cholera, not a beggar or prostitute was to be seen on the streets of Maputo. Machel traded openly with South Africa, and having been brushed aside by the West, worked closely with Moscow without becoming a Soviet satellite. He was willing to take help wherever he could find it.

But Machel insisted that his was the only way. "When a class imposes its will," he once said, "those who refuse to accept this imposition must be forced to conform. Those who oppose this will be repressed."

Such words don't leave much room for compromise, and for just that reason Machel is unlikely to be typical of the presidents who will lead Africa into the twenty-first century. In the years ahead Africa will need more compromise and consensus, not less. And it will need far more room to maneuver than his rigid Marxist system allows.

Despite Machel's accomplishments, Mozambique was in dreadful shape in 1984, and Marxism had retarded, not stimulated its development. As in Tanzania, there were no economic incentives and the Mozambicans responded by producing little besides a small crop of cashew nuts. The two hundred "people's stores" set up in the countryside, though relatively effective in controlling prices and black marketeering, were pitifully short of goods. In the cities, women had to stand in lines for hours to buy a pint of milk or a loaf of bread. Agricultural production had fallen 70 percent since independence, and factories were limping along at 30 percent of capacity. The tourist industry, once worth millions of dollars every year, no longer earned the country a single nickel.

Additionally, the mountain of regulations and restrictions affecting every Mozambican often made life intolerable. To change his place of residence, a Mozambican needed a dozen permission slips. To buy a ticket for a flight within the country, he needed authority from the ministry of immigration and had to wait for hours at the country's single, nationalized travel agency. To hire, say, a lathe operator, an employer needed approval from five levels of worker committees. During the days it took them to decide if that particular individual deserved the job, the lathe stood idle.

"The thing that history will record as the principal contribution of our generation," Machel said during the liberation war, "is that we understand how to turn the armed struggle into a revolution, that we realized it was essential to create a new mentality in order to build a new society."

But recognizing the need for change, and finding the means to effect it, are, as Machel must have discovered by now, very different challenges.*

The evening is breathless with heat, and vultures huddle in the mango trees overhead. From a distant mosque the singsong call to prayer rolls across the White Nile, but the dozen Europeans sitting on the veranda of Juba's only hotel pay no attention. They are drinking beer with ice and swatting at the flies and cussing the inattentive service, and they give nary a glance at the procession of seven-foot-tall Dinkas moving silently through the shadows nearby. The Dinkas have shed the shirts and pants they wore to their daytime jobs, and now they are nearly naked, their bodies smeared with cattle dung and red ochre. Drums throb in the darkness. The Dinkas slip toward them, just as they have for centuries. Once they reach the field where the drums are pounding, they will work

* Machel was killed in 1986, when his Soviet-piloted plane crashed inside South Africa on a flight from Zambia.

themselves into a melodic trance, dancing until dawn, bodies glistening in the moonlight, jumping and writhing amid a guttural chorus that fills the night with a thousand voices: "*Umppah, umppah, umppah.*"

This is the Sudan, Africa's largest country, nearly a third the size of the continental United States. But this is "the other" Sudan, the southern Sudan. The north is Arabized and wealthier and more developed. The south is African, a Christian and pagan region as big as Texas and New Mexico combined where there are only 17 miles of paved roads and where government workers still tap out Morse code messages to Khartoum, the nation's capital in the north, a thousand miles away. The economic and cultural differences between the north and south led to 150 years of distrust and bloodshed, culminating in 1955 in the south's seventeen-year war for autonomy. The conflict, largely ignored by the world and given scant attention in the international press, claimed the lives of 400,000 Sudanese and created a million refugees.

One of the prominent southern guerrilla leaders of the war, Mading Degarang, was sitting with us on the hotel verandah in Juba that evening. He heard the Arabic chants and he saw the African dancers ambling toward their ceremonial grounds. Two different worlds, two different cultures, two different religions thrown together in a single country. But, he mused, the peace was holding. It was a fragile peace, but it was holding. The Arabs and the Africans had found room for compromise and understanding. The wounds of the continent's second longest civil war (the Eritrean war in Ethiopia is the longest) were slowly healing.

"Ten, even five years ago, no one thought it could work this well," Degarang said. "Of course, one man was really responsible for ending the war and one man is responsible for keeping the peace, and if something happens to him—well, we could only hope."

That man is Jaafar Numeiri, a dictator president who practices compromise and conciliation, a rare pastime for an African leader. Numeiri, a strict Moslem who believes Allah chose him to lead the 18 million Sudanese people, prays five times a day and has given up the occasional glass of whiskey he once enjoyed. His father was a messenger for a British company during the colonial era, which ended in 1956 in the Sudan, and the young Numeiri's rebelliousness was always something of an embarrassment to his family. In 1946, when he was seventeen, he led a political strike that closed down his secondary school for seven months, and in 1957 he was suspended from the army for sixteen months for leading an abortive coup. He staged another coup in 1969—this one succeeded—and three years later made the concessions no previous Sudanese leader had dared to make, thus ending the civil war and sowing the first seeds of unity between the Arab-dominated north and the black south.

Rather than insisting on absolute victory, he granted the south regional autonomy in most matters except defense and external affairs. The two warring armies became one peacetime army, the two very different regions became one nation, held together by the leadership of a single man. Later, in 1978, Numeiri took another unprecedented African step as part of a national-reconciliation program and granted a general amnesty to dozens of Sudanese who had emerged in the postwar years as his political enemies. It made him a circus ringmaster surrounded by unpredictable and potentially dangerous tigers, held at bay by one man with the whip.

Every Thursday, Numeiri plays polo with a former soldier who devoted a good deal of his time to planning Numeiri's assassination. "That away, Sadiq, you're looking good," Numeiri will call when his elegantly attired former adversary makes a skillful shot. Sadiq al Mahdi, a former prime minister and head of a group of fanatical Moslem warriors, was condemned to death for plotting the overthrow of the Numeiri government—and the death of Numeiri—in 1975 and 1976. But Numeiri asked him to end his exile in London and return home to work toward building a united Sudan. At about the same time, Numeiri freed the Sudan's twelve hundred political prisoners and permitted his former enemies to run for the People's Assembly. Several were elected.

On the nights when he cannot sleep—which are most nights—Numeiri rises by four o'clock, slips out a back door of State House and wanders alone and unannounced through Khartoum, whose streets are laid out in the pattern of the British Union Jack. He pauses by the bridge spanning the confluence of the Blue and White Niles—referred to in Arabic poetry as "the longest kiss in history"—and strolls into the open-air marketplaces that are just beginning to stir.

Dressed in a white Moslem robe, his bronzed face bearing traditional self-inflicted tribal scars of his initiation into manhood, he stops to question the surprised merchants, asking them about their lives, their problems, their hopes for the Sudan. "What are your children learning in school?" he asks one woman selling cabbages.

"They must be educated, you know. The country will need them."

Numeiri, though, is no soft touch. He retains the rank of army general, and for years used a network of spies and informers to keep track of his enemies. In 1975 he approved the execution, after trial, of ninety-eight Libyan-recruited black mercenaries who tried to overthrow him. In 1983, after government troops crushed a mutiny near Juba, he had the rebels shot in "batches of six," his ministry of information announced. He maintains strict control over the national press in his one-party state and remains very much in charge of the Sudan's day-to-day affairs.

What sets Numeiri apart from other African presidents is his willingness to experiment and his ability to change. While other presidents have solidified their power, Numeiri has loosened his. While other presidents tend to blame colonialism for all Africa's problems, Numeiri believes the causes of failure are rooted closer to home. Numeiri flirted with Marxism until a Soviet-inspired attempted coup almost succeeded in 1971; then he moved abruptly out of the Moscow camp. He nationalized the economy, and finding that the move stifled development, once again encouraged free enterprise, thus attracting considerable foreign investment from the Arab and Western worlds. He may not have produced any miracles—agriculture remains stagnant, the bureaucracy inefficient, the South a potential flashpoint, the international aid projects generally unproductive—but he nevertheless has given his people a precious gift, a sense of unity and purpose that grew from the ashes of a shattered nation.

One of the first lessons a Western journalist learns in Africa is not to make predictions; they are usually about as reliable as weather forecasts in New England. Perhaps Numeiri has been too liberal and the tigers wait only for an unguarded moment. Perhaps the Sudanese peace rests on the shoulders of just one man, and if he fails, so will the country. But I would like to think that there is no turning back for the Sudan. It has gone too far at too great a cost to fail now.

Numeiri has shown his people the benefits of conciliation. His benign dictatorship could be the forerunner, instead of the tombstone, of a democratic, socially just political system. It is, I believe, the Numeiris, not the Bokassas or Machels or Nyereres, who symbolize Africa's hope for the future. For Numeiri has made national contributions that will outlast the man himself, and that is the mark of a worthy president on any continent.

THE GHOST
OF IDI AMIN

▲

Hitler was right about the Jews, because the Israelis are
not working in the interests of the people of the world,
and that is why they burned the Israelis alive with gas
in the soil of Germany.

—IDI AMIN,
former Ugandan president

THE DATE WAS JANUARY 25, 1971, and by the tens of thousands
Ugandans poured into the streets of Kampala to celebrate the overthrow of their president, Milton Obote, a hard-drinking tyrant who
had ruled the country since independence. The mastermind of the
coup d'état had once been, as is often the case in African revolts, the
president's trusted ally. He was a military man who had worked his
way up through the ranks, establishing rapport with his troops and
keeping his distance from politics and ideology. "I am not a politician but a professional soldier," the general said in his first address
to the nation. "I am, therefore, a man of few words, and I have been
brief throughout my professional career." He went on to say that his
was only a caretaker administration, that power would be transferred
to a civilian government as soon as elections could be organized.
Ugandans were relieved. Neighboring African countries were reas-
sured. The West was pleased. Almost everyone, in fact, agreed that
this new man, Idi Amin, would make a steady, decent president.

Idi Amin was forty-six years old then, a mountain of a man with a
cheery disposition and an earthy, barracks-style sense of humor. He
had a second-grade education and spoke the smatterings of five languages, but handled only his tribal tongue with any degree of fluency. His former commanding officer in the British army, Colonel
Hugh Rogers, remembers him as "a splendid and reliable soldier
and a cheerful and energetic man." Others described Amin as a man
with neither pretense nor ambition. What no one mentioned,

though, was that Amin had all the qualities that make a dangerous leader in Africa: his instincts were primitive, his loyalties tribal, his orientation military.

Strange things started happening in Uganda almost from the day he took over. First, Brigadier General Suleiman Hussein, the army chief of staff and a potential rival to Amin, "disappeared." Permanently. Then Uganda's chief justice, Benedicto Kiwanuka, was dragged from his chambers in broad daylight by Amin's soldiers and was never seen alive again. The vice chancellor of Makerere University also disappeared, and the beaten body of Amin's personal physician was found dumped along a road. Bodies floated down the Nile and turned up by the hundreds in Mabira and Namanve forests. The prisons filled up and prisoners were forced to stand in line and beat each other to death with ten-pound sledge hammers; the last man was shot. Entire villages populated by the Lango and Acholi tribes, which had supported Obote, were wiped out. The screams emanating each night from Amin's secret-police headquarters became so regular and so blood-curdling that the French ambassador, who lived next door, lodged a complaint, and his wife, unable to sleep for nights on end, returned to Paris. Cabinet ministers, university professors, Christians, Asians, Jews—almost everyone except Amin's inner circle of Moslems and Kakwas—experienced the wrath of a man gone crazy with power, a man obsessed with reducing Uganda to the lowest common denominator, his own.

Ugandans coined a word—Aminism—to describe the terrible happenings in their country, and by the time the Aminisms ended in 1979, an estimated 300,000 Ugandans—or one Ugandan in every forty—were dead. The carnage was tantamount to murdering the entire population of Louisville, Kentucky. It was as though Amin had studied presidential protocol in Papa Doc's Haiti or Pol Pot's Cambodia. And in the process the Ugandan people learned how to survive but forgot how to feel. "Killing was so commonplace," a grocer in Kampala told me, "that if you heard your brother had been picked up by the police, you knew that was the end of him. You'd say, 'Too bad,' and you'd feel bad for a few days, then you'd just go back to work and forget about him." A single human beast, as playful as a kitten, as lethal as a lion, had managed almost single-handedly to destroy a nation of 13 million people.

Eight years after the celebrations that marked Amin's rise to power, Ugandans once again returned to the streets of Kampala in joyous revelry. Old friends embraced, and surprised to find the other alive, exchanged an eerie greeting: "You still exist!" Their nightmare was over. Amin—the nonpolitician who became president-for-life, the professional soldier who became a common murderer—had fled to Libya, chased from Uganda by a ragtag army of invading Tanzanians and a handful of Ugandan rebels. It was V-J Day in Times Square, African style, and standing there on the steps of the parliament building, among thousands of dancing, singing Ugandans, I thought I was witnessing the rebirth of a nation. I felt good for Uganda and good for Africa. If ever an African nation had a chance and a reason to set aside personal ambitions and tribal suspicions in order to reconstruct a heritage, Uganda did.

The sun had just broken through a heavy overcast in Kampala that afternoon, April 11, 1979, and from the shadows of Parliament House an elderly man stepped forward, removed his glasses, bowed his head and asked his gathered countrymen to pray silently "for those who have died at the hands of Idi Amin." The crowd fell silent in prayer.

Yusufu L. Lule's fingers fidgeted at the side of his blue safari suit as he prepared to take the oath as Uganda's interim president. His eyes swept the crowd in Parliament Square and he spoke slowly, his voice quivering. The horror, he said, had ended. With the overthrow of Amin a new era of national reconciliation had begun. Lule, a distinguished academic who had come home from exile in London, stepped down and the throng went wild. They hugged, cheered, kissed and hoisted the Tanzanian soldiers to their shoulders, snaking through the parliament courtyard to the beat of drums. The leader of the Ugandan guerrillas, David Oyite-Ojok—who Amin once said was the "only man besides God" he feared—waved his rifle overhead as he was swept onto a mass of shoulders and a thousand voices joined in the country's new national anthem: "O Uganda, the land of freedom, our love and labor we give . . ." In the distance a church bell sounded. Then another and another, until finally a clanging chorus from the steeples swelled through all Kampala.

"If they will only bring Amin here," shouted a former Kampala city councilman, Rashid Kawawa, "we will eat him on the spot. Yes, we'll roast him and sear his skin and pass around chunks of him. He was a cannibal, so he would understand what we were doing."

Amin's modest four-bedroom home was in the hills overlooking

Kampala, only a mile or so from Parliament Square, and the next morning I walked through its open front door. I felt as though I were entering a hallucination.

His bedroom, like that of a child, was covered with pictures of military aircraft, scotch-taped to the walls. There were cartons of hand grenades under Amin's bed and bottles of pills for venereal disease on his bureau. One closet was stacked with reels of "Tom and Jerry" cartoons, and a file cabinet was stuffed with black-and-white photos of tortured Ugandans, gaunt, maimed creatures who hardly resembled human beings at all. Amin's health records were strewn about the floor; they contained no mention of the degenerative syphilis that an Israeli doctor claimed he had, but they showed that he had been suffering from gout and obesity for years. "You need a rigid exercise program," one doctor advised. Piles of never opened letters from foreign governments and his own embassies abroad littered the room.

"I think it is safe to say that medically Amin was crazy," Solomon Asea, a doctor who had been Amin's ambassador in Washington, told me. "He had a split personality. He could kill a person one minute and the next he'd be laughing and playing the guitar and he had no recollection of what he had done. In a medical sense, he wasn't responsible for much of what he did. He should have been a patient, not a president."

Sadly, the euphoria that engulfed Uganda in those first days of life without Idi Amin was short-lived and it soon became clear that there would be no miracles of reconstruction or reconciliation in Uganda. One nightmare had ended but another was about to begin. Uganda itself was about to complete the mission of destruction on which Amin had embarked.

The Tanzanian army that had come to save Uganda now set out to ravage it, the unpaid soldiers taking at gunpoint what they wanted. Soon every soldier had a Seiko watch and a shortwave radio. The economy collapsed, the food supplies ran out, the morgues filled up, and the stench of death hung about. Honest men became thieves, and gangs of Ugandan bandits roamed the cities, killing and looting to survive. Western diplomats armed their homes with shotguns, German shepherds and grenades, and on occasion fought off attackers from their bedroom windows. Matts Lundgren, a United Nations representative, stationed two guards with machine guns in the garden of his Kampala home, and Joseph Bragotti, a Roman

Catholic priest, started packing a .38-caliber revolver under his cassock. Chaos had given way to anarchy.

At Makerere University, professors stopped showing up for classes and spent their days scrounging for food. The hospitals ran out of medicine, and operations ceased because there were no anesthetics. Emergency supplies of food and medicine from international relief agencies poured into Uganda by the truckload but were hijacked almost as soon as they crossed the border. In the north, where drought and famine held the people hostage, and the cows seemed to have fared better than the humans, the Karamojong cattle herders routinely tossed the withered corpses of their little boys outside the villages each night. There were so many that the hyenas grew fat and lazy and the packs no longer fought and squealed over each feast. The boys were allowed to die because, when rations are meager, the Karamojong give the available food to their girls, who can be traded for cattle.

From their exile homes in Europe and the United States, thousands of young, ambitious and intelligent Ugandans answered President Lule's call to come home and help rebuild their country. But the task overwhelmed them and, in the end, defeated them. The law of the jungle had reclaimed the soul of Uganda. There were no obtainable national causes left, only personal ones, and within weeks of becoming cabinet ministers and presidential advisers, the former exiles were demanding their 20 percent off the top of foreign grants and contracts. When someone spoke of "my people," he didn't mean Ugandans in general; he meant the people of his particular tribe. If he said things were improving, he wasn't referring to the national economy; he was talking about his overseas bank account.

Lule was the one man who had a chance to save Uganda. He was honest, intelligent and, at the age of sixty-seven, cared little for the trappings of power. More important, he was a Baganda,* Uganda's largest and best educated tribe, and thus commanded the allegiance of the majority. Had he been a dictator instead of a humanist, he might have succeeded. But Julius Nyerere, the Tanzanian president and Uganda's de facto ruler, had installed Lule as his socialistic stalking horse. When Lule started speaking with a voice that was both independent and capitalistic, Nyerere spirited him out of

---

* The kingdom is Buganda, the people are Baganda, their language is Luganda.

Uganda, locked him up in a room without a telephone in Dar es Salaam and announced that Uganda would have a new president.

That man was Godfrey Binaisa, an attorney who had lived in New York and fallen on tough times, handling not much more than an occasional divorce case. I met him in the lobby of Kampala's International Hotel, just after he had returned to Uganda. A once important official in the pre-Amin government, he was now portly and balding, and he wore a rumpled suit. Asked by an American journalist how to pronounce his name, he replied, "Be nisa to me." He hung around the lobby, bumming cigarettes, chatting with the Western reporters, saying no, he didn't know what he would do now that he was back, but he hoped he could find some work. The next day he was as surprised as anyone to learn that he had a job—as president of Uganda, having been appointed by a local committee, which decided that he seemed as harmless and as reliable as anyone available. One of his first moves was to hire an American public relations firm for $400,000 to clean up Uganda's tarnished international image. An account executive from Washington, D.C., flew into Entebbe, brimming with confidence, carrying business cards that bore the notation "We can solve any problem." He left a few days later, shaking his head. What Uganda needed was a mortician, not a flack.

The cycle was soon to be complete. Binaisa was ousted from office by Nyerere, and the military returned to power.* Idi Amin was thrown out of Libya after his bodyguards had a shoot-out with some of Muammar Qaddafy's soldiers. He moved to Saudi Arabia, with two wives and twenty-three of his children, and announced his willingness to return to Uganda "for the good of my people." Meanwhile Obote, whom Nyerere had kept in waiting for just such a moment, had come home from Tanzania, won a fixed election and became Uganda's president for a second time.† "Today we raise the banner of democracy once more and proclaim the rule of law," he said at his swearing-in ceremony. "The past is gone. We start a new

---

* By the summer of 1982, Binaisa was back in New York, trying to resume his legal practice. Lule had returned to his exile home in London.

† Obote's people were in firm control of the ruling Military Commission. Even before the Ugandans cast their first ballot, the electoral commission simply awarded seventeen seats in parliament to Obote's Uganda People's Congress Party. When early returns showed Obote trailing, the chairman of the Military Commission, Paulo Muwanga—a front man for Nyerere and Obote—announced that he alone would count the ballots and decide the validity of the election. Two days later Obote was declared the winner.

future." This time, though, there were no celebrations. Within a few weeks Obote re-established the State Research Bureau, the security agency that was to Amin what Savak had been to the Shah of Iran. Torture became common again in the crowded prisons, people once more started "disappearing." The newly independent newspapers were closed down, dissent was muzzled, the International Red Cross and resident Western journalists were expelled. Uganda teetered on the brink of civil war that would pit tribe against tribe, and in the outlying districts a new guerrilla group, composed mostly of Baganda, launched its first attacks against the government installations in an attempt to bring down the Obote regime.

Had the psychology and attitudes of an entire nation changed during its long nightmare?

"No," the vice chancellor of Makerere University, Senteza Kajubi, told me one day after some thought, "I wouldn't quite say that Uganda has produced a generation of moral cripples. But on the other hand . . ."

He fell silent, searching for the words. "On the other hand," he repeated at last, "we obviously have been greatly affected by the experience of Amin and what came afterward. We have fallen so low that I wonder if we can ever climb back."

To realize just how far Uganda did sink, it is worth taking a brief historical look at the country Winston Churchill described as "the pearl of East Africa." Landlocked Uganda is one of Africa's most beautiful countries. It is a fertile land of high plateaus and lush green foliage that reach from the shores of Lake Victoria—the source of the White Nile—to the dry plains of the north. Blue crater lakes are tucked among the terraced hillsides, and within a day's drive of Kampala, like Rome a capital built on seven hills, some of the most splendid wildlife herds in all Africa roamed through national parks as large as Rhode Island.

"Uganda is a fairy tale," Churchill wrote in 1908 after arriving by train from the Kenyan coast. "You climb up a railway instead of a beanstalk, and at the top there is a wonderful new world. The scenery is different, and most of all the people are different from anywhere else in Africa."

The early Ugandan people were farmers and warriors who developed five centralized, prosperous kingdoms: the Buganda, Bunyoro, Busoga, Toro and Ankole. From the mid-nineteenth century through to independence in 1962, the Baganda dominated Uganda. They were a proud, elitist people who considered themselves superior to other Bantu kingdoms in the Lake Victoria basin and to the Nilotic cattle-herding tribes of the north, the Acholi and Lango. They were ruled by a *kabaka* (king) and represented about 20 percent of Uganda's population.

In 1894 Uganda became a British protectorate, and colonial administrators, utilizing the policy of "divide and rule," bestowed special favors on the Baganda. They became the backbone of the civil service and the vehicle for carrying out colonial policies. The other tribes sought, but did not receive, similar privileges. Unable to win responsible jobs in the bureaucracy or to dent the Baganda-dominated commercial sector, these outsiders had the choice of remaining neglected or finding new avenues into the mainstream of civilization. The Acholi and Langi, for instance, cast their lot with the military and became the tribal majority in the colonial army.

Unlike neighboring Kenya and Tanzania, Uganda moved toward independence without any united nationalistic front. Indeed, the Baganda even considered secession rather than risk the loss of dominance in a new nation. This absence of central authority would later prove to be a major obstacle to political stability. But Milton Obote, a Lango schoolteacher, promised the Baganda autonomy and managed to put together a loose coalition that led Uganda to independence, with himself as prime minister and the *kabaka* as president.

It soon became apparent Uganda was missing another element that was to become important in Kenya's success—European settlers. There were 43,000 whites in Kenya at independence, and more than 5,000 of them were farmers who had settled in the highlands north of Nairobi. Kenya was their home and they had a stake in making the new republic work. In Uganda the 8,800 whites were administrators, professionals and technicians. They would stay for three or four years, then move on when their contracts were up. The settlement of whites in Kenya had been a conscious decision of the British government for two reasons: Kenya was on the coast and more accessible to travelers than landlocked Uganda; and Kenya's farmland, though not as fertile as Uganda's, was less densely populated and thus did not require the displacement of large African groups. If the British had settled Uganda instead of Kenya, it is entirely possible there would have been no Life-President Idi Amin and no socioeconomic debacle in Uganda—and no mini-miracles of progress in Kenya. For, however much European settlers retarded the Africans' advancement, their presence represented strong authority, law and order, political stability—concepts that African colonies could carry with them into independence.

As it turned out, Obote had no intention of sharing power with the *kabaka*, Freddie Mutesa, a slight, elegant figure who had once served as a lieutenant in England's Grenadier Guards. Obote wanted absolute control, and his accord with the Buganda kingdom erupted into confrontation; secession again became the Buganda cause. In 1966 Obote called on his army chief, Idi Amin, to put down the rebellion with minimum force. Instead Amin blasted through the *kabaka*'s palace with tanks, and King Freddie, the last in an unbroken line of ruling royalty dating back to the sixteenth century, escaped over a wall and fled to London, where he died a penniless alcoholic five years later. The monarchy was abolished, Obote became president, and Amin was now a man to be reckoned with.

Despite tribal rivalries, Obote's misdirected leadership and the absence of exploitable minerals, Uganda had a great deal working for it in those early days of independence. Makerere was a superior university, referred to as "the Harvard of Africa." The economy, based on agriculture and buoyed by the presence of 70,000 Asians, was healthy, the tourist industry was booming. The health system was one of the finest in the Third World: there were forty-eight hospitals, several hundred rural dispensaries staffed by paramedics, a surprisingly sophisticated facility for psychiatric care, a tropical-medicine institute of international note, and black Africa's best city hospital, Mulago in Kampala. There were excellent hotels and game lodges, 1,000 miles of paved roads, and an extensive rail network that stretched to Mombasa on the Kenyan coast, six hundred miles away. Even more important, there were the Baganda, a people far less primitive than most other Africans in the neighboring countries.

The man responsible for Uganda's destruction was born in 1925 to peasant parents who scratched a meager living from their two-acre plot. Idi Amin was a Moslem and a member of the small backward Kakwa tribe, a people noted for little except their lack of education and their penchant for soldiering. His parents separated shortly after his birth and Amin was raised by his mother, who lived sometimes in the barracks, with a succession of military men.

In 1946 Amin joined Britain 4th King's African Rifles as a kitchen helper. Knowing that the British did not favor the Kakwa, he listed his tribe on the registration forms as Acholi. Amin never fought in India and Burma, as he later claimed to justify the medals dripping from his uniform, but by all accounts he was a tough, courageous, unquestioning soldier. He fought well during the Mau Mau Emergency in Kenya in the 1950s and later was promoted to lieutenant, an unusually high rank for an African in the discriminatory colonial promotion system. "Idi was a fine chap," one of his British officers remembered, "though a bit short on the gray matter."

By 1962, the year of independence, Amin had displayed the first signs of the brutality that was to become his trademark. As a platoon commander, he was assigned the task of ending a tribal war between two neighboring people, the Turkana of Kenya and the Karamojong of Uganda. He accomplished that job, but a month later several bodies were disinterred from shallow graves in the village where Amin's unit had operated. Villagers had been tortured and beaten to death; others had been buried alive.

"Some pretty fearful things have been going on in Turkana," Kenya's deputy governor, Sir Eric Griffith-Jones, said, "and it looks as if there is some evidence apparently that one of the Uganda army people has so brutally beaten up a complete Turkana village, including killing, that I think we shall have to take criminal proceedings against him."

The name he mentioned was Idi Amin. But Sir Walter Coutts, the British governor of Uganda, on the advice of Prime Minister Obote, quashed the charge. Amin was one of only two African officers with the British army in Uganda, and with independence only weeks away, a court-martial could have been embarrassing to all concerned. It was the gravest misjudgment the British made during their sixty-eight years in Uganda.

The Uganda flag replaced the Union Jack over Kampala on October 9, 1962. The new banner bore the national emblem, a crested crane, and a series of horizontal stripes: a black one for Africa, a yellow for sunshine, a red for brotherhood. There was irony in each symbol, for in time Obote's country would slaughter much of its wildlife for food and profit, Africa would turn its back on Uganda, sunshine alone would not be sufficient to make the farmlands flourish, and brotherhood would become fratricide.

Obote was a resourceful and strong-willed man, a socialist and a theoretician. A decade earlier he had been offered a scholarship to study law in the United States, but the colonial authorities refused him an exit visa on the grounds that knowledge of American law would be useless in Uganda. Now Obote had his chance to experiment. He crushed the monarchy and nationalized the economy. He got his attorney general—the Bagandan who would later resurface as president, Godfrey Binaisa—to rewrite the constitution, consolidating virtually all powers in the presidency. Uganda, Obote said, was putting distance between itself and the stereotyped European systems. Indeed it was. And the tribes grew restive, the economic foundations quivered, the army waited.

In January 1971 Obote flew to Singapore for a Commonwealth meeting to rally support against Britain's decision to sell arms to South Africa. Before he left he made a fateful mistake: he ordered Amin and his defense minister, Felix Onama, to explain in writing the disappearance of $4 million in army funds and weapons. The demand hastened the inevitable, and on January 25 Amin and his soldiers seized power. The result was tantamount to arming a mob of twelve-year-olds and telling them they were now running a country.

Perhaps not surprisingly, it was Amin the buffoon, not Amin the butcher, who first caught the world's attention. A hulking six-foot-four 240-pounder, he raced around Kampala in a red sports car, plunged fully clothed into swimming pools during diplomatic functions and promised to make Uganda more prosperous than Japan. He divorced three of his five wives en masse in 1974—the dismembered body of one of them, Kay, was later found in the trunk of a car—and fired his winsome foreign affairs minister, Elizabeth Bagaya, accusing her of having had sexual intercourse in a lavatory at Orly Airport in Paris.

"The problem with me," Amin said, "is that I am fifty or a hundred years ahead of my time. My speed is very fast. Some ministers had to drop out of my government because they could not keep up."

To students at Makerere University he said: "Now I have got a couple of rockets for you. You are responsible for teaching people hygiene. You must make yourself very smart, very clean, very healthy. I find that the VD is very high. If you are a sick man, sick woman, you had better go to hospital, make yourselves clean or you will find that you will infect the whole population. I like you very much and I don't want you spoiled by gonorrhea."

And to Lord Snowdon, after the breakup of his marriage to Princess Margaret, he wrote: "Your experience will be a lesson to all of us men to be careful not to marry ladies in very high positions."

The world chuckled, Africans applauded, and Ugandans died, often at the rate of 100 to 150 a day.

From politician to peasant, no one was immune. Education, money or influence was enough to mark a person for death. Social gatherings, even close relationships, were best avoided because Amin's spies were everywhere, in the ministries, the shops, the airports, the bars, the hotels, the taxis, the schools. To survive, one stayed quiet and unnoticed, melting into the crowds regardless of his station in life.

"Sometimes my husband and I would talk quietly in our bed about what was happening to Uganda," said Judith Mulondo, the mother of two young boys. "But we'd never mention our feelings or Amin's name in front of our children. They might have let it slip at school. Then there would be a knock on your door, and those knocks were the same as death notices."

One undercover agent, in a document I found in Amin's house, used these words to pass along an execution order to his superiors: "This person is so close to me that I cannot take any action on him. So if action is to be taken, it should be carried out in such a way that I am not discovered."

An attorney told me of walking to work every morning in a T-shirt and tattered slacks so that he would not draw attention to himself as a member of the upper class. A businessman left his Mercedes-Benz in the garage and bicycled to work for the same reason. University students interviewing for jobs would identify themselves as high school dropouts because Amin apparently was intent on eliminating the country's intelligentsia.

Big Daddy, as the international press called him, evoked a peculiar response in black Africa and became for a time a sort of perverse folk hero. Savage though he was, he had qualities that Africa's unsophisticated leaders rather admired: he dealt with anyone who crossed him as casually as a child would squash an ant; he said all the right things about nationalism, economic development and human dignity, and the fact that what he said was either outrageous or spurious was immaterial to his presidential peers; he humiliated the Asians, expelling Uganda's entire community of 70,000 in 1972;* and he toyed with the Europeans, once forcing British resi-

* Amin gave the Asians' shops and businesses to his army cronies. As happened in Zaire, many of them simply sold the existing stocks and closed up permanently. The Asians were never compensated for the loss of their businesses.

dents in Kampala to carry him on a thronelike chair. Many African presidents would have loved to have the gall to be as crudely blunt.

But the price Uganda paid! Amin declared himself a doctor of philosophy and the chancellor of Makerere University, and the one-time "Harvard of Africa" became a university of semiliterates, acquiring not a single book for its library or classrooms between 1976 and 1979. Inflation rose more than 1,000 percent during Amin's eight-year reign, while basic wages went up only 54 percent. By the time Amin was overthrown, a man earning the minimum wage of $34 a month had only enough money to buy ten loaves of bread.

The roads cracked and filled with potholes; the factories closed; the wildlife herds were machine-gunned by soldiers for meat and ivory; the coffee plantations stood idle; Mulago Hospital became a scandal, its toilets stopped up, its water taps dry, its sixty-bed wards jammed with three times that many patients and filled with rats, cockroaches, lice, fleas and bedbugs. The country's sixteen psychiatrists—along with as many as 100,000 other Ugandans—went into exile, the rural health clinics closed, the tourist industry evaporated.

Even in its dying days, Kampala was a lovely city, laced with tree-lined avenues, waving palms and municipal gardens. The skyline was dominated by the sixteen-story International Hotel and a fine mosque. The Anglican and Roman Catholic cathedrals stood atop two of Kampala's hills, and on a third, Kasubi Hill, were the tombs of four *kabakas*, including King Freddie, whose body Idi Amin had had exhumed in England and flown home to Uganda in an early attempt to win Buganda backing. On the sides of the hills, just a five-minute drive from the downtown square, were some of the most gracious suburbs in all Africa, their stately mansions covered with ivy and set back from the road, surrounded by gardens that seemed always in bloom. There were sidewalk cafés such as Chez Joseph to enjoy on warm summer nights, frequent choral and dance performances at the National Theater, and the campus grounds of Makerere University were as pleasant and as pampered as those of any rural American college.

If you had flown over Kampala in a helicopter, the capital would have looked as tranquil and attractive and everyday normal as, say, Medford, Oregon. It was only on ground level that you realized what was happening. In the shop windows were impressive stacks of cans of paint, cartons of small electric appliances, boxes of liquor; but the contents all had been emptied and the displays were only ø façade. The 300-room International Hotel—formerly called the Apolo, Obote's middle name—looked like any Holiday Inn, but the restaurant served only bread and instant coffee. The electrical generators had broken down and guests huffed up fourteen flights of stairs by matchlight. The water system was out of service too, and if you wanted to take a bath, you pulled the fire hose down the corridor and filled your tub from the emergency tank on the roof. The performances ended at the National Theater; waiters in white jackets stood in the cafés with soiled napkins over their arms but with no customers to serve; the large clock in Independence Square stopped, ticking off not a second over the course of several years.

Amin's Entebbe State House on the shores of Lake Victoria—the Ugandan equivalent of the White House—appeared immaculate outside to passers-by. Inside, though, sofas were covered with cigarette-burn holes, drapes had been pulled off the windows, beer bottles cluttered the closets, grease covered the kitchen floor and bullet holes dotted the ceiling of the living room, where Amin regularly used to blast away with his revolvers to summon his staff.

The worse things became in Uganda, the more adaptable and accepting the Ugandans seemed to become. If there was no food in the stores, they picked fruit and ate steamed, mashed bananas, which are served with local spices and are known as *matoke*. If the phones didn't work, they did their business in person. If friends and relatives died for making ill-chosen comments, they became silent. If there was no public transportation to get them to their city jobs, they walked. They did so without complaint or apparent anger. "*Shauri ya Mungu*," they said—Swahili for "It's God's will." To a Westerner, such fatalism might be dismissed as passivity. But there is more to it than that. Like so many Africans, the Ugandans had lost control of their lives. They lived in a feudal-style system in which one's well-being depended on an allegiance to a man or a group of tribal barons, and that attachment did not include the right to question. The tradition of giving all power to a village chief, the era of colonialism, and the repressiveness of men like Obote and Amin had taught them obedience, even servitude. They had learned the art of survival.

Tragically, Amin would not have lasted as long as he did if Africa had had the courage to isolate him, and if the East and West had cared less about their own interests and more about Uganda's. But Libya helped train Amin's army and sent military advisers and civilian technicians. Saudi Arabia promised Amin $2 million in the dying days of his regime in the name of Islamic brotherhood. The Palestine Liberation Organization provided personal bodyguards as a reward for Amin's anti-Israeli ravings. Egypt, Pakistan and Bangladesh sent university professors for Makerere, doctors for Mulago, engineers and other professionals. The Soviet Union gave sophisticated weapons, East Germany trained the secret police.

The West's interests were economic. The United States—which to its credit did institute a trade embargo shortly before Amin was toppled—was for years the biggest purchaser of Uganda coffee. Western companies supplied the country with petroleum. Britain, Uganda's largest trading partner, sold Amin everything from radio technology to drugs to military uniforms. It was not until Amin ordered the murder of Uganda's Anglican archbishop and two senior cabinet ministers in 1977—Amin said they died in a car accident— that world opinion turned solidly against the man who had once seemed such a good-natured oaf.

Amin was facing pressures at home, too, at the time he killed the archbishop. His army was restless, and tribal fighting broke out in the barracks. Amin needed to put his soldiers to work. The solution he came up with was to start a war. On October 30, 1978, the Ugandan army invaded northwest Tanzania, annexing 710 square miles without opposition. The occupation, Amin announced, was "a record in world history," completed in the "supersonic speed of twenty-five minutes." Julius Nyerere responded that Amin was a "snake" mentally damaged by syphilis. He summoned his generals and ordered a counterattack. The initial results were a case study in how not to wage war.

The first day the Tanzanians mistakenly shot down three of their own planes. A week later the counteroffensive had to be halted entirely because no one was sure where the ammunition stockpiles were. One Tanzanian battalion never got the word of the delay and headed off for Rwanda, planning to veer north into Uganda. But the unit got lost in the Rwandan forests and wandered for days, unable to find its way either into Uganda or back to Tanzania. Most of the Tanzanian military vehicles broke down, so the generals had to commandeer buses, Land-Rovers and cars in Dar es Salaam, 850 miles from the front. The convoy finally got rolling. Many of the vehicles ran out of gas en route. The soldiers abandoned them and finished the journey on foot.

When the two armies at last caught up with each other a few weeks later, there was little enthusiasm for any fighting. Soldiers just set up camp on either side of the Kagera River. Nyerere, though, was determined to complete the job, and in the spring of 1979 he brought the twenty-eight Ugandan exile and liberation groups to a conference in Moshi, Tanzania. They included Marxists and monarchists, socialists and capitalists, tribalists and nationalists, men who were united only in their resolve to rid Uganda of Amin. Nyerere scraped together a 50,000-man people's militia, composed largely of illiterate youths pulled off the streets and out of the bush. It was more a mob than an army, for its members had no rank and little training, but together with a handful of Uganda rebels they pushed north, crossed the Kagera River and moved into Uganda. Amin's soldiers—supposedly the best armed and trained in East Africa—threw down their weapons at the first sound of gunfire and fled. Several hundred Libyan soldiers, dispatched to Uganda by Colonel Muammar Qaddafy in an eleventh-hour attempt to save Amin, took up the front-line positions around Kampala. They broke and ran too, and the capital fell without a battle. Amin escaped on a military flight to Tripoli, and Yusufu L. Lule stepped out of the shadows of parliament to speak about the new beginning that was never to be.

Uganda no longer exists today as a viable nation. It has disintegrated into a cluster of tribal states. Its cities have become frontier towns, terrorized by bandits who will kill for a Seiko watch. Its government is a collection of outcasts and misfits serving only themselves. Most of the bright young Ugandans who came home after Amin's overthrow already have returned to exile. There was nothing left to rebuild. The economy, the governmental infrastructure, the spirit of reconciliation had all been destroyed. The Ugandans had committed national suicide and by the summer of 1983, upwards of 200 people a day—most of them women and children—were dying as government troops and antigovernment guerrillas leveled villages, ambushed buses, shot up churches, raided houses and did their utmost to make sure the legend of Idi Amin was not forgotten.

I telephoned Amin one day that summer at his modest villa outside Jidda, Saudi Arabia. He was living on a dole from the Saudis, did his own sweeping and cooking—"I'm an excellent chef now," he said—and spending his ample free time studying Islam. Every

Friday he prayed at Mecca or Medina, unrecognized in his Muslim robes and lost among the crowds. Wherever he went, he carried a satchel filled with world maps which he would spread on a table when he wanted to discuss a particular region.

"I'll tell you this," he told me. "I have studied a lot here, and I am convinced that democracy is much better than being—what is it the press called me?—a dictator. People in the United States and the United Kingdom have the freedom to express themselves. This teaches me a good lesson.

"That's what Uganda needs—democracy. Of course, I can see that democracy would not work immediately in Uganda. It would take two or three years. Security is very bad there now, and there are many problems. But a tough person with military knowledge like me could teach the people discipline and prepare them for democracy.

"I think you will see from this example that I was not responsible for what went on. Obote is in power now, right? Can anyone say that he himself is killing all those people? No. I found myself in that same particular situation.

"The problems in Uganda are tribal, economic, selfishness. Obote should sit down with me and the opposition, and we could discuss Uganda's problems. But this Obote man"—and on the phone line from Jidda there was an impish chuckle—"he is very afraid of me. If he even heard my voice on the telephone, he would be scared."

Uganda raises many troubling questions. Is it an isolated case or is all Africa destined to follow the same course of self-destruction? Can Uganda ever recover? What should the role of the West be? What lessons should Africa have learned from watching the sorry spectacle of a prosperous country fall a millennium behind the times?

To be sure, Uganda represents the ultimate horror of what a tribalistic, misled, primitive country can become. But it would be unfair to say that Uganda has any more lessons for Africa than Northern Ireland does for Europe. The failing is a human one, for no continent has a patent on the injustices man inflicts on man. Africa produced Amin, but Europe gave us Hitler. Uganda, a nation for only two decades, dug its own grave; Cambodia, part of a great empire dating back eleven hundred years, dug a bigger one. The lessons of Uganda are for all mankind, not just for Africa.

Because of its great agricultural potential, Uganda has an economic base that could be revived with foreign assistance. That alone holds out hope that Uganda could, in a generation or two, forge some kind of meaningful nationhood. Recovery, though, can never begin until the Ugandans themselves are given control of their national destiny and the Obotes and Nyereres retire to the sidelines.

A first step in this direction would be to bring in a foreign peace-keeping force—from the United Nations, the British Commonwealth or Africa itself—to supervise fair elections, an exercise Uganda clearly is incapable of handling on its own. The country should be disarmed, and a new army reflecting a tribal balance should be formed. Only then can tribalism be diminished, for until all thirteen major Ugandan tribes believe they have a stake in their country's political and economic future, there can be no Ugandan nation. Uganda had this opportunity when Lule became president and Julius Nyerere took it away in imperial style. But Africa is a land of second chances, and the choice is still Uganda's.

The United States and other Western powers quite wisely curtailed their promised financial assistance when Uganda's rulers started playing musical chairs. To invest a nickel in Uganda, other than that needed for emergency food and medicine, would have been to throw good money after bad. This was not the time to build dams or repair roads. To think that Uganda's problems could be solved with money was about as foolish as giving King Freddie another bottle of whiskey to cure his alcoholism. Uganda is a derelict and no one can get it to the rehabilitation center but the Ugandans themselves.

One afternoon before Obote's return to the presidency, I stood on the patio of a young accountant's home, talking about the demise of Uganda. I remembered how good I had felt when Lule took office, and I now knew I had been naïve. Uganda had individual concerns more pressing than national integrity. There was, it seemed, nothing any outsider could do to alter the inevitable. I suddenly felt detached, as if I had been walking through the Bowery in New York and knowing that that alien world belonged to no one but the unfortunates who inhabited it.

I asked Richard Mulondo, the accountant, how it had all happened. He had no explanation for the past, he said. But what he did know was that the present was terrifying. He had sold some of his furniture to get food—he was still working but the Uganda shillings he earned were worthless—and at night he and his family slept in the backyard, wrapped in newspapers. They armed themselves with machetes and they took turns standing guard, ready to flee at the sound of a breaking twig or a whispered word. Kampala belonged to the thugs with guns. As we talked, a yellow dump truck moved slowly along the street. It was full of corpses and on its door someone had scrawled in red: "Kampala City Body Removal."

Mulondo watched the truck stop. Two men sauntered out of the cab, picked a body off the curb and flung it onto the pile of corpses. It bounced off and tumbled back onto the pavement. The men grumbled and tossed it on again. This time it stayed and the truck moved on. Mulondo remained silent for several moments. Finally he asked, "What can you say except that Amin turned us all into savages?" Then he went inside and locked the door.

IN SEARCH OF UNITY

▲

These summits are a waste of time. All anyone does is
talk. Sometimes, sitting there, listening to all the talk, I
think I will scream.

—PRESIDENT EL HADJ OMAR BONGO OF GABON

EVERY SUMMER in early July, fifty men who hold the world's riskiest
political jobs gather in an African city to discuss the affairs of the
continent. This is the annual summit of the Organization of African
Unity, and for the heads of state it provides a forum to confront—or
more often, side-step—the immense problems retarding Africa's development: war and famine, superpower intervention and border
disputes, failing economies, inadequate leadership, ideological differences, human rights violations, political instability, soaring birth
rates. The meeting starts with brotherly embraces and pledges of
unity and ends three days later with the presidents and generals flying home in a huff, having accomplished little except the denuncia-
tion of apartheid in South Africa, and having found no consensus
other than agreeing to disagree.

"Trying to get these people to agree on anything," said Sir
Harold Walter, the foreign minister of Mauritius, after one OAU
summit sesson, "is like trying to play a violin by pissing on it."

The OAU was founded in 1963 roughly along the lines of the
United Nations. All African states, except white-ruled South Africa,
are members.* In the ideal, the OAU gives black and Arab Africa an
opportunity to speak with a single voice and provides a forum to
study and resolve African problems. Among the purposes stated in
its charter are the "total advancement" of the African peoples

---

* In 1982 the OAU admitted as the fifty-first member the Polisario, a guerrilla movement
fighting for the independence of the Western Sahara (known by the Polisario as the Democratic Arab Republic of the Sahara).

through political and economic development, the eradication of colonialism in all its forms, and the promotion of African unity. It is an important marketplace for the exchange of ideas, and however few its achievements thus far—its major one is simply to have survived—it does hold out hope that all Africa one day may move with a common resolve to right the injustices and inequities of past and present.

Unlike the United Nations, though, the OAU has no Security Council and no provisions to give its decisions teeth. It must depend on persuasion rather than punishment, or consensus through cooperation rather than correction through condemnation. Its authority is all but crippled by a charter clause stipulating that member states cannot interfere in each other's internal affairs. The intention is a good one, but by interpreting the clause literally, African leaders have denied the OAU any mechanism to settle wars, impose sanctions, pressure barbaric rulers or encourage unity.

When President Idi Amin kills upwards of 300,000 Ugandans, as he did between 1971 and 1979; when six wars engulf Africa, as they did in 1981; when Ethiopia stuffs its jails with 30,000 political prisoners, then the OAU's loudest response is silence. To speak out, individually or collectively, would be internal interference, violating an unwritten code in the fraternity of Africa's presidents: Leave me alone to run my country the way I want, and I'll leave you alone to do the same; that way we'll both stay in power a lot longer.

The code was tested when Tanzania invaded Uganda in 1979. Nigeria and the Sudan protested the action at the OAU summit meeting, not because they had sympathy for Idi Amin, but because Tanzania's Julius Nyerere had set a dangerous precedent. If he had assumed the right to decide who was qualified to govern next door, what would stop other presidents from making similar decisions? There were two stern speeches condemning the invasion, then the summit moved quickly on to other business. Interestingly, no one challenged Libya's Muammar Qaddafy, who also had intervened, sending combat troops to bolster the crumbling Ugandan army. The lesson was clear: Intervening to keep a president in power is acceptable; meddling to unseat him is not.

To understand precisely how chancy the career of an African president is, consider the fate of the original OAU signatories. Thirty heads of state signed the charter in Addis Ababa, Ethiopia, in 1963; by 1980, only seven were still in office. Of the others, two were murdered by their own soldiers, seventeen were overthrown in military coups but survived, two died natural deaths.

One of the reasons the presidents greet one another so warmly at each OAU summit is that it's always a mystery who will be around from one year to the next. When President William Tolbert hosted the OAU summit in Liberia in 1979, billboard-sized photographs of Africa's rulers lined the route to the conference hall. Half a dozen signs bore only the country's name but no picture because events had moved too fast for the summit organizers. Since the meeting a year earlier, Uganda had gone through three presidents, Ghana had publicly executed three former heads of state; the Congo had placed its ruler under house arrest, charged with, among other things, stealing $1 million to buy a solid-gold bed; Chad had seen its president sneak out of the capital at night and flee into exile; Mauritania's prime minister had been killed in a plane crash, Equatorial Guinea's life-president had narrowly escaped a coup attempt (but was overthrown and killed three weeks later), and two presidents, Jomo Kenyatta of Kenya and Houari Boumédienne of Algeria, had died of natural causes.

People had tittered at the summit in Khartoum a year earlier when the chubby President Tolbert, then sixty-five years old, was seen jogging around the Hilton Hotel pool, dressed in a white tropical suit and matching hat. Three feet in front of him and three feet behind were his security agents, moving at a sprightly pace, their walkie-talkies crackling. His entourage of seven brought up the rear, panting. Worries for his safety were well founded. Twenty months later he was murdered and disemboweled in his bedroom by a group of army enlisted men. Tolbert at the time of his death was chairman of the OAU, the most prestigious position on the continent, and as such represented the voice of black Africa.

The summit is held in a different capital each year with the host government shelling out huge sums it doesn't have (Gabon spent $1 billion in 1977, Sierra Leone $200 million in 1980) to build a conference hall, chalets for the heads of state, hotels and new roads from the airport to the downtown area, and to buy limousines for the presidents, buses to shuttle the press, and BMW motorcycles for the policemen. (Liberia bought thirty-six motorcycles for the 1979 summit. Within three days, the unsteady escort officers had wrecked twenty of them.) When a summit ends, the conference hall is usually boarded up, the hotels are closed or subsidized by the government to operate with a minuscule occupancy rate, the chalets are abandoned. Guinea turned down a chance to host the 1981 summit on the sensible grounds that the expenditures outweighed the benefits, for the time being at least. Most governments, though, justify the investment because it gives them an excuse to spruce up their capitals, and more important, because it offers many small insignificant countries and their presidents a brief moment in the limelight.

President El Hadj Omar Bongo—who also serves as Gabon's minister for defense, information, telecommunications, planning and national guidance, popular education, civil service, specialized party organs and women's advancement—celebrated the hosting of the 1977 summit in his country by putting the finishing touches on a $800 million palace right out of *Star Trek*. From his elevated thronelike marble chair behind a long marble-topped desk, the tiny statesman (Bongo is four feet eleven) has a panel of buttons that can make walls recede, doors open, rooms turn and lights dim. Although Gabon produces excellent marble of its own, Bongo imported the marble for his palace, and for the $23 million OAU conference hall from Italy, because the local quarry could not guarantee a delivery date.

Bongo's palace also has a night club, a banquet hall for 3,000 persons (which represents about 1 percent of Gabon's population) and a bathtub big enough to swim several strokes in. For good measure, there are two theaters, separated by a central viewing room which Bongo can rotate at the push of a button to make his choice of presentations.

Borrowing heavily against his country's modest oil revenues, Bongo turned his summit into as flashy and chaotic an event as Africa is likely to see for a while. Presidents roared through Libreville, the somnolent capital on the Atlantic coast, in Mercedes-Benzes and Cadillacs with sirens wailing, each jammed into the back seat between his bodyguards. (Bongo, like President Mobutu Sese Seko of Zaire, used Moroccan bodyguards, not wishing to trust his safety to local soldiers; Idi Amin used Palestinians.) The Gabonese honor guard, wearing red velvet capes and holding gold swords, lined the entrance to the conference hall. Gabonese soldiers in full combat gear patrolled the corridors, carefully checking each reporter's tape recorder to make sure it wasn't some kind of secret device for sending coded messages.

There was no laundry service in Libreville that week because the city's women had been recruited to perform traditional dances in honor of the arriving presidents. Nor were there any working prostitutes because Bongo had swept the streets clean with the warning to the nation's ladies of the night: "Open your hearts during the summit, but not your bodies." As a sign of African solidarity against the white South African government, Bongo also ordered the temporary suspension of flights between Libreville and Johannesburg and passed the word that the Rhodesian beef the restaurants were serving really came from Botswana.

When a journalist arrived at the airport and said he was from Salisbury, he was promptly deported. It was not until two days later that someone discovered he meant Salisbury, England, not Salisbury, Rhodesia. Two diplomats from the Asian nation of Bangladesh on the same flight asked for observer credentials to the summit. The welcoming committee, thinking Bangladesh was the name of a new African liberation group, assigned them delegates credentials instead. On the other hand, when the delegation from the little-known African island republic of São Tomé and Príncipe (population 90,000) arrived, no one on the committee could quite place the country. "Are you sure that's in *Africa?*" one official asked. The São Tomé group had to endure other indignities as well. In the OAU handbook the purported picture of the country's president was actually that of the former health minister, a political dissident who had fled to Europe. Public relations officers scurried around and pasted into the booklet a proper portrait of President Manuel Pinto da Costa.

For the seventy or so journalists who converge on every OAU summit—only five or six are Africans, the others are Westerners— the three-day spectacle is an exercise in patience and an ordeal of frustration. All but the opening and closing sessions of the OAU are conducted in secrecy; OAU officials operate on the premise that if you don't give the reporters any information, perhaps they won't write anything at all; and accommodations are, well, dicey. In Gabon some journalists arrived at their assigned hotels and found buildings still under construction; the hotel had no employees, doors, water or electricity, and the guests' $50-a-night "rooms" were nothing more than open space in uncarpeted corridors, to be shared with bags of cement. In Sierra Leone, members of the press were relegated to cots in the "visiting" locker room of the national soccer stadium. Liberia tried to solve its accommodation problem by bringing in a forty-year-old cruise ship, the former S.S. *America*, and turning it into a hotel for journalists and low-ranking delegates. The public was allowed aboard to drink, gamble and sightsee, and on the summit's final night so many people from Monrovia showed up that the Italian captain ordered the decks cleared, for fear that the ship might sink. But everyone was having too good a time to leave. The Liberian police were called, and the helmeted officers waded aboard in riot gear with billy clubs flailing. Within an hour the liner had been abandoned by all but the crew.

When journalists have problems during a summit, they are free to try to locate an OAU representative euphemistically referred to as the press spokesman. But the man filling that job during the three summits I covered, Peter Onu of Nigeria, seldom showed up for even his own briefings. At one point he disappeared for thirty-six hours, and when he finally did appear at the podium, he had only one announcement: "No questions, I'll take them at the evening briefing." Later, the evening briefing was canceled. When an Agence France-Presse reporter filed a story that displeased him, Onu announced that the entire four-man AFP bureau would be expelled from Gabon, an edict that Bongo overruled. All right, then, Onu said, delegates would no longer be allowed to talk with journalists.

One of the best sources for finding out what is going on behind the closed conference doors comes from the West, not from Africa. The United States, Britain and Australia all send young diplomats specializing in "OAU-watching" to the summit. They manage to obtain press credentials and to keep several key African delegates on their payroll. During nighttime meetings in parking lots and bathrooms, the diplomats receive copies of the classified documents under debate from their African agents. The issues might involve proposed recognition for the liberation-group fighting in the western Sahara or Tanzania's invasion of Uganda or formation of a human rights policy. There is little conclusive action, but the documents enable the diplomats to cable their governments in Washington, London and Sydney with an accurate assessment of the OAU's thinking.

Inside the conference hall the façade of unity crumbles as soon as the doors are locked, and each year there is usually at least one memorable fistfight on the floor between warring delegations. While presidents boo and hiss one another and translators work feverishly inside four glassed-in booths* and the chairman shouts "Order, order!," Africa breaks into the various factions that divide a continent: there are the so-called moderate countries, friendly to the West, and the so-called progressives, aligned with the East; there are the Moslem countries and the Christian countries; the Arabs and the blacks; the wealthy oil producers such as Nigeria and Libya, and the impoverished international beggars such as Rwanda and Tanzania; the French- and English-speaking countries (as well as five Portuguese-speaking countries and one nation, Equatorial Guinea, that speaks Spanish); the countries that harbor their neighbors' dissident groups and the lucky few that have formed alliances of friendship across their borders. The Hilton Hotel in Khartoum once made the mistake of checking the delegations from Zaire and Angola into rooms on the same floor. The countries weren't getting along at the time and heavily armed security men from each nation patrolled the corridor in their undershirts, glaring at one another so fiercely that the hotel manager (a German) moved the Angolans to another floor to avoid a shoot-out.

What quickly becomes apparent at a summit is that there is more that divides Africa than binds it. In 1982 Africa was so divided over the fate of the Western Sahara and Muammar Qaddafy's pending chairmanship of the OAU that most heads of state boycotted the annual summit. The presidents who did show up hung around Tripoli for a day, then went home because the quorum necessary to take any action never materialized. They tried to hold another summit in Tripoli a few months later, but this one, too, was aborted, this time over which of the two delegations from Chad was the legal one. It wasn't until 1983, in Ethiopia, that they managed to finally convene. Qaddafy was so infuriated at being denied the chairmanship that he stormed out of the conference, flew home to Libya with his entourage of female bodyguards and launched an attack on Chad to overthrow the government. The spectacle led more than a few pundits to suggest that the OAU should be renamed the Organization of African Disunity. Its members share the humiliation of their history and the bewilderment of their future, but beyond that, their unity is, in any continental sense, largely an imaginary concept, an idea whose time has come and gone. The Marxist Mozambicans and the capitalistic Senegalese, for example, live in two worlds 4,200

* European, not African, languages are spoken by delegates during the official sessions. The ones translated are English, French, Portuguese and sometimes Spanish and Arabic.

miles apart. The nomadic Tuareg of West Africa and the Kikuyu farmers of East Africa are as different as are Indians and Eskimos of North America. Robert Gabriel Mugabe, the scholarly, disciplined prime minister of Zimbabwe, wouldn't have much to talk about with Chad's semiliterate former head of state, Goukouni Oueddei, even if they could speak the same language. The Ethiopians and Somalis have been shooting at one another for a millennium. Individual countries have tried to overcome the diversity within their borders and found that nationalism cannot be created. For a continent of fifty-one countries (including South Africa) to do what a single nation cannot is an improbable assignment, given the depth of the linguistic, ethnic, cultural, philosophical and religious schisms in Africa.

If Africa's quest for unity has failed so far, if Africa's presidents get along no better than the European powers did with one another during the colonial period, no one, least of all the historians, should be surprised. Let's step back a century to the time when Africa was Balkanized and brought under European domination. It happened in Germany at a conference that not a single African attended.

The European powers, wanting trade routes, new markets and natural resources, were scrambling for influence in Africa. The competition was stiff and they often used chicanery and deceit to achieve their ambitions. France was pushing toward Timbuktu (now part of Mali), attempting to surround all British possessions in West Africa with a continuous band of French territory; Germany was secretly preparing to take possession of regions more than three times the size of Alaska; Britain was promising that its occupation of Egypt was only temporary (it would later become permanent); Italy was quarreling with France over Tunis; King Leopold II of Belgium was financing expeditions by the explorer H. M. Stanley, who secured treaties with African chiefs that would enable the king to personally control a million square miles.* Leopold soon instituted a system of monopolies in the Congo Free State that prevented inter-

* Leopold's will, published in 1889, bequeathed his Congo estate to Belgium. After much criticism, Leopold transferred the Congo to Belgium while he was still alive, in 1907.

† The countries represented at the Berlin Conference were Austria-Hungary, Belgium, Denmark, France, Germany, Great Britain, Holland, Italy, Portugal, Russia, Spain, Sweden and Norway (Norway was then part of Sweden), Turkey and the United States. The only important European state that did not attend was Switzerland. All fourteen countries signed the Berlin Act, but only the United States failed to ratify it.

national competition, and his rule was as tyrannical and corrupt as any African president's in the 1980s.

The acrimonious disputes, though all were solved peacefully, caused much apprehension in Europe, and it was finally decided that the world's powers had better sit down to determine some game rules for Africa. Delegates from fourteen countries assembled for the Conference of Great Powers in Berlin in October 1884.† Four months later, on February 26, 1885, they signed the General Act of the Berlin Conference, which provided that any power that effectively occupied African territory and duly notified the other powers could thereby establish possession of it. The Berlin treaty, along with other accords signed during the next fifteen years, defined "spheres of influence," which partitioned the continent among European governments and reduced their rivalry for domination. After a flurry of public debate, anticolonialist protests subsided in France and Italy. Conservative governments ruled in England and Germany. Policies of mercantilism were prevalent from Rome to London. Europe was assertive and nationalistic. Its mood favored colonialism.

The effect of the Berlin Conference was to divide, not unify. The colonial boundaries were artificial and illogical. They ignored the cultural cohesion of tribal Africa and separated the peoples of ethnic mini-nations held together for centuries by their common heritage and language. No sensible grouping of people remained.

The Masai, a proud, nomadic, warlike tribe, was split between German-ruled Tanganyika and British-ruled Kenya. And on the other coast, right through the middle of French-speaking Senegal, a narrow strip was inserted that followed the Gambia River from the Atlantic Ocean into the interior; that wormlike intrusion is The Gambia, an English-speaking country smaller than Connecticut. The Portuguese sold trade rights to the river to English merchants, and England later formalized its presence in a treaty with France. The accord divided the Mandingo and Wolof peoples into two colonies with different languages and different European masters.

In 1900, Africans living in Europe convened the First Pan-African Conference in London. The move was mainly aimed at providing a sense of community for Africans abroad, but more important, it represented the first step in Africa's search for African unity. The two world wars—in which 700,000 Africans fought on the side of their colonial masters—brought Africa more into the world's mainstream, and by the late 1940s the continent's leaders were turning their attention from the concept of Pan-Africanism to independence. A few leaders still hoped that the continent could merge into a United States of Africa, or at least into regional groups of English- and French-speaking nations. But Africa's new nations opted at independence to recognize the colonial boundaries rather than try to redefine new national entities. The result was a hodgepodge of countries, and today no one talks anymore about combining sovereignties.

Most African leaders will admit privately today that the OAU does not work in its present format and needs to be overhauled if it is to be anything more than a symbolic reminder of Africa's dim dreams of finding an identity and a unity. First, the charter needs to be amended to allow the OAU the authority to influence and even control African events. Second, the power of the heads of state (who are the OAU's "supreme organs" and the only decision-making body in the organization) should be diminished and partly transferred to the secretary-general, giving him the strength to act independently on urgent matters. And third, member states must stop hiding behind the mask of unity that dictates that any criticism of an African or an African country is detrimental to the well-being of Africa.

Unfortunately, though, Africa, like the Third World as a whole, expresses itself mainly in clichés and slogans. Most African leaders believe that if they talk long enough and loud enough, someone will listen and take them seriously. But words have lost their meaning. What is said publicly has nothing to do with what is thought privately. People talk at each other, not to each other.

President France Albert René of the Seychelles drew a warm response at the OAU summit in 1979 when he condemned the new constitution and called for penalties against African countries doing business with South Africa. The logic of such statements defies understanding. At the time, 60 percent of the Seychelles' trade was with South Africa, and René had suspended his own constitution after coming to power in a coup that overthrew a man who had twice defeated him in free elections.

In OAU summit after OAU summit, the delegates quite rightly condemn the injustices of apartheid in South Africa. Yet how much credence can those words have on a continent where more than a million people have died at the hands of their own governments in the first two decades of independence? How credible can the voice of the OAU be if it expresses outrage at the death of activist Steve Biko in South Africa and utters not a word of protest while President Idi Amin slaughters Ugandans like cattle during an eight-year rule of terror?

"The OAU's silence has encouraged and indirectly contributed to the bloodshed in Africa," a Ugandan Anglican bishop, Festo Kivengere, told me. "I mean, the OAU even went so far as to go to Kampala for its summit [in 1975] and make Amin its chairman. And at the very moment the heads of state were meeting in the conference hall, talking about the lack of human rights in southern Africa, three blocks away, in Amin's torture chambers, my countrymen's heads were being smashed with sledge hammers and their legs were being chopped off with axes."

One of Amin's successors, President Godfrey Binaisa, made the same point in the 1979 summit in Liberia. "There's no use criticizing others' human rights records when we are doing the same things," he said. Binaisa went on to condemn the Central African Empire, where Emperor Bokassa I had recently beaten to death eighty disrespectful schoolchildren, and Equatorial Guinea, where Life-President Macias Nguema Biyogo had murdered one eighth of his country's population.*

The conference fell silent as Binaisa delivered his address in soft, reasoned tones. Nodding heads bobbed awake. Empty seats filled. Delegates fidgeted uncomfortably. Never before had an African head of state actually condemned by name another African country for violating its people's human rights. The delegates were shocked and none too pleased. There was no applause when Binaisa returned to his seat ten minutes later. "He is either a drunk or a traitor; I do not know which," a delegate from Benin later muttered in the corridors. Binaisa was neither, but the speech was to be his last at an

---

* Macias ruled Equatorial Guinea from independence in 1968 until he was ousted by his cousin in 1979 and executed. Western human rights organizations estimated that 50,000 Guineans were murdered during that time. Another 100,000 Guineans escaped into exile. Macias, a member of the majority Fang tribe, directed most of his brutality against the Bibis, the best-educated and wealthiest of the country's ethnic groups. A Catholic-turned-atheist, he celebrated Christmas Eve in 1975 by ordering the shooting and hanging of 150 prisoners in the national soccer stadium. During the spectacle, loudspeakers blared a recording of "Those Were the Days."

OAU summit. Ten months later he was overthrown.

Perhaps one day the OAU will feel secure enough to admit that more divides its members than unites them, that candor and criticism can be as healthy as they can be disruptive, that countries with differences can still act as one when the common good is threatened. Perhaps Africa and the outside world simply expected too much too soon from the OAU.

As Emperor Haile Selassie I of Ethiopia said in his opening remarks at the OAU's founding in 1963, twelve years before he, too, was overthrown, "The Union which we seek can only come gradually . . ." No one today would contest the wisdom of that comment.

COUPS AND
COUNTERCOUPS

▲

I am your god and teacher. I am the divine way, the
torch that lights the dark. There is no god but Ali
Solih.

ALI SOLIH, *the late president of
the Comoros, speaking to his people*

THE MOST REMARKABLE ASPECT of Africa's coups d'état is not how
many there are, but how small their impact is on the average citizen's life. They are usually staged in the name of economic reform
and social justice, yet they seldom accomplish either. And when the
African awakes, turns on his radio and hears the voice of an unknown general saying that the government has just been taken over,
he treats the matter casually. Chances are he has heard it all before.
He accepts the change in leadership without debate, hopes for the
best and does as he is told.

True, countries may undergo a radical shift in political orientation, as happened in Ethiopia when Haile Selassie's feudal, pro-
Western government was toppled by a clique of soldiers who were
both Marxist and murderous. But except for the land-reform policies the sergeants instituted, the Ethiopian peasantry would hardly
have known there was a new government in Addis Ababa. Even in
Uganda, the leadership exchange between Milton Obote and Idi
Amin did not greatly affect life in the rural areas, where about 80
percent of the population lives. This separation between city rulers
and rural subjects helps explain why Africa does not have revolu-
tions in the sense of popular uprisings. It has coups in which power
is merely transferred within an inner circle of cousins, friends and
soldiers. The procedure is so routine that the coup d'état has become to Africa what a presidential or parliamentary election is to
the West—except that the loser often ends up dead or in prison instead of in comfortable retirement.

In Sierra Leone, army generals brought down the civilian government in 1967; within a matter of months they were overthrown by other senior officers, who in turn were driven from office by a sergeants' revolt. Benin (formerly Dahomey) endured five military coups d'état, ten attempted coups, twelve governments and six constitutions between 1963 and 1972.* Junior military officers staged a "coup of conscience" in Ghana in 1979 and executed three former heads of state for corruption in the space of a few days, and never managed to bring about a single lasting reform. No sooner had the firing squads laid down their rifles than the black market reopened, government officials began taking bribes again and smuggling of cocoa to neighboring countries resumed. Fifteen countries in Africa have had one coup since independence, thirteen others have had two or more. By 1983, no fewer than fifty governments had been overthrown in independent Africa, and twenty-eight of Africa's countries had experienced coups d'état. Most coups were politely welcomed by the African citizenry whose lives were already so difficult that any change was viewed as an agreeable alternative.

It is worth noting that sub-Sahara Africa did enjoy political stability for the first six years of the independence era (1957-1962). But in 1963 the founding president of Togo, Sylvanus Olympio—whom President John F. Kennedy called "one of Africa's most distinguished leaders"—was assassinated at the gate of the United States embassy in Lome while seeking refuge. Olympio was a political moderate and fiscal conservative. He had managed to invigorate his fledgling country's agricultural sector, balance its budget and end its French subsidy. But he paid with his life for refusing to increase the size or salaries of his 250-man army. The soldiers were amazed—and so was the rest of Africa—how easily they had gotten their way. A few shots and they were in business. The precedent was set. With

---

*The fifth coup, in 1972, was engineered by a young French-trained paratrooper, Mathieu Kérékou. He and a group of soldiers surrounded the presidential palace, where the ruling ministerial council was gathered at siesta time. In a matter of seconds the ministers' status of governors changed to one of prisoners.

Kérékou decided that the country's 3.3 million people needed a Marxist "revolution." Christmas and Easter were abolished as legal holidays, the Jehovah's Witnesses were banned and their officers were ordered to undergo "demystification" training. Kérékou also forced sorcerers into special asylums—an unpopular move because witchcraft is still commonly practiced in Benin. Voodoo, in fact, was born in Benin and spread from there to Haiti and other parts of the world.

Kérékou was still in power in 1984. He had given his country a decade of political stability, but only at the cost of widespread repression and steady economic deterioration.

Olympio's death began a period of continental instability unmatched in the modern world.

Africa has no tradition of government such as, say, China has had, so as often as not the coups lead to a complete breakdown in effective administration. Why, then, does Africa keep having coups when the results are so seldom positive? Part of the reason is historical, entwined in the same forces that stymied nationalistic causes: tribalism, linguistic diversity, colonial boundaries, unsteady economic foundations. And part is contemporary, reflecting the character of the men at the top:

▶ In their insecurity, African presidents closed the safety valve of public expression. Dissidents and creative thinkers were killed, jailed or exiled. Newspapers and radio stations were brought under government control. People who did not pay homage to their president, no matter how misguided his ways, were considered traitors. Discontent built, tension rose. Each country became a sort of pressure cooker. There was no escape for the steam. And when the pressure became too great to contain, there was an inevitable explosion.

▶ Colonialism ensured stability. It was the symbol of continuity, of law and order. When that era ended, there was a void with no strong central authority, except perhaps the military. Uneducated, ambitious men stepped into the vacuum, and the only power base they could immediately establish was built on the strength of the gun. In civilian countries the army became, in effect, the opposition party, waiting in the wings for an opportunity to test its theories on how to run a government.

▶ The European powers, as I mentioned earlier, imposed on Africa a political system that did not work. Parliamentary democracy was a luxury for Africa's young, uncertain governments. When the inherited systems broke down, neophyte presidents disposed of the Old Guard, but they had not thought out any sensible substitute. They tried to write new rules without understanding the old ones. The first coup usually settled nothing; it only led to another.

▶ A man who gains power in Africa does not surrender it voluntarily. In the West a president can be impeached or voted out of office, a prime minister can be brought down by a vote of no confidence. Although some countries such as Kenya do have "no confidence" provisions in their constitutions, no such tradition of succession exists in Africa. Presidents become life-presidents (one even became emperor). However overdue their departure, they stay until they are killed or driven from office, believing that, as with a village chief, their right to rule is inalienable.

There are three specific coups d'état, each representing a different dimension of how and why governments are overthrown, that deserve a closer look. Two of the coups symbolize the extremes: in the Comoros the horrors preceded the coup; in Liberia they followed it. The third coup, in the Seychelles, comes closer to the norm, for it was a harmless, foolish affair that need not have happened at all.

The Comoros islands are only a speck in the Indian Ocean, four volcanic islets that, from the window of an airplane, look no bigger than icebergs, lost and adrift in the choppy seas. The islands are very beautiful and very poor and are known primarily, if at all, for their *ilang-ilang*, an exotic flower whose extract is widely used in French perfumes. But except for the *ilang-ilang*, the fine sandy beaches and the soft ocean breezes, the Comorian people can count few blessings. Resourceless, destitute and disease-ridden, their island republic is the waif of the French colonial empire, the stepchild of an independence movement that promised so much and delivered so little.

Potable water is still a luxury on the islands, collected during the rainy season in masonry cisterns. Illiteracy among the 400,000 Comorians tops 90 percent. Bananas make up 20 percent of the people's caloric intake, and half the children die before the age of five. There are only 14,000 paid jobs in the entire country, and it was not until 1976 that the Comoros manufactured its first farm implement, a wooden hoe. The islands had nine doctors and no working telephones when I arrived in Moroni, the capital, on a rattling DC-3 from Dar es Salaam, Tanzania, four hundred miles away. The only dentist had left two years earlier, and an old travel guide I picked up in my hotel—where I was the only guest—advised: "If you fall seriously ill on the Comoros, fly to Paris."

The Comoros—comprising only 693 square miles, one-sixth the size of Yellowstone National Park—declared unilateral independence from France in July 1975, thus becoming a republic and, later, the 143rd member of the United Nations.* France retaliated

---

* The 38,000 residents of one of the Comoros' four islands, Mayotte, voted to remain an overseas territory of France when independence was declared. Mayotte has the only deep-water port in the Comoros, and because of its association with France, is more prosperous than the other three islands: Grande Comore (where the capital is located), Anjouan and Moheli. The Organization of African Unity contends that France's presence in Mayotte is colonial and illegal.

by promptly withdrawing its $18 million annual subsidy and five hundred technicians. Disaster was inevitable. Twenty-eight days after the French flag was furled, the Comoros had its first coup d'état. Attempted coups followed in each of the next three years, including one masterminded by the president's press attaché. People died, the prisons were filled, paranoia gave way to a national insanity. The *période noire*, as it became known, had begun, and what happened next was as bizarre as anything modern Africa has ever seen. It was a drama whose cast of characters included a demented president, a white mercenary looking for a winning side after twenty-three years of fighting for losers, and two wealthy Comorian exiles, one of them an ex-president, plotting their return to the islands from the seclusion of a penthouse apartment in Paris.

Ali Solih had seemed normal enough when he first came to power in a coup six months after independence. He was thirty-nine years old then, balding with a slight paunch. He had three attractive wives and he gave each her due share of attention. He was an atheist and a moderate drinker, despite his early Moslem upbringing, and was known as something of an idealist, frequently extolling the virtues of the Chinese revolution. His record as a senior civil servant in the ministry of agriculture was undistinguished. On the surface at least, there was nothing to suggest that this mild-mannered, bland government official would soon be transformed into the Madman of Moroni.

"Do not believe all you hear about Ali Solih; my son was a good boy," his seventy-nine-year-old mother, Mahamouda Mze, said one afternoon, receiving me in her tiny tin-roofed home a few miles from Moroni. Her living room was dark and cool behind the frayed blankets she had nailed across the open windows. An old Marconi radio sat in the corner, useless because her village had never had electricity. She had placed a rear-view auto mirror and a vase of plastic roses on a table near the radio for decoration. She lit her kerosene lamp, the blazing sun outside invisible in the blackened chamber she seldom left.

"You know," she said, "Ali would come every month to bring me food and a few francs, and he was always talking about how he wanted to do something for his people. He said Communism was best for a poor country like this. He said experiments with it failed in Tanzania and all over Africa, but he was going to make it work and all the world would look to the Comoros.

"When he made the coup, I was scared. I did not want him to be president because I knew he would make many enemies." She paused, taking a sip from the warm Coca-Cola bottle she held. Then she went on, "Now you tell me something. How could this thing happen? What went wrong?"

Clearly, some great change came over Ali Solih. Some say it was the drugs and alcohol that changed him. Others believe he had a mental breakdown. Whatever the reason, the pressures of the presidency far exceeded the limits of his abilities. His fuzzy notion of national goals grew dim in the glow of personal power and the pleasures it could bring. The men with the brains to think or the courage to speak went to jail or to their graves until only the sycophants were left. The Comoros became Solih's personal toy, and like a child with a new Christmas present, he played and experimented and manipulated, ending one game and starting another whenever he became bored.

Boasting that he had "changed the people's mentality," he put together his own parody of the Chinese revolution. He fired the 3,-500 members of the civil service and turned the government over to teen-age dropouts, the group he could most easily indoctrinate. He lowered the voting age to fourteen, burned 134 years of French administrative records and declared himself a prophet. He closed the hotels ("Foreign influence corrupts," he declared) and nationalized everything from the taxi cabs to the bread shops. He brought in Chinese advisers to guide him and Tanzanian soldiers to protect him. He denounced religion as a curse and forbade Moslem women to wear black veils. Once he stormed into a mosque and raged at the worshipers, "Go ahead. Call on God! See if He answers."

For days at a time he refused to leave his white stucco palace. He divorced his wives and kept steady company with a bevy of young girls in his second-floor bedroom, drinking whiskey and smoking hashish and watching movies on his 16mm projector until the sun came up and the light of morning calmed his nerves. During the day he popped Valiums. His eyes grew bloodshot, his mumbled words became incoherent.

Through the streets of Moroni, past the little whitewashed homes and the clusters of empty shops and the shuttered high school, roamed the youth brigade that Solih had sanctioned. Its members were illiterate toughs, and the so-called revolution—of which they had not the vaguest understanding—had bestowed upon them their first taste of authority. They had no ideology other than the power of the gun, and they killed and terrorized and raped. Petty criminals and "counterrevolutionaries" were marched through the narrow, winding streets, dressed in burlap grain sacks, their heads shaved and their faces painted with white stripes. A member of the youth brigade followed each procession with a megaphone, announcing the prisoner's alleged crimes to the Comorians who lined the way.

One such procession was forming at the airport at the precise moment a West German diplomat arrived in Moroni from Madagascar on a chartered flight. He had come to discuss a large agricultural grant the Bonn government was considering for the Comoros. He watched bewildered as the prisoners were herded and whipped into a single line. Not having been met by any Comorian official, he caught a ride to Moroni with the driver of an old French army truck. He entered the ministry of foreign affairs, where he had been expected, and found himself in consultation with two ranking officials. They were about seventeen years old, and of course, neither could read or write. "It was a very astonishing exercise," the diplomat recalled. He was airborne within the hour. There was no further mention of the German grant.

"We can't go on running the country like this, with teen-agers in charge, with so many people in jail," the prime minister, Abbas Jusuf, told Solih one day. "People are starting to say we are crazy. The country is paralyzed."

"Silence," Jusuf remembers Solih screaming. "Do you not realize that I have visions, great visions? That is is I who guide our destiny?"

The next day Jusuf's seventy-five-year-old mother was marched through the streets in a burlap sack and imprisoned on unannounced charges.

Solih, though, did have a great vision one night and he spoke of it often afterward. It was of a man and his dog and they had come to kill him. Solih awoke sweating and trembling the next morning, his cook told me, and after a breakfast of sausages and brandy, issued a presidential decree: all dogs on the Comoros were to be killed immediately. The youth brigade carried out the order that day, butchering hundreds with their machetes, dragging others to death behind Land-Rovers.

The Comorian people displayed a remarkable reaction to the national delirium: silence and quiescence. It was as though Los An-

geles had made Charles Manson mayor, and then sat back to casually watch the chaos. But the Comorian response was not unique,
for Africans as a whole show a remarkable capacity for tolerance
toward their leaders. Presidents can get away with murder, literally
and figuratively, and no voices are raised in protest. They can pilfer
the treasury bare, have the blood of a thousand men on their hands,
govern like medieval monarchs—and still command the obedient
servility of their people. Fear is a powerful master. At some undefinable point, though, when corruption and craziness become too
overt, a president places himself in jeopardy. Both his job and his
life are on the line. And in the spring of 1978, that moment was fast
arriving for Ali Solih.

There was a man in Solih's past named Bob Denard. He was fifty
years old and referred to himself as a military technician. His profession had carried him from Indochina to Africa during more than
two decades of warfare, and in many African countries there was no
more hated or feared name than his. Bob Denard was one of *les af-
freux* (the terrible ones)—a French-born white mercenary who, for a
fee, would do the dirty work for Africans they couldn't do for themselves. There were not many jobs left for "the dogs of war" by the
time Solih's enemies contacted Denard; in fact, there were not
many mercenaries left either. Most had gone into retirement, slipping quietly from the limelight. They were middle-aged men left to
reminisce about the Biafras and Katangas and Stanleyvilles. But
Denard had never fought for a real winner, and he wanted one last
curtain call for a dying profession.

"African armies are much better than they used to be," Denard
lamented with a trace of nostalgia. "There was a time when our services were really needed, but that time is passing now. I think I am
the only person left who could have mounted an operation like
this."

Denard was no stranger to the Comoros. He and a handful of
hired guns had helped stage the coup which brought Solih to power.
An avowed anti-Communist, Denard later pulled out of the islands
and moved to Paris when his employer began espousing radical
causes. Now he had the tacit approval of the French government,
and two new employers: Ahmed Abdallah, the exiled first Comorian
president, and Mohammed Ahmed, a wealthy Comorian businessman who mortgaged his penthouse apartment in Paris to help
raise the $2 million Denard needed for the operation. It took De-

nard three months to put together an invasion force of twenty-nine men, mostly French and Belgian, each with a military specialty ranging from communications to munitions.

In April 1978 they set off from Europe in a rusting thirty-year-old trawler, the *Masiwa*, under the guise of making mineral surveys in Argentina. When they reached the Cape of Good Hope they simply turned left instead of right. Shortly after midnight on May 13, the *Masiwa* slipped through the mist to Grande Comore, where it stopped offshore. At the front of the trawler stood Bob Denard and his German shepherd.

The island's largest hotel, the 25-room Itsandra, was, as usual, empty and the twenty-one-year-old bartender and night custodian, Youssouf Zoubeir, had wiled away the evening playing Ping-Pong in the lobby with the cook and watching lizards scurry along the walls in search of insects. "Every night seemed as long as a lifetime in those days," Zoubeir later recalled.

Down the road, at the seaside military camp, Abdul Mdahuma, the exiled president's former senior adviser, was finishing his second year of imprisonment in Room 10 of a windowless cell block with mud floors, cement walls and thick wooden doors. He had eaten his daily ration of rice and beans and settled down with the three former ministers with whom he shared the six-by-six-foot cubicle, wondering if the whispered rumors of an impending coup were true.

Ali Solih had heard those rumors too. But his fears were dispelled by Jean Guilsou, a French mercenary who had come to the Comoros with Denard in 1975 and had stayed to train the president's bodyguards. Guilsou, who had become an accomplice in the new plot, convinced Solih that the threat was coming from the next island, Anjouan. Now betrayed by even his most trusted friends, Solih dispatched his 2,000-man army to Anjouan, leaving Moroni open to attack.

Solih was in his hilltop villa the night Denard arrived. The president's two teen-age mistresses were upstairs. Until well past midnight Solih sat at the mahogany dining-room table drinking brandy with Olacharry Christian, a French shipping agent who had invited himself for an evening of idle conversation. Christian had ended up on the short end of the stick in several business deals with Solih and now his allegiances had changed; they belonged to Bob Denard, who at that moment waited a mile offshore with his band of mercenaries.

Shortly before four o'clock, Denard received the radio message from Moroni that Solih had fallen asleep, full of brandy. The mercenaries, their faces blackened with charcoal, their hands holding sawed-off shotguns and grenades, slipped into three rubber rafts and paddled ashore, landing on the beach near the Itsandra Hotel, where Youssouf Zoubeir had become bored watching lizards and dozed off. Worshipers in the mosque across the street stared in disbelief, said nothing and returned to their prayers.

The mercenaries split into three groups. One moved on foot along the coastal road to the radio station—always the first target in any African coup; another filed up the hill to Solih's villa; a third headed north to the military camps where, after a brief fire fight, the guards were killed and the wooden doors holding Abdul Mdahuma and three hundred other prisoners were swung open.

In three hours the mini-war was over. Thirty men had captured a country.

The skirmish claimed the lives of ten Comorian soldiers. The others, along with their eighty Tanzanian advisers, fled or threw down their weapons. The operation cost the mercenaries a single sprained ankle. By breakfast time, Denard was on the phone to Abdullah in Paris.

Solih was under house arrest. The army had surrendered. The people were dancing in the streets. "You can come home," Denard told Abdullah, "as soon as we clean things up a bit."

Two weeks later, after Abdullah had returned to a rousing welcome, Solih was shot to death by the mercenaries, who said he had tried to escape from his villa, where he was awaiting trial for misappropriating millions of dollars of aid money from China and Kuwait. Denard loaded his body into the back of an open Land-Rover. There were two chest-high bullet holes in Solih's white shirt. The vehicle moved through Moroni, Solih stretched out in the back. Small crowds gathered to hiss a farewell. Just outside of town, past the abandoned parliament building, Denard turned off the paved road and headed up a rocky track toward the 7,600-foot-high volcano, Kharthala.

Solih's mother and sister, Fatime, waited there. "Here is Ali Solih," Denard said, dragging the body from the vehicle and letting it fall to the ground. "If you need some of my men to dig a hole, I will get them. But I do not want a lot of people at the burial." Only a couple of curious youngsters showed up, and Solih was interred in his mother's backyard with his name scratched into the wet cement of a simple grave marker.

Africa reacted with shocked indignation. The OAU summit refused to recognize the new Comorian government and turned back Abdullah's delegation, refusing to issue its members the credentials they needed to enter the conference hall. Once again white men had used their authority to determine the destiny of a black people. African sovereignty had been held up to ridicule. The mercenaries' presence in the Comoros was like rubbing salt in an open wound, reminding African governments how little control they really had over their own future. "We've got to send these people packing," said the Seychelles president, Albert René, who, in fact, had come to power a year earlier with the help of black mercenaries from Tanzania. (That had been acceptable as far as the OAU was concerned.)

"I don't know what the African countries are so upset about," Denard said. "At least they know where I am. If they send me away, I will disappear, and who knows where I may show up next?

"All my life people have accused me of fighting for wrong causes, of backing the wrong side. Now I have done something that gets rid of a crazy president who ruined his country. We get a sensible anti-Communist government back into power. I am on the right side. And people still accuse me of doing wrong. I don't understand why Africa isn't grateful."

But if Africa brooded in anger, the Comorians themselves were overcome with joy. Denard had ended a nightmare and to them he was a hero and a liberator. They cheered him on the streets, and Denard responded with exaggerated military salutes. They sold T-shirts emblazoned with his name. Children reached out to touch him, the elderly moved respectfully aside to let him pass, the new government gave him the run of the islands.

"A man reaches a point in his life when he sees it's time to settle down and he selects a place," Denard said. "Here in the Comoros, I can eat well, I can drink, sleep and make love. There you have it. If the people want me, it will take a hundred thousand Cubans to get us off the islands."

Bob Denard had indeed found a home. He bestowed Comorian citizenship and the rank of colonel on himself. He took the Moslem name Moustapha Mouhadjou and announced that he was hanging up his gun and settling down on his islands in the sun. The young bartender at the Itsandra Hotel introduced him to a receptionist there named Mazna, and Denard promptly married her.

By that time the mercenaries had taken over control of the key ministries, including defense and communications. They got the

mail flowing in the once empty post office and started fixing the telephones. They supervised the removal of garbage from the streets,
staffed a health clinic and made the Comorians whitewash their
scruffy homes. They formed a new army, and they moved into the
villas where French colonialists and later Solih's henchmen had
lived. For the first time in Africa's history, an independent country
was being run by European mercenaries.

I arrived in the Comoros not long after Solih had been killed. In
the course of a few weeks, as often happens in black Africa, an entire
people had changed its personality. It was spooky. The immigration
officials who greeted me so warmly and politely at the airport were
the same men who would have jailed or beaten a foreign journalist a
month earlier. The Comorian officials who spoke of the need for reform were, in some cases, the same men who had enforced Solih's
Draconian rule. The amiable youngsters who chatted so openly
about the horrors of life under Solih were the same fellows who only
recently had marched prisoners through the streets. How could
there be such a complete transition so quickly? People would shrug
indifferently. "We did what we were told to do," explained a young
man who had been a member of the youth brigade.

The Comoros under President Ahmed Abdullah rapidly returned
to what it had been before Solih. The economy was denationalized,
close relations with France were re-established, elections were held,
the children were sent back to school, adults again became civil servants. I arrived at Abdullah's house for an interview one sultry afternoon in a bullet-riddled Renault that had been shot up during Denard's coup. The government driver had picked me up an hour late,
and when we pulled into the president's driveway I saw an elderly
man sitting alone by the garage. He was drinking a glass of ice
water and smoking a Marlboro cigarette, and he had his bare right
foot tucked in his lap, yoga style. His sandals were on the ground
nearby.

"Please tell the president that I apologize for my tardiness," I
said. "There was some confusion over the time of the interview."

"That won't be necessary," the man replied, "I am the president."

Abdullah was a gracious and articulate host. His coup, he said,
had been the first in Africa waged in the name of democracy and
capitalism. He lit another cigarette with his gold Dunhill lighter. An
ocean breeze stirred the coconut palms, and the only sounds were
those of the waves nearby and the expressions of Abdullah's opti-

mism. "After every storm," he said, "there is a calm, and if we do not get bogged down in ideology, our islands can again be peaceful and prosperous. For us, this is like starting our independence all over again."

As for Bob Denard, the Comoros had agreed to let him stay, but it had become obvious from Africa's reaction that his presence would create too many problems and would politically isolate the Comoros. Denard accepted the decision and agreed that, yes, he was obliged to go. Abdullah hosted a lavish state banquet with French wine and Kenyan beef for Denard.

"Whatever some people in the world say," Abdullah told him, "you leave here a national hero. You can hold your head high. You can come back to the Comoros any time—but if you do, please come as a tourist."

The next morning Denard bought up all the T-shirts in Moroni bearing his name, drank his last bottle of orange soda pop, kissed his Comorian wife goodbye, collected the Zairian wife he had met during another war who had flown from Paris to join him in Moroni, and, dressed in civilian clothes and lugging a duffel bag, drove to the airport in the Land-Rover that had carried Ali Solih to his grave. A cargo flight hauling Rhodesian beef to Paris had been ̍diverted to Moroni to pick up Denard because no other African country would have given him a transit visa.

And four months after he had arrived on a fishing trawler, Denard climbed aboard the jet, offered a crisp salute to the gathered ministers and government officials and was gone, a winner at last but still a man without a home.*

Here's what one man who should know says about the leadership in Africa today: "There are some pretty shameful things going on, in no small part because Africa has such mediocre leadership. Everywhere you look, there are guns and unhappy people. The promises of independence have been a fake in most countries, and I can tell you this: a lot of people in Africa preferred the colonial days. They had more freedom.

"All this shouting about neocolonialism and imperialism is just

---

* After reading the story about the Comoros I wrote for the Los Angeles Times, Clint Eastwood located Denard in France, flew him to Hollywood and bought the rights to his life story for an undisclosed price. Eastwood was going to play Denard, but the actor was unhappy with the script he had commissioned and the movie was put on ice before filming started.

silly jargon. It's an excuse to divert attention from national short-comings. Black Africa devotes so much attention to South Africa and the apartheid there that it forgets the real problems are right there on its own doorstep."

The speaker was James ("Just call me Jimmy") Mancham, who for eleven months and seven days was president of the Seychelles, a peaceful cluster of islands (population 60,000) in the Indian Ocean, a thousand miles from Kenya. He had been overthrown by his prime minister, Albert René, and sixty Tanzanian soldiers and now he was sitting at his usual corner table in his favorite London restaurant, Mr. Chow, sipping white wine with Perrier water and reminiscing about the error of his ways.

"You know, right before the coup two people from the outside—I can't tell you where they were from—came to me and said that if I didn't do René in, he was going to do me in.

"I said, 'What do you mean—do René in?' And they said I had to kill him if I wanted to stay in power. That I couldn't do. I never even held a political prisoner. Maybe that was my weakness, because if you're going to be president in Africa, you've got to be ruthless to survive. If you don't have the stomach for violence, then you're going to lose your job, sometimes your life."

Mancham was living with an attractive Australian journalist in a penthouse near Hyde Park. He was a nonpracticing lawyer, educated in Paris and London, with sufficient business interests back in the Seychelles to live comfortably. (He spoke cautiously about René, not wanting to lose those interests.) In his spare time he wrote poetry—a sort of upbeat version of Rod McKuen—and he spoke in a touching way about his need to share friendship and make people around him happy.

The last time I had seen him was three years earlier, a few days before the coup. The bearded Mancham, then only thirty-seven years old, had entered his office in State House wearing an embroidered Mexican shirt open to the third button, flared slacks and loafers with no socks. A gold chain hung loosely around his neck. He rubbed the night-before's party from his heavy eyes and winked at us. "I don't believe in self-denial," he said, by way of introduction. "All the world leaders would like to live like I do, and if they could get away with it, they would." He winked again, leaned back in his chair and burst into song: "Tonight, tonight . . ."

I had to pinch myself to remember that this was a presidential interview. I had never had one quite like it. But then, I had never met a president quite like Mancham either. He tooled around his little island nation in a blue Rolls-Royce convertible, often in sneakers and shorts and usually in the company of beautiful women from Europe and the United States. Recently divorced from Heather, an Englishwoman, he made no secret of his desire to have a different first lady in State House each weekend—a desire he frequently fulfilled—and he made no attempt to separate his private life from his public one. "Is it a crime to be happy and have fun?" he would ask.

At State House he had put a quick end to the stuffy formalities inherited from the British colonial administrators. He entertained in open-neck sports shirts and filled his mansion that overlooked the Indian Ocean with orchestras and his favorite French wines. Almost every night the house echoed until the early hours with the sounds of laughter and singing.

On overseas trips, which he made with great regularity, he banged out press releases and telexed them back home to the local newspaper. At home, when the disc jockey at the local radio station overslept, he would slip on shorts and sneakers, drive to the station and spend a couple of hours reciting his poetry, reading the news and playing records.

And when a British gossip columnist got wind of an extramarital affair just before his twelve-year marriage broke up, he had an unusual response. He called a meeting of the islands' political leaders, held up a picture of the model involved and said, "This is the woman. Now, have I done anything wrong?" Apparently his people thought not. In the election three weeks later, his party won thirteen seats; René's got two.

But if Mancham pursued the good life with gusto, he also worked tirelessly on behalf of the Seychelles. He was a one-man public relations agency, traveling the world and telling anyone who would listen about the beauty of a nation very few people had ever heard of. He opened an international airport. Several luxury hotels sprang up. The tourist industry boomed. Visitors arrived from the distant corners of the world to enjoy this tropical paradise, whose president had a political credo he called "the Singing Philosophy"—just be happy as a person and a nation. His goal, Mancham declared, was to put a boy with a guitar under every palm tree.

"We are a small, quiet country," Mancham said. "We should not pretend to be anything else. We do not need great doses of political ideology. Let us just be what we are."

That, however, is not easy for an African country. Mancham headed off for London in the summer of 1977 to attend the Commonwealth Conference. René bid him farewell at the airport and that night sent his Tanzanian military "advisers" to the radio station. They played Peter, Paul and Mary records, and in the morning René made a simple announcement through a spokesman: Mancham had been overthrown and would not be allowed to return home. The Seychelles was just twenty-three days short of its first anniversary of independence.

René criticized Mancham's flamboyant life style, saying he spent too much time jet-setting and not enough minding the affairs of state. And perhaps Mancham should have been a good-will ambassador-at-large, not a president, but if any country had an opportunity to achieve the dreams of independence without a coup d'état, it was the Seychelles, Africa's smallest country in terms of population. Its per capita income of $650 was among the highest in Africa. So was its literacy rate (75 percent for persons between fifteen and thirty years of age), and its life expectancy at birth (seventy years for a woman, sixty-three for a man). The islands were completely free of malaria and the other diseases that have brought such misfortune to the rest of Africa. The people, mostly descendants of French settlers and their African slaves, were racially harmonious. (Mancham himself had Chinese and Creole ancestry.) Their life was so quiet, so seemingly secure, that the Seychelles didn't even have an army.

"It's no big heroic deed to take over the country," Mancham said. "Twenty-five people with sticks could do it."

Without Mancham the Seychelles might have remained an isolated backwater. But his great failing was naïveté, his belief that his country was entitled to something that did not belong to Africa—an age of innocence. René moved the Seychelles to the left politically and started tampering. He partly nationalized the economy, locked up a few opponents and formed an army, advised by the same Tanzanian soldiers who had turned Uganda into a shambles. The influx of tourists slowed, the economy weakened, the free press died. By 1980 the Seychelles was observing the third anniversary of the coup with a military parade through downtown Victoria, the capital. There were uniformed soldiers, armored personnel carriers and lots of weapons everywhere. The palm trees along the route swayed in the balmy breezes, and under them were young men who had forgotten their guitars and now carried guns.*

"Look at it this way," Mancham said when we met in London a few days before he set off to lecture on a Lindblad tour of the South Pacific. "I'm alive. That's more than a lot of ex-presidents in Africa can say. Besides that, everyone had fun when I was president, and how many ex-presidents can say that?"

The United States Congress in 1816 chartered a white philanthropic group known as the American Colonization Society. Supported by a $100,000 congressional grant, the society began organizing ship caravans of freed slaves who wanted to return to the Africa of their forefathers. Six years later, after being refused admission to Britain's Sierra Leone colony, the first shipload of freedmen landed near the mouth of the Mesurado River on the West African coast. With them was an agent of the society and a U.S. Navy lieutenant who persuaded the local chiefs, at gunpoint, to sell them the site for $300 worth of assorted hardware, knickknacks and biscuits.

Over the next years 45,000 former slaves—or black pioneers, as they called themselves—returned to West Africa.† They named their new home Liberia (for "liberty"), and their capital Monrovia (in honor of U.S. President James Monroe). In 1847 Liberia became Africa's first republic. It had an American-style government, a striped red, white and blue flag with a single star, and a national motto of "The love of liberty brought us here."

The new settlers adopted the only desirable life style they knew—that of the ante-bellum whites who had ruled them—and

* In November 1981 a group of wealthy Seychellois living in exile recruited, for $1,000 each, fifty-two white mercenaries from South Africa, including Michael (Mad Mike) Hoare, a notorious Irishman who had fought in the Congo in the mid-sixties, to bring Mancham back to power. The bargain-basement mercenaries flew into Victoria on a commercial jetliner, pretending to represent a sports and drinking club called the "Ancient Order of Foam Blowers." A customs official discovered their weapons while checking baggage, and after a fire fight at the airport the mercenaries hijacked an Air India jet and flew back to South Africa, the coup attempt nipped in the bud. (Five of the hired gunmen were captured and imprisoned in the Seychelles. The surviving mercenaries flew into Johannesburg, where they were later tried on hijacking charges. Some, including Hoare, were sentenced to prison.) Mancham denied having anything to do with the affair. He also said he was not involved with a coup attempt in 1982, which René put down with the help of Tanzanian soldiers.
† Ships brought African slaves to the United States until 1860, and the society's accomplishments were small. It gradually lost support and came under attack from abolitionists such as William Lloyd Garrison. They looked on Liberia as a palliative to ease the conscience of whites who refused to deal with the real issue: slavery.

they turned the sixty indigenous tribes into an underprivileged majority, referring to them until the 1950s as "aborigines." The pioneers and their "Americo-Liberian" descendants became a black colonial aristocracy. They controlled the commerce, ran the government and sent their sons abroad to be educated. The men wore morning coats and top hats, drank bourbon, joined the Masons and formed a secret society called Poro that acknowledged no African heritage. They passed on to their children their American names such as Christian Maxwell, George Browne and Barton Bliss—the army's chief of staff in the late 1960s was General George Washington—and a member of their True Whig Party was as conservative as any Southern Republican back in the United States.

Even today, urban Liberia seems more like William Faulkner's South than Africa. The official currency is the same U.S. dollar bills used in New York or Chicago—though they are faded and wrinkled and long ago were taken out of circulation by American banks. Policemen wear summer uniforms discarded by the New York City Police Department, and townships have names such as Louisiana, New Georgia and Maryland. On Sundays, when the strip joints on Broad and Gurley streets in Monrovia are closed, American gospel music fills the radio stations, and the accents in the packed Baptist church on Center Street are distinctly Deep South.

For a long time Africans poked fun at Liberia, disparaging it for adopting attitudes and importing values not in keeping with African traditions. But there was one aspect of Liberia no one mocked: stability. While governments fell like dominoes throughout Africa, Liberia seemed as solid as a rock politically. It was the essence of permanence and internal strength. By 1980 it had known 133 years of stability not marred by a single coup d'état. On top of that, it had become the first black African country to experience a peaceful, constitutional transfer of power when in 1971 President William V. S. Tubman died in office and was succeeded by his vice president of twenty years, William Tolbert. "We can take pride in the fact that this nation stands today as a true example of stability," the new president said.

Then fifty-eight years old, Tolbert was the grandson of a freed American slave and the son of a wealthy rubber baron. He had begun his government service as a typist in the treasury in 1935. He was an ordained minister and the first black man ever elected president of the Baptist World Alliance, and would later become chairman of the Organization of African Unity. He called his political philosophy Humanistic Capitalism and he lectured his people in preachy homilies.

"In a world of rising expectations and accelerated change," he said, "the lofty goals of national destiny still require and demand that Liberians harness and channel all their resources . . . in order to achieve a sustained upward thrust for ever-escalating rounds of distinction—yea, higher heights."

Tolbert was a decent man who, though certainly not untouched by corruption and nepotism, ruled more capably than many African presidents and more benignly than most. There were three main problems his administration had to come to grips with. First, Liberia had to be moved more into Africa's political mainstream. Second, accommodation had to be made with the indigenous Africans who had become increasingly resentful of their second-class citizenship. Third, the economy—based on iron ore, timber, rubber and the registration of the world's largest ghost fleet of ships*—had to be buoyed and restructured. Never having been a colony, Liberia had missed out on the benefits of colonialism (schools, roads, hospitals and a trained bureaucracy) as well as those of postcolonialism (huge European grants and foreign investment). The very independence that made Liberia unique had also cost its 1.8 million people dearly.

Tolbert made modest progress on all three fronts. He rode to his inauguration in a Volkswagen Beetle and wore a white safari suit to show that Tubman's stuffy, top-hat era had ended. He sold Tubman's $2 million yacht (it was never clear what happened to the proceeds). He brought more people who weren't the privileged descendants of slaves into the government, started a liberation fund to combat white rule in southern Africa and spoke out against the brutalities of Uganda's Idi Amin, one of the few African presidents to do so. He introduced universal suffrage, advocated free university education and amended the constitution so he could not run for another term, something no president had ever done on the continent.

---

* Liberia has only two ships of its own, but more than 2,500 vessels ply the seas flying Liberia's flag of convenience. Registration fees for the Liberian merchant fleet earn the Monrovia government $16 million annually. For the shipowners, about one third of whom are American, the savings run into the hundreds of millions of dollars. The Liberian flag enables them to hire low-paid, nonunion crews and to forgo some of the strict safety regulations that are imposed by nations such as the United States and Britain.

"We've been so lucky in Liberia," a businesswoman in Monrovia, Ruth Phillips, told me one day. "This is one of the few places in Africa that has known political stability and has respect for the rights of the individual. If you blame other presidents for what they did to their countries, then you have to credit Tolbert for what happened to Liberia."

Mrs. Phillips, who owned the West African Travel Agency, had come to Liberia from her home in Washington, D.C., in 1954. She was a nurse and had intended to stay for only six months. But she fell in love with a young Liberian businessman who was bright and industrious and eventually became the country's minister of finance. They were married and Mrs. Phillips took out Liberian citizenship.

"This is home now," she said. "I still go back to the States frequently on trips, but Liberia is where my heart is. My husband has done well financially and he's a respected member of the government. He's very intelligent. Tolbert relies on him a great deal."

During his nearly three decades as vice president and president, Tolbert's people sang his praises and sought his favors. His generals obediently carried out his commands. Then, as often happens in Africa, he was given the kiss of Judas and buried like a dog.

Late one evening in April 1980 he left a reception for religious and diplomatic guests in downtown Monrovia and returned to his seven-story Israeli-built mansion overlooking the Atlantic. It was almost midnight and he went directly to his penthouse suite. He changed into pajamas, presumably said prayers (as he always did), and crawled into bed. Two hours later, with the help of rebels in the presidential guard, a twenty-eight-year-old army sergeant named Samuel K. Doe scaled the mansion's iron gate with nineteen colleagues. They overpowered the few loyalist soldiers on duty, and in the fire fight a stray bullet severed the telephone line to the military barracks. It was the million-to-one shot that prevented Tolbert from summoning his army. Doe and his colleagues broke down Tolbert's door and found him in bed. They gouged out his right eye, disemboweled him and fired three bullets into his head.

Two days later, as Monrovia slumbered under the army-imposed curfew, a big yellow bulldozer crashed through the wrought-iron fence surrounding the Palm Grove Cemetery, and in a corner section used for dumping garbage, cut a shallow trench long enough to hold twenty-eight bodies. Tolbert's corpse, still clad in pajamas, was collected from John F. Kennedy Hospital, where it had lain unattended on a slab. Soldiers who had served their commander in chief loyally threw the body into the back of a truck, drove to the cemetery and dumped it into the unmarked grave along with the bodies of the men killed defending him.

Many Liberians came to peer into the open pit, but there were no prayers or eulogies for the ordained Baptist minister who was chairman of the OAU. Instead, before wandering back to town, the people threw stones and spat at their late president. "Pig," shouted one youth, hurling his beer can at the corpse.

Meanwhile Sergeant Doe, the semiliterate head of state, by this time had moved into Tolbert's mansion and was riding around town in Tolbert's chauffeured black Mercedes-Benz. (Tolbert had long since given up his VW.) Doe held a press conference to say there would be no witch hunting. "Our responsibility is to build a new society for the benefit of all our people," he said. But *all* the people really meant *some* of the people, and first there were some old debts to be repaid.

Swaggering soldiers patrolled the streets, shaking down civilians and looting shops. One group of drunken soldiers stormed into the Ducor Inter-Continental Hotel, and in a room-to-room foray, robbed foreign delegates who had been attending a Lutheran conference. The houses of Tolbert's associates were attacked and sacked, and ninety-one of his top officials were arrested on charges ranging from corruption to human rights violations.

The trials began on a Wednesday in a second-floor conference room at the military barracks on the outskirts of Monrovia. The public jammed into the stark cement-walled room, staring wordlessly at the accused, who faced the five-man military tribunal. None was permitted a defense counsel. Overhead fans cut through the heavy, stale air, and outside, hundreds of civilians watched gleefully while former cabinet ministers were paraded through the camp, wearing only their underpants. On the sandy beach nearby, nine telephone poles were erected in the sand, a sure sign that some of the accused had already been judged guilty and would be executed.

I arrived at the barracks in a taxi, expecting to be turned back as soon as I identified myself as a journalist. Instead the soldiers at the gate nodded and waved me through. A few minutes later I was seated in the second row of the makeshift courtroom, where Frank Stewart, the budget director for Tolbert's government, was pleading for his life.

Stewart's hair was flaked with sawdust from ten days of sleeping on a cement floor, and a gray stubble covered his chin. He wore a T-shirt, baggy brown trousers with no belt, and sandals. Someone said he was fifty but he looked much older. He sat on a wooden straight-back chair, squinting and sweating in the glare of camera lights from the local government station. He hunched forward to hear the accusations from the military tribunal. When the honking horns and rumbling traffic in the streets outside became too loud, he cupped his hand to his ear.

His five accusers were army officers with spit-shined shoes and steel-cold eyes. Two weeks earlier they had been the country's loyal servants. Now they were part of the ruling elite, sitting as judge and jury. To their left, a young army private wearing sunglasses labored unsteadily over a typewriter, recording the proceedings. In the back of the small auditorium several soldiers with rifles slumped sleepily against the unused bar. One of them kept bringing Stewart bottles of ginger ale, which he would empty in a single gulp.

It soon became clear that Stewart had stretched his annual government salary of $18,000 a long way. He earned $32,000 a year from the rental of three houses, and he owned twenty-eight lots, a supermarket, a farm and other scattered investments. Everything, he insisted, had been obtained legally, and if the tribunal would only allow him to bring his records, he said, he could prove his innocence. But no, an officer replied, that would only be a waste of time. So Stewart presumably knew he had already been judged guilty and the only question was whether he would be killed or jailed.

"Mr. Stewart," an officer said, "for the benefit of this tribunal, please state how many houses, lots and farms do you own."

"I will answer that by telling a story about how I happened to get—"

"We are not interested in stories. How many houses you got?"

"Well, houses . . . there are, let's see—four."

"Four," repeated the officer accusingly, holding up four fingers. "You got that down?"

"Got what down?" asked the typist.

"Four houses. Mr. Stewart got four houses."

"Four houses, yeah, I got it."

"Yes," Stewart said, "but in 1957 the price of cement was very cheap, so my wife, who was earning one hundred and twenty-five dollars a month at the Justice Department, and I—my salary was two hundred and fifty dollars—we used small loans from the bank, and for seven years we worked building the blocks we needed to construct—"

"Holy Christ," an officer said, "cut this short or we goin' to be sittin' here right through lunch."

"No, let him finish," another said. "Mr. Stewart, is it right for a government official to build a house, like you did, and then lease it back to the government? That's a question."

"What's the last part?" the typist asked.

"I said, 'That's a question.' You don't have to write that down."

"None of it?"

"No, just the last part, the part about the question."

"My answer to that," Stewart said, "is that it depends on the demand and the need and the government policies in force."

"How about your water bills, electricity, things like that. They up to date?"

"As far as I know."

"I ask that 'cause I don't ever know no government people who pays their utility bills."

"Mr. Stewart," said an officer, reading from a prepared question he had struggled over for some time, "according to the history of Liberia, this is the first coup d'état in history. If this is correct and true, please refresh your memory and tell this tribunal from your keen observations what the progressive differences are between the administration of the late president Tubman and President Tolbert. I want you to evaluate the different administrations as far as serving the masses and the importation of goods."

"The importation of goods?" Stewart replied. "Well, I'm not really in a position to evaluate that—"

"To what?" the typist asked.

"Evaluate. E-v-a-l-u-a-t-e. I really can't evaluate that. Certainly, during the Tubman years goods were cheaper and the cost of living was less."

"So," the officer said, "you indirectly made us understand that the Tubman administration better managed the affairs of the nation, particularly"—and he kept repeating "particularly" while the typist put in a new piece of paper—"particularly in regard to the masses, commonly referred to as the poor people."

"Yes."

"May we then conclude that the coup of April 12, 1980, was necessary to relieve the people of Liberia of their suffering?"

"Not only was it necessary—"

"Wait," said the typist. "Not what?"

"Not only was it necessary, it was long overdue."

The questioner smiled and nodded in agreement. "This trial is recessed so we can get some lunch. Mr. Stewart, you are finished."

"Finished? How do you mean? Will I be coming back again?"

"Maybe," the officer said with a shrug.

The next morning Sergeant Doe, the new head of state, held his first press conference for the forty or so foreign correspondents who were now in Monrovia. He strode into the ballroom of Tolbert's mansion wearing a wide-brimmed army ranger hat, crisply pressed fatigues and combat boots. He carried a ceremonial sword, a .357 magnum revolver and a walkie-talkie. In halting English he read a prepared statement, handled two brief questions and sat down. "Ladies and gentlemen," his new information minister, Gabriel Nimely, announced in a casual voice, "you are invited to some executions at two-thirty."

Back at the Barclay Training Center, where the trials had been held, the mood was festive. Thousands of civilians had packed the beach, and hundreds of soldiers, many of them drunk, danced and pranced around a small white mini-bus in which thirteen condemned officials of the Tolbert regime were locked. They pounded on the windows and kicked at the doors, laughing and jeering at the men inside.

"Hey, there, Cecil boy," one soldier shouted at the former foreign affairs minister, "I'm going to get the first shot. If I don't kill you, don't worry much. We'll let you die slow."

Sergeant Doe's motorcade arrived with a roar and nine of the condemned men were dragged from the bus—the remaining four would witness the spectacle and be pulled out later—and bound to the telephone poles. They wore only underpants. The soldiers taunted them and tickled them during the twenty minutes it took the firing squad to get organized. The officer in charge cursed as he tried to unjam his rifle.

Cecil Denis, the distinguished foreign affairs minister whom I had known well over the past few years, glared with disgust at his tormentors. Frank Tolbert, the late president's brother, fainted. Frank Stewart glanced about wide-eyed, as though it were all a nightmare from which he would suddenly awake. James Phillips, the finance minister and the husband of my travel-agent friend from Washington, D.C., wet his underpants.

"Squad, fire!" the commander ordered, his rifle finally functioning properly. For three minutes the executioners unleashed volley after volley. Bullets smacked into Phillips' arms and shoulders before one struck his forehead. Stewart was hit in the stomach, then thirty seconds or so later, in the heart. Denis continued to stand upright, eyes closed, as one bullet after another zinged harmlessly by. Finally a soldier stepped out of the ranks and killed him with a burst of machine-gun fire. A great shout of joy rose from the mob: "Freedom. We got our freedom at last!" The soldiers rushed forward to kick and pummel the corpses.

One of Doe's first moves as head of state was to double the wages of soldiers and civil servants, whose support he needed to retain power. The treasury was already in the red, though, and the $34 million annual expenditure for the salaries only heightened Liberia's economic crisis. Before long it became evident that the people's ecstasy at the executions had been premature. Power had changed hands but little else changed. Sergeant Doe promoted himself to General Doe, and each morning a hairdresser came to the executive mansion to fluff up his Afro. He raced around town with an escort of motorcycle cops, and he took care of his opponents at secret trials and public executions. In no time at all, he became quite comfortable with his new job as head of state, and the United States, not wanting to lose its toehold of influence in West Africa, courted him like a hero.

But in killing Tolbert, Doe and his soldier-politicians had merely identified the symptoms of Liberia's discontent. The causes remained. Running a government, they found, was more demanding than staging a coup; formulating remedies for national illnesses was more complex than shooting government officials bound to telephone poles. Freedom, the people learned, did not come from the barrel of a gun. Only one thing seemed certain as a result of the army takeover: Liberia's first coup d'état would not be its last.

The Liberian coup unnerved every president in Africa. If the chairman of the OAU could be murdered by a gang of enlisted men, who was safe? The answer was: No one. Political stability is largely an illusion in sub-Sahara Africa and almost any government can be overthrown as suddenly and as easily as Tolbert's. And below the paper-thin veneer of civilization in Africa lurks a savagery that waits like a caged lion for an opportunity to spring.

Tolbert's downfall was founded on the same mistakes that have led to the overthrow of so many other African presidents. First, he raised his people's expectations and aspirations, economically and socially, but delivered little of what he promised. Second, he allowed governmental corruption and the gap between rich and poor to grow beyond that undefined limit which Africans accept and tolerate. And finally, he misread the pretense of obedience that Africans pay almost any man with authority as a sign of love and respect for him. In the end, he was destroyed by the system he had helped create and try to liberalize.

Like many presidents, Tolbert said all the right words, but he didn't hear the rage building and he couldn't see the pillars of stability tumbling. The lessons of African history escaped him.

Sadly, there is little to suggest that history won't keep repeating itself. If any trend is likely, it is that Africa will have more coups, not fewer, in the decade ahead, because few presidents have addressed themselves to the causes of instability. Tolbert made reforms, but they were too few, too late, and their main effect was to give the opposition more room in which to agitate. For just that reason, most presidents are afraid to liberalize their own rule. But by refusing to do so, they create the very conditions that eventually lead to what they fear most—the loss of power.

The shortcomings that resulted in Tolbert's murder and Doe's ascendance exist in virtually every African country, usually far more acutely than they did in Liberia. And if national economics continue to wither and presidents continue to keep closed the safety valves of public expression, there can be only one conclusion: Africa's era of instability is just beginning.

THE COLONIAL HERITAGE

▲

I'll tell you this: those old days were incredibly good for
the European. There was no law, so we made it. *We*
were the law.

—LATHAM LESLIE-MOORE,
a ninety-year-old British settler in Kenya

THE EUROPEAN EMPIRE that once stretched the length and breadth
of Africa had, by the summer of 1977, shrunk to a Vermont-sized
chunk of coastal desert known as the French Territory of Afars and
Issas, a wretched wasteland France had colonialized 115 years earlier as a refueling stop for its Saigon- and Madagascar-bound ships.
Located on Ethiopia's northeast border, the territory—commonly
referred to by the name of its capital, Djibouti, which means "my
casserole" in the Afar language—was a resourceless and penniless
land that cost France $100 million a year to operate. It had only two
factories, one for bottling Coca-Cola, the other for bottling Pepsi,
and almost everything except a few home-grown tomatoes was imported: table salt from Holland, vegetables and eggs from Ethiopia,
meat from Kenya, drinking water from France. The population of
320,000 Afar and Issa tribesmen included three university graduates, no doctors and one *fille de joie*, Madame Fatima, a toothless
Somali who ran the Red Arrow brothel frequented by French Legionnaires.

Djibouti, the capital and only city, was a wonderfully seedy place
where Peter Lorre and Sydney Greenstreet would have felt right at
home. There was a dingy square, Place Menelik, surrounded by
cafés and bars nestled under urine-drenched arches. French soldiers
and civilians sat at the tables there, shirts unbuttoned to the waist,
sweating in the 100-degree evening heat, swilling lukewarm beer
and chasing away the swarming beggars with a wave of the hand. At

night the foreigners retreated behind louvered shutters in shabby villas on streets like the Rue de Beauchamps and Avenue Pasteur. The Africans lived on the other side of town, in shacks made of packing crates. Beyond the African quarter was a barricade of barbed wire forming a ten-mile necklace around Djibouti. After President Charles de Gaulle was greeted by riots on a visit in the 1960s, the French erected the barricade to control the swelling city population.

The atmosphere of Djibouti was reminiscent of Saigon circa 1950. The elegance was gone, but a faded charm lingered. Everything needed painting and sweeping. The sun beat down like a hammer, and everyone moved slowly, concerned with little except the arrival of siesta time, which stretched from eleven-thirty to four. Even the mosquitoes were lethargic, so sluggish that you could catch them in flight with your bare hand. The one hotel in town without cockroaches, the 39-room La Siesta, had only a single spigot in each bathroom which produced, naturally enough, hot water. In the hotels and bars, ceiling fans groaned overhead but the air was too heavy to move, and at night Frenchmen lay on their bedroom floors under the fans and poured bottles of water over their bodies and hoped they would fall alseep.

There were 15,000 Frenchmen in Djibouti—soldiers, businessmen, civil servants, expatriate wanderers—and by early 1977 most had already started packing their bags, having lost another home away from home. Indochina was gone. West Africa was gone. Soon Djibouti would be gone too, and the Frenchmen would drift on to Tahiti or New Caledonia, even back to France. The end of the European colonial era in Africa came on a June night, dripping with heat and humidity, in a capital city surrounded by barbed wire, and it would come without tears or toasts, farewells or nostalgia. Africa's newest nation would be launched into independence in a sad little ceremony that rated hardly a line in the international media and attracted not a single head of state.

The president-to-be, Hassan Gouled Aptidon, had been handpicked by France. He was sixty-one years old, a former nomad and a camel herder with a sixth-grade education. I arrived unannounced at his door one afternoon before independence, and rising from the couch where he had been napping, he welcomed me with a bottle of Coke and a French cigarette. His was a tidy cement-block house with three bedrooms, no air conditioning and a few pieces of old furniture in the living room. He seemed not at all worried by the future when I asked him how a country that was 90 percent desert and produced nothing could survive economically.

"Ah," he replied, puffing on his cigarette, "but when you were born, you had no money, correct? Then you worked and got some money and you lived better. We will do the same because we will find solutions when we are free to meet our responsibilities.

"We have many possibilities—salt, tourism, atomic energy, maybe a duty-free port like Hong Kong, and"—after a pause— "French aid."

There was no great sense of excitement on that June evening in 1977 as five centuries of European colonialism in Africa dwindled down to their final few seconds.* Several hundred chairs were lined up near the piers for the ceremony and a handful of buildings were whitewashed at the last minute. The new airport passenger terminal opened and the La Siesta hotel put up a "No vacancy" sign. The French aircraft carrier *Foch* anchored a few miles out to sea in the unlikely event an evacuation of the expatriates would be necessary, and Madame Fatima bolted the Red Arrow at 6 P.M., mumbling aloud, "Mercy, what will I ever do without the Legionnaires?" There was a shooting outside the barbed-wire perimeter that claimed one life when something called the Front for the Liberation of the Somali Coast—an outfit pledged to overthrowing the government that had not yet even taken office—demanded permission to enter Djibouti. Gouled smoothed out the problem with some skillful negotiating, and most of the front's 3,000 members were left milling outside the barricade with their camels and guns. By eleven o'clock the invited guests were in their seats. The women, stout and big-chested, wore colorful print-cloth dresses, and the men sat glassy-eyed, chewing khat, a narcotic weed imported from Ethiopia to which virtually every adult male in Djibouti is addicted.

At precisely one minute past midnight, France's high commissioner, Camille d'Ornano, offered a crisp salute as the French tricolor was lowered and folded for the last time in Africa. Hassan Gouled Aptidon, who would move out of his little home and into

---

* In a strange turn of events, one country, Rhodesia, would later return briefly to a colonial status. The white population there had declared unilateral independence from Britain in 1965. In late 1979, when it became apparent the whites could not win an intensifying guerrilla war, Rhodesia reverted to a colony ruled by a British governor. In April 1980, Rhodesia became the independent nation of Zimbabwe.

the French governor's seaside mansion the next day, was now the president of Africa's fiftieth independent nation, the Republic of Djibouti. A bugle sounded from somewhere in the darkness, a cannon roared twenty-one times from the French armada in the harbor, and fireworks danced through the skies, illuminating the ramshackle port city overlooking the Bab el-Mandeb strait that leads from the Red Sea to the oil routes of the Indian Ocean. Polite applause rippled through the audience and then everyone moved off into the night. Soon Djibouti was empty and silent. The torch had been passed.

John Gunther was no supporter of colonialism as an institution. But in *Inside Africa*, published in 1953, he shared the prevailing Western view that the European presence had been largely positive:

> The Europeans may have ravaged a continent, but also they opened it up to civilization. Colonialism made today's nationalism possible, and opened the way to democracy. The Europeans abolished slavery, and ended tribal warfare. They created communications, improved the standard of living, developed natural resources, introduced scientific agriculture, fought to control malaria and other diseases, established public health controls, gave natives only an inch away from barbarism stable administration and a regime based in theory at least on justice and law. (The white man's law, of course.) Most important, they brought Christianity and western education . . .

In reading those words today one gets the impression that Gunther probably spent too much time talking to British governors and not enough to Africans. The benefits he mentioned were not lasting. They vanished almost as soon as the Europeans left. The Europeans built artificial foundations for Africa's fledgling nations, and when the tide changed, they crumbled like sand castles. Only one aspect of colonialism was strong enough to survive the transition to independence—economic enslavement.

True, the two black African countries that were never colonized, Liberia and Ethiopia, remain among the most backward on the continent, and officials there often attribute their undeveloped condition to the fact that they missed the material benefits of colonialism. But the overall effect of colonialism on Africa was overwhelmingly negative. England, France, Portugal, Belgium, Germany and Spain divided up the continent like poker players sharing a pot. Their interests were economic: slaves, ivory, raw materials, bunkering ports such as Djibouti, new markets for European goods and, in Portugal's case, a dumping ground for more than one million of its citizens, most of them unskilled and semiliterate. Europe had not the slightest concern for the advancement of Africa—if that advancement did not profit Europe. As long as law and order were maintained, all other considerations were secondary.

To lessen the drain on treasuries back home, the colonialists introduced cash-crop economies: cocoa was planted in Ghana, peanuts in Senegal, tobacco in Malawi, coffee and tea in Kenya, sisal in Tanzania, cotton in Angola. These were export crops, and they neither fed Africa nor reduced Africa's dependence on Europe. Thus Africa was cast into independence with no industrial base. Each economy was based on one-crop harvests that were irrelevant to Africa and were subjected to wild price fluctuations on the world markets. Kenya, for instance, enjoyed a financial bonanza in 1977 when coffee prices soared following a frost in South America. That year Kenya earned $482 million from its coffee crop. Two years later world prices returned to normal and Kenya's earnings shrunk to $265 million. But Kenya had overspent during the boom days as though the windfall were permanent, and it was soon back on the international dole, its ambitious development plans wrecked.

The European powers, already having established borders that ignored tribal demarcations, now further divided the Africans in each colony into haves and have-nots, the former being a small, select group, often from a particular tribe, whom the colonialists deemed worthy of assuming limited bureaucratic authority. At independence the goal of the privileged few was to grow into a dominant bourgeoisie as quickly as possible. To do this, the African elite had to accumulate wealth and influence, and this new class set about manipulating public power for personal enrichment with remarkable ingenuity. The gap between the few and the many grew.

Throughout the five hundred years of European domination in Africa, dating back to the early Portuguese settlements in Mozambique and Angola, the whites governed as though colonialism would last forever. It was not until the final years of Africa's subjugation that Europe took any serious steps to prepare the continent for nationhood. By then it was too late. The new countries inherited economies and governmental infrastructures and sophisticated jobs that were designed by a European society to meet the needs of a European society. The untrained Africans could not cope. Twenty-five years ago they did not drive cars, let alone fly airplanes. They did not dream of becoming bank managers or corporate directors—positions that only whites filled—and the highest advancement an African could expect to make during the colonial era was to the level of senior civil servant, a job that would be closely supervised by a more senior white civil servant.

Djibouti had fewer than a hundred high school graduates at independence. The Congo had but a single senior African civil servant. Mozambique had an illiteracy rate of 90 percent. Zaire, a country as large as the United States west of the Mississippi, had only a dozen university graduates among its 25 million people. Several countries, such as Guinea-Bissau and Cape Verde, had not one African doctor, lawyer or accountant. No country, except perhaps Nigeria, had a middle class that had risen on its own merit.

But Africa's preparedness for independence was no longer the question by the mid-1950s. The moral climate in the world had changed. The colonies had become expensive to run and only Portugal was willing to risk a land war to keep its empire intact. France and Britain preferred simply to pack their bags and hope that the new states would remain within the structures of international capitalism, that they would respect their inherited Western-style political systems, that they would settle easily into the rhythm of responsible national behavior. In 1957 Britain's Gold Coast became the Republic of Ghana, black Africa's first ex-colony.* The next year France's Guinea became the second. In 1960 seventeen new countries with a population of 198 million were born.

Freedom Year, as 1960 was known, began with a prophetic speech by Britain's prime minister, Harold Macmillan. Addressing both houses of South Africa's white-only parliament in Cape Town, he said: ". . . The most striking of all the impressions I have formed since I left London a month ago is of the strength of this African national consciousness. In different places it takes different forms, but it is happening everywhere. The wind of change is blowing

---

* The Sudan, administered by Britain and Egypt, became independent in 1956. Its population is largely Arab, and although I have included it in sub-Sahara Africa, many people lump it with the Saharan countries. But black Africa's independence era is generally referred to as having started with Ghana in 1957.

through this continent, and, whether we like it or not, this growth of national consciousness is a political fact. We must all accept it as a fact, and our national policies must take account of it."

What if that speech had been given a hundred years earlier and Europe had decided not to colonize Africa? What condition would Africa be in today? First, remembering that the ancient Mali Empire stretched over what is now nine countries, it is reasonable to assume that Africa would have formed viable regional entities—just as the principalities of Germany and the city-states of Italy did in the 1800s. The strong would have risen to impose their language, culture and rule on the weak. This would have reduced tribalism— though not without bloodshed—and Africa in time would have been led by legitimate presidents or monarchs. A sense of nationalism would have followed.

Second, even without colonialism, Africa would have been no more isolated from Western influence than is, say, Asia. The Dutch would still have settled South Africa and instituted their policies of white supremacy. The missionaries would have come and, later, so would businessmen from London, New York and Tokyo seeking markets and resources. Africans would still have gone off to Europe and the United States to be educated, and returned home to understand their continent's problems. Certainly they would have been as capable of building schools and hospitals as the colonialists. Africa would not have inherited the European political systems and thus would probably have outgrown its age of instability long ago. A member of the Third World it might still be, but if Africa had had the opportunity to develop naturally at its own pace, it seems unlikely that there would ever have been such a place as Djibouti.

The colonialists left behind some schools and roads, some post offices and bureaucrats. But their cruelest legacy on the African continent was a lingering inferiority complex, a confused sense of identity. After all, when people are told for a century that they're not as clever or capable as their masters, they eventually start to believe it.

No group nurtured this confusion and uncertainty more than the white missionaries. They came to Africa as the soldiers of the holy Gospel, bringing Christianity and culture to a pagan people, and the revolutionary doctrine they preached ultimately changed the character of the entire continent. The message of these missionaries who arrived by the handful in the mid-1800s and by the thousands a few decades later was that the European and his ways were superior to anything the empty heritage of Africa had to offer. Civilization, they contended, was possible only through assimilation.

"It is dangerous," the Italian novelist Alberto Moravia said in 1972, writing about Africa, "to destroy a religion at a single blow, rather than allow it to die from old age and unreality, especially a primitive religion, which is at the same time both a faith and a culture.

"I believe, in fact, that there is no greater suffering for man than to feel his cultural foundations giving way beneath his feet."

For better or worse, though, the missionaries did not fail in their assigned task: they planted the seeds of Christianity deep. And today, despite great obstacles erected by repressive presidents and Marxist governments, the Christian church is probably the most powerful institution in sub-Sahara Africa, an institution that is influenced by the West but is, at its core, indigenous.

Almost every president in Africa is the product of a missionary education, and many remain closely associated with the church. President Hasting Banda of Malawi is a minister, as was the late Liberian president William Tolbert. President Kenneth Kaunda of Zambia is a lay preacher. The former prime minister of Rhodesia, Abel Muzorewa, is a United Methodist bishop. The socialist president of Tanzania, Julius Nyerere, and the Marxist-oriented president of Madagascar, Dikler Ratsiraka, are devout Catholics, and Jomo Kenyatta, the late Kenyan president, as a boy gave up herding his father's flocks in favor of life at a nearby Church of Scotland mission.

"You have to understand," Canon Burgess Carr, the former head of the All-Africa Conference of Churches, said, "that for the generation of men now in power, my generation, the churches provided the only opportunity available. When I was growing up in Liberia, none of us could think of being engineers or chemists. The only path was the church."

The Portuguese and Spanish brought the first seeds of Christianity to Africa in the fifteenth century. But they did not survive in the face of disease, warfare and primitive conditions. Four hundred years later came the Germans and the British. The European missionaries were instrumental in getting slavery abolished; but by preaching assimilation they also helped create the climate for colonialism and the undermining of African cultures. They were the harbingers of the white man's economic and social domination of a black continent, and as they pushed inland, they brought to the African interior, often for the first time, forces and values that emanated from another continent.

"I beg to direct your attention to Africa," David Livingstone, missionary and explorer, said at Cambridge, England, in 1857. "I know that in a few years I shall be cut off in that country [sic]; Do not let it be shut again. I go back to Africa to make an open path for commerce and Christianity."

Under their religious banners, the missionaries provided schools, churches and hospitals and eventually translated the Bible into four hundred African languages. They denounced what they considered the evils of African traditions such as polygamy and female circumcision and were authoritarian and paternal in their approach to Africans. One African convert recalls an Anglican missionary in Uganda known as Bwana Botri who frequently descended from his pulpit during service to cane African latecomers.

"The Negro is a child," Dr. Albert Schweitzer wrote in 1921 after his first years of work in Africa, "and with children nothing can be done without the use of authority . . . With regard to Negroes, then, I have coined the formula: I am your brother, it is true, but your elder brother."

Schweitzer (1876–1965), a French Protestant clergyman and physician who won the 1952 Nobel Peace Prize, used to pay his African workers in bananas, seven bananas a day per man. John Gunther once asked him if the Africans would work better if they received eight bananas. "No," Schweitzer replied, "that would disturb discipline and morale." The bush hospital Schweitzer built from scratch—practically with his bare hands—after arriving in Africa in 1913 operates to this day in Lambarene, Gabon. It is a modern facility with two air-conditioned operating rooms, staffed by both Europeans and Africans. Schweitzer is buried in a grassy patch out back.

Although spending most of his adult life in Africa, Schweitzer never learned to speak an African language. Today the young white missionary coming to Africa certainly speaks a local language, and he is more likely to be a specialist (perhaps a linguist or a doctor) than an evangelist. He needs a work permit in most countries, just as other expatriates do, and he seldom devotes his entire career to Africa as did his predecessors. His life may be Spartan and occasionally dangerous—thirty missionaries were killed in the 1970s during the Rhodesian civil war—but the missionaries still come in great numbers, apparently motivated by the same pioneering flame that has burned for more than a century. In Zaire alone, there are more than 5,000 white missionaries, in Kenya 3,000, and in many countries the demand for missionaries is higher than the churches can meet.

Unlike the West, where the congregations of many churches have been dwindling for years, Christianity in Africa is growing so fast that by the year 2000 the continent may have the greatest concentration of Christians in the world. Their current strength is nearly 200 million or forty-four percent of the population. Another 100 million Africans are Moslems; the remainder follow animist or traditional beliefs.*

David Barrett, a Nairobi-based Anglican researcher completing a multivolume study on world religions, estimates that each year about 6 million Africans—or more than 16,000 a day—are added to the Christian rolls. About two fifths, he says, are converts; the rest are the result of population increase. (Islam grows in Africa by about 3.6 million members a year, virtually all because of population increases.)

That Christianity should be undergoing such a numerical expansion in Africa is something of a miracle in itself, for in few places in the modern world have the church and its leaders been subjected to such humiliation and perils. But although many African presidents have managed to cripple the spirit and dreams of their own people, none has ever succeeded in breaking the church.

In Uganda, Kabaka Mwanga, a Moslem king of the 1880s, murdered scores of young Christian converts and an Anglican missionary, Bishop James Hannington, for what he saw as an attempt to establish Christian hegemony. Under Idi Amin, also a Moslem, the Christian majority did not fare much better. Amin kept lists of all clergy, ordered the murder of the Anglican archbishop and often had Ugandans tortured for the simple reason that they had attended church.

"You would leave your home in the morning on God's work and

---

* The largest denomination is Catholicism, which has upwards of 75 million followers and twelve cardinals in Africa. (Ten of the cardinals are African, two are European.) The Protestant Church has an estimated 50 million members. The majority of Ethiopia's 31 million people are members of the Coptic church. In many areas the Africans' denomination depends solely on which missionaries got there first. In northwest Kenya, for example, almost everyone is a Quaker.

not know if you would come home that night," Silvanus Wani, the successor of the slain Ugandan archbishop, told me. "Each morning was one of thanksgiving. The next day you went out in faith again."

In Ethiopia, Emperor Haile Selassie forced clergymen to recite his name as part of mass. In Guinea, Archbishop Raymond Marie Tchidmbo was arrested in the 1970s on trumped-up charges of being implicated in a coup, and despite the pleas of two popes, kept in jail for nine years. Sixty-five missionaries in Burundi were given two days' notice to leave the country in 1979 for "preaching tribalism," and most missionaries have been expelled from the Marxist states of Ethiopia, Mozambique, Angola and Benin. Jehovah's Witnesses have been persecuted in Kenya and jailed by the thousands in Malawi.

The president of Equatorial Guinea, Macias Nguema Biyogo, a Catholic-turned-atheist, decreed in the late 1970s that mass must end with the congregation chanting, "Forward with Macias, always with Macias, never without Macias." He later closed all the churches in his country. When he was overthrown by the military and executed in 1979, the soldiers' first order of business was to reopen the churches.

Church services were segregated in colonial days and names such as "Native Anglican Church" were common. But most Africans do not view Christianity as a white, imported religion. Jesus is depicted as a white man on some church murals, as a black on others. The interpretation is the artist's to make. Nevertheless, the Catholic and Protestant churches have remained largely traditional, failing to "Africanize" either their hymns or sermons, and in the past two decades there has been a move away from the Western orientation toward breakaway Christian sects of a purely indigenous nature. By 1982 the number of separate denominations operating in Africa had passed six thousand.

Some of the new sects have fewer than a hundred members. Their church may be under a mango tree or in the corner of a city parking lot, and every Sunday, cities such as Nairobi come alive with groups of singing, chanting worshipers, swaying to the beat of drums, often dressed in white robes with caps bearing the insignia of their sects. Western Christians would find little familiar in the service, the hymns or the prayer books.

Despite the growing number of converts throughout Africa, there is reason to question whether their commitment is really as deep as the numbers suggest. The church, I think, is primarily expanding because it represents a modern rather than primitive force, exerted at the very time Africa is preoccupied with the future. After all, Jean-Bédel Bokassa, the former president/emperor of the Central African Republic/Empire used to swing between Christianity and Islam, depending on his current source of foreign aid. For the average African, Christianity legitimizes a belief in miracles and a respect for mystery, and that alone is sufficient to attract a following of millions.

However valuable the church has been in assisting Africa's five million refugees, in helping during times of drought, famine and sickness, it traditionally has acted as a tool of the white establishment. The church did not play an active role in supporting the Africans' struggle for independence, largely because white clergy in Africa were racist in attitude and approach. White missionaries did not speak in protest when barbaric governments killed hundreds of thousands of innocent Africans in places such as Uganda, Burundi, Rwanda, the Central African Empire, because, they reasoned, Africans have always killed Africans. "I'd hate to think what they would have done to each other if it hadn't been for Christianity," an American missionary in Burundi told me. The church also has failed to follow its own doctrine in South Africa, where many of the Ten Commandments are ignored as part of national policy.

But not long ago, a large congregation gathered in Germiston, South Africa, for the funeral of Christian Smith, a white who had been assistant manager of a plastics factory. The mourners included blacks, coloreds (people of mixed blood) and Indians, some of whom had worked with Smith for as long as fifteen years. The minister, Rev. J. J. du Toit, mounted the pulpit and looked out over the congregation in his normally white-only church. His eyes narrowed and his words came slowly: there would be no service until the blacks left the church.

Robina Smith, the widow, stood and led the entire congregation, black and white, out of the church, leaving the minister alone in the pulpit. An undertaker conducted an informal gravesite service. "And just to think that we have the nerve to call ourselves Christians," Mrs. Smith said.

The incident occurred in a church belonging to Nederduitsch Harvormde Kerk, the most conservative of South Africa's three Dutch Reformed churches. The three have a white membership of about 1.8 million, or 40 percent of the country's white Christians. At a 1974 synod, the church dropped its openly racist theology and now nominally supports racial equality. But it holds that apartheid is morally acceptable, saying that "the New Testament does not regard the diversity of peoples, as such, as something sinful." Remarkably enough, the Dutch Reformed churches in South Africa have almost a million black members, who, not allowed to sit with white congregations, have formed their own separate churches.

There is a little island called Goree off the Senegalese coast in West Africa, and here one finds more scars of the colonial heritage. Goree's streets are sandy and narrow. They wind past rows of tidy houses, their blue shutters drawn tight against the sun's afternoon assault, and meander up a hill where rusting cannon point out to sea. Near the cannon, at the foot of Saint Germain Street, stands a rambling weather-beaten structure built by the Dutch two hundred years ago. Its empty basement cells are filled with silence. The ocean beats against their stone foundations and from their windows you can gaze out across the Atlantic toward the New World, so far away.

For millions of West Africans—the ancestors of what would become the United States' largest minority class—this is where freedom ended and serfdom began. It was here, in the dark, dank slave house, that Arab traders bartered and bickered with European shippers, here that the Africans spent the last weeks in their homeland, chained to a wall in underground cubicles, awaiting a buyer, a boat and, at the end of a long, harrowing voyage, a master.

In the weighing room below the trading office, the men's muscles were examined, the women's breasts measured, the children's teeth checked. Those were the qualities—muscles, breasts, teeth—on which human worth was judged. The slaves were fattened like livestock up to what was considered an ideal shipping weight, 140 pounds, and those who remained sickly or fell victim to pneumonia or tuberculosis were segregated from the rest by an Arab doctor, led into a corridor whose open door overlooked the ocean and tossed out for the sharks. The selection process was similar to the one the Nazis would use two centuries later in World War II death camps.

I took the thirty-minute ferry ride one day from Dakar, the modern capital of Senegal, with a group of black American tourists. Goree, named for an island in the Netherlands and once a French naval base, is a quiet, peaceful place with only 500 inhabitants and no cars or crime. In the streets, African children tugged at our sleeves, saying, "You need guide? I take you. I show you where you become slave."

The slave house was turned into a museum some years ago and the Senegalese curator, Joseph Ndiaye, greeted us by the open door. The tides below smashed against the same rocks on which the visitors' forefathers had trod onto vessels with names such as the *Five Brothers*, the *Diane* and the *Regina Cook* for the trip with no return. One of every seven Africans who took that journey died at sea, a victim of disease or maritime disaster.

Unlike Goree, most of Africa's slavery monuments have been allowed to fall into disrepair and slip quietly into an unobserved past. The stone blocks in Zanzibar on which slaves were auctioned are now occupied by vegetable sellers. The forts used to protect trading routes along Ghana's Gold Coast are crumbling. All that remains in Lagos, Nigeria, are a few chains and spikes pounded into buildings on Breadfruit Street. In Freetown, Sierra Leone, the immense cottonwood tree around which former slaves rallied to proclaim their freedom still stands in the main square, but no one attaches much historical significance to it anymore. African children, in fact, are given only a cursory glimpse of slavery in their history classes. It is a chapter of the past most Africans would rather forget.

The black American visitors were as respectfully silent as worshipers in a cathedral while Ndiaye led us through the slave house, talking about three centuries of trade in human cargo, dangling handcuffs and tools of torture in front of us like a courtroom prosecutor. For slaves who tried to escape there were anklets with a spike that was driven through the foot. For the verbally defiant there were oval rings through which the lips were pulled and sealed by a spike. The Yoruba tribe of Nigeria called the device an *itenu*, meaning "shut your mouth."

"I'll tell you," said Geraldine Fair of New York City, "it'll take a long time for this to sink in, before I know what I really feel inside. It's a lot different, a lot more real than the half-assed way they teach it in the history books at home. Most of all, I think, seeing Goree, seeing West Africa, helps me establish my own identity, just knowing way down deep that I did have a homeland."

Although no precise figures are available, the number of slaves transported from West Africa to the Americas from the sixteenth to the nineteenth century is believed to have ranged between 10 million and 15 million. The trade reached its peak in the 1790s, when about 70,000 slaves were landed annually in the Americas. In East Africa, where slavery continued from 1770 to 1896, between 1.2 million and 3 million slaves were exported, mainly to the Middle East. (Some historians place the total number of slaves taken from Africa at 50 million.)

Slavery as an institution came rather late to the United States. The first shipload of slaves did not arrive in Virginia until 1619, and as late as 1681 there were only 2,000 black slaves in the colony, compared to 6,000 European indentured servants. But slaving soon boomed as the United States sought cheap labor for its tobacco, sugar and cotton plantations, and in 1860, on the eve of the Civil War, the U.S. census showed 4.4 million blacks among a total population of 36 million people. Thus the percentage of blacks in the U.S. population was precisely the same in 1860 as it was in 1970, 8.1 percent. (The percentage was 11.7 in 1980.)*

The Africans themselves—as well as the Arabs—were no less guilty than the whites in making sure that places such as Goree remained well stocked with merchandise. For the most part the Arab traders did not venture far into the interior to capture slaves. That service was provided by African kings and chieftains who, unable to adjust to the new economic temptations of a changing world, subjugated and sold their people for the luxuries and essentials they had only recently been introduced to: cloth, metals, beads, spirits, tobacco, firearms. The slave trade made kings rich in the interior, and along the coast created a new class of African merchants.

African wars in those days were fought for power and wealth. Land had little economic importance, and although territorial control and natural resources were of some value, the prime measure of one's strength was manpower. As a result, wars were waged as much to increase the size of a chieftain's human flock as to gain new land or settle old scores. Many of the Africans sold into bondage were prisoners of war. Others were criminals, debtors and those who simply had been outcast for various reasons from the extended family system. Some were the unfortunates who had strayed unknowingly across tribal boundaries and were captured. But it was the African himself who made slavery possible: he seized and traded his people

* For census purposes, a slave counted as two thirds of a white American in 1860.

to the Arabs, who in turn sold them to the Europeans. Everyone shared the burden of shame.

The Europeans argued that the acquisition of slaves was a natural consequence of Africa's warfare. It was better, they said, to ship the African off to a Christian master in the civilized world than to leave him at the mercy of kings in a primitive, pagan society where he perhaps would be killed as a human sacrifice. The Christian church never condoned the morality of selling human beings—there were scattered antislavery protests in Europe as early as the 1700s—but the pillage of a continent's human resources generally was not a topic of sustained debate.

Interestingly enough, the steps to abolish slavery were taken outside Africa, not in it. Denmark barred its citizens from slave trading in 1803, Britain followed in 1807, the United States in 1808 and France in 1818. Despite the ban, U.S. citizens continued to buy slaves, and slaving still flourished in many areas of the world because African and European merchants were unwilling to sever this lucrative economic link. Britain meanwhile had set out to enforce its abolishment decree, establishing a twenty-ship antislavery fleet that patrolled the West African coast and stopped vessels suspected of carrying slaves. Between 1825 and 1865, Britain detained 1,287 slave ships and liberated 130,000 slaves. But during that period, ships carrying 1.4 million slaves still managed to slip through the British patrols and land their cargoes in the Americas.

The decisive factor ending the trade was the U.S. Civil War and the resultant emancipation of slaves. That left only Cuba and Brazil as legal slave importers and the risk of transporting to just two markets became too great for the shippers. One sad era in Africa's history had ended. Soon another one, a subtler form of bondage known as colonialism, would begin.

I know of no studies that adequately describe what long-range effects slavery had on Africa, a continent where up to 50 million people, mostly males between the ages of fifteen and thirty-five, were forced to migrate to other worlds. The migration had influenced events economically, politically and socially in the United States to this day. In Africa, one could argue that the economic impact of depopulation was relatively minor. The economy was a subsistence one, there was ample land and the young women left behind continued to produce large families. Africa, though, had been robbed of its masculine strength. Families were torn apart, tribes saw their warriors disappear, the white man became the symbol of a superior force that was evil enough to be feared and powerful enough to be respected. Psychologically the effect was devastating.

Europe later met great resistance confronting the Moslems in northern Africa. France needed 30,000 troops before Tunisia yielded to colonialism. Britain fought pitched battles with the Egyptians and spent a dozen years fighting in the deserts of the Sudan. But black Africa lost its first confrontation with the white man in the most humiliating way. It surrendered without a struggle, with hardly a bow raised in protest. It had been as passive as the Indians were fierce in defending their rights and land in the United States. The first seeds of the uncertainty and inferiority Africa still feels in its dealings with the outside world had been planted. If Africa had had the means to resist the slave traders, then the era of colonialism might never have spread to its shores. As it was, the course of African history had been changed unalterably.

"Sometimes I sit down and try to think what my life, my family's life, would be like if I'd been born two hundred years ago," a civil servant in the Gambia, Abdulla Secka, told me one day as we traveled by boat up the Gambia River to the village of Juffure, where author Alex Haley found his "roots" and later wrote a book that sold more than 20 million copies and was translated into thirty-two languages.

"I really can't imagine it. Maybe somebody would be trying to sell me or my children. Or maybe I'd be trying to sell someone for some rum or beads. It's all too distant, too impossible, to imagine. It's just not something we talk about or think about anymore. God has been kind. He has let us forget the past."

Africans can no more forget the past than can the 25 million Americans for whom Africa is the distant motherland, beckoning her children home with promises of black dignity, cultural affinity, a sense of belonging. Tens of thousands of these Americans answered that call during the past decade as the reorientation of black Americans gained momentum, signaling a shift from self-criticism and even self-hatred to fascination and pride in black origins. The return to Africa brings joy to some Americans, disillusionment to others. But for almost all, whether expatriate or tourist, there are two overriding impressions: first, the blackness of one's skin does not guarantee immediate acceptance; second, Africa may be the homeland, but the United States is home.

"I think we're perceived as Americans first, blacks second," said David French, a Boston doctor who ran a twenty-county health program in West Africa for the World Health Organization. "When I first visited Africa eight or nine years ago, I had the feeling there was some disdain on the part of Africans toward black Americans. We were suspect because we ended up in the United States in the first place, and because we put up with all we did for three hundred years.

"Now I get the impression that Africans are asking themselves, 'Where are the most educated, prosperous, technically trained blacks in the world?' Well, they're in the United States. And the Africans are saying, 'If you've got something to offer, come on over and join us.' "

In the 1960s a group of Black Panthers from the United States went to Kenya, hoping to learn the tactics of revolution. It was in Kenya, after all, that the Mau Mau guerrillas fought black Africa's first war of liberation and the Panthers expected to find many sympathetic brothers there. Not so. They were ignored by the government, harassed by the police, laughed at by the university students and never even saw an Afro haircut. The Panthers' intended revolution was a luxury of the middle class in a free society. But in Kenya they were outsiders in an impoverished land of passive people and conservative government. They found no audience at all and within a week were on their way back to the United States.

In Ethiopia, black U.S. Peace Corps volunteers always had a difficult time finding acceptance; they were looked down on, as are most Africans, by the European-featured Ethiopians. And in many capitals, African government officials are distinctly displeased when Washington assigns an abundance of black diplomats to its forty-two embassies on the continent. At one point in the late 1970s when the ambassador, aide director and Peace Corps director at the U.S. embassy in Kenya were all black, a ranking Kenyan official remarked at a cocktail party, "Why doesn't Washington send us its *top* diplomats, instead of sticking us with all its blacks?" The assumption was both unfair and incorrect; the black American diplomats I met in Africa were on the whole no better or worse than the white diplomats. But most Africans are still imprisoned by a colonial mentality, believing that a European—as all whites are called in East Africa—is somehow more capable than a black. This attitude is not surprising when you consider that most whites an African encounters are in positions of authority, or at least are involved with missions that can bring change to Africa: they are doctors, businessmen, diplomats dispensing advice and money, missionaries, relief agency workers, journalists, highly trained technicians and professionals with skills in communications, construction, aviation, agriculture and finance.

The African experience for American blacks is a more poignant and moving one than a white American would experience traveling for the first time to, say, England. But blacks are not immune to the lethargy, frustrations, inefficiency and ignorance in Africa, and no small number merely throw up their hands in disillusionment. "Thank God my granddaddy got aboard that ship," said a member of Muhammad Ali's entourage during the 1974 Ali-Foreman fight in Zaire. And on a continent where individual liberty is the privilege of a chosen few, there is also the realization that the American black has more dignity, freedom and security at home than most Africans have ever known in their own lands.

"I'll tell you what I tell blacks who write me, asking if they should come to Africa," said Clifford Sharp, a Detroit mechanic who moved to Guinea in West Africa in 1968. "I tell them: If you want to come to Africa for fun, don't come. If you have a superior attitude, don't come. If you expect to have no problems here, don't come. But if you want to aid the development of the black race, if you care, then come. But you must have pioneer spirit and missionary zeal, because you're certainly going to have some problems getting by day to day."

Sharp was sixty-six years old when I met him in Conakry, as depressing, dilapidated and filthy a capital as you'll find anywhere in Africa. He had maintained his U.S. passport and voted Democratic on an absentee ballot in each U.S. presidential election, but he considered himself a "returned African," not an American. He and his wife, Laverna, lived simply on his monthly $404 Social Security check, which he supplemented by tending to President Sékou Touré's fleet of cars. Touré had run one of the most repressive regimes in Africa for more than twenty years, but the Sharps had remained apolitical, not meddling at all in local affairs, and they spoke with great pride of being black people in a country run by a black president.

Back in the early sixties, when Sharp had decided "I just wanted to be with my own kind," he and Laverna, a teacher, had started saving their money for a "return" to Africa. They wrote to four countries asking about the possibility of immigrating. Nigeria never bothered to reply; Ghana responded that the Sharps had flunked the examination for entry, although they had never taken any test; Liberia said it did not need mechanics or teachers; and President Touré had written back personally, saying; "Come. We welcome any brother who wants to help us develop our country."

"I'd never even seen a black president before we arrived," Sharp said. "I found it hard to believe there really was such a thing. But just after we got to Conakry, we were ushered into President Touré's chambers. They were beautiful chambers, and he rose to receive my wife and me. A president of a republic rose to receive us!

"He extended his hand and said 'Bon jour'—we had a translator with us who said that meant 'good day'—and when we left after about ten minutes, President Touré rose again and led us to the door and opened it for us. Can you imagine how proud we felt as black people."

Sharp said he had no interest in politics or revolution and he had nothing more than a nodding acquaintance with another American living in Conakry, black activist Stokely Carmichael, who moved to Guinea in 1968. Was there anything Sharp missed in the United States? Sharp thought for a moment as he climbed into his battered 1971 Peugeot. "Chicken," he finally said. "A good succulent chicken, not the scrawny little ones we got here. How much does a good succulent fried chicken cost in America now?"

By late March the monsoon winds along the Kenyan coast have started to die, leaving the air breathless and heavy with humidity, and on the piers of the Old Port in Mombasa bare-chested stevedores sweat and strain, their backs piled high with cases of dried fish. They struggle up the slippery gangplanks and onto the decks while the captains of the great wooden dhows look anxiously out to sea, hoping to detect even the softest breeze that would carry them home to India on their last journey of the season.

The dhows have plied the waters of the northern Indian Ocean for two thousand years, connecting Africa with Asia and the Persian Gulf states as trading partners. In the early years the dhows brought glass bottles and iron tools to Africa and returned to Arabia with slaves, ivory, animal skins and timber. The single-masted, lateen-rigged ships would slip by Fort Jesus, the fourteenth-century Portuguese bastion that guards the entrance to Mombasa's port, with drums beating and flags flying. The crews would throw up their hands in thanksgiving and shout their greetings to friends who had arrived earlier on other vessels. The port would be so packed with dhows that you could hardly see the water.

As recently as 1945, more than four hundred dhows used to call every year at Mombasa and Zanzibar. But trade routes and markets changed, transportation moved into the age of jetliners and supertankers, and today the long-distance dhows, like the monsoon winds in March, are dying. No more than a dozen now make the treacherous five-week journey from Kuwait or Bombay to Mombasa in any given year, and they glide quietly into the empty port with no pounding music or cheering crews. Their time is past, though their role in history is not. For the dhows remain a symbol of another foreign people who affected the character of Africa—the Asians. (The term "Asian" in Africa refers to all brown-skinned people, usually Indians, Pakistanis and Goans.)

For more than a century the Asians in Africa have lived in a twilight zone: half citizen, half refugee, not quite belonging anywhere. They came as traders and sailors and indentured servants, and although the Europeans treated them with contempt and the Africans with suspicion and disdain, they did not succumb to the discrimination and hostility of their new world. Instead they did what the African had been unable to do. They scaled or sidestepped the barriers and emerged as Africa's first nonwhite entrepreneurial class of money brokers and professionals.

The Indians arrived in their dhows in the 1700s, setting up trading posts along the coast, and before long they were the dominant commercial presence in Mombasa and Zanzibar. Many trafficked in slaves. Others pushed into the interior on foot and in ox carts. They established small shops—an important factor in the development of East Africa—that catered to the African and later to the white settler. In many cases the Indian merchant was the first permanent commercial or foreign contact the African villager had with the outside world. The Asian considered the African slothful and did not hesitate to exploit his ignorance for personal profit.

When slavery was abolished and Africans refused to continue to work on the plantations, even for wages, thousands of Indians were brought in as indentured workers. Nearly 32,000 were imported in 1896 to build the railroad from Mombasa to Uganda that opened up East Africa for the European settler. Others went to Mozambique to build a rail line from Beira to Southern Rhodesia. Disease, insects, heat and wild animals killed thousands of them.

After the two world wars, new waves of immigration, encouraged by the British, brought thousands more Asians to East Africa. They were dubbed "passenger" Indians, and they came for the same reasons that their forefathers had stayed—a better standard of living. Colonial governors argued that their segregation in residential and commercial zones was essential for sanitary reasons until they learned the "European way of life."

The Asians were industrious and economically aggressive and they soon controlled a large part of the East African economy.* They became the merchants, the artisans, the financiers and they garnered large fortunes. To the African, the Asian was an exploiter; to the Asian, the African was culturally inferior and lazy.

"I could start out from scratch tomorrow and I'd be rich again in three years," an Asian jeweler in Somalia said. "The competition of the Africans is negligible. They don't know how to work like we do. Even if I had to work twelve or fourteen hours a day, Saturdays and Sundays, I wouldn't mind."

In the 1950s, Indian Prime Minister Jawaharlal Nehru urged the Asians in Africa to give their active support to the black nationalist movements that were sweeping the continent. Few did. They had every reason to hate colonialism, but they had learned how to prosper within the system and they feared that independence would threaten the limited privileges they had won.

The Asians' hesitancy to accept local citizenship after independence—the same wait-and-see attitude that many white settlers had—seemed to confirm what the Africans believed, that the Asians were unwilling to throw in their lot with the national inspirations of newly emerging black countries.

By the early 1970s, with governments trying to "Africanize" their economies and job markets, the Asians were under pressure almost everywhere. To many black Africans their presence became known simply as "the Asian problem." In 1971 Uganda ordered a special census of Asians. They were lined up at counting centers throughout the country and made to sign documents with an inked thumbprint. The ink signing was deliberately intended to humiliate them

---

* The Lebanese, numbering more than 200,000 in Africa, control the economies of several West African countries as tightly as Asians control those in East Africa.

because most, unlike their African census takers, were quite capable of writing their names.

Ten months later President Idi Amin began an address to his nation with the words: "My government believes that one of its primary duties is to ensure the welfare of all members of the community." He went on to say that all Asians had ninety days to leave Uganda, so that control of the economy could be given to "indigenous people." Seventy thousand people, one third of them Ugandan citizens, were suddenly homeless.

President Nyerere of Tanzania drew parallels between the expulsion of the Asians and Hitler's treatment of the Jews. President Kenneth Kaunda of Zambia said the action was "terrible, horrible and abominable." But they were in the minority. Most black Africans enjoyed the spectacle of watching disenfranchised Asians searching for refuge in other African countries and in India, Canada, Britain and the United States. The Asians, many felt, were only getting what they deserved.

Malawi in the 1970s canceled Asians' licenses to grow tobacco. Tanzania nationalized their businesses and their sisal plantations. South Africa officially bestowed second-class citizenship on its 1 million Asians. Kenya confiscated thousands of shops owned by Asians who had not taken Kenyan citizenship and forbade them from doing business in the rural areas. Kenya's assistant minister for home affairs, Martin Shikuku, echoed the popular sentiment when he said in the early 1970s: "The Asians should go home."

What seemed clear in those days was that the Asian had no future in Africa. He was an alien in a land he had helped build with sweat and ingenuity, and he lived with his bags packed, his money banked abroad, his destiny squarely in the hands of the new black authorities. He was a conspicuous, vulnerable minority that numbered nearly 1.5 million.

The last few years have seen a significant mellowing in the African's hostile attitude toward the Asians. Though he is still discriminated against, far more than whites or any other minority in black Africa, the Asian today seems to have earned a permanent and fairly secure role in the future of the continent. His presence has quietly ceased to be an issue. There are two likely reasons: the indigenous African feels less threatened today than he did a decade ago; and national economies have suffered greatly—and in Uganda's case, collapsed—when Asian participation was eliminated.

"I'm convinced there couldn't be another repeat of what happened in Uganda, although I wouldn't have told you that a couple of years ago," an Asian friend, Abdul Hamid, told me over lunch one day in Nairobi's Red Bull restaurant, where the hundred or so predominantly male customers were about evenly divided between Africans, Asians and Europeans. Hamid, who was forty and ran one of the biggest printing companies in East Africa, was a Sunni Moslem, one of the 200,000 members of Kenya's Asian community, the largest and most economically and politically influential in black Africa.

"I mean, my kids' generation can't identify with India anymore. They don't even care about learning the language. All our ties are to Kenya, not India. My family's been here over a hundred years. The Asian is a tribe of Africa now."

Hamid was raised in Mombasa in a house with sixty relatives. The men, women and children ate in shifts. His marriage was arranged. His grandfather was an uneducated dhow repairman. But like almost all Asians in Africa, Hamid escaped the mire of poverty, insufficient education and tradition that his ancestors had known. Economically and socially, he outdistanced his African counterpart.

"When I moved to Nairobi from Mombasa eight years ago," Hamid said, "I came with nothing. Absolutely nothing. I lived on bananas and a pint of milk a day for two years, putting every shilling into my business. An African wouldn't do that. But I wasn't afraid to work and I wanted to make money for my children. I will admit the Asians collect money almost as a hobby. We are the Jews of Africa and that's why the Africans resent us."

In the colonial era when Hamid grew up, the Asian in East Africa was the man in the middle, caught between white and black, with neither the privileges of the former nor the burdens of the latter. He lived in special Asian residential zones and was not allowed to send his children to European or African schools. In the mid-1950s the British administration in Kenya spent an average of $180 a year for the education of each white child, $65 for each Asian and $5 for each African. In the Ugandan public service, according to government records, the Asian earned six times more than the African and a third less than the European.

"People forget what this place was like twenty-five or thirty years ago," said John Karmali, an Asian who is chairman of the Nairobi Rotary Club and a graduate of the University of London. "When I came back to Nairobi from London in 1946 with an English wife, it was one of the first mixed marriages Kenya had ever seen. There were only a few places where I could buy land, and no hotel in Nairobi or up-country would serve you a meal or a drink. If you went out for a drive with your children, you couldn't stop anywhere for a cup of tea. Apartheid was very strong, much like South Africa's."

Karmali was one of the original agitators for Asian rights. In 1950 he and his wife, Joan, founded the first multiracial school in Kenya, and in 1958 he became the first Asian member of the all-white Rotary Club. He had been blackballed twice previously, and his acceptance prompted two white members to resign on the spot. In 1980, when he was elected chairman, there wasn't even a ripple of protest.

"I wouldn't deny that substantial discrimination still exists against the Asian," Karmali said, "but I honestly think the tensions that we used to know between European, African and Asian have pretty much disappeared. As far as the discrimination goes, there are a number of reasons. One, the element of jealousy—the Asian community as a whole is rich. Two, the Asians tend to keep to themselves and don't mix, something I fault us for. And three, the Asians and Africans are strangers to each other's way of life.

"The African is in the position of strength now and he is using that position to pay back some old scores. That's human enough. I can appreciate the fact that he was downtrodden for so long he finds some pleasure on trodding down a bit on someone else now. It's hardly unusual."

The discrimination he mentioned takes many forms, subtle and overt. At Jomo Kenyatta International Airport in Nairobi, African and European travelers are waved through customs and immigration formalities in a flash, but Asians are shaken down like petty criminals. Their suitcases are opened and each garment is unfolded and waved about. Their wallets are searched and their pockets frisked. The African customs official gloats as he carries out this ritual and the Asian stands patiently by his luggage, stoic and polite, doing exactly as he is told.

If an African and an Asian with similar credentials apply for a public service job or for entrance to a university, the African will be given preference, even though both are citizens of the country. The handful of Asian officers in the Kenyan army have little hope of being promoted beyond the rank of a major, and when a nineteen-year-old Asian student applied for architecture school at the University of Nairobi, she was told quite bluntly by the dean that she was the wrong color. Kenya wanted black architects, not brown ones.

"Sure it makes you bitter," said the girl, who is now a secretary, "but if you're an Asian in Africa, you don't rock the boat. If there are no waves, there's no controversy. We're pretty good at not rocking the boat, you know. We've had a hundred years here to practice."

But unlike the Africans, the Asian today shows no visible wounds from the colonial experience—or from the postcolonial discrimination. For the most part, he mastered the same system that defeated the African. When many of his shops were looted and burned by rioting mobs during Kenya's attempted coup in 1982, the Asian simply shrugged and started rebuilding.

"I suppose the reason we don't feel as bitter about the colonial period as the Africans do," an Asian jeweler in Kenya said, "goes back to one basic thing: we made a lot of money off the Europeans."

The political fortunes of independent African nations were not discernibly dependent upon which European country colonized them. The number of wars, coups d'état and military governments that former French Africa has experienced since independence are almost exactly the same as former British Africa has seen. Both colonial powers produced presidents who became distinguished statesmen and others who became savage madmen. Both produced nations that did well economically (Ivory Coast and Kenya), that failed economically (Guinea and Tanzania), that disintegrated into tribal mini-nations (Chad and Uganda), that enjoyed political stability (Senegal and the Malawi), that broke down in constant political turmoil (Benin and Ghana). It is, I think, fair to conclude that colonialism did nothing for Africa that Africa could not have done for itself.

What is apparent, though, is that the legacy of French colonialism is much stronger in Africa today than that of Britain. France, in fact, retains an extraordinary influence in its former colonies and in many cases remains the paramount economic and cultural force dominating their affairs.

In the West African country of Senegal, former President Léopold Sédar Senghor makes no bones about his love for what, one suspects, he still considers the motherland, and that love for France has withstood the pressures of nationalism and the vicissitudes of independence. Across from his palace is a towering statue honoring one of the previous French colonial rulers of Senegal. And Senghor himself, who was educated in Paris and spends his holidays in France, is one of the world's leading authorities on French grammar. He is an eminent poet, a former minister in the French government, and an unabashed admirer of anything bearing a French label.*

Such an affinity would be inconceivable in a former British, Belgian or Portuguese colony. But France's method of colonial administration was designed to pay long-range dividends, and today ties between Paris and France's old colonies are so strong that when an African says he is going home, he is as apt to mean France as he is Senegal or the Ivory Coast.

Unlike other colonial powers, France governed through a policy of assimilation or, as some have called it, cultural imperialism. Its rule was direct, authoritarian and centralized, with limited powers invested in appointed chiefs. More significantly, while Britain trained bureaucrats, France trained leaders. The British came to settle the land—one third of the English expatriates in Kenya were farmers—but the French came to administer. The British farmers spoke Swahili; the French administrators spoke French. The British dealt with traditional chiefs through a series of treaties; the French created a new elitist class whose members were educated in Paris, imbued with the culture of France and had all the rights of a Frenchman, including citizenship.

If France's emphasis in its colonies was cultural, Britain's was economic. In the course of exploiting those interests, Britain built—and later bequeathed to its colonies—a superior infrastructure: better roads, schools and communications, a more efficient civil service. Those, however, did not represent emotional ties, and the former British, Belgian and Portuguese colonies have gone out of their way to sever all visible links to their European past. One of the first things Zairians did after independence was to pull down the statue of King Leopold II in Kinshasa. In Nairobi, Livingstone Drive, named for the British explorer, long ago was renamed Gen. Mathenge Drive to honor a Mau Mau leader. But visit almost any

* On New Year's Eve 1980, after twenty years as chief of state, the seventy-four-year-old Senghor did something no African president had ever done: he stepped down voluntarily, handing over power to his prime minister, Abdou Diouf. Senghor's presidential term had been scheduled to expire in 1983. (Cameroon's founding president, Ahmadou Ahidjo, similarly retired in 1982 after twenty-two years in office.)

capital in the old French West Africa and you'll find statues honoring Frenchmen, and bridges, squares and streets named for Frenchmen. When Jean-Bédel Bokassa seized power in the Central African Republic in 1966, his first words were "*Vive la France!*" And when he attended Charles de Gaulle's funeral, he sobbed "Papa, Papa" and had to be helped from the grave site.

France, again unlike other European powers, has proved willing on several occasions to use military force to change or keep in power African governments—and has continued to provide its former colonies with touches of the good life—which, of course, benefit the expatriates far more than the Africans. In Bamako, the capital of dirt-poor Mali, you can buy French food, flown in twice-weekly from Paris, including ice cream at $24 a gallon. In the Ivory Coast, where 50,000 Frenchmen live and work, you can sit in a sidewalk café, eating a freshly baked croissant and reading that day's edition of *Le Monde*. In Ouagadougou, capital of one of Africa's poorest countries, Upper Volta, there is a store that sells nothing but fresh flowers from the fields of France. In the Central African Republic, France subsidizes half the annual $70 million budget, pays for the telephone system and covers 20 percent of all government salaries. In Gabon the government and the commercial sector are run, for all intents and purposes, by the 30,000 resident Frenchmen. There are more weekly airline departures from Niamey, Niger, to Paris than to anywhere in Africa. If you want to telephone another African country from the Congo, your call is routed through Paris. Throughout most of French-speaking Africa, the common currency is the African franc, backed by France.

In 1958, with the nationalistic movement gaining momentum in Africa, Charles de Gaulle gave France's colonies a choice: continued association with France and the financial support that went with it, or independence. Only Guinea chose immediate independence. "Guinea prefers poverty in freedom to riches in slavery," said the president-to-be, Sékou Touré, then a thirty-six-year-old trade-union leader. De Gaulle stormed back to Paris, canceling a dinner party in Guinea with Touré. With De Gaulle went Guinea's annual $17 million stipend. Said Senegal's Senghor: "Poor Sékou. Never again will he stroll up the Champs Elysées."

Given all he has had to endure from the beginning of slavery to the end of colonialism, the African displays a racial tolerance that is nothing short of amazing. He holds no apparent grudge against the

European as an individual, and it is rare indeed for any white person to experience even the slightest indignity because of his color. There are virtually no urban areas in Africa that are off-limits to whites as are, say, parts of Harlem in New York or Roxbury in Boston. There are no hostile stares, surly responses or epithets like "whitey" or "honky." In the Ivory Coast, the white population is five times greater than it was at independence in 1960. In Kenya, 5,000 former British citizens have taken out Kenyan citizenship. In Mozambique and Angola, white citizens of those countries hold high-ranking positions in government. The African has forgiven, if not forgotten. He fought and negotiated for his independence for no greater reason than to end the pain of prejudice. Having won, he proved himself far more magnanimous than his colonial masters had ever been. He may have harbored animosities toward the Asians, but if you were white, it was your personality, not your pigmentation, that counted.

Kenya provides an illuminating illustration of the changing relationship between black and white in Africa. For it was in Kenya during the 1953–1956 Mau Mau "emergency" that Africa first took its independence struggle to the battlefield. It was in Kenya that an old man named Jomo Kenyatta emerged from the colonial prisons to preach a message of racial harmony to those whites who would "turn and become Africans in your hearts." And it is in Kenya, particularly in the highlands north of Nairobi where the war was fought, that Africans, both black and white, have set down their guns, buried the past and now farm side by side. They have reached an accommodation with one another that is based on neither love nor hate. Rather, its foundation is the simple recognition that times have changed. But no matter how deep their roots in the land, the whites can never again be anything more than guests.

The highlands are a two hours' drive from Nairobi. Just outside the capital, the four-lane road headed north thins to two lanes; the city horizon, dominated by the Hilton Hotel and the Kenyatta Conference Center, fades in one's rear-view mirror and the world again belongs to rural Africa. The red earth turns brown, and the plains start to roll and dip like a rough sea. The road climbs higher and crosses the equator. Trailer trucks hauling Kenyan beer and rickety buses packed with passengers and loaded down with bicycles, produce and mattresses career around blind corners and down steep hills at a frightening clip. The streams, alive with trout, tumble off snow-capped Mount Kenya, and the dark pine forests hide large herds of elephant and occasionally the rare, moose-sized antelope, the bongo. Harvested coffee beans dry by the tonload on acre after acre of elevated screen frames. Little farming plots are carved into and up the slopes of every hill. Roadside vendors hawk sheepskins and straw baskets to tourists dashing by in safari mini-vans painted in zebra stripes. It is a beautiful land, reminiscent of New Hampshire. The air has a bite of mountain chill, and everything feels clean and fresh and gentle.

The Europeans did not penetrate the Kenyan highlands until the 1890s. It was the home of the Masai, the graceful nomadic warriors, and their battles with the Kikuyus and other intruders were sufficient to discourage the entry of slave traders, missionaries or settlers. But as the railway from Mombasa on the coast pushed through Nairobi and west toward Uganda, the isolation was broken. The Masai were driven south and the Europeans soon became masters of the highlands (and of the Africans who remained), farming land that had not been cultivated before and enduring hardships that belied the image of colonialists living in splendor.

In those days, the valleys and ridges reaching to the foothills of Mount Kenya were known as the "white highlands." They were a white preserve in a black land. Today the region is called merely "the highlands" and fewer than a hundred white settler families remain. The white-owned farms are being bought by African cooperatives and subdivided into five- and six-acre plots for subsistence farming. As far as the eye can see, the once empty glades are bursting with little mud homes whose tin roofs glisten like mirrors in the noontime sun. Near the village of Mwega there is a fork in the road, and if you bear to the left, you leave the pavement behind and bounce over a dirt track for a mile or two until you pass through a wooden gate. On a grassy knoll just beyond the gate is the Aberdare Country Club. There are two men there—one black, one white—who symbolize all that has happened to Kenya.

One of the most fearful of the Mau Mau commanders, a man who helped change the balance of power in the highlands, was Frederick Ndirangu. He was a general at the age of twenty-nine and for nearly four years he lived in the Aberdare Forest with his men, burrowing into the earth by day to protect himself from British bombing raids and leading attacks by night against white homesteads and African villages whose people had refused to support the Mau Mau.

Ndirangu, a big man with graying hair and a viselike handshake, works at the Aberdare Country Club, a one-time settler home that is now an inn catering mostly to tourists and white expatriates living in Kenya. The fight, he says, was worth fighting. He has land today, and two of his sons are electricians in Nairobi. His other seven children are all in school. He says "sir" to no one. Once the vanquished, he is at last the victor.

"We have a tradition in our Kikuyu culture," Ndirangu said as a waiter served us tea on the club's lawn. "If you quarrel, you can never be friends until you fight. But once you fight, all the hatred is finished.

"Before the Mau Mau, there were no good Europeans. They abused us and they never gave us a chance to advance our intelligence. Today things are different. This is our country now, not theirs, and the relationship is pretty good. I remember the past, but I do not carry it with me."

Sam Weller was a young British army captain when the Mau Mau terrorist attacks began, and he and his men spent many months in the Aberdare Forest trying to track down and capture or kill General Ndirangu. "I had the old boy in my sights a couple of times," chuckled Weller, who manages the Aberdare Country Club and employs Ndirangu as his driver. "But he always managed to slip away . . . Really, though, unless a visitor like yourself brings it up, you don't hear anyone, black or white, talk about the Mau Mau anymore up here. It was so long ago.

"Why has it been forgotten? Well, partly I think, because the African isn't capable of the depth of emotion that the European has. He doesn't love his women or hate his enemies with the same intensity. You look at a good solid white hatred and it can last for generations. Africans don't hate that way."

After the war Weller became a farmer, then a professional hunter and guide, and when convinced that the European, of his generation at least, did have a future in Africa, a Kenyan citizen. He lives alone in a comfortable one-bedroom bungalow, up the hill from the country club. He offered me a brandy. Logs crackled in his fireplace, and his two Labrador retrievers, Mark and Rebecca, stretched out at his feet. The living room was full of fishing tackle and there were books everywhere, on African butterflies, African flowers, African animals, African history.

In the corner an ancient shortwave radio, as big as a dishwasher, was tuned in to 1542 kilohertz, a custom followed in almost every expatriate's house at this hour, for the eight o'clock news: "This is

London, BBC World Service ... The British governor is leaving
London for Rhodesia ..."

Weller raised his eyebrows, shrugged and said nothing. Another
white bastion had crumbled. It was clear that white-run Rhodesia
was about to become black-run Zimbabwe. The vestiges of white
privilege had slipped away almost everywhere, and as Weller knew,
places like the Kenyan highlands were now an anachronism on a
continent obsessed with outdistancing the past.

The early settlers who preceded Weller to Kenya were not gentlemen farmers. They were hard men, independent, self-sufficient, an
African version of the early American settlers who trekked West and
took the Indians' land. They traveled in wagons pulled by oxen,
made soap from rhinoceros fat and often went weeks at a time without seeing another European. Their attitude toward the African was
at best paternal, at worst brutish, and right up to the dawn of independence, they apparently never gave the slightest thought to the
possibility that one day someone else might farm their land.

For those willing to work, the highlands were indeed an adventurous attraction. Just before World War I a poster circulated in
England advertising for new settlers and listing these enticements:
passage from England cost $80 and wages for farm helpers in Kenya
were $14 a month "until the customs of the country have been
learned."

"The soil is fertile," the poster announced, "the pasturage rich,
the water abundant. Ostrich feathers sent to Port Elizabeth realize
remarkable prices, locally cured bacon sells readily and is highly re-
munerative ... The healthiness of the highlands as a home for
white men, women and children has been proved beyond all
doubt."

It was said in those days that the British army officers who wanted
to settle in Africa came to Kenya and the enlisted men went to
Rhodesia. One of the bluebloods who staked his claim in Kenya was
Sam Weller's father, an accomplished artist, poet and violinist. He
arrived in 1925, after a career as a builder of railways in India, to establish a vocational training school for Africans.

In his book, *Kenya Without Prejudice*, Henry Owen Weller
wrote in 1931:

> There can be no happier, healthier life than that of the set-
> tler. Even when the future does not smile for a time ... it is
> easier to carry a heavy heart with a gun under the arm and a

buck to be shot on a hillside than to hang on a strap in the foul air of the "tube" after lunching on a bun and a cup of tea. It is better to drive a car through colonial mud than to dodge buses in Trafalgar Square.

... As [white] children grow up they must be kept from familiarity with Africans. Girls must never be left alone with male natives. At boarding school this matter receives careful attention. To neglect it at home would be asking for trouble.

... The African responds well. It is unlikely that he will reach the intellectual plane of the European or even the Indian, but he will get the chance of doing so, and it is hoped that he will settle down to working quietly when he has reached his ceiling.

One morning, twenty-two years after that book was published, a white farmer in the highlands awoke to find two hundred of his cattle mutilated, their eyes gouged out, their legs severed. A few weeks later, twenty-one Kikuyus loyal to the colonial government were massacred. It was March 26, 1953, and the Mau Mau uprising had begun.

"We knew the forests—that was our great advantage," General Ndirangu recalled. "But the European was a better soldier. If an African soldier got a hold of you, he would kill you. A white soldier would arrest you and take you to court to be tried. There was more justice under the Europeans."

The Mau Mau were almost exclusively Kikuyu, the dominant Kenyan tribe. They took secret ritual oaths of loyalty, operated in small guerrilla bands throughout the highlands, and were not content to merely kill their victims. The whites surrounded their homesteads with flares and booby traps, started carrying side arms and drew their drapes each evening at dusk. They sealed off the second-floor living quarters with iron barriers, still used and known in Kenya today as Mau Mau gates, and dismissed their Kikuyu servants because suddenly no one knew who the enemy was. "If you made it through soup, you figured you were safe for another day," one settler remarked, referring to the Mau Mau's habit of attacking at dinnertime.

More than 20,000 Kikuyus were placed in detention camps, where the British tried to "re-educate" them politically. But the Mau Mau raids continued, more often directed against uncooperative Africans than white farmers, and by the time the British managed to subdue the Kikuyu in 1956, the death toll stood at 11,500 Mau Mau guerrillas and African civilians, 2,000 African troops fighting for the British, 58 members of the British security forces and 37 British settlers. It was, though, too late for military victories. The war hardened the attitude of some whites. "This is our country," they would say. "Without us, there'd be only savages here." But any sensible man, European or African, knew that a new reality was at hand. The day of white supremacy was ending and the possibility of sharing power had passed. The 43,000 whites in Kenya were outnumbered 190 to 1: the voice of the majority was growing louder.

In Nairobi three European-led political groups emerged: the Federal Independence Party, which wanted to partition the country between blacks and whites; the Coalition, which advocated the protection of European rights; and the multiracial New Kenya Group, headed by the colonial minister of agriculture, Michael Blundell, which supported a transfer of power to a democratically elected African government. Blundell estimates his party had the support of only 30 percent of the expatriates when the Lancaster Conference opened in England in 1960 to decide the future of the Kenyan colony.

Blundell returned to Nairobi from one of the Lancaster negotiating sessions to find an angry crowd of whites waiting for him at the airport. They pelted him with rotten eggs and ripe epithets. Security officers hurried him through the terminal. Near his car a man rushed forward and tossed a small brown package at him. Blundell started to dive, thinking it was a bomb. The parcel burst open at his feet and out rolled thirty silver coins.

"Traitor," shouted the white man, "you sold us out!"

"I was spat upon and ostracized," said Blundell, who is now Sir Michael, in his seventies, and a Kenyan citizen. "For two or three years, my wife and I couldn't even go into our club. It was really rather unpleasant.

"Some people have never forgiven me. But, you know, it's a funny thing—most of the people who hated what I stood for the most will now admit, especially over a drink or two, that I was right, that there is a place in Africa for the European who has African interests at heart."

As the Lancaster Conference progressed, the exodus of whites from Kenya increased. Most of the Afrikaners who had come north from South Africa after the Boer War and thousands of British settlers hurried off to Rhodesia, South Africa and Australia. There they became known as the "Whenwe Tribe," because there was much talk of the good old days and every sentence seemed to begin with "When we were in Kenya . . ."

The British government agreed at the conference to provide the new Kenyan government—independence was scheduled for December 1963—with $100 million in loans and grants to buy out European farmers whose three million acres in the highlands had been reserved exclusively for whites. Payment would be in pounds sterling, not Kenyan shillings. To encourage the continued presence of whites—and thus ensure a smooth transition and much-needed expertise in agriculture and government—Britain privately said that it would, if requested, restore the British citizenship of those who became Kenyans. There were no special guarantees for the whites in the new constitution, and elections were to be conducted on a one-man, one-vote basis.

On the evening of August 12, 1963, four months before independence, several hundred European farmers and their wives packed the Nakuru town hall, a few miles from the Aberdare Country Club, to hear what they thought would surely be their marching orders. Nakuru has just one wide street, with a row of shops and general stores on each side. By the time the meeting started, a funeral-like stillness had fallen over the town; everyone, it seemed, was either in the wooden hall or gathered around it, straining to hear what was going on inside.

Jomo Kenyatta, the spiritual leader of the Mau Maus whom the British had imprisoned at hard labor for seven years, walked to the stage. He was seventy years old and he leaned on his walking stick. He talked quietly, his voice slowly gathering strength.

"We want you to stay and to farm well in this country," he told the settlers. "This is the policy of this government . . . What the government needs is experience, and I don't care where it comes from. I will take it with both hands.

"Continue to farm your land well, and you will get all the encouragement and protection of the government. The only thing we will not tolerate is wasted land.

"Kenya is large enough, and its potential is great. We can all work together harmoniously to make this country great, and to show other countries in the world that different racial groups can live and work together."

The whites stirred uneasily, looking at one another to make sure they heard the old man correctly. Then they stood and cheered.

Most of the whites have left the highlands since then, reluctantly but more or less voluntarily. The pressure for land is great in over-populated Kenya and the huge white-owned ranches are being bought by the cooperatives, the land is being fenced and the whites have moved closer to Nairobi or Mombasa or gone back home to England. The hundred or so white settler families who remain—representing one of the largest white farming communities in black Africa—speak little today of their future, hoping only that they, if not their children, will be able to stay on the land that was turned green and productive through the sweat of their forefathers. If they can't, it will not be because the African subjected them to the same discrimination that they inflicted on the African. It will be because land is the most sacred possession in Africa—land rights was the original issue in the Mau Mau war—and if the government is to maintain the support of its people, every rural African must eventually have his plot.

I have always found it strange—not unsettling, just unusual—to land on a grassy runway in the highlands and be greeted by a cluster of barefooted, blond-haired white farm children who were as African in their understanding of life as the blackest child of Africa. It seemed a flashback to another era. But the highlands are full of scenes frozen in time, and in the autumn of 1979, 300 white Kenyans gathered at Charlie Stone-Wigg's 45,000-acre Gianni Ranch for the marriage of his daughter to Frederick Brendan, son of another old-time settler family. The little town of Nyeri, a few miles from the Aberdare Country Club, had seen many such weddings in the past but would not see many more.

Two small-boy ushers, one wearing a kilt and both with clean, slicked-down blond hair, stood by the stack of wedding programs. The European soloist sang "The Holy City" and the European vicar called upon the congregation to ask for Jesus' help in time of need. The new Mrs. Brendan wore a homemade white dress and a lace shawl and she blushed as she walked down the aisle with her husband. The bride and groom both were born in Kenya and, given their choice, they both one day would be buried in Kenya.

In the drizzle after the ceremony, the guests crowded onto the verandah of the Stone-Wiggs' home. This was the last of the settler community, second- and third-generation white African farmers, and everyone knew everyone else—the Nyeri crowd greeting the people from Naivasha and Nanyuki, the Kitale families joking with their friends from Nakuru and Gil Gil and Naro Moru. Their faces were tanned from the African sun and their hands were callused and their laughter could be heard a long way off.

An old Kikuyu woman wandered up the road. She was barefoot and stoop-shouldered beneath the load of firewood on her back and her tattered dress was hardly more than a rag. She stood on the lawn for a few minutes, unnoticed, a black face in a sea of white. Then, losing interest, she moved on toward her village several miles away.

Three months after the wedding the Stone-Wiggs left Gianni Ranch, which soon would be divided into as many as ten thousand subsistence plots. The red oat grass that Stone-Wigg had nurtured so skillfully for his merino sheep and boran cattle would disappear, and the region's delicate ecological balance would be threatened.

The division of Kenya's large export-producing ranches for pint-sized subsistence farms, each supporting fifteen or twenty people, is a worrisome omen for a land with no mineral wealth and the world's highest birth rate. With the division comes a decline in agricultural production and a diminishing tax base for the government. (In 1975 Kenya was self-sufficient in wheat; in 1980 it had to import half of the 280,000 tons of grain needed to feed its people.) The government in Nairobi says that the subdividing must stop, that the white farmer must continue to produce if Kenya is to prosper.

But the pressure for land makes the destruction of the big farms inevitable. In the same way, the pressure for housing eventually will result in the destruction of the white-owned urban estates. And the pressure for jobs will lead to fewer and fewer white-held positions. Almost all white Kenyans now send their children to school in Europe, preparing them for a life very different from the one they have grown up with.

As one of the settler farmers told me, "I don't want my kids to learn to love Africa too much."

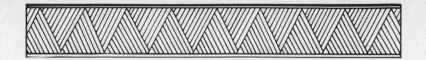

FROM LISBON WITH LOVE

▲

We're producing 600 tires a day in Angola, but God knows how we're doing it. The workers come in the morning and push the buttons, and if everything works, fine. If it doesn't, they just go home.

—*A U.S. executive of General Tire & Rubber Co. after touring the company's plant in Luanda, Angola, where absenteeism runs 50 percent a day*

IT'S HARD TO BELIEVE NOW, but only a few years ago Luanda was known as the Rio de Janeiro of Africa. And Angola was a place of prosperity and abundance. Ask a Portuguese what life was like in that colony on the South Atlantic coast and he will smile, close his eyes and blow a kiss.

Angola, he'll say, was a much better place to live than Lisbon. Savor it for just a day and you would know that Thomas Wolfe was only half right: it wasn't that you *couldn't* go home again; it was that you *didn't want* to go home again. There were weekends on the beach, eating fresh lobster and prawns; chic shops stuffed with gourmet foods and the latest European fashions; luxury high-rise apartments overlooking the bay, summer homes at Lobito—an African version of Florida's West Palm Beach; and, almost right up to the end, not the slightest hassle with the "natives." And then there was Luanda.

Luanda, the capital, was built on hills that rose gently from the bay. The sidewalks were paved with mosaic tile, and the streets were wide and lined with trees. There were parks everywhere, neatly clipped and ablaze with flowers, and throughout the city there were 170 restaurants and night clubs, open from dusk to dawn. The skyline, stretching from the twenty-five-story President Hotel to the seventeenth-century Dutch fort a few miles away, was like nothing else in Africa. There was, in fact, no more striking urban view—and no more pleasing life style—on the entire continent.

One of the best things, as far as the Portuguese were concerned, was that you didn't have to be rich or even literate to enjoy the fruits of this good life. You only had to be white. For with a resident population of 500,000 Portuguese, Angola was the "whitest" colony in all Africa. Like Portugal's other African colonies—Mozambique, Guinea-Bissau, Cape Verde, and São Tomé and Príncipe—it was the exclusive domain of white men who thought they would stay forever. Even menial jobs such as driving a taxi, cutting hair, tending bar, were held by the Portuguese. About the only jobs available to the 7 million black Angolans were as servants, janitors or plantation workers. At independence in 1975, after five centuries of Portuguese domination, 98 percent of the Angolans were illiterate and scarcely more than a handful had any technical skills, much less a university education.

Independence coincided with the collapse of the Portuguese overseas empire, which left in its wake a cluster of revolutionary, and often Marxist, independent states stretching across Africa. The whites became fearful, expecting the Africans to turn on them with vengeance. And in a panic of settler hysteria, they fled to Europe or South Africa in the largest white migration Africa had ever known. They brought with them everything they could carry or ship. More than twenty thousand cars were put on vessels; hundreds of others were totaled in drunken games of "chicken" on the streets of Luanda so that none would be left for the Angolans. The fishing fleet sailed off to Lisbon or down to Walvis Bay in Namibia. Telephones were ripped from the walls, typewriters were packed, plantations abandoned, mansions shuttered. Doctors walked out of the hospitals and professors emptied their desks at the university. In the course of a single week, 95 percent of the employees of the Bank of Angola departed, leaving junior clerks and janitors to run it. By the time the exodus ended, Angola had been stripped bare: all that remained were 25,000 whites and the carcass of a nation. "I'm not proud of what we did, but we didn't leave voluntarily, you know," a Portuguese exporter told me.

To refer to Portugal's colonial history as disgraceful would be to give Lisbon the benefit of the doubt. Portugal stood for all the evils of colonialism and none of the good. It took but did not give. It milked its two largest African colonies, Angola and Mozambique, as dry as a dead cow and bequeathed them nothing but the guarantee of economic disaster.

Today you can still stand on the patio of the Panorama Hotel and gaze out across the bay at Africa's most beautiful skyline. But not much else is the same. The hotel's entrance is guarded by a young woman wearing fatigues and double-buckle Soviet combat boots and carrying an AK-47 assault rifle. The harbor is full of Soviet ships, but cargo stands rotting on the piers while dock workers doze in the shadows nearby.

The mosaic sidewalks have cracked, exposing large gaps of stones and dirt, and garbage fills the streets. The high-rise apartments are occupied by squatters; the corridors reek of urine, and laundry hangs from the balcony railings. Rats scurry through the deserted restaurants, torn and filthy awnings hang limply in the stifling afternoon heat. The parks are overgrown, rusting frames of wrecked cars litter the alleys, and promptly at 5 A.M., when the curfew ends, women start queuing for a loaf of bread or a can of powdered milk imported from Brazil.* By noon, the lines stretch for blocks.

Walking through Luanda alone one afternoon, I was struck by the eerie notion that I had entered a living ghost town, that here was the African city of the twenty-first century. It had people but no sense of life or purpose. Block after block of stores were closed, their windows broken and boarded up. Neon signs flashed mysteriously above IBM, Sony and Singer showrooms that had been empty for years. Hotel employees snoozed at the reception counters, and government workers slouched behind desks that were barren of telephones, typewriters, pencils or paper. Elevators were stuck where they had jammed two or three years earlier, and air conditioners coughed and sputtered and threw out blasts of hot air.

In my $40-a-day hotel room a sign advised: "The great difficulty we are finding in replacing lost or deteriorated objects forces us to make this special request. Should you need a towel, please request same at the porter's desk." But the hotel had no porter, no porter's desk, no running water, no food in the dining room except soup and bread.

One morning from my hotel window I noticed what appeared to be a Peugeot convertible, moving ever so slowly along the beachfront road. When it finally drew even with the hotel, I saw that the owner had cut off the car's top, gutted the inside and attached a

---

* Brazil, a former Portuguese colony, has become a major trading partner with black Africa, seeking in particular to capitalize on its cultural and linguistic ties with Angola and Mozambique. Trade between the Brasília government and Africa increased fourteenfold from 1970 to 1980. Among Brazil's major exports are vehicles and food products.

yoke to the front axle. The $10,000 Peugeot had been turned into a cart and was being pulled by oxen.

"I'd grant you that we're not in a very happy state of affairs," a senior police official told me. "I wouldn't suggest for a minute that anyone would want colonialism and the Portuguese back, but certainly, unless you're an important party official, you were a lot better off in 1970 than you are in 1980."

His conclusion seemed reasonable enough, for Angola was a wounded and fragile country in a state of utter deterioration. Yet, like so many African countries, its resources were immense and its possibilities for development great.

Angola (the name comes from an early king, N'gola) is fourteen times the size of Portugal, or as big as Spain, France and Italy combined. Once you leave the flat narrow strip along the coast, the land rises quickly into a shrub-covered plateau, often a mile high or more, which forms one of Africa's great watersheds. The rains are generous throughout much of Angola and the climate is temperate. Though there are millions of acres of fertile, unused farmland, agricultural development has been retarded by a variety of tsetse fly whose bite is so painful that domestic animals become uncontrollable. As a result, there are no horses or beasts of burden in all of southern Angola, an area twice the size of Colorado.

In terms of natural resources, Angola is one of the two or three potentially wealthiest countries in black Africa. Its offshore oil platforms, operated by Gulf, earn Angola about $5 million a day. (Sixty percent of the oil ends up in the United States, even though Washington has never recognized the Marxist government in Luanda.) Its exported coffee crop and its diamond mines (which are covertly run by South African interests) were at independence among the world's most productive. Its iron ore exports used to bring in $75 million annually, its sisal and cotton crops another $51 million. Additionally, Angola earned $100 million a year from traffic fees paid by Zaire and Zambia on the Benguela Railroad. But by 1980, Angola had little more than its petroleum income, and most of that was being used to pay for its war against antigovernment guerrillas in southern Angola.*

---

* Except for its oil, in 1980 Angola was not producing much more than six hundred rubber tires a day and some textiles. It was importing half its food, and its agricultural exports had tumbled. Coffee production, for example, fell from 205,000 metric tons in 1974 to 25,000 tons in 1980. The diamond mines were earning less than a quarter of the $80 million they

Angola had been crippled by its abrupt transition into independence and by the Portuguese exodus, by the continuing civil war against South African–backed guerrillas, by a bewildered Marxist government which thought the nation's problems would go away if it recited enough slogans, by a bored, obedient population that was not trained to provide the skills a new nation required. Angola had become a victim of both past and present, exploited by the colonialists and misled by the nationalists. It was the tragic symbol of what Africa is and a case study of what, with luck and planning, it could be. One day, perhaps, the chasm between those two extremes will no longer be worlds apart.

The first European to reach Angola was the Portuguese explorer Diogo Cão, who landed at the mouth of the Congo River in 1483. The people he found there were of Bantu stock, representing a hundred different tribes, and the land was under the rule of an African monarch, the King of the Kongo. Seven years later the Portuguese sent a small fleet of ships to the kingdom, carrying priests, skilled workers and tools. The mission was received warmly and in return for the Portuguese favors, the king accepted Christianity and agreed to send his son, the future King Afonso, to Lisbon for schooling. Thus began, on a note of mutual respect, Portugal's African presence. It would end nearly five hundred years later with the Portuguese losing liberation wars in Angola, Mozambique and Guinea-Bissau and fleeing the continent in panic.

Relations between Lisbon and King Afonso soon deteriorated. The Kongo kingdom was racked by internal revolt and gradually disintegrated. The slave traders came and military clashes were frequent. The Portuguese meanwhile extended their contacts southward along the coast and in 1575 founded Luanda. In 1641 a Dutch fleet seized Luanda and another slaving port, Benguela, forcing the Portuguese to retreat into the interior. Seven years later an expedition from Brazil returned the coast to Portuguese control.

Why had Lisbon fought so determinedly for a coastal strip on a primitive, mysterious continent? Its incentive was economic—slaves. For during three centuries an estimated three million Angolans were shipped to plantations in Brazil, providing the foundation of that Portuguese colony's economic growth. The slaving industry

had brought in at independence. Most of the Benguela Railroad had been knocked out of operation by the antigovernment guerrillas. The government had not even published a budget since 1977.

in Angola was made possible by the willing participation of chiefs from two tribes: the Chokwe, a mobile, aggressive group living in eastern Angola, and the Ovimbundu, the largest ethnic group, which ranged through central and southern Angola and represented 40 percent of the total population.

Portuguese soldiers and settlers faced sporadic but continuous warfare in Angola for more than a century after the founding of Luanda, and it was not until the late 1800s that Lisbon was able to extend its control into the high plateaus of the interior. By then the European imperial powers had begun their "scramble for Africa." Portugal, industrially and technologically backward, was the light-weight of the group which met in Berlin in 1884–1885 to establish the boundaries of Africa. Largely because of Britain's support, Portugal was granted the "right of occupation" in Angola. At the same time it was forbidden to move into the central African lands of Northern Rhodesia (now Zambia), Southern Rhodesia (Zimbabwe) and Nyasaland (Malawi), all of which were placed in Britain's sphere of influence.

Most of the white settlement before this century was comprised of *degredadas*—criminals sentenced to Angola rather than to jail in Portugal. As recently as 1950, half the white population in Angola had never attended school, and another 40 percent had completed no more than four years of primary school. Unlike, say, the Kenyan highlands, which were settled by upper- and middle-class Britons, Angola had become a dumping ground for illiterate European peasants. And a miserable lot they were. Unable to find suitable work in the cities, many drifted into the villages, took up with African peasant women and "went native," living as bare a subsistence existence as the poorest black farmer.

The Portuguese did two things unique to European colonialism in Africa: they built beautiful cities, such as Luanda and Lourenço Marques (now Maputo) in Mozambique, and they intermarried to such an extent that their former colonies today are among the most multiracial countries in Africa.

"God created the whites and the blacks," old settlers in Angola used to say, "but the Portuguese created the *mestiço* [person of mixed blood]." The racial mix, however, probably had more to do with promiscuity and sexual ratios than tolerance. There were, for instance, eleven white men for every white woman in Angola in 1846.

Ninety-nine of every 100 Portuguese in Angola lived in the cities.

This meant that Lisbon's influence in the countryside was limited and Angola's farmlands were not developed to anything approaching their full potential. The Portuguese did not have the attachment to the land or the commitment to national development that the British had in Kenya. Their emotional ties belonged to another continent, and it was as easy for them to leave as it had been for them to come. Lisbon tried numerous schemes to reverse the white urbanization. At one point in the 1950s it even offered every married Portuguese farmer over thirty years of age a free fifty-acre plot with a cow, sheep, a pig, six chickens, six ducks and some rabbits. Scarcely more than a hundred Portuguese a year took advantage of the opportunity.

By the early 1960s, France and Britain were cutting their colonial ties to Africa. But Portugal's premier, António de Oliveira Salazar, the last of the West European dictators, refused to even consider eventual independence for his African colonies, contending that they formed an integral part of Portugal. (A sign outside the city hall in Lourenço Marques announced: "Here is Portugal.") In 1961, black nationalists took up arms against the colonial authorities, and Lisbon found itself fighting two separate independence wars in Angola, one against a movement advocating Marxism, the other against an organization whose orientation was pro-Western and capitalistic. As so often happens in Africa, the nationalists themselves were divided by tribal and ideological differences, and once the Portuguese were defeated, they turned their guns on one another. Three movements figured in the liberation war and the civil war that followed:

▶ The Popular Movement for the Liberation of Angola (MPLA), Marxist and supported by the Soviet Union, was formed in 1956 with the help of the Portuguese Communist Party. Its principal guerrilla bases during the fourteen-year independence war were named Hanoi II and Ho Chi Minh. Its key figures were mostly *mestiço* urban intellectuals. Agostinho Neto, the MPLA leader and later the first president of Angola, visited Washington in 1962, seeking economic help from the West. But U.S. economic and political interests in Africa had always lain with the colonial powers, not the black liberation movements, and the Kennedy Administration snubbed Neto. The slight pushed this man, who would become one of Africa's most important revolutionary leaders, further into the Soviet camp.

▶ The National Front for the Liberation of Angola (FNLA) was formed in 1962 and soon set up a government-in-exile in neighboring Zaire. It was backed by Western countries, including the United States, and led by Holden Roberto, who was named for a British Baptist missionary and was a descendant of the Kongo monarchy. It had the largest guerrilla army in the independence war, about 15,000 men.

▶ The National Union for the Total Independence of Angola (UNITA) was formed in 1966 after a split in FNLA. It was supported at various times by China, the United States and South Africa and led by a bulky, bearded, Swiss-educated guerrilla named Jonas Savimbi, a member of the dominant Ovimbundu tribe.* UNITA was the only faction in the war committed to the electoral process. Savimbi was shunned by black Africa after he called on South Africa for military help and the Pretoria troops, both black and white, swept to within seventy-five miles of Luanda on the eve of independence.

The military coup in Lisbon in April 1974 led to major policy shifts, including Portugal's decision to grant early independence to its African colonies. Just before the panicked white exodus, Lisbon worked out a complicated agreement with the three factions in Angola to form a tripartite transitional government. The deal was a failure. Neto's MPLA sought a military victory over the two pro-Western groups and asked for Cuban assistance. Help was quick in coming, and within a matter of weeks Neto had 20,000 Cuban combat troops and more than 1,500 Soviet and Eastern-bloc advisers on Angolan soil. The choice Washington faced was to sit by and watch a Marxist government come to power or to step up its covert support for Roberto and Savimbi, enabling one of them to make the final push into Luanda and establish himself as the head of a pro-Western government. President Gerald R. Ford and Secretary of State Henry Kissinger favored the latter course, which would have represented a major setback to the Soviet interests in Africa. But the U.S. Congress, weary of another Vietnam-type involvement, was unwilling to confront the Eastern bloc for African real estate and after long debate it cut off funds for Roberto and Savimbi. (Up to that point, Washington had pumped about $40 million into Roberto's and Savimbi's movements.) South Africa, whose

---

* Like Neto and Roberto, Savimbi was the product of a missionary education. But he was the only one of the three who spent most of his time in the bush with his troops. Neto and Roberto lived outside Angola during the war years.

invasion of Angola had been encouraged by Washington, withdrew, quite rightly feeling betrayed. For Neto, the dream was at hand. And in a somber ceremony on November 11, 1975, with enemy African soldiers almost within gunshot range of Luanda, Neto became president of Africa's forty-eighth independent nation.

Neto had been imprisoned four times by the Portuguese for anticolonial activities. He was a recipient of the Lenin Peace Prize. He had the credentials of a true revolutionary, and indeed, by planting Marxism on the doorstep of South Africa, he changed the political balances across the southern third of Africa. But Neto ("Our Immortal Guide," as the Angolans called him) was certainly not the ogre the West had expected. He was a published poet, a physician, an articulate spokesman for the rights of the underprivileged. His rule was neither corrupt nor overly repressive, and even Neto's harshest critics were surprised at his willingness to compromise: he invited the thousands of Angolan exiles in Portugal to return home and help rebuild the country; he reached an accord of friendship with Zaire, which had harbored his enemies; he flew off to Guinea-Bissau for a cordial three-day meeting with Portugal's president, António Ramalho Eanes. Before he died in 1979 in Moscow of cancer at the age of fifty-six, Neto had come to realize that he needed economic assistance the Soviet Union could not provide. He started inquiring about the West's willingness to help and told confidants he was uncomfortable with the realization that his government's survival depended on the military presence of a foreign country, Cuba.

During the 2,000-mile trip I made through Angola, most of the Cubans I encountered in Luanda and the major rural areas were civilians—teachers, doctors and government administrators. They approached me with curiosity, not hostility. But as I traveled south, into the rural areas of central Angola, Cuban soldiers were very much in evidence and my government translator made no attempt to steer me away from them. In Huambo, a once lovely farming town that had turned into an unsightly slum in less than ten years' time, I saw military convoys rumbling toward the front with uniformed Cuban soldiers. Others strolled through the streets in small groups and some played baseball in an open field strewn with garbage. I tried to find out how many Cubans had died defending the Angolan government. No one would answer in anything but the vaguest term, though it is pretty well established that Cuba's casualties numbered in the thousands.

Most Western governments were responsive to Neto's overtures for help. Washington, however, saw a Communist under every Angolan bed and refused to even recognize the Neto regime or that of his successor, José Eduardo dos Santos. It said formal relations could not be established until the Cubans started withdrawing and Savimbi was included in a new government. The demands were as absurd as if Angola had told a U.S. President whom to put in his Cabinet and had insisted that he start pulling American troops out of West Germany. The United States would have been much wiser to have recognized the Angola government and assisted it with a modest aid program aimed at economic recovery. Such moves would at least have made Angola realize that it did have options in choosing its foreign friends. As it was, the United States only succeeded in convincing Angola that Washington was more concerned with the Soviet presence in Africa than with a country's economic development, an assumption that was probably correct.

On the eastern side of Angola, facing the Indian Ocean, was Portugal's other important African colony, Mozambique. It, too, gained independence in 1975 after a long guerrilla war, and its government, like Angola's, is Marxist and closely aligned with the Soviet Union. Though Mozambique is not blessed with great mineral resources— its major export is cashew nuts—the country's deterioration has been less dramatic than Angola's for two reasons: first, Mozambique maintains close economic ties with its prosperous neighbor, South Africa; and second, despite some antigovernment guerrilla resistance, President Samora Machel has not had to contend with a major civil war like the one Jonas Savimbi continues to wage in Angola.

This has given Mozambique a little breathing space. In Maputo, a capital nearly as beautiful as Luanda, I was impressed to find the streets spotlessly clean and amazed to see volunteer work crews collecting garbage at dawn each morning. "People's committees" had taken over the hotels and restaurants and performed their duties with a smile, if not efficiency. In the countryside schoolhouse, lights burned late as many thousands of adults learned to read and write in one of Africa's most ambitious literacy campaigns. When I asked a farmer if he was embarrassed to be in the first grade studying the alphabet at the age of fifty, he replied, "No. I am thrilled. I can write my name."

Machel's goal is to create in Mozambique what he calls "The

New Man" of Africa—an educated, politically aware nationalist who works for the common good. Those who do not conform to this vision are sent to one of the country's eight re-education camps, modeled after similar centers set up by the Communists in Vietnam. Mozambican officials won't say how many people are in the camps but Western intelligence sources place the number at about twelve thousand. On one visit to Mozambique I was given the rare opportunity as a foreigner to visit a camp called Codzo, seventy miles from the Zimbabwe border. I was accompanied by a government escort officer and a government translator, so no doubt I saw only what Mozambican authorities wanted me to see. Nevertheless, I found nothing to confirm the stories of barbaric treatment that trickled out of the camps in the early months of independence.

Codzo was a prison with no walls, no gates, no clanking steel doors. Approaching it on the dusty road that pushes through head-high elephant grass, I saw what looked like a typical African village. Mud-walled, thatch-roofed bungalows were clustered near the little schoolhouse. Chickens scurried along the dirt paths. A Mozambican flag fluttered from a stick poked into the ground. In the fields, men wearing baggy black uniforms and blue sneakers toiled over patches of turnips and potatoes. The camp commander told me none of the guards carried guns, but I saw at least a dozen who did.

There were eight hundred male prisoners, ranging in age from sixteen to the mid-thirties. Some were petty criminals or drug addicts, others were described as enemies of the revolution. None was ever charged or tried in court, and none knew how long he would stay. One teen-age boy I talked to had been imprisoned merely for getting drunk and forgetting his identification card. Everyone in Codzo spent ninety minutes a day in sessions devoted to self-criticism and Marxist orientation, and everyone was taught a trade, from carpentry to farming.

President Machel bristles at criticism about the camps, pointing out that Mozambique, unlike some African countries, has chosen to educate its dissidents, not kill them. Besides, Machel says, the camps are but one minuscule aspect of a revolution designed to reconstruct a country. And the problems that revolution faces are indeed great.

Educated administrators are in such short supply in Mozambique that youths fresh out of college are made provincial directors (governors); agricultural production has tumbled since independence and foreign investors have been scared away by radical fiscal policies; government red tape turns the smallest daily chore into an obstacle course of frustration; 70 percent of the population is under the age of eighteen, and most are so unsophisticated that when thousands of them moved out of the slums and into seaside apartments and lovely old homes abandoned by—or nationalized from—the Portuguese, Machel warned, "Remember, you must not keep chickens in your new homes."

There were 200,000 Portuguese in Mozambique before independence, and although Mozambique was not a penal colony, they managed to ravage the land and retard the Africans' growth as thoroughly as had their counterparts in Angola. The country had a healthy industrial output of $40 million a year at independence and only 10 percent of the food was imported, but the economy was built by and for the European settler. White-oriented services such as banking, insurance and tourism accounted for a staggering 63 percent of the economy; agricultural, mining and industry for only 37 percent.

Machel, though, had learned the lessons of African history. Despite all that his people had endured at the hands of the colonialists, despite the bitterness of the liberation war, he asked the Portuguese to stay on after independence, knowing that a European exodus would cripple an already wounded country. "We want harmony among the races," Machel said. "For the sake of national construction, we must have the support of all people on every continent and of every race."

His message was reminiscent of the one Jomo Kenyatta had delivered to the white farmers in the Kenyan highlands just before independence. But in Mozambique, Machel's words fell on unbelieving ears, and the jittery Portuguese started packing. "We really believed that Machel's movement was a terrorist organization and that the terrorists were going to kill civilians and rape our wives and eat our daughters," a Portuguese merchant who left told me. Within a few months all but 20,000 of the Portuguese had gone. Their departure devastated Mozambique as thoroughly as the white exodus did in Angola. There was, incidentally, never any recrimination or retaliation against the Europeans, and Machel's closest advisers soon included blacks, Indians and whites. (On my last visit, three of his cabinet ministers were white Angolans.)

Why did the whites stay in Kenya and flee from Mozambique and Angola?

▶ First, the British settler was a person of much higher caliber than the Portuguese expatriate. He had an attachment to the land and a stake in the country's prosperity. Africa really was his home, and his own future depended on making it work.

▶ Britain had won its war against the African freedom fighters; Portugal had lost its. In Kenya, there was a seven-year hiatus between the end of the Mau Mau emergency and the birth of nationhood. The Europeans and Africans had time to work out their differences and establish a structure for majority rule. In Mozambique and Angola, the liberation wars led directly to instant independence, and the guerrilla movements became the governments.

▶ Independence in Kenya did not bring a radical shift in political and economic philosophies; Mozambique and Angola became Marxist. Economies were nationalized, farming cooperatives established, one-party systems created, the free press dismantled. (Colonial Angola had seventeen radio stations, sixteen newspapers and fifteen magazines; independent Angola has two newspapers and one radio station, all under government control.) There was no room for Europeans who were not committed ideologues.

Marxism has failed in Mozambique and Angola—just as it has failed everywhere in Africa. Everywhere it has been tried, national economies have stagnated, the masses have been kept ignorant of their right to question, Soviet influence has grown beyond any reasonable limits, repression has become a key government tool, over-bureaucratization has destroyed what little efficiency existed in the public and private sectors. Africa, unlike, say, China, does not have the tradition of central government so essential to the propagation of Communism. It has no history of placing common welfare above that of the family or tribe. It has no experience in being industrious in any endeavor unrelated to individual survival. The tenets of Marxism are alien to African culture.

Marxism failed in Somalia and Algeria because nationalism and an adherence to Islam proved stronger than any dedication to a political system. Ghana, Guinea, the Sudan and the Congo all flirted with it but found that economic realities carried more weight than visionary ideals. Ethiopia is still trying it but has accomplished little other than the death of many of its people in a government terror campaign against "counterrevolutionaries." President Julius Nyerere's dreams of a socialistic Tanzania sounded fine in the classroom but in practical application did nothing to advance his country economically. Political ideology, whether it is imported from East or West, does not fill empty stomachs or rebuild abandoned factories. It merely usurps energies that should be devoted to national development. It leaves a numbed people mumbling foolish slogans at the command of their presidents, and if that ideology is Marxist, it removes all individual economic incentives. The result is that an untrained, uneducated people have no motivation, and care little about increased production. The tropical sun gives them warmth, the fertile earth gives them food, the tribe gives them protection. Surrounded by decay, denied the opportunity to rise above the crowd through industriousness and ingenuity, they do what they must to survive, but not much more.

At Angola's only functioning cotton mill, Africa Textile, outside Benguela, so many workers were showing up three and four hours late each day that the company sold everyone a bicycle at cost and began rewarding punctual workers with cloth at reduced prices. Absenteeism still averages 30 percent.

When production falls at the General Tire plant, a party meeting is called and the workers vote, usually unanimously, to declare a "Red Saturday"—an extra workday, which they donate without pay. General Tire had a Red Saturday during my visit, and only 3 of the 150 employees showed up—two foreigners and a party official.

"Our production was really hurt by all the political meetings the workers hold at the drop of a hat," a foreign executive at Africa Textile said. "Now, finally, we've convinced the party to ban meetings, except after five P.M. on Friday. I told the party, 'Look, you've got the only mill still operating in Angola. Why not leave it alone?' "

For most Angolans, ideology is just something they must live with. They cannot escape it, but they don't pay much attention to it either. In one of the few factories operating in Luanda I asked a worker what he thought of an uncomplimentary drawing of President Carter scrawled on the nearby wall. "Who did you say that is?" the worker asked, puzzled. Then, after a lengthy pause, he added, "Is he Communist?" The bookstores are among the few shops still open in Luanda, but they sell only Communist literature. The newspapers are filled not with news but with propaganda. The ruling party exhorts the hungry masses to labor for society's benefit while weeds and jungle reclaim the plantations, mothers nurse their babies on tea and sugar, and the standard of living deteriorates by the day.

"Angola, Angola, Angola!" a navy lieutenant exclaimed, throwing up his hands in exasperation one day when most of his men didn't show up for a training exercise. "What is this thing we have created?"

SHADOW FROM ABROAD

▲

The United States better start taking care of things it knows how to take care of. We know so little of Africa, the 800 [*sic*] and some tribes that make up Africa . . . I say it is like a different world.

—SENATOR HUBERT HUMPHREY,
1976

ONCE IT WOULD have been easy simply to forget Africa. But no longer. By the 1980s the world had come courting and the stakes were high: Africa's untapped mineral reserves were among the most plentiful in the world; its location was a strategic one from which a military power could control the West's major oil-shipping routes as well as the Red Sea, gateway to the Suez Canal and the Mediterranean; its strength as a political bloc was sufficient to affect decisions made in the United Nations; its growing markets were absorbing billions of dollars in foreign goods every year and demanding more; its untilled farmlands were fertile and huge, a potential breadbasket for millions of people at home and abroad. Yet for all its riches, Africa was still virgin territory, vulnerable to internal pressures, susceptible to external influence. It was an inviting prospect for foreign suitors who came calling with gifts of guns and money.

And from Moscow to Washington, from Rio de Janeiro and Havana to Paris and Tokyo, governments jockeyed for influence, for a stake in the future of this continent, which twenty or thirty years from now might carry the weight to tip the world's balance of power, one way or the other. The first "scramble for Africa" occurred a century ago when the European powers met in Berlin to carve up the Dark Continent for themselves. This new "invasion" was more subtle but its aims were similar: economic and strategic domination. So far, Africa has fallen into line. It needs money from the West to survive and weapons from the Eastern bloc to fight the enemy of the moment. And in accepting those dollars and guns, it has become as beholden to and dependent on foreign governments as it was in the final days of colonialism. It speaks of being left alone to find African solutions to African problems, but when there is a problem, military or economic, the summons for help immediately goes out to Paris or Moscow or London or Washington. It speaks of being nonaligned, but with the exception of oil-rich Nigeria, has not the clout to act or speak independently. So a new division, this one ideological, has appeared in Africa, dividing the continent in half. One group, the so-called progressives, looks to Moscow as its patron saint; the other, the so-called moderates, has cast its lot with the West. The groupings are helter-skelter, not regional, and as cross-border rivalries heighten, the potential for superpower confrontation increases.

There is a saying that you cannot buy the allegiance of an African government—you can only rent it for a day. And that pretty well sums up the risks involved for those investing in Africa's future. Governmental loyalties change overnight and are sometimes available to the highest bidder. Moderate presidents are overthrown by progressive ones, who are toppled by army generals, who are ousted by army sergeants. Economies are nationalized and denationalized, foreign communities are expelled and invited back.

No foreign power should know this better than the Soviet Union. But the Russians are slow learners—and the most racist of all the foreigners in black Africa.* They live in compounds surrounded by high stone walls, seldom mix with Africans except at diplomatic functions and do not hire Africans for even the lowliest embassy job. They bring their own receptionists, cooks and chauffeurs from home. In Mogadishu, Somalia, and Lobito, Angola, special beaches were set aside for the Russians. In Conakry, Guinea, the Russians rode from their fortresslike embassy to their residential compound in buses, even though they could have walked the distance in five

* About 11,000 Africans have scholarships to study in the Soviet Union—one of the few forms of aid Moscow offers without any strings attached. Most have encountered there stronger racism than what they saw at home during the colonial period, and over the years thousands have left Moscow before the completion of their studies, deeply disillusioned. If you want to make an African into a capitalist, the saying goes, send him to school in Moscow; if you want him to be a Communist, send him to Paris.

minutes. One day, strolling through an outdoor market in Mogadishu with a group of Western journalists, we were surrounded by an angry crowd. The people shook their fists at us and glared and repeated over and over, *"Ruusk, Ruusk, Ruusk."* Finally our translator said something in Somali. The mood softened and the crowd pulled back to let us pass. "Don't worry," our guide said. "They thought you were Russians."

Such hostility should surprise no one. Almost every African country that formed an intimate relationship with Moscow—among them Egypt, Ghana, Guinea, Somalia and the Sudan—eventually discovered that they were on the wrong end of an unbalanced deal; the heavy-handed Russians were sent packing. The Soviet policy in Africa is based on capitalizing on regional instability and on providing the military hardware—but not the developmental assistance—needed to buy the dependence of various radical factions. Throughout the seventies, Moscow was content to probe for weak spots and to collect a few pieces of real estate here and there, adding Ethiopia, Mozambique and Angola to its current cluster of allies. For the eighties, Moscow's goal appears to be the extension of a Soviet-influenced belt that would reach across southern Africa from Mozambique to Angola and would isolate pro-Western South Africa, the continent's only industrialized nation. It is a policy of opportunism that benefits only the Soviet Union.

The worry to the West is not that one or two African countries will become Communist; it is that a Soviet presence in any country has a destabilizing effect on the entire region. Economic growth and political stability do not give rise to radical regimes; poverty and turmoil do. A peaceful Africa, prosperous and steady, is to the advantage of the West—and, of course, Africa itself—but not the Soviet Union. Take a map of Africa and put a red pin in every country where the government is especially repressive, where warfare engulfs the land, where the economy is a shambles. And wherever there is a pin, that's where the Soviet Union's influence is the strongest.

Few African countries have ever benefited from that relationship. Moscow's first "developmental" gift to Guinea, a tropical West African country where few homes have running water, consisted of two snowplows and ten thousand toilet seats. French-speaking Chad got twelve Soviet university professors, who knew only one language—Russian. In Somalia, Moscow constructed a meat-packing facility, but the bulk of production went to the Soviet Union at discount prices. In Tanzania, Moscow built the last thing that backward country needed—a $30 million air-missile system to protect Dar es Salaam. Ethiopia had to mortgage its coffee crop for the next ten years to repay Moscow for the $1 billion arms airlift of 1977–1978. Guinea-Bissau buys fish taken in its own waters by Russian fishermen and packed in cans labeled "Caught in the Soviet Union." In Mozambique, Spain pays $2 million annually for fishing rights; the Soviet Union gets them for nothing. Under terms of an agreement favorable to Moscow, the Soviets "vacuum-clean" the fish from the Mozambique Channel, keeping the best 75 percent of the catch and selling the leftovers to Mozambique's Marxist government. In Angola, sixty cents of every dollar the government earns goes to the military or to repay Soviet debts. For each Cuban teacher or technician in Angola, the government pays Havana $600 a month. It also pays for the Cubans' housing and utilities. Even to comrades, Moscow gives nothing for free and at some point it always calls in its debts.

The Soviet Union has become by far the largest arms supplier to Africa, providing eleven times more weapons than the United States and four times more than France. This alone gives Moscow considerable clout; without those guns at least two governments, Angola's and Ethiopia's, would not be in power today. But the Soviet Union's biggest advantage in Africa is historical and psychological: Washington backed the colonial powers in Africa right up to the dawn of independence; Moscow supported the liberation movements. It is, though, naïve to take this tradition one step further and say that therefore the Soviet Union is Africa's "natural ally." But I met more than a few educated Africans, many of them Ethiopians schooled in the United States, who believe precisely that. They resent the economic and political strength of the United States, its backing of South Africa, its bullylike tactics in international forums, its professed concern for human rights abroad while having given its own minority groups at home much to complain about.

There's an interesting point here. These same Africans speak with respectful awe of the American Revolution, considering it the model of an oppressed people's triumph over colonialism. They know the U.S. Constitution better than most American schoolchildren do and mention it often as a document that reflects the dreams of all mankind. And if the United States and the Soviet Union both lifted visa restrictions and invited free immigration, Washington would have to send a larger fleet than it used in the Normandy invasion to carry the exodus out of Africa. Moscow wouldn't be able to fill a

Boeing 727. Why? Because Africans know the United States offers an individual something they can't find at home or in the Soviet Union—an opportunity for economic advancement in a free society.

Washington has never known how to react to this love-hate affair. Nor has it ever been sure how to deal with Moscow's clumsy, militarily aggressive posture in Africa. It had a chance to confront Moscow in Angola in 1975, in the Horn of Africa in 1977 and in the Rhodesian civil war that led to the birth of Zimbabwe in 1980. Each time, it backed off and sought political rather than military solutions. As it turned out, having no policy or at least a nonbelligerent policy proved to be the best policy of all. Zimbabwe became independent with a Marxist head of state, Robert Mugabe, who was thoroughly distrustful of Moscow. Angola and Ethiopia sunk deeper into internal warfare and economic chaos, making the Soviet Union's investment an expensive one that was unlikely to return any dividends for a long time. If you accept the premise, as I do, that Communism is not a long-range threat to black Africa, it is entirely possible Moscow may never get any return on its money at all.

No doctrine, in fact, is more in conflict with the inherent character of Africa than Communism. First, Africans are religious, whether that religion is Christianity, Islam or animist. Second, Africans are capitalistic, collecting cattle or money as greedily as any Western entrepreneur. Third, Africans are historically democratic, choosing their village chiefs and clan elders by varying forms of consensus. Fourth, Africans are individualistic, willing to labor for themselves or their tribe, but seldom showing much interest in the broader, abstract concepts of nation or state. Fifth, Africans simply do not work or produce when they are not rewarded with economic incentive.

The United States can capitalize on this natural antithesis toward Communism by convincing Africa that economic development and security are interdependent, that the longer-term advantages of economic assistance are far greater than the short-term ones of military support.

To accomplish this, the United States and its Western allies must provide the technical and financial aid that African countries, even Marxist nations such as Ethiopia and Angola, need to arrest their deterioration and to develop economic and political self-reliance. That in turn will make Africa less dependent on outside meddlers. At some point Africa's radical states will realize that posters of Karl

Marx or Friedrich Engels hanging in their main squares look as foolish and as un-African as would portraits of Adam Smith or Thomas Jefferson. Until that happens, Africa will continue to take its guns from the East, its money from the West. But one president after another has learned that the expertise and financial resources needed for tomorrow's growth are available only in the West, and if Africa is to develop a skilled, enterprising propulation, it is to the West that the continent must turn, just as it always has in the past.

▶ The Soviet Union pumped $1 billion worth of weapons into Ethiopia in 1977 and 1978 to help that country gain a military advantage over two different antigovernment guerrilla movements, in the Ogaden and in Eritrea. When a severe drought struck the Ethiopian provinces of Wallo and Tigre a few months after the arms airlift, Moscow gave nary a ruble for relief. Marxist Ethiopia turned to the West and emergency assistance poured in, including $2.5 million from the United States. Drought struck again in 1983, and again it was only the West that helped.

▶ The Gulf Oil Co. suspended production in Angola during that country's civil war in the mid-seventies. One of the first moves of the Marxist government that came to power was to ask Gulf to resume production, which the company did. Gulf's complex is located in the Cabinda region, and security for the U.S. interests there is provided by none other than Fidel Castro's Cuban troops. And who did Angola retain as its economic consultants? The Boston firm of Arthur D. Little.

▶ The UN Security Council pledged $385 million in 1976 to help Mozambique counter the financial drain of closing its border with Rhodesia, a move Mozambique hoped would help bring down the white-minority government in Salisbury. Only about $100 million of the pledge was ever delivered to Mozambique, but every cent of it came from the West.

▶ In the late 1970s, the Soviet Union attempted to expand its political influence in the eight West African nations that comprise the constantly drought-stricken Sahel. Moscow increased the size of some of its embassy staffs, but not the amount of its donations. Again, economic assistance for the region came from the West, $1 billion in 1978 alone, of which the United States gave $67 million.

Until the arrival of the Carter Administration, the United States had displayed a remarkable insensitivity toward and ignorance of black Africa. Washington professed support for the aspirations of the emerging nations but its real sentiments lay with the white man in Africa—the Portuguese, South African, Rhodesian. In 1962, for instance, the United States voted for a UN resolution criticizing Portugal's colonial rule in Africa. But then, because Washington wanted continued access to Lajes Air Base in the Azores, Presidents Kennedy and Nixon both strengthened U.S. support for Portugal and voted with the Portuguese on almost every issue involving colonialism.

President Nixon continually refused to receive African heads of state visiting Washington or New York, and Secretary of State Henry Kissinger wouldn't even see African ambassadors in Washington except as a group, an oversight that African statesmen quite properly found demeaning. To justify his boredom with Africa, Kissinger maintained privately that it was impossible to formulate an African policy. The place was too diverse, too politically incohesive, he said; you would need forty or fifty policies, not just a single one.

He was wrong. The Carter Administration gave top priority to forging a more equal partnershp with the Third World. Carter visited Nigeria in 1978—the first U.S. President ever to pay an official visit to a black African country. His Administration was actively involved in the settlement that ended the Rhodesian civil war and led to the independence of Africa's fifty-first nation, Zimbabwe. And Washington began putting some distance between itself and the white supremacist regime in South Africa. Carter and his UN ambassador, Andrew Young, paid so much attention to Africa, in fact, that the British prime minister, James Callaghan, remarked, "There seems to be a number of new Christopher Columbuses setting out from the United States to discover Africa for the first time. Africa has been there for a long time."

Foreign aid represents a reasonably accurate barometer of Washington's interest in an area, and Callaghan might have been surprised to learn that sub-Sahara Africa did not rank high, despite all the time Carter and Young spent discussing it.* In 1979 Washington budgeted only $265 million in developmental assistance for black Africa. That represented seventy-one cents per recipient, or 17 percent of Washington's total world-wide aid commitment. Israel, on the other hand, recieved $785 million that year, and Egypt $750 million. One footnote worth mentioning here: four fifths of Wash-

* Between 1953 and 1981, sub-Sahara Africa received 6 percent of the economic assistance and 1 percent of the military assistance that the United States provided to foreign countries.

ington's aid to black Africa is nonmilitary, while most of the Soviet's is military.

The United States, with an aid budget of $4.7 billion in 1979, remained the biggest contributor in the world, but it was far from the most generous. If you measure aid against wealth, the United States contributes only 0.2 percent of its gross national product to the Third World. That ranked it fifteenth among the seventeen members of the Organization for Economic Cooperation and Development, a grouping of industrialized democracies. (Only Austria and Italy gave proportionately less of their gross national product.) The United States' contribution has grown steadily smaller over the years, falling from 0.5 of GNP in the Eisenhower-Kennedy years, to 0.32 in 1970 to its current low.* The decline has continued under the Reagan Administration, causing former Secretary of State Edmund S. Muskie to remark that the United States "can no longer afford to act as if foreign aid were charity, and as if diplomacy were a diversion. They are as vital as defense."

Black Africa is also important to U.S. business, although it is still a largely untapped market. U.S. investment in black Africa totals only $2.5 billion, with another $1.5 billion in South Africa. (In Latin America, which has fewer people and fewer resources, U.S. investment is six times more; in Brazil alone it is $8 billion.) American exports to black Africa are only $3.4 billion (and $1.3 billion to South Africa), but imports, ranging from oil to coffee to cashew nuts, are $13.6 billion from black Africa (and $1 billion from South Africa). Nearly half the global U.S. trade deficit is with African countries, an imbalance that will continue until the United States makes a greater effort to link its own economy with Africa's developmental priorities.

A peaceful, prosperous Africa serves everyone's interests except the Soviet Union's. But, sadly, Africa has not known a single day of peace since the independence era began. From the deserts of West Africa to the Horn of Africa in the east, this troubled continent

* The most generous nations statistically are Sweden, the Netherlands and Norway, each giving above 0.9 percent of its gross national product. Members of the Organization of Petroleum Exporting Countries provided $5.2 billion of aid in 1979, but many Third World recipients complained that the growth of OPEC's aid has not been as steep as the climb in its oil revenues. The Soviet Union gave $1.4 billion in aid in 1979, the great bulk going to Vietnam, Cuba and North Korea. Collectively the Communist countries give only 0.04 percent of their combined gross national products to developmental aid.

enters the 1980s in a scramble to arm itself with the best weapons it can beg, borrow or buy. Armies across the continent are growing, defense expenditures increasing, armaments becoming more sophisticated. According to the London-based International Institute for Strategic Studies, military spending in sub-Sahara Africa, excluding South Africa, rose between 1975 and 1978 from $1 billion to $3.5 billion. It was the largest defense expenditure for any Third World bloc outside the Middle East. The number of black Africans under arms rose during that period from 475,000 to 750,000, and in 1983 no fewer than ten wars were being fought in Africa.* They ranged from wars of secession to wars of liberation, and they pitted Marxists against Marxists, Western-backed factions against Soviet-backed factions, whites against blacks and blacks against blacks.

"The big powers made our continent a battleground and our people the cannon fodder for their wars," said the Sudan's president, Jaafar Numeiri. "I fear that our continent will go the same path that Asia has taken for twenty years of war and destruction."

Sub-Sahara Africa, with the exception of South Africa, does not manufacture its own weapons, so its wars are waged with weapons imported from abroad. It is, though, an oversimplification to blame the superpowers, as Numeiri did, for Africa's inability to live at peace with itself.

True, the artificial colonial boundaries Africa inherited at independence did exacerbate cross-border hostilities. But even if those borders had never been established, even if the superpowers had not armed the newly independent states, chances are Africa would still be fighting wars, with bows and arrows if necessary. Centuries-old traditions do not change in a decade or two. Nor do men become presidents and generals in Africa by making concessions. They assume and maintain power for the most part because they mastered the arts of guile and force. They do not negotiate with enemies when they can banish or jail or kill. Their solution may be crude and

* Ethiopia was fighting two wars, one against secessionist guerrillas in Eritrea, its northern province, the other against Somali inhabitants of its western region known as the Ogaden. Morocco was fighting an Algeria-supported group called the Polisario for the phosphate-rich Western Sahara (formerly the Spanish Sahara). Spain had pulled out of the area in 1976 after ceding the northern two-thirds to Morocco and the southern third to Mauritania; South Africa was fighting SWAPO (South-West Africa People's Organization) guerillas for Namibia (formerly South-West Africa), a one-time German protectorate that South Africa administered illegally under an outdated (1920) League of Nations mandate. Angola was fighting Jonas Savimbi's guerrillas. Chad was battling Libyan-backed rebels. Zimbabwe, Uganda and Mozambique were combatting antigovernment insurgency movements.

only temporary, but it is an essential tool of governments that have not wielded a consensus among their people and of presidents who have not included in their inner circle those of differing political, tribal or religious persuasions. These outcasts make their voices heard with gunfire, not words.

"The storm has not struck yet," South Africa's Prime Minister John Vorster said in 1977 of the continent's increasing military problems. "We are only experiencing the whirlwinds that go before it."

Even though the majority of Africa's 455 million people do live in peace, Vorster's words were prophetic, and bloodshed under the banners of liberation, secession, religion, nationalism and territorial integrity, increased while the Organization for African Unity watched helplessly, having neither the mechanism to impose its decisions on member states nor the will to condemn member heads of state.

When the OAU mediation committee met in Nairobi in 1979 to discuss the eight wars Africa was then fighting, the secretary-general began the session with these words: "Our task today is to bring a smile back to the lips of our African brothers."

A few delegates groaned. But such bromides were as close as the OAU ever came to taking a stand on anything, except apartheid. Several weeks later the committee sent a group of representatives to Dar es Salaam to consider the Tanzania-Uganda war that eventually resulted in the downfall of Idi Amin. A few hours after arriving, they were headed back to Nairobi for dinner, having said they could not linger because they had forgotten to pack their nightclothes.

"As far as I can tell, they were more interested in wearing pajamas than in settling a war," said Tanzania's foreign minister, Ben Mkapa.

Covering African wars presents Western journalists with some unusual obstacles because the wars themselves are usually shrouded in mystery, secrecy and falsehood. The lack of reliable information from the governments involved and the inaccessibility of the battlefronts make it difficult if not impossible to determine who is winning, who is dying, who is supporting whom, who gets what spoils. Not only is it frequently difficult to tell the players without a scorecard, but sometimes it is impossible to get a scorecard. These jottings from a notebook I kept during the 1979 Tanzania-Uganda war—a war journalists had to cover from neighboring Kenya—illustrate the often undefinable line between fact and faction:

March 10—Libya denies that it is shuttling military supplies into Uganda to bail out President Amin.

March 11—Two Libyan transport planes land at Entebbe air base in Uganda loaded with military supplies and soldiers.

March 19—Amin announces that Palestine Liberation Organization commandos are fighting beside his soldiers on the front lines.

March 25—A PLO official calls a press conference in Tanzania and says: "I want to assure you that no Palestinians are involved in the fighting in Uganda."

March 26—Radio Uganda reports that Amin is trapped in his residence, that the highway from Entebbe to Kampala has been cut, that enemy tanks are closing in on the president's home.

March 27—Radio Uganda makes no mention of the previous day's broadcast, saying only that everything is calm in Uganda and Amin is with his troops.

One British journalist sent from London to East Africa to cover the war succumbed professionally to the lack of information. He couldn't get a visa to enter Uganda and he didn't learn anything very topical from the Ugandan refugees pouring into Kenya, so he sat in his room at Nairobi's Inter-Continental Hotel, haphazardly moving toy tanks on a map of Uganda spread out at his feet. Then he wrote a story based on his map maneuvers. A more enterprising American journalist managed to get through on the telephone to Amin's residence. He identified himself and was told by the official on the other end: "I know you're CIA, so plug me into President Carter first, and we'll give him something to rock 'n' roll about."

The result of this double-talk and no-talk is that reporters frequently must cull their information from second-hand sources—refugees, Western embassies, government radio broadcasts and, all too often, one another. But using your ingenuity can be dangerous in Africa, and the risk is often not worth the value of the story. I remember four European journalists who came through Nairobi a few weeks before Idi Amin was chased out of Uganda by the invading Tanzanian army. One of them had been told by his editor to photograph and interview Amin. The assignment was both absurd and impossible, for Uganda was a scary, paranoid place, closed to the civilized world. Still, the four journalists were determined to get into Uganda by any means possible. Those of us based in Nairobi told them, "You're crazy. Don't try." They went anyway, renting a fisherman's rowboat in Kenya and slipping across Lake Victoria to a small village near Entebbe. Several Ugandan soldiers greeted them politely there, took them to the local police station, and shot them dead.

On a map of Africa there is a region in the east that resembles a rhinoceros horn, jutting into the Gulf of Aden between the Red Sea and the Indian Ocean. This is the so-called Horn of Africa. It consists of three countries, Ethiopia, Somalia and Djibouti, occupies an area slightly larger than Alaska and Oregon combined and has a population of 35 million people. To the west of the mountain spine that cuts Ethiopia in half some of the world's best coffee is grown.* To the east the riverbeds quickly run dry and the scrub-covered plateaus give way to an endless expanse of desert that stretches to the coast. This is the home of the Somalis, a nomadic people, defiant and tough, imbued with both a sense of fatalism and a knowledge of survival, qualities they learned in living with the rhythm of the desert and the beat of war.

Unlike most other Africans, the 4 million people of Somalia are fiercely nationalistic. They share a common language and a common culture and a common belief that their Moslem leaders are descendants of Aquil Abu Talib, cousin of the prophet Mohammed. Isak Dinesen, in her book *Shadows on the Grass*, compared the Somalis to the ancient Icelanders of the Nordic sagas. The Somalis have faced expansionist threats from the Portuguese, Ethiopians, Egyptians, French, English and Italians and never willingly yielded an inch or lost an ounce of spirit. In 1921 the British subdued one Somali leader, Muhammad Abdullah Hassan, only after they bombed his forts. "It is wonderful," said a British officer, "how little we have yet managed to impress the Somalis with our superior power."

For years the Horn of Africa has been synonymous with crisis.

---

* Many etymologists believe the word "coffee" comes from the name Kaffa, a province in southwest Ethiopia that is reputedly the birthplace of coffee.

Wars have dragged on here for centuries longer than the white man has been in Africa. The Soviet Union and the United States, wanting access to the horn's strategic coastal location, have confronted each other here. Christianity and Islam, Marxism and pro-Western socialism have collided here. The evils of poverty and repression fester here. In almost any direction you travel from Mogadishu, the Somali capital, the paved road soon turns into dirt and sand and before long you will happen onto a makeshift camp, where rows of straw huts stretch as far as the eye can see. And there you will find another product of Africa's wars and harsh governments—the refugee, one of five million Africans on the run.

For all her thirty-three years, Dol Abdu Husein has lived in the shadow of war and drought. Planes rain death from the skies and artillery shatters the desert stillness. Water holes go dry, the earth cracks, cattle die. Children whimper with hunger and the camels grow restless, sensing that it is time to move on.

Husein, a tall, graceful Somali woman who has mastered the art of survival, shrugs. She dismisses these forces that control and buffet her life—and that have made her a refugee—with a single, brief observation: "The fates are powerful."

Until a month before I met her in a Somali refugee camp known as Gialalassi, home for Mrs. Husein and her four children had been the Ogaden, the barren Ethiopian province where Somali nomads and Ethiopian farmers have been fighting each other for a thousand years. It is a vast, empty place, full of deprivation and despair. In all her life, Mrs. Husein has never tasted a glass of ice water, never seen a city or flipped an electric switch.

"I would not have left but finally I got too scared," she said, holding her youngest child close to her breast. "The Ethiopian planes came often, bombing our villages and water holes, and many died in their attacks. There are Cuban soldiers everywhere, trying to drive us from our land. It was time to run."

And so under the cover of darkness one night, leaving her soldier husband behind to continue the guerrilla war against Ethiopia, she gathered her children, wrapped all her belongings in a blanket, draped the blanket on her camel's back and headed for Somalia. Thirteen days later she crossed the border. The nomad had officially become a refugee.

"It is very difficult for these people to adjust," the commander of the Gialalassi camp, Colonel Abdullah Haji Ahmed, said. "Their whole way of life has changed and they may never be able to reclaim what is gone.

"All their days they have lived free, unrestricted, moving with their herds to the good grass and water. Now they have no herds and no room to roam and we tell them they must dig latrines for sanitation. They don't understand that."

All across Africa there are similar scenes at camps where people like Mrs. Husein live on charity and sufferance. They have fled from tyranny, revolution, tribal animosity, apartheid, poverty, war and drought, and their displacement has caused what the United Nations calls the greatest refugee problem the world has known since World War II.

The African refugees—one of every 100 persons on the continent is a refugee—represent more than half the world's nine million homeless people. They are larger in number than the combined populations of Benin, Burundi, Chad, Botswana, the Central African Republic, Djibouti, Gabon, Gambia, Liberia and Swaziland.

In 1965, when 535,000 Africans were classified as refugees, the All-African Conference of Churches blamed the exodus largely on racial discrimination in white-ruled southern Africa. The conference issued a new report in 1979, noting that the majority of today's refugees are black Africans victimized by black dictatorships.

"Many Africans in positions of power—the power elite—are not genuinely interested in making their people aware of the basic human rights in society," the report said. "Given the present situation with human rights on this continent, anyone in Africa can become a refugee."

In many cases the flight of refugees follows no logical pattern, reflecting the artificiality of Africa's national boundaries. About 400,-000 Angolans, for example, have fled to Zaire, and 200,000 Zairians have taken refuge in Angola. Thousands of Burundians have escaped to neighboring Rwanda, and thousands of Rwandans have moved into Burundi. In all, twenty-five of Africa's fifty-one countries have sizable refugee populations. Among them are deposed presidents, former cabinet ministers and guerrilla leaders, wealthy businessmen and university professors and, by the millions, peasants and nomads, whose only crime was to be in the wrong place at the wrong time.

Tragically, Africa's refugee problem is of more concern to the international community than it is to Africa itself. The same is true of food shortages, population growth and the misfortunes wrought by droughts and other natural disasters. It is, in fact, to most African presidents' advantage to keep their countries in a constant state of emergency, because then they can parlay the crisis into a windfall of monetary assistance and can justify the repressive measures they use in the name of national survival. In one particularly bad harvest year, for instance, Kenya sold 80,000 tons of wheat to Zambia, then declared that it had been struck by an emergency shortage. Western donor agencies filled the quota, and everyone was happy: Kenya banked the proceeds of its sale to Zambia, received free wheat to make up the difference and didn't have to go through the hassles of planning for the storage and distribution of its crops. And the donor agencies once again had been able to explain their existence by ticking off statistics on how many people they had saved from starvation.

President Julius Nyerere of Tanzania nicely summed up this crisis mentality, telling the United Nations High Commissioner for Refugees Poul Hartling: "I love the refugees. They cultivate the country for me. But I have no money. You bring in the money."

Of all the countries I visited in Africa, none remains etched more clearly in my memory than Ethiopia. A land rich in history and full of international intrigue, Ethiopia today is the fulcrum for the balance of power in the Horn of Africa, and it is here, as much as anywhere on the continent, that one learns just how fickle political alliances can be.

The name Ethiopia is derived from the Greek words "to burn" and "face"—the land of people with burnt faces. Except for Egypt, Ethiopia is the oldest independent state in Africa. The fertile mile-high plateaus of the interior are surrounded by craggy mountains that shoot almost straight up from the desert floor below. These mountains formed a natural barrier that enabled the Ethiopians to repel outside penetration and, living in isolation, to develop their own culture over more than two thousand years. The mountains made Ethiopia so inaccessible that it was one of only two countries (the other being Liberia) in black Africa never colonized by Europe. And it is the only country where Christianity (Coptic) is indigenous and not imported by European missionaries.

According to legend—and it is only legend—the first Ethiopian ruler, Menelik, was a descendant of King Solomon and the Queen of Sheba. Many Ethiopians have European facial features, and the dominant ethnic group, the Amharas (from a Hebrew word meaning "mountain people"), look down on other black Africans as inferior. Long before the rest of East Africa had discovered the wheel, Ethiopians were recording their history in a written language, Amharic.

So isolated was Ethiopia that in Homeric times the Ethiopians were known as "the farthest away of all mankind" and their country was supposed to be the place where the sun set. It was not until 1895 that the Ethiopians faced their first major challenge from abroad, an Italian invasion. But the Italians were soundly defeated at the Battle of Adowa and forced to withdraw, marking the first time any European army had been vanquished in black Africa. Ethiopia's independence continued uninterrupted until 1935, when the country was conquered by Italy's fascist dictator, Benito Mussolini. The emperor, Haile Selassie, forced into exile and living in Bath, England, during the Italian occupation, took his case to the League of Nations. The league ignored his plea for assistance.

"Outside the kingdom of the Lord," Selassie said in an address to the league in Geneva in 1936, "there is no nation which is greater than any other. God and history will remember your judgment."

Selassie returned from exile in 1941, after British, Indian and Ethiopian troops had driven out the Italians, and moved back into his hilltop palace around which thirty lions roamed free. From the palace in Addis Ababa ("new flower" in the Amharic language), Selassie looked down on a sprawling capital where, as time went on, slums and modern office buildings stood side by side and the past seemed forever in conflict with the present.

Even today, caravans of donkeys plod each morning down the rough streets of Addis Ababa, their backs piled high with wheat, their masters stopping from time to time at the mud homes where an empty tin can placed on a stick by the door indicated that homemade beer is for sale inside. Like other old men in Ethiopia, a donkey driver would coat his head with butter to cure a headache and wrap his limbs with religious scrolls to heal wounds and scare away evil spirits. When he returned home at day's end, his tired feet were washed and massaged by his wife.

Emperor Selassie made every decision, controlled every cent in the treasury and never held a real election. But unlike some of Africa's modern-day authoritarian rulers, the Lion of Judah, as he was called, did bring some positive reforms to Ethiopia. He spent one-third his budget on education, built some excellent hospitals and schools, and by African standards, was not brutally repressive, holding fewer than a hundred political prisoners in the mid-fifties. He was a stuffy man of dignity and grace, at home in the company of presidents and prime ministers. With the help of the United States, Selassie brought Ethiopia to the threshold of modern times.

The conservative, anti-Communist emperor had turned to the United States as his chief ally partly because Washington had money to spare and partly because Washington had never recognized the legitimacy of the Italian conquest. From 1954 to 1977 Ethiopia was a client-state of the United States. At one time Washington had key Americans posted in the ministries of foreign affairs, finance and commerce. Washington armed and trained Ethiopia's army. Washington ran top-secret communications and intelligence-gathering military facilities staffed by Americans. Washington gave Selassie $2 million to buy a yacht.

But while Selassie and the royal family lived in splendor, the Ethiopians in the early 1970s languished in poverty with an annual per capita income of $90 and a literacy rate of 7 percent. They labored, virtually as slaves, on land owned by imperial princes and princesses. Occasionally, there were rumors of unrest in the army and whispered talk among young men educated in England or the United States that Ethiopia and Africa were not in step. But Selassie seemed firmly in charge and several attempts to unseat him were amateurish affairs that hardly got by the planning stage. Then, in 1973, a drought swept Wallo province. The government tried to keep the disaster a secret, not wanting to admit it was unable to care for its people's needs. More than 200,000 people died. At about the same time Selassie, then eighty-one years old, was photographed tossing scraps of fresh meat to his two Great Danes. The stories of discontent in the barrcks were no longer rumors.

Selassie was overthrown the next year, after forty-four years as emperor, by a group of enlisted men. If any African country needed a revolution, Ethiopia did; unfortunately, though, it got a Marxist group of revolutionaries whose style was murderous and vindictive. Under the military junta, headed by Mengistu Haile-Mariam—a five-foot-five member of the dark-skinned Galla tribe that had long been dominated by the Amharas—hundreds of Ethiopians with ties to the royal family were executed; scores of Selassie's relatives were murdered or chained to walls in the wine cellars of the imperial palaces; thousands of suspected "counterrevolutionaries" were gunned down on the streets; an estimated 30,000 persons were jailed. When one member of the junta questioned the government's terror tactics at an official meeting, Mengistu calmly leaned back in his chair, pulled out his revolver and shot him in the head. Dissent diminished.

Selassie was locked up in a wing of his palace. For a while the junta put out occasional releases on his health, giving the unlikely explanation at one point that he had gone on a hunger strike. Then the releases stopped. No official announcement was ever made, but word was passed through Addis Ababa that the emperor had died of poisoning. Haile Selassie, the most enduring and eloquent head of state modern-day Africa had produced, was buried in an unmarked grave whose location is known only to the tough young soldiers now running the ancient empire.

The thirty-eight-year-old Mengistu, who looked as innocent as an ROTC cadet when he attended OAU summits dressed in a Western business suit, turned out to be an unpleasant fellow with no pretense of compassion. When Eritrean secessionists threatened to kidnap his wife and children, he snapped, "Go ahead. Boil them in oil for all I care." Before long, he replaced Selassie's portraits that hung throughout Addis Ababa with his own and started living in the grand style of the deposed emperor. His underlings became as sycophantic as had been Selassie's. A new cult had been born.

The coup gave the Soviet Union a grand opportunity. The junta was speaking with an increasingly radical voice and was embarrassed by its close military and economic relationship with the capitalistic United States. And the junta needed two things Moscow had plenty of: guns to put down the secessionist movement in Eritrea province* and the guerrilla war waged by Somalis in the Ogaden; and guidance on how to turn a feudal society into a Marxist state.

But the Soviet Union had a problem. Ethiopia and next-door So-

* Eritrea was an Italian colony from the nineteenth century until 1941. A United Nations resolution in 1952 ended British administration, and Eritrea was federated with Ethiopia under an agreement that gave it considerable autonomy, including the right to elect its own parliament. In 1962 Haile Selassie abolished the federation unilaterally and absorbed Eritrea as Ethiopia's fourteenth province. About 40,000 Arab-backed, Marxist-oriented Eritreans have been fighting for twenty years to regain their independence. The guerrillas are divided into three factions, which have battled one another when there are no Ethiopians in the area to fight.

malia were bitter enemies who had been fighting periodically in the Ogaden since time immemorial, and Somalia was Moscow's most important ally in Africa. Moscow could hardly be friends with both Ethiopia and Somalia. It was going to have to choose, and in many ways Ethiopia and its 31 million people presented a more inviting target: Ethiopia was nearly twice as big as Somalia and its potential for development was far greater; it offered two major ports on the Red Sea, Assab and Massawa, and possession of the main source of the Blue Nile, the heartline of Egypt.

Somalia, in 1974, had become the first black African government to sign a treaty of friendship and cooperation with the Soviet Union, and the 6,000 Russian soldiers and civilians there ran the place as though they were operating out of a mini-Kremlin. They controlled the ministries of defense and information, the secret police and an important military facility at Berbera. They turned the ragtag Somali army into a 25,000-man fighting force, armed with heavy artillery and AK-47 assault rifles. They supplied the Somali air force with MiG fighters, and the schools with teachers who taught more political theory than mathematics. They put together an impressive military parade each May Day, and they spent their weekends sunbathing by the Soviet beach house, shooing away barefoot Somali children who tried to sell them seashells and homemade sandals.

And the Americans? Well, they had rushed into Somalia after independence with millions of dollars of aid money, but now they were unwelcome ogres, the victims of their own alliance with Ethiopia and of a propaganda campaign orchestrated by the Soviet Union. Peace Corps volunteers were stoned in the streets of Mogadishu, and in 1971 the organization was forced to pull out of Somalia entirely. U.S. diplomats were spat upon, and by 1977 Washington had closed down its aid mission—none of its agricultural projects had done much good anyway—and had reduced its sizable embassy staff to just three envoys. "There's nothing to do on this assignment except catch up on my reading," one of them said. Posters of Uncle Sam being stomped by Somali peasants were all over the capital, and the residence of the U.S. ambassador, John Loughran, was broken into, probably in an attempt to find documents that would discredit him. The U.S. embassy phone was tapped, its mail was opened, and Somali civilians were forbidden by presidential decree from talking to foreigners. Any Somali who dared set foot inside an American's home would immediately have been branded a spy.

The xenophobia reached its peak in the spring of 1977 as Somalia prepared for a full-scale invasion of Ogaden to fulfill its long-standing territorial claim. Once again the Horn of Africa was to become a battlefield. But this time the combatants would include Cubans, Russians and, indirectly, Americans, and the Ogaden war would lead to the most extraordinary flip-flop of superpower partnerships independent Africa had ever seen. It might be useful to take a brief historical look at the Ogaden to understand what was about to happen.

The Ogaden is an arid Montana-sized plateau reaching from the eastern deserts to the inland mountains that flow in the shape of a crescent through Ethiopia. The land is of little use to anyone except the nomads who wander there with their camels and cattle, and from the tenth to the fifteenth centuries these nomads—Moslems from the Arabian peninsula who would eventually be known as Somalis and Christians from the Ethiopian kingdom—battled for control of the Ogaden's waterholes and grazing lands.

Somalia was carved up by the European powers in a series of treaties that followed the Berlin Conference of 1884–85. One chunk was given to the British to form the northern third of Kenya, another to France as the Territory of Afars and Issas (now Djibouti) and a third—the Ogaden—to independent Ethiopia. (Emperor Menelik of Ethiopia signed treaties in 1897 and 1908 with Britain and Italy, respectively, formalizing his jurisdiction in the Ogaden; the Somalis were neither consulted nor present at the signings.) What remained of Somalia after its dismemberment was divided into Italian Somaliland, with its capital at Mogadishu, and British Somaliland, with a capital at Hargeisa.

In 1934 Italian-led Somali troops clashed with Ethiopian soldiers at a watering hole for camels in the Ogaden known as Wal Wal. Mussolini used that battle as an excuse to conquer and occupy Ethiopia. He detached the Ogaden from Ethiopia, ruling it as part of Italian Somaliland. (Later, in 1941, the British defeated the Italians in East Africa and established a military administration to govern the Ogaden.)

Britain proposed in 1950 at the United Nations that the five parts of Somali be reunited. Ironically, that proposal was shelved largely because of opposition from the Soviet Union—which two decades later would be instrumental in preparing Somalia for its ill-fated attempt to win back the Ogaden militarily. Rebuffed at the United Nations, Britain returned the Ogaden to Ethiopia in 1955 at the insistence of Selassie. Five years later British Somaliland and Italian Somaliland were united to form the independent republic of Somalia. Though not supported by black Africa—which considers the colonial boundaries inviolable (i.e., the boundaries they inherited at independence)—the Somalis still want to reclaim their missing chunks as part of a "Greater Somalia." Each of the white star's five points on the flag represents one of the regions populated with the homogeneous Somalis. So when one speaks of the hostility between the Somalis and the Ethiopians in the Ogaden, he is talking about a hatred implanted in a thousand years of strife.

Throughout the 1970s Moscow prepared the Somali military for its invasion of the Ogaden, which was lightly defended by the American-backed Ethiopians. But then, in 1977, with Selassie dead and Ethiopia under the control of young revolutionaries, the Russians began to have second thoughts. They virtually begged Somalia to scrap its planned attack and proposed that Somalia and Ethiopia merge into a Marxist federation. Mohamed Siad Barré, Somalia's Moslem president, scoffed. The Russians started leaving Somalia in large numbers, and Barré secretly dispatched an envoy—his American dentist, who lived in New York—to Washington to see if the Carter Administration had anything to offer. Yes, the Administration said, the United States was willing to give Somali "defensive" weapons if Barré cut his ties to the Soviet Union. Barré told Moscow it would have to choose—it could back Somalia or Ethiopia, but not both—and just before dawn one June morning, he sent his army across the border and into the Ogaden. The Ethiopian defenses crumbled. Within two months Somalia had captured 90 percent of the region, and Barré's dream of reuniting all his people under a single flag seemed within reach.

Until then, Somalia had been one of Africa's most isolated countries, as closed to the outside world as North Korea and completely off-limits to Western journalists. Suddenly, though, Barré had something he wanted to tell the world and Somalia started passing out visas like supermarket discount coupons. A group of us descended on Mogadishu, looking for a way into the Ogaden. We hung around the Uruba Hotel, a new place with a lovely seaside view and toilets that overflowed when flushed, permeating every room with an outhouse smell. We pestered the government for transportation to the

Ogaden, scraped together some interviews around town and went to a press conference in which Barré denied that his troops had invaded anything. All the fighting, he said, was being done by Somali inhabitants of the Ogaden. And where did these peasants get their tanks and heavy artillery? Barré, a former policeman who was born in the Ogaden, said he wasn't sure; they must have "borrowed" them from the Somali army.

Barré claimed, not without some justification, that the Ethiopian presence in the Ogaden was a colonial one. And there was no doubt that the Ethiopians had been harsh rulers, intent on driving the Somali nomads back across the border. The Ethiopians had poisoned water holes and on occasion, according to some Somalis we talked to, cut off women's breasts to deprive children of milk. The Ethiopians collected taxes at gunpoint and maintained administrative control with second-rate soldiers and policemen who had been more or less exiled to the Ogaden by the government in Addis Ababa.

"I have lived under three colonial powers—the British, the Italians and the Abyssinians [Ethiopians]," said a seventy-one-year-old Ogaden peasant, Husein Liban, a frail man with a wispy white beard, watery eyes and a single tooth. "The Italians and the British exploited us and harmed us, too, but they did it gradually. The Abyssinians were quick and primitive. If you have to have an injection, you will choose the one that only hurts a little rather than the one that goes deep into your body."

We had met the old man in Jijiga, a one-street desert town the Somalis had just captured from the fleeing Ethiopians. Jijiga had no running water and no electricity, and what was known as the Genet Hotel was nothing more than a large windowless room with a sand-covered floor, a battered sofa and three cot beds. We had reached Jijiga after a five-hour drive in Land-Rovers provided by the Somali government, traveling straight across the desert on a moonless night to avoid detection by Ethiopian war planes. Everything seemed so mysterious, so distant from any people or place I had ever seen before—the solitary figures wrapped in robes who appeared with their camels out of the icy blackness and watched us pass with silent stares, the little towns that emerged as an outline of mud shacks and disappeared into the night as though they had been only an illusion, the rutted desert tracks that seemed to have no end and no direction but which our driver negotiated as surely as if he were reading a city street map.

It was just past three in the morning when our three four-wheel-drive vehicles arrived in the abandoned Ethiopian army camp on a rise overlooking Jijiga. The sand turned to rocky earth, and our driver cut off the track, heading overland to a small dark building made of mud and cement blocks. A candle burned inside, beneath an Italian-charted map of the Ogaden, and half a dozen Somali guerrillas with rifles rose from a long dining table to welcome us in halting English. The rebel leader, Abdullah Abdi, motioned us toward the table, where a roast of freshly slaughtered goat had been placed in our honor. Like our hosts, we pulled off the greasy meat with our fingers. The meat, which was barely cooked, was chased down with gulps from a bottle of dust-covered Scotch that one of the Somalis had taken from an ammunition box. Stomachs churning, we reclined in a corner to wait out the night.

Word of our presence spread quickly through Jijiga, and early the next day the entire town gathered outside the Genet Hotel to demonstrate for us their hatred of the Ethiopians. The people, perhaps 2,000 in all, came from out of nowhere in a rush. One moment the place was as lifeless as a ghost town, the next alive and teeming, swirling with a carnival-like motion and color. The crowd moved as a single body, dancing and prancing, surrounding us and carrying us with it. "Victory to the front!" they shrieked, their cries echoing through the desert valley. Old men, barefoot and spindly, waved their spears and daggers and machetes and odd assortments of old rifles in our faces. The children laughed and flung rocks at stray "Ethiopian" dogs, chuckling gleefully when one was struck and limped away yelping. The women swayed among their menfolk in a hypnotic trance, their delicately featured faces wreathed in smiles, their pounding drums and tribal war calls melting into the clamorous welter.

For twenty minutes the euphoric crowd reeled along the sandy, unpaved street, falling quiet only when Abdullah Abdi jumped atop a 1959 Chevrolet sedan outside the hotel. "Back to your homes now," he shouted, cupping his hands to his mouth. "We do not want a big crowd on the streets, because this is the time of day when the planes like to come, and you know . . ."

But the warning was too late. The Ethiopian war planes had come from the north, graceful and silent against the soft blue Ogaden skies. In the streets below, where we stood with our notebooks and cameras, the Somalis neither heard their high-level approach nor sensed that death was once again imminent in Jijiga.

Suddenly the planes veered and plunged, hurtling straight for the hotel. And in the split second it takes for disbelief to turn to horror, they were upon us, two silvery American-made F-5 fighters leading the attack, a poky old British Canberra Bomber bringing up the rear. Bombs thudded and cannon barked like firecrackers and people screamed, diving and tumbling and elbowing their way to the ground in a panic of confusion. I dove toward the old Chevrolet, my camera and cigarettes and sunglasses all headed in different directions. I clutched my notebook with both hands and squirmed to make myself as flat as possible. There were moans and cries all around me and I remember thinking that I had seen—which I'm sure I hadn't—the face of one of the pilots, smiling as he flashed by fifty feet above. I had an absurd reaction, wanting to stand up and scream, "For God's sake, don't hit *me*! I'm an *American*!"

Four times the planes passed over us, engines shrieking, guns rattling, the ground trembling. At the end of the first three passes they pulled straight up at the outskirts of town, circled high above Jijiga for what seemed like a tantalizing hour—but was actually only a few seconds—and dove again upon us like hawks seeking their prey. Then, after a fourth pass, they were gone, streaking back to the north.

The first strafing run decapitated a Somali nurse named Sarah outside the ramshackle eighty-bed hospital. It also blew away a ten-year-old boy in a mud home across the street. The hospital's only doctor was critically wounded by shrapnel as he rested in his bed, and outside one ward a civilian patient writhed on a stretcher, his stomach and head torn open. He moaned his final prayers to Allah, then his body quivered and relaxed. The man who had been comforting him removed the plasma tube from his arm and walked toward the toolshed that in times of crisis also served as a temporary morgue.

In all, seven Somalis were killed; twenty or thirty were gravely wounded. The attack was apparently designed not to destroy Jijiga, but only to demoralize the people there. Indeed, seven deaths were not many for a people so inured to never-ending war. In the Ethiopian air attack a few days earlier, three had died; in the one before that, nine. And over ten centuries of warfare between the Somalis and Ethiopians, fought first with spears, then with multimillion-dollar war machines supplied by foreign allies, those small numbers had grown large, and the hating had become very deep.

"We have lived with war for many years," said a blacksmith, Mohammed Heeban. "For as long as I can remember, as long as my grandparents can remember, there has been war in the Ogaden. We are used to death. It is not a big price to pay if our people can get our land back from the Abyssinians."

Chances are good that Heeban's children may not know much peace either. For one Saturday night that November, shortly after we left the Ogaden, American spy satellites detected an unexpected massive movement of Soviet aircraft heading for the Horn of Africa. The Russians had made their choice. Fifteen thousand Cuban troops and $1 billion worth of Soviet weapons were on the way to Ethiopia. Soon Soviet-advised Ethiopian troops, spearheaded by Soviet tanks and Cuban infantrymen, would sweep back into the Ogaden, recapturing Jijiga and the other desert towns lost during the Somali offensive. The Somali guerrillas would drift back into their mountain hideouts to restock arms and prepare for hit-and-run nighttime attacks, just as their forefathers had been launching for generations.

The arms lift resulted in a stunning shift in the Horn of Africa's military balance, international loyalties and political ideologies. President Siad Barré threw out the Russians—most of whom simply moved to Ethiopia—and never again uttered a favorable word about Marxism. He ordered the removal of all anti-American posters in Mogadishu, ended the surveillance of American diplomats and asked for assistance from Washington, which had reneged on its promise to give Somali "defensive" arms. The Americans returned with a diplomatic mission of sixty-nine persons and $86 million for military, developmental and refugee assistance. They moved into the residences and offices abandoned by the Russians and began negotiations to take over the former Soviet military base at Berbera. The Ethiopians meanwhile expelled the Americans, smeared Addis Ababa with grotesque caricatures of Uncle Sam, signed a treaty of friendship and cooperation with the Soviet Union and announced their intention to become black Africa's first authentic Communist state. Washington's closest African ally was now a Soviet satellite, and Moscow's African stepchild was under the tutelage of the United States. Ethiopia and Somalia had put themselves on the open market and sold their allegiances to the highest bidder with the best deal. One day, no doubt, the arrangement will come unhinged and the loyalties will change again.

The flip-flop in the Horn underscored once more that Africa's fortunes rest in the hands of the Eastern and Western factions and that both blocs consider Africa important enough to make substantial military and economic investments in the continent. The Russians have been willing to fight to the last drop of Cuban blood, the Americans to counter Soviet expansionism with guns if not surrogate troops. Certainly Africa's strategic location and potential wealth—as well as its inability to defend itself—make it vulnerable to outside manipulation that could lead to foreign confrontation.

Although I have had few kind words about the Soviet role in Africa, each African country should, I think, be free to choose its own form of government. Marxism has been no more a disaster in Mozambique than capitalism has been in Ghana, but by its very nature, Marxism denies the Africans the economic advancement and individual dignity they seek to become a free people. To counter this, the West must continue to provide the financial assistance Africa needs to develop, even if much of that money is filtered off by corrupt presidents and ill-conceived projects. And, sadly, it probably will have to continue to provide the guns Africa needs to secure its borders even if some of those guns are used by despotic presidents to perpetuate their own rule. The alternative is to let Moscow take Africa piece by piece, exploiting the fragility of individual countries and choosing Communism for these people, who would not have chosen it for themselves.

SEPARATE ROADS
FOR TWO NEIGHBORS

▲

To those who speak of a Pan-African union, I ask,
What are we supposed to share? Each other's poverty?

—President Félix Houphouët-Boigny
of the Ivory Coast

For the first twenty years, we in Guinea have concentrated on developing the mentality of our people. Now
we are ready to move on to other business.

—President Ahmed Sékou Touré
of Guinea

THE IVORY COAST AND GUINEA in West Africa share many things,
among them a common border. Both countries are former French
colonies, both have had but one president, both have recognized the
importance of agricultural development, both have enjoyed political
stability, both are struggling to reach shared goals of economic
growth, individual dignity and national self-reliance, and both were
born as nations in the same era, the Ivory Coast in 1960, Guinea in
1958.

Back in the dying days of colonialism, Guinea was the rich child
of the French family and was, most agreed, destined to become the
wealthiest nation in black Africa. It was Africa's leading banana exporter, and its verdant farmlands fed much of French-speaking
West Africa. Its earth held one-third the world's known bauxite reserves, more than two billion tons of high-grade ore, and enough
diamonds and gold to fill a dozen Fort Knoxes. Its three major rivers
offered great potential for hydroelectric development, and its capital, Conakry, a tidy white-washed little town perched on Tumbo Island and surrounded by blue ocean, attracted thousands of French
tourists. The beaches were lined with palms, the restaurants were

staffed by chefs from Paris, and a deluxe room in the seaside Hotel de France cost no more than a bottle of inexpensive Chablis.

The Ivory Coast had no such good fortune. Its heavy surf, treacherous harbors and lack of minerals discouraged the early European settlers who pushed on east and established their forts on the Gold Coast (now Ghana). The dense forests of the southwest were virtually impenetrable, and the dry red earth of the north yielded little except dust. At the end of World War II, the Ivory Coast had a one-crop economy, coffee, which accounted for two thirds of its exports, and a capital, Abidjan, with a small expatriate population and 20,000 African residents who lulled away the tropical days in their mud huts, seldom bothering to even catch a fish for dinner in the nearby lagoon. The Ivory Coast, everyone thought, was destined to join the line of international beggars.

But the predictions were wrong. From the first day of independence, the Ivory Coast and Guinea set off on divergent roads, the former pursuing a capitalistic course heavily influenced by France, the latter a radical philosophy—"Marxism in African clothes," President Sékou Touré called it—under the sponsorship of the Soviet Union. In each case just one man—the president—was responsible for deciding the path his country should take toward national self-reliance. Those decisions made more than twenty years ago have produced dramatically different results. They offer a fascinating insight into the role of ideology in the Third World and into the power of a single man to determine the fate of his nation for generations to come.

President Félix Houphouët-Boigny of the Ivory Coast is an uncommon figure amid the tumult and violence of Africa, speaking with a soft, reasoned voice, forgiving those dedicated to his downfall (even those who have tried to kill him), telling his people, "We must go slowly, my children, for we are in a hurry."

A devout Catholic who never drinks or smokes, Houphouët-Boigny wears black homburg hats and three-piece suits and meets secretly with South African leaders, believing that dialogue solves more problems than diatribe. He has a great fondness for France—dividing his summers between an apartment in Paris and an estate in Switzerland—and he disdains the radical rhetoric that has become so characteristic of African politics. He welcomes Western journalists, issuing visas to all who apply, because, he says, the Ivory

Coast has nothing to hide. Which, in fact, it doesn't: not one execution has ever been carried out in the Ivory Coast since independence and the country doesn't even hold a single political prisoner.

Félix Houphouët-Boigny (the name Boigny means "the ram") was born in 1905, the son of a wealthy Baoule chief. He made his way through the French colonial education system, studying medicine in Dakar, Senegal, and became a respected public health official and prosperous planter before entering politics in 1944. That year he created the Ivory Coast's first agricultural union, which later became the forum for planters demanding minimum prices for coffee and cocoa crops, denied them by the colonial regime's discriminatory laws.

At the end of World War II he went to France for the first time, as the Ivory Coast's representative in the Parlement. Within a few years he had become a minister in the government of Prime Minister Guy Mollet, the first African colonial to hold a cabinet post in a European government. As late as 1959, the year before independence, he was still declaring that the Ivory Coast was not ready for nationhood. "Perhaps my grandchildren . . ." he said.

But he returned home and immediately ensured his popularity by abolishing the single most hated feature of colonial rule, a labor law that allowed the French planters to conscript workers from any village in the country. He may have been in France all those years (1946 to 1958), but his heart remained in Africa; although his debts to France were great, he probably never made a presidential decision—including the expulsion of the Russian embassy from Abidjan in 1969—that was designed to please the French rather than to benefit the Ivorians.

Houphouët-Boigny competed successfully with the French on their own terms. He mastered their colonial system and he learned how to use the European. Despite what his critics say, he didn't sell out to France; he simply used France's resources—money and people—for his country's betterment and he did it at a relatively small cost to the Ivorians.

It is a mark of Houphouët-Boigny's confidence that he does not surround himself with the symbolic trappings favored by other African presidents. He doesn't wear a leopard-skin cap or carry a fly whisk or wave a white handkerchief. He doesn't display his Africanism on his sleeve because, in competing with the French and succeeding, he has no hangups about the Europeans or the Africans. He knows precisely who he is.

Houphouët-Boigny is a short, stocky man in his mid-seventies, respectfully called Le Vieux (The Old Man) by his countrymen. If he appears out of step with mainstream Africa, as he often does, it raises some questions about what beat Africa is marching to. For Houphouët-Boigny has presided over a country that has enjoyed the fastest, steadiest growth of any non–oil producer in sub-Sahara Africa (except South Africa). The African backwater has become the African miracle, and passengers landing at Abidjan's gleaming, air-conditioned international airport often shake their heads, thinking they must be debarking on the wrong continent. As the saying goes, Abidjan is very nice and very convenient to Africa.

From its modest beginnings it has grown into black Africa's most luxurious metropolis, as clean and orderly as it is modern. Pastel-shaded office buildings soar twenty stories high, superhighways carry trucks laden with export produce to the port, the elegant shops and bustling markets are awash with goods, the restaurants are perhaps the best in all Africa. Abidjan even has its own Club Méditerranée and its own artificial-ice skating rink (the only other one is in South Africa) and a booming tourist industry that pumps many million francs into the economy each year.

Of course, skating rinks and $80-a-day hotel rooms may be fine for the visiting Westerner, but they don't mean much to the underpaid resident Ivorian. Indeed, the skeptics are quick to scoff at the Ivory Coast, saying its rapid growth is superficial, that its prosperity is dependent on the continued presence of French nationals, that development dollars have been concentrated in the cities, not the countryside. Their suspicions were heightened in 1982 when, for the first time since independence, the country experienced zero industrial growth. Just as alarming, the foreign debt was growing and students were openly questioning whether democracy was possible in a one-party political system. But the Ivory Coast had still moved lightyears ahead of its neighbors. Even in the villages, a traveler sees telecommunications lines and paved roads and running water and tin roofs for the one-room huts. They are the milestones by which progress in rural Africa is judged.

Largely because the Ivory Coast has avoided political adventurism and shunned hefty expenditures on defense and wasteful projects, the country has been able to devote 20 percent of its budget to education, and school attendance has risen from 22 percent to 55 percent since independence; literacy is a remarkably high 60 percent, more than twice the continental average.

The country's gross national product—the sum of all goods and services produced—has tripled since 1965. Palm-oil production has increased sevenfold, making the Ivory Coast the world's largest producer. Per capita income has jumped from $70 to $1,000, the highest of any non–oil producer in Africa (except for South Africa and the Seychelles), making the country so well off that it is not even eligible for United States' developmental assistance.

Most significantly, the Ivory Coast has been one of the few African countries that has been able to expand and diversify its agricultural sector, the lifeblood of its economic gusto. Coffee production, for example, has tripled, although coffee's share of export earnings has fallen from two-thirds to one-third. The dry northern quarter of the nation is now a major sugar producer; the forests of the southwest have been conquered and harvested for timber export; the lowlands of the swampy, sweltering south have been transformed into plantations that have made the Ivory Coast Africa's leading exporter of bananas and pineapples; a canal has been cut through the sandbanks and lagoons to create an excellent artificial harbor at Abidjan. The Ivory Coast, in short, has done what every African country talked about doing in 1960 but which none, with the possible exception of Kenya, managed to accomplish.

Houphouët-Boigny, who calls himself the nation's "No. 1 Peasant" but lives in regal fashion, admits privately that he took a calculated risk back in the sixties. Instead of being caught up in the nationalistic fever of the day, he opened his doors to foreign investors and expatriate residents with laws that imposed few restrictions on transfer of profits and capital. He resisted the temptation to industrialize, believing it more important to develop the country's agricultural resources first, and then to concentrate on providing efficient ports, good roads, communications and power.

To Africa's new breed of young, radical leaders, Houphouët-Boigny is an anachronism. He is too French, too bourgeois, too paternal to suit the mood of the 1980s. He is not, in their parlance, a revolutionary, yet what he accomplished is nothing less than a revolution, a fundamental change in his country's socioeconomic structure. It is a revolution in which no one died, and no one had to go into political exile. And to those who call him a neocolonist and to those who denounce his use of palaver instead of power, he replies huffily, "Nobody more than I, and no people more than the Ivorian people, aspire more toward peace through dialogue. I have given every proof of this and at a great risk."

Consider these examples of conciliation and compassion, all but unheard of in Africa: in 1961 a group of army officers arrested for plotting a coup were startled to receive daily visits from the president they had tried to overthrow. H.B., as his friends call him, sat on their steel bunks hour after hour, trying to convince them that their judgment was flawed. All were eventually released. Five years later Houphouët-Boigny released three former cabinet ministers and ninety-three others who had been convicted of trying to assassinate him in another coup attempt. He reduced the death sentences of ten others involved in the plot to six years in prison. One of those sentenced to death was Jean Baptiste Mockey. H.B. released him, befriended him, attended his daughter's wedding and later made him minister of health.

When university students went on strike in 1977, Houphouët-Boigny didn't call out the army, as most African presidents are wont to do in similar situations. He spent three days talking with the students, hearing their grievances, urging them to return quietly and proceed with their education, which they did.

The composition of the country's population also offers some telling evidence of the political and economic atmosphere in the Ivory Coast. Unlike many African countries from which thousands of nationals have fled to escape repression and poverty, as many as one quarter of the Ivory Coast's 8 million people originally came from other African nations. Most are laborers who immigrate for several years to build financial nest eggs, working in the factories and forests and plantations, where they can earn perhaps $800 in a single season. When they drift back home, to the millet fields of Mali, to the idleness of Guinea, or to the overgrown cocoa plantations of Ghana, they carry with them radios and shirts and cans of cooking oil, goods often unavailable at any price in other African countries.

From the inland Sahelian countries of Upper Volta and Niger come the cattle herders, moving with their animals along the shoulder of the roads toward the Abidjan slaughterhouses. They gather in the flat, treeless plains near the international airport, the gleaming Abidjan skyline in the distance, bulldozers and dust all about as ground is prepared for new factories and new office buildings and new roads. They have made this journey of hundreds of miles because their cattle will fetch a higher price and be in greater demand in the Ivory Coast, and gathered there, among their milling, restless cattle, they talk of money. Given the opportunity, almost everyone in Africa is a capitalist.

While Houphouët-Boigny was the force that gave the Ivorians

their opportunity for growth, France was the strength that enabled them to capitalize on it. France provided the capital and the manpower that transformed the Ivory Coast, and today Frenchmen are everywhere, their numbers and influence overwhelming. More than 50,000 French nationals live in the Ivory Coast, five times the total at independence. The World Bank estimates that they hold 80 percent of the jobs in those occupations that require a university degree. French businessmen control up to 40 percent of the investment in the Ivory Coast's industry and 50 percent of its trade (although the agricultural sector remains in Ivorian hands). Six hundred French soldiers provide the backbone of the Ivory Coast's external security, thus necessitating little more than token defense spending by Houphouët-Boigny, and French civil servants play key decision-making roles in every governmental ministry. If you walk through the ministry of planning and development, you will find that the minister and his two or three top deputies are African and the janitors are African, but almost everyone in between is French. In other African countries, Europeans are no longer permitted to fill jobs that Africans are capable of handling; in the Ivory Coast, there are French bartenders, French maître d's, French store clerks.

Their presence rankles many young Ivorians, particularly those with education who cannot find jobs. They contend that the Ivory Coast is in a constant state of tutelage, that despite the impressive statistics the country is still dependent on foreign labor, foreign investment, foreign technicians, foreign markets for its crops. If the French pulled out of the Ivory Coast tomorrow, the country would collapse. The resultant turmoil would not be on the magnitude of Angola's when the Portuguese left overnight, because the Ivory Coast has developed a monied, propertied, educated class of capable people. But still, without the French, there would be no Ivory Coast miracle.

There are some other problems as well. Corruption is widespread, the gap between rich and poor is very large, and because education is free and in the hands of expatriate teachers, it costs at least twice as much to educate an Ivorian child as it does a child in the neighboring countries. All of this could make Houphouët-Boigny vulnerable. But the one issue the opposition could seize on is the French presence. A skillful propagandist could blame any national shortcoming on it and probably muster the support of the Ivorian majority. One other potential problem: Houphouët-Boigny has not groomed an heir apparent, and if he dies in office, there could be a leadership vacuum and a resultant struggle for power.

Houphouët-Boigny dismisses the skeptics, particularly those critical of the French presence, saying, "If I could have twice as many Frenchmen as we have to help us build the Ivory Coast, I would take them." Given the striking progress his country has made, the nation's "No. 1 Peasant" answers his critics with a single suggestion: Look at the economic and political stagnation that imprisons neighboring Ghana, Upper Volta, Mali, Liberia and Guinea, and consider the alternatives.

The flight from Abidjan to Conakry, capital of next-door Guinea, covers 700 miles and brings you back to a more familiar Africa. The little airport terminal is stuffy and dirty, and scattered alongside the runway are the rusting skeletons of six DC-4s (once used by Air Alaska), which the United States gave Guinea nearly twenty years ago. The Guineans flew them until they ran out of spare parts or crashed, then junked them at the airport.

Throughout most of the 1970s, Guinea was as isolated from the Western world as Albania. Having escaped numerous attempted coups, including an invasion by Portuguese mercenaries in 1970, President Touré had shut his country's doors to concentrate on internal security and what he called the "mental development" of his people—a euphemism for training the uneducated masses to think as one and to see the world as he wanted them to see it. For years no tourists came to Guinea and all non-Communist journalists were declared *personae non grata*. Nevertheless, every four or five months I used to write Touré from Nairobi on *Los Angeles Times* stationary, requesting a visa. The first eight letters went unanswered. Then, much to my surprise, I received a reply one April morning from his minister of foreign affairs saying that yes, of course, President Touré would be pleased to receive me anytime. The letter had been sent via surface mail rather than air mail, and had taken four months to reach me. Its unspoken message was clear: Touré wanted to end his seclusion from the West and my newspaper was to be his initial sounding board.

To arrive in Conakry, after having breakfasted that morning on fresh-baked croissants and strong French coffee in one of Abidjan's sidewalk cafés, is to turn back the calendar fifty years. The narrow, potholed road from the airport to town winds past the dingy De Donka Hospital (where bedpans are routinely emptied out the windows), past decaying French plantations where trees grow in the living rooms of abandoned manor houses and local villagers collect overripe mangoes that have fallen to the ground, past rows of empty shops, their doors hanging at crazy angles on broken hinges. The state owns everything in Guinea, and in the government's largest department store, Nafyaya (meaning "plentiful"), there is nothing for sale except some Chinese shaving brushes, some pineapple juice and a few boxes of macaroni. The cold-cut counter, covered with an inch of dust, is empty and unrefrigerated. At one end of the store, which is as big as a basketball court, there is a picture of Fidel Castro, and at the other there is a banner saying: "To Suffer is to Succeed."

The entire foreign community in Guinea numbers only 350, so there's not much need anymore for the amenities to which Conakry was once accustomed. Only one restaurant of note remains, Petit Bateau, but diners must bring their own bottled water and order their meals a day in advance so the proprietress has time to shop for food in the outdoor market. Trash litters the streets and the trees that once lined the boulevards are dying, but no one seems to notice, or if they do, they apparently don't mind; everyone is very laid back in Guinea. There is no bustle or sense of urgency or feel of movement. Life is a sun-bleached blur of unchanging conformity.

On my second day in Conakry, word was passed to me through the American embassy that my request for an interview with Touré had been granted; I should be at the presidential palace promptly at 4 P.M. A little after 6 P.M., acknowledging me with a nod, President Touré emerged from his residence, cigarette in hand, a white cap perched jauntily on his head. He is a big, vaguely handsome man, and he walked with long, hurried strides down the stone steps, his eyes moving constantly, catlike, absorbing everything.

At the base of the steps, near his sporty Renault sedan, Touré paused. His entourage of cabinet ministers and other aides paused too. An honor guard snapped to attention, a bugler sounded his salute, and eight security men kicked the starter pedals on their big BMW motorcycles. The backfires filled the courtyard like claps of thunder.

The cavalcade moved out of the palace grounds with Touré at the wheel of the lead car and me squeezed in the backseat between two bodyguards. Along the streets the peasants stood three deep, applauding this man they had learned to respect and fear. Touré responded with waves of his white handkerchief, his eyes ignoring the road ahead until an aide reached over to steady the wheel. "He is a better president than he is a driver," a bodyguard whispered to me.

The horns of many ships flying Guinean and Russian flags blared in anticipation of the presidential visit at the nearby port. Suddenly

Touré made a quick, unexpected turn to the left. His motorcycle escort, unprepared, sped off in the wrong direction. Touré chortled with mischievous delight. His aides laughed too. For these were relaxed times; Guinea was ending its repressive, Marxist ways and looking for new friends and new directions.

Ever since 1958, longer than any other black head of state in postcolonial Africa, Touré has ruled Guinea like a boot-camp sergeant, crushing his enemies, organizing his people into 2,500 cells known as village councils, sacrificing all for the revolution he believes one day will lift his country from the bondage of poverty, ignorance, apathy and disease.

So far, visible accomplishments are few, but Touré—an uncompromising and scrupulously honest former union leader once known as *l'enfant terrible* of French West Africa—has, for better or worse, done it his way, and in doing so has managed a remarkable feat: he has survived.

"I don't know what people mean when they call me the bad child of Africa," Touré says. "Is it that they consider us unbending in the fight against imperialism, against colonialism? If so, we can be proud to be called headstrong. Our wish is to remain a child of Africa unto our death."

I had submitted a list of fifteen questions to one of Touré's aides prior to the presidential interview that had been scheduled after the port inspection. The aide went over each question carefully. *What have been the benefits of your relationship with the Soviet Union?* I had asked. "Irrelevant," the aide said, crossing the question off the list. *What economic changes do you envision as a result of the recent rebellion against you by the marketplace merchants wanting to set their own prices, free of state control?* "Disrespectful," the aide said, his pencil active again. *How would you compare the progress Guinea has made since independence with that made by the Ivory Coast?* "Immaterial," the aide said. Finally seven questions were approved for submission to the Clairvoyant Guide, as the president likes to be called, and I was seated next to Touré on an old blue sofa in the palace reception room. The entire cabinet and a film crew from the government's television station had been summoned—a normal procedure in Africa—and were gathered around us. All eyes were on me. I flicked on my tape recorder and prepared to ask the first question.

"Not now," an official behind me whispered mysteriously. "The time is not right. You have to leave." Knowing how a leper must feel, I walked across the large hall and down the stone steps. "We'll reschedule the interview, don't worry," the official called out cheerily.

But he never contacted me or answered my messages, and five days later I made the 3,300-mile trip back to Nairobi, having no hint of what had gone wrong. Waiting for me was a seventeen-page, single-spaced telegram from Touré with answers to my seven questions.

Touré's voice is an abrasive one, and one that has been difficult to ignore. In 1958, when France gave its African colonies the choice of independence or continued association with France, only the Touré-led Guineans voted (by 97 percent) for immediate independence. President Charles de Gaulle flew to Conakry in an attempt to sway the thirty-six-year-old Touré, who, in effect, told De Gaulle to get lost. Within a month, on De Gaulle's orders, all but twenty of the 4,000 French colonial administrators—including doctors, teachers, judges and technicians—had pulled out of Guinea. They took everything, from the country's maps to medical supplies in the hospital, even the china plates from the governor's palace, where Touré now lives.

The Guineans rejoiced at the French departure. But Touré banned demonstrations and snapped, "This is no time for dancing." Guinea was alone and adrift, an outcast even among its more conservative neighbors. Touré, closely associated with the French Communist Party and later winner of a Lenin Peace Prize, searched for assistance in the West and found only hostility. Only the Soviet Union seemed eager to help. It was an error the West would make often in the years ahead, as it brushed aside Angola's Agostinho Neto and Mozambique's Samora Machel and other influential African leaders merely because their political orientation was radical. They were left with nowhere to turn to but Russia.

From Moscow came Guinea's first aid contributions: snowplows, porcelain toilet seats and six giant combine harvesters, which no one knew how to drive. Moscow built a sports stadium, a few small office buildings, a military academy (now empty), and the longest runway in West Africa (which Guinea never found much use for, but which served the Russians well as a staging area during the Angolan civil war in the mid-seventies). Moscow sent high school teachers (who spoke only Russian), built a big compound where Russian diplomats could live and work behind a stone wall and not have to mix with the Guineans, and negotiated some tough bargains that must have left Touré feeling a little short-changed.

Among them was one for fishing rights in which the Soviet Union keeps, without charge, 60 percent of the fish caught in Guinean waters and sells the remainder to Guinea. More important, the Soviet Union developed Guinea's bauxite, the raw material of aluminum, and buys the ore with unconvertible rubles at far below the world price. Under the agreement, 90 percent of the ore from one of the major mines must go to the Soviet Union, while all Guinea's income from the mine goes toward paying off its Soviet debts. (Another mine, operated by a Western consortium, earns more than $100 million a year in hard currency for Guinea, representing 70 percent of the country's foreign exchange.)

Twenty years after independence, Touré was becoming increasingly bitter about the inadequacies of Eastern-bloc aid. He grumbled privately that the Soviets were "more capitalistic than the capitalists"; to prove his contention, he pointed to the $25 million a year Guinea was repaying Moscow for its early loans and "assistance." On top of that he made his first trip to the Ivory Coast—he had once dismissed Houphouët-Boigny as a French colonialist—and was dumfounded by the progress he saw. Then Touré did what so many African leaders have done in times of need: he turned to the West for capital and expertise. He invited Valéry Giscard d'Estaing to Conakry for a visit and greeted the French president like a lost brother. He toured the United States and marveled at the sophistication of farming in the Midwest. He started easing out of his alliance with Moscow and toned down his Marxist rhetoric so that his philosophy became an African blend of socialism, nationalism and Islam. He even reduced the repression that had characterized his regime.

But in his search for international respectability, Touré had a hard time living down the past. He had always been single-minded and ruthless in his pursuit of revolutionary goals. His authority was unquestioned. His cabinet ministers might suggest, but only Touré decided. The state, the presidency and the party were all one, and politics were discussed only in hushed tones. None but the foolhardy challenged the Clairvoyant Guide.

Thousands of Guineans who tried to go against the tide had been imprisoned or killed. Torture was as common as the waving of Touré's symbolic white handkerchief. By the best count available, seventeen of Touré's cabinet ministers were shot or hanged between 1958 and the late 1970s, eighteen others were condemned to life in prison at hard labor. Several years ago the bloated bodies of five hanged officials were left to sway from the downtown Castro Bridge for two days as a lesson to the masses. Touré's murdered victims included Diallo Telli, the secretary-general of the Organization of African Unity. As many as two million Guineans—a staggering total of 40 percent of all the Guinean people—have escaped their homeland to live in exile in other African and European countries.

When Amnesty International accused the Touré regime of practicing torture, the president replied in a word: "Rubbish." He offered to open his prisons to any African president who was prepared to open his own to the same inspection. None accepted.

In his telegram to me, Touré said:

Those who have criticized Guinea [in connection with human rights] have never known its realities.

We consider them "sick doctors" for they pass judgment on people on whom they have never set eyes.

...Defining the rights of man is an abstraction, for that right differs from country to country. But what one should demand in the name of humanity, justice and human dignity is the nondiscrimination between men of the same country, and in Guinea there exists no discrimination.

Men and women are treated equally, really equally. Tribal differences have been erased. There is no distinction between colors or religions. The rights of the people are safeguarded better in Guinea than in many other countries of the world. We need not apologize to anyone.

Touré has a point, for there have been some intangible benefits from his decision to go it alone. Even though only 12 percent of the farmland is cultivated now and Guinea is forced to import most of its food, even though the per capita income of $210 has, in real terms, dropped since independence, even though signs of Guinea's great potential wealth are nowhere to be seen and the country has only 300 miles of paved roads, Guinea is a country virtually without crime, corruption, prostitution or beggars. There is not a single foreigner holding down any key government position. There has been no disruptive rural exodus in Guinea because there is nothing in the cities to attract people. There have been no unfulfilled aspirations in Guinea because to know nothing else is to want nothing more. Guineans do not travel freely to the Ivory Coast to see how that country has changed. They do not listen to radio stations or read newspapers that give them access to uncensored opinions. They know only the world Touré has created for them, and in that world, there is no gap between rich and poor because everyone is poor. Even Conakry's few businessmen live in dirt-floor hovels shared with chickens and goats.

If Guineans expect more, they do not show it. They express, in fact, a pride in their nationhood that is rare in Africa, an awareness that Touré, regardless whether he courts the Russians or the French, has not compromised his revolutionary principles during more than two decades of independence. Touré has done it his way and he is indebted to no one. If all 350 foreigners left Guinea tomorrow, the country would be no worse off than it is today. Touré's emphasis has been nationalistic, not tribalistic, his concerns have centered on what he calls human development, not on economic growth.* Rather than being resentful, the Guineans have accepted Touré's priorities and have become more secure in their own identity than most African people, more comfortable with the paucity of amenities than others.

That has been the major accomplishment of black Africa's senior statesman, who once proclaimed, "All Africa is my problem." It is, though, a modest accomplishment compared with the huge cost the Guineans have had to pay for a president who gave his people poverty and repression along with the promised freedom.

After my visit to Guinea, I wrote a long story about Touré that appeared on page one of the Los Angeles Times. I felt sure he would be offended by my description of the repression and economic sluggishness in Guinea. On the contrary, Touré told a U.S. diplomat in Conakry that he was delighted with the article, the he felt it was a fair and balanced assessment of Guinea's place in Africa. Those were adjectives a Western journalist does not often hear from an African president, and they just went to show that Touré had no apologies for anything he had done. Indeed, some Africanists believe Touré has chosen a wiser long-range course for his country than has Houphouët-Boigny. They say he has disciplined and organized his people, has given them a sense of nationhood and has contained the temptations, greed and self-interest that can erode the foundations of nationhood.

But what would happen if the Guineans had a choice? What would happen if they had a chance to get a piece of something rather than being assured a slice of nothing? If they could speak their mind without fear of reprisal, if they were given the freedom to question and ponder, what would they say?**

---

*The fact that Guineans are less tribal than most Africans is partly attributal to the country's relative absence of ethnic diversity: three major tribes—Foulah, Malinké and Soussous—and fifteen minor ones.
**Touré died of a heart ailment in March, 1984. The next week the army overthrew Guinea's caretaker government, accusing Touré of running a ruthless dictatorship and promising a return to democracy.

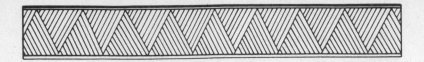

CULTURE SHOCK

▲

In Africa the clock is always at five minutes to twelve.
—ANONYMOUS

GENERALLY, THE LESS INTELLIGENT the white man is, the more backward he thinks the African is. "But they didn't even have the *wheel*," old settlers will say, implying that if it weren't for the European, Africa would still be the Dark Continent. This simply isn't true. The African devised systems—political, social, economic— that worked fine for him. It was only when he was thrust into a Western-oriented world that those systems started to break down. The African culture shock that an outsider encounters has to be considered in that context because everything is tainted by the newness of the African's confrontation with the modern world.

Most Western tourists who visit the continent are pretty well isolated from the mind-bending frustrations of Africa. They are whisked from the airport to a Hilton or an Inter-Continental Hotel to a game-viewing lodge to a tour of Nairobi's city market and back to the airport for a flight to London or Rome. But if you linger, you quickly realize that all those things you learned in the West about punctuality, efficiency and rational thought processes don't have much to do with Africa. Africa can only be explained in terms of Africa. It is a different world where the shortest distance between two points is seldom a straight line, where patience is more than a virtue; it is a necessity for survival. Africa has taken all the worst aspects of European bureaucracy, combined them with ignorance and indifference, and come up with a system that is as undirected, as lethargic as a rudderless dhow in a rough sea. Niceties aside, Africa just doesn't work very well.

In West Africa the expatriates have a word to describe their losing battles with life's daily encounters. The word is WAWA, an acronym for West Africa Wins Again. It is a reminder that to avoid stress, you move with the system, not around it or through it. If the phone doesn't work, the hotel is out of food, the air conditioner sputters and dies, the government official shows up three hours late for his appointment with you, the plane doesn't arrive on the scheduled day, much less the appointed hour, you merely shrug and dismiss your travails with the words, "I was WAWAed." The malady is rarely fatal.

The African is mystified when a Westerner gets upset with these inconveniences, considering such signs of impatience a peculiarity of the Europeans and Americans. The African doesn't live his life by a clock and he doesn't get ruffled if things move slowly or not at all under the warm tropical sun. He will wait quietly in line for three or four hours to pay his water bill and obediently help fill stadiums to hear his leaders drone on for an afternoon about political philosophies he doesn't understand. He will queue all day at a hospital to see a doctor and move on without a word of protest—to return the next day—when told the doctor isn't seeing any more patients. What's the rush? he will ask. Time is the one thing in life there is an abundance of.*

The most enduring memory of Africa I have is of idleness (not laziness): of thousands of Kenyans stretched out dozing on every inch of grass in Nairobi; of crowds sitting in city squares, of block-long lines outside government offices, of a hundred or more people waiting silently in a hospital emergency room, some with broken bones or festering wounds, hoping to see a doctor. Sometimes I would return to my Nairobi office after lunch and find a dozen people sitting there with my Ugandan secretary. They would be staring at the wall, no one talking, their hands folded in their laps. They had nowhere to go and nothing else to do. There were few jobs. Even for those who did work, the economic incentives in Africa are so small—a Tanzanian farmer receives ten cents from his government for producing the pound of freshly roasted coffee beans you pay $5 for in an American supermarket—that idleness is a tolerable alternative to work. And in those circumstances life is not lived by a clock.

* In the Swahili language of East Africa, time is measured by the sun. Each day begins at one o'clock (late dawn), which on a Westerner's watch is seven o'clock. This six-hour difference continues throughout the day and night, and explains why a taxi I once told to pick me up at noon showed up at six in the evening. Most educated urban Africans, however, use Western time, not Swahili time.

But, curiously, if you put an African behind the wheel of a car, he is transformed. Speed becomes crucial. White-knuckled and seemingly as intent as a race-car driver, he careens at breakneck clip down hills and around corners, his vehicle inevitably as jam-packed as a Tokyo subway car. Posted speed limits are ignored by drivers and not enforced by policemen, vehicle safety inspections are not required, seat belts are virtually unknown. The result is a highway carnage bloodier than most old tribal wars.

In Zaire the road from the airport to Kinshasa is littered with scores of smashed cars left to rust. In Nigeria the new sixty-mile freeway linking Lagos and Ibadan resembles a deadly carnival game of bumper cars with kamikazelike drivers whizzing by left and right, roaring up behind other vehicles, swerving or jamming on their brakes at the last second. In Uganda, army trucks tear down the middle of the potholed roads, and oncoming traffic is expected to head for the shoulders.

Kenya has less than 2,000 miles of paved roads, yet about 1,500 persons die on them each year. After forty-four people died in one pile-up outside Nakuru in 1979, the police commissioner, Ben Gethi, announced a campaign aimed at the "control of drinking habits when using roads." If Californians drove the way Kenyans did, and you took into account the number of registered vehicles and the miles of usable roads in both places, the annual death toll would exceed 120,000.

South Africa's National Road Safety Council says that whites own 72 percent of the country's four million vehicles and account for 21 percent of the road fatalities. Blacks own 12 percent of the vehicles and account for 62 percent of the deaths. In an attempt to reduce the slaughter, the council buys space in newspapers aimed at black readers and publishes a comic strip called "The Crazy Adventures of Bobo." The hero is a black, naïve about the perils facing him when he takes the wheel.

It is difficult to find a satisfactory explanation for the Africans' propensity to pass on blind curves and drive at out-of-control speeds. The best one, I suppose, is that an African does not conceptualize a potential problem the way a Westerner does. The Westerner says, If I do this, that might happen. The uneducated African does A without reasoning that it could lead to B. If an oncoming car has to swerve off the road to avoid his vehicle, and there is no collision and no injuries, the African does not say, Next time I'd better not do that. He will do exactly the same thing because he has, after all, accomplished his objective of getting from one point to another without major mishap. He does not deal with the unexpected on a sophisticated level because to do so is, again, a quality of education and training, and the automobile is a new device to most Africans.

One evening the body of a pedestrian was lying on the four-lane highway near our house in Nairobi. The rush-hour traffic veered around it at high speed, but no one stopped. Occasionally a car would neglect to swerve and would strike the body. The driver would continue on, his accelerator pushed to the floor. A friend from the United Nations passed the scene and stopped at a pay phone to call the police. He had this conversation:

"Hello. I want to report that there's a body lying on the highway. Just beyond Riverside Drive."

"How many are there?" the police dispatcher asked.

"How many what?"

"How many bodies are there?"

"One. There is one dead man on the road who was run over."

"Is he carrying identification?"

"Look, I don't know anything except that I've stopped up the road at the petrol station to call you."

"I see. And this man, how long has he been dead?"

The conversation dragged on for another half-minute before the dispatcher asked one final question: "How many did you say there were?"

Such an exchange may unglue a Westerner, but often what is unfathomable to him makes perfect sense to an African. And who's to say one is right and the other wrong?

On December 8, 1978, for instance, two Zaire air force Mirage jets approached Kinshasa from Bangui. The tower radioed the pilots, Major Uzapango Kanzeka Mba and Captain Luamba Nguy Wanguy, not to land because of limited visibility. Baffled, the pilots abandoned their jets and parachuted to safety. The planes ran out of fuel and crashed into the Atlantic ocean. They had solved the problem.

Then there was the Interpol conference in Nairobi, which attracted top law enforcement officers from throughout the world. At the session I attended, the topic was a broad overview of international counterfeiting and the first speaker was an FBI agent from the Washington headquarters. Midway through his presentation the Ivory Coast's delegate started frantically waving his hand from the rear of the room. He was recognized and proceeded to read out a list of the serial numbers of all stolen bills in his country.

Or ask my friend Greg Jaynes about WAWA. A correspondent for the *New York Times*, he had been stationed in Nairobi for only a few days when there was a coup in the Central African Empire. His foreign editor told him to get there as quickly as possible. The Inter-Continental Hotel in Nairobi booked him into the "new" Inter-Con in Bangui, and Jaynes, setting off on his first out-of-town African assignment, was relieved to know that at least a clean room awaited him. He flew from Nairobi to Paris to Bangui—the quickest way to get from East to West Africa is usually via Europe—and arrived in a taxi at the address of the Bangui Inter-Continental Hotel, clutching his confirmation slip. All he found there was a hole in the ground. Construction had not yet started. The driver shrugged and suggested he come back in a year. Jaynes shrugged and found an un-air-conditioned room at the nearby Rock Hotel.

Jaynes had discovered what more experienced travelers already knew: there are few burdens in Africa greater than trying to get from here to there in a hurry. Trains opened up Africa for the adventurous traveler, but now, because the rails are unreliable or inoperable, the roads frequently impassable, and interstate highways all but nonexistent, you must fly. The real function of Africa's airlines, though, has little to do with providing service or turning a profit. They were established originally to bring a sense of identity and prestige to fledgling nations, so the first priority for most governments at independence, even before expenditures on education and health, was a spanking new airport and an international carrier bearing the new flag.

Air Burundi, for example, had two international flights a week when I lived in Africa, both to Nairobi. It lost $12,000 on each round trip, but Burundi, one of the world's ten poorest nations, refused to suspend the service because it wanted the prestige of being an international carrier. Air Tanzania needs hard cash so badly that it doesn't accept credit cards; and in most countries a foreigner buying a plane ticket cannot use local currency—pounds sterling or dollars only, please. Ghana Airways, once an efficient little carrier with twenty aircraft, was down to four operable planes at last count, including an ancient VC-10 with clogged toilets and faded upholstery. It was known as "Old Faithful" and was used on the prestigious run to London.

Black Africa has twenty-eight national carriers, all of whom lose money, except for Gambia Airways, which has no airplanes. Gambia, a pleasing little West African country that lives by its wits and within its means, owns two flight ramps and runs an office that sells Gambian Airways tickets for transportation on other airlines, thus earning the nonexistent carrier a tidy $250,000 annual profit. As for the other government-owned airlines, well, most have more pressing needs than carrying passengers. Those needs include shuttling presidents and cabinet ministers around the world, ferrying troops and war supplies to various battlefronts, as Ethiopian Airlines does, or transporting coffee to the international marketplace, as Ugandan Airlines' lone Boeing 707 does. If passengers get bumped as a result, they should expect neither an apology nor a hotel voucher. "I don't understand why you're so upset," I once heard an airline clerk tell a stranded passenger on a Wednesday. "There's another flight Saturday."

One morning the phone rang in the Nairobi home of an American journalist. It was Air Zaire and the clerk informed him that his flight to Kinshasa had been delayed two days for technical reasons. How, my friend asked, could the airline be so precise about the length of the delay? "Oh, the president has the plane," the clerk said, "and he's promised to return it by Tuesday."

Sure enough, President Mobutu Sese Seko of Zaire had flown off to Europe with the airline's only Boeing 747. His wife had taken the DC-10. No matter that Air Zaire flights QC 011 and QC 073 failed to show up those days for scheduled stops in Nairobi, Brussels, Paris and Bujumbura. (Not long afterward, the country went broke, and the planes were repossessed.)

Even if a plane does show up, that's no guarantee it will stop. Three diplomats I knew were waiting in Bujumbura, Burundi, one day for a long-overdue Air Zaire flight; finally they saw it approaching in the distance and let out a cheer. But the jet was at 37,000 feet and there it stayed, zooming by right overhead. What my friends didn't know was that airlines ignore scheduled stops in Bujumbura if there are fewer than four passengers to be picked up.

Things don't happen in Africa the way they do in the United States or Western Europe, and if you expect otherwise, nervous indigestion may be your only reward. What may seem impolite or crude to a Westerner is not intended to be that way at all by an African. What may seem inefficient actually may prove to be very direct and practical. Again, the African takes care of A but doesn't worry about the ramifications of B.

I remember seeing seventy-five American tourists check into the Kilimanjaro Hotel in Dar es Salaam to start a one-week safari through Tanzania. The next day the government needed rooms to host a conference on apartheid in South Africa. While the Americans were out exploring the slovenly capital, their bags, clothes and personal belongings were collected from each room and tossed into a huge pile in the corner of the lobby. They returned to the hotel to discover that they had been checked out.

"You *can't* do that!" stormed one American, his face red with anger.

"You don't understand," the receptionist replied, very calmly and rationally. "We need the rooms. All the other hotels are full in Dar, so if we don't take your rooms, where is the delegation going to stay?"

EAWA (East Africa Wins Again). The tourists cut their Tanzanian trip short and caught a flight to the Seychelles.

There is, though, one unsettling aspect to the casualness of the African system: it is often controlled by men who have guns but not the training to use them sensibly. Confronted with the unexpected, they react unpredictably. Their authority far exceeds their ability to exercise their power wisely or even humanely.

During the final days of Idi Amin's rule in Uganda, Dave Wood of *Time* magazine and Bob Caputo, a free-lance photographer, drove with me in a rented car from Nairobi to the Kenya-Uganda border. We hoped to pick up some color for our stories, interview a few refugees coming out of Uganda, perhaps find a Kenyan authority knowledgeable on events in Uganda. No Western journalist had been allowed into Uganda for months at that time, and we remembered the four European journalists who had recently been murdered after crossing Lake Victoria in a boat.

We reached the Kenyan border town of Malaba shortly before lunch. Refugees were streaming out of Uganda, old men and women in tattered rags carrying their few possessions, and on the Kenyan side, scores of trailer trucks were parked bumper to bumper, their drivers unwilling to enter the area a few miles ahead where pro- and anti-Amin forces were battling.

A small cement bridge spanning a dry riverbed marks the actual border. A hundred yards farther on is a guard shack and police station that serves as the Ugandan regional immigration post. We parked our car and crossed the bridge on foot, thinking the Ugandan dozing in the shack would merely tell us to go back to Kenya, which, after all, was only a thirty-second walk away. He awoke with a start, adjusting his reflector sun glasses and grabbing his rifle in one motion.

"*Jambo,*" I said, the Swahili greeting for "hello." "We just wondered how things were going on the border. Any chance of getting a visa?"

The man stared back wordlessly.

"Well, glad to see everything's quiet," Wood said, getting a bit uneasy. "We might just as well get back to Kenya. Sorry for the bother."

The man kept staring at us, his face a mask that showed neither recognition of our presence nor awareness of our words.

"Shall we run or walk?" Caputo said under his breath.

The man motioned us with the barrel of his rifle in the direction of the police station. The groans of a man being beaten inside reached our ears. I swallowed hard and terrible visions filled my mind.

We were led into an interrogation room by a member of Amin's State Research Bureau (a euphemism for the national murder squad); there was dried blood on the unpainted cement floor and a single lamp bulb was hanging by a cord from the ceiling. Beneath the light cord was an empty desk, and the man who sat there, dressed in shabby fatigues and muddy boots, stared at us impassively, his eyes invisible behind large sunglasses. He began his remarks by saying that mercenaries and CIA agents were not welcome in Uganda. We assured him that we understood this and said we were journalists. What was the difference? he asked.

There really were no answers for the questions he asked, and each jumbled response seemed to increase his suspicions. What did we mean, he asked, that we had *rented* a car? Couldn't we afford to *buy* a car? If California was my home, how could I also live in Nairobi? If I was a journalist, why didn't I have a typewriter with me? If we wanted to know something about Uganda, why didn't we just call the ministry of information in Kampala? Had we ever been in the U.S. Army? Had we ever been in Israel? How about South Africa? The answer to all three of the last questions was yes. He led us into separate rooms and told us, "Write down everything you know about Uganda, where you learned it, who told you, and who you are." He gave us each a pad of yellow scratch paper and a ball-point pen.

I filled a page. He read it with great difficulty, his lips mouthing each word, his pencil moving along each line. "That's not long enough," he finally said. "Write more." So I filled another half page, mostly about what a lovely drive it had been from Nairobi. That satisfied him, and he took my pad with a grunt, disappearing down the corridor. I could hear him shouting over an apparently static-filled phone line to Jinja, the military command post a hundred miles west. He was asking for instructions on what to do with us and I could imagine the voice on the other end saying matter-of-factly, "Kill them."

He returned a few minutes later. The icy glare had given way to a friendly smile. He had removed his sunglasses. He embraced us like old friends, shaking our hands and patting our backs. He had received his instructions, and his demeanor, before and now, was only a guise, a façade that gave not the slightest hint of his real emotions or feelings.

"You are free to go now," he said, still pumping our hands. "I have been asked to tell you that your interest in Uganda is deeply appreciated and we hope you will return soon. You will always be welcome."

We crossed back into Kenya, feeling like condemned prisoners who had won a reprieve. The young men on the bridge tried to sell us Ugandan shillings at a discount rate. The old women peddling tomatoes and turnips glanced at us with a faint trace of curiosity. We got into our car, knowing that the man back in the police station could have killed us just as casually as he had sent us on our way. He would simply have done whatever his boss had told him to do.

In many ways, the longer I stayed in Africa, the less I really understood the nuances of the African character, and any Westerner who says he feels differently is probably being less than honest. Before going to Africa, I had lived for four years in Asia and for two in Australia, and when I left those continents, I felt I had a grasp of who the people were, how they would react to certain situations, why they responded in particular ways, what they thought about the world around them. But the African often becomes a deepening mystery. It is rare that he will reveal his inner emotions or talk about his beliefs in more than superficial terms. As often as not, he will tell you what he thinks you want to hear rather than risk offending you with an opinionated view. He does not often defy authority and he will follow anyone who asserts himself as a leader, however inept, with an amazing alacrity. His resilience extends beyond any logical human limits; his crops can fail, his children can die, his government can treat him grievously and the African still carries on, uttering no protest, sharing no complaints.

For a people who have had to tolerate so many injustices over the centuries, yet have remained basically gentle, polite and racially equitable, I was constantly shocked to see the cruelty, even sadism, that Africans inflict on one another so willingly. In Zaire, mobs will pull the driver from a car that has struck a pedestrian and beat him to death on the spot. The U.S. embassy there has this advice if any of its personnel are involved in an accident: Drive off fast and don't stop until you get to a police station. In Kenya the victim of, say, a purse-snatch has only to holler "Thief!" Every bystander will take off after the culprit, and in a carnival-like atmosphere, punch and kick him to death. In a single week a few summers ago, nine Kenyans who had been stealing from merchants in the Nairobi markets were stoned and kicked to death in various incidents.

One day after our house had been burglarized, my wife, Sandy, went to the neighborhood police station to file a report. A middle-aged Kenyan, shoddily dressed and wearing only one shoe, was stretched out semiconscious behind the sergeant's desk. Sandy started writing out a list of our stolen items, but the sergeant seemed preoccupied. "I wish this guy was dead so I didn't have to fill out the form," he said to no one in particular. "Yeah, he ought be dead," said one of the sergeant's subordinates. For the next twenty minutes, every time a policeman walked by the prostrate man, the officer kicked him in the head or groin. It was done casually, without comment, as offhandedly as getting a drink at the water cooler.

The sergeant apparently felt he owed Sandy an explanation. He pulled a rumpled pack of imported Benson & Hedges cigarettes (available for $2 a pack anywhere in Nairobi) from the man's pocket. "See," the sergeant said, "he's a thief. Otherwise he couldn't afford these."

I'll never find such behavior easy to explain, whether it happens in America or Africa. But in trying to understand the African character, you have to start with an awareness of how debilitating everything in Africa is. The heat, the diseases, the shortage of jobs and the absence of free expression all drain the energies, making the African—even those who are Christian—a fatalist, intent on his own survival but caring little for those who are less fortunate. Some people told me that the Africans' violent reaction to thievery reflected the heritage of the village, an open society where property rights are respected, stealing is considered a violation of the group's welfare, and instant justice is meted out. That was, though, a weak argument. The fatal beating of thieves was, I thought, indicative of only one thing in the life of urban Africa: boredom.

If the African is often inexplicable to the American or European, so must the outsider be to the African. Indeed, many of the whites who have made Africa their home are a peculiar lot, and some could not survive in a society where life was more rigid and regulated. They live in a small, self-centered world, often immune from change, isolated from much human contact, pursuing whatever it is—perhaps gorillas or ancient bones—that brought them to Africa in the first place. My first introduction to this community was as full of culture shock as anything I ever encountered in any African home.

At a little Tanzanian village called Makuyuni, the paved road turns to dirt and for the next hundred miles it twists and tumbles through the vast plains in the shadow of Mount Kilimanjaro, finally ending as a narrow track, rough and rutted, at the home of Mary Leakey.

Mrs. Leakey, now nearing seventy, appeared at her door, cigar in hand. A gusting wind raced through her compound, kicking up thick layers of fine, red dirt and churning into groaning motion the two windmills out back which were used to generate electricity. She shielded her eyes from the blowing dust to watch our car approach her home—so far from anywhere but the fossils of the past.

The home, located in the splendid isolation she cherishes dearly and protects fiercely, rests on a small hilltop overlooking the Serengeti Plains. A few miles away is the fabled extinct volcano, Ngorongoro, and below, almost at her doorstep, is Olduvai Gorge, the anthropological treasure chest that has yielded to the Leakeys and other scientists so many secrets about early man.

Mrs. Leakey eyed Sandy and me wordlessly. She does not like intruders, and although she had approved our visit and we had brought her a box full of groceries, a bottle of whiskey and two flagons of wine, there was no greeting and no smile. "It's not usually blowing this much," she said simply. Then Mrs. Leakey, widow of Dr. Louis Leakey and herself a gifted anthropologist, disappeared behind the closed door of her den to get back to work. There she works for months on end, disregarding weekends and holidays, immersed in her solitary world.

Unlike her husband, who relished the public attention earned by his warm personality and professional achievements, Mrs. Leakey, a feisty, independent woman, is reticent beyond the point of coldness. She makes no attempt to hide her displeasure with any interference in her work at Olduvai and she bristles at what she considers the ignorance and impertinence of journalists, tourists and other strangers who occasionally pass her way. "If I could just go back to my maiden name, Mary Nicol," she said in one of her more expansive moments, "I could get a lot more work done. Living with this so-called Leakey legend becomes quite a tiring burden. I don't see why everyone always wants to talk about it."

But the remarkable Leakeys have built a legend that will live on. Louis (who died in 1972 at the age of sixty-nine) and Mary Leakey showed that the evolution of man probably took place in East Africa, and the 1.75-million-year-old primate skull—known as Zinjanthropus—that she found in Olduvai Gorge in 1959 pushed back by nearly one million years the accepted date of man's evolution. It took her eighteen months to piece together the skull's five hundred pieces of bone fragment in what many scientists called some of the most detailed anthropological work ever done. Of their three sons, Jonathan operates a snake farm in Kenya and has made his own important anthropological discoveries in East Africa; Richard, a civil servant of the Kenyan government, is director of national museums; Philip is the only white man in the Kenyan parliament.

Mrs. Leakey avoided us all afternoon, and by dinnertime I was getting nonplused. I went out to our car to get a pack of cigarettes, accidentally locked my keys inside, and had to break the window with a rock to retrieve them. I had visions of making the rough twelve-hour drive back to Nairobi the next day, calling my editor in Los Angeles, and saying, "No story. She wouldn't talk."

Mrs. Leakey's home was a low, rambling structure, made of wood and tin, and built piecemeal over the years. The open-air living room was an extension of the patio, and Sandy and I sat there, waiting. The wind still blew outside and no one else was about except the servants. Finally, from the evening shadows beyond the patio, Mrs. Leakey appeared, a glass of whiskey in one hand and a thin cigar in the other. She settled into an old stuffed chair and asked, "Now, what is it you want to know?" Each question was met with a penetrating eye and a terse phrase, followed by stony silence.

Well, I asked, was each of the Leakeys' children encouraged to follow his own path as a youth, independent of his parents' fame? "I don't know what you mean," she replied. "We were just a normal family." (Just like any other family, I guess, growing up in Olduvai Gorge, a hundred miles from the nearest Europeans and fifty from the closest town.)

Was there anything she could add to the story about the hippopotami that used to bathe and urinate in the Leakeys' only water source at Olduvai, thus polluting the precious supply of drinking water? "I don't know where you got that," she said. "There hasn't been a hippopotamus around here for four hundred thousand years." She was right: I had meant to say "rhinoceros."

How did she feel about the changes she had seen during her forty-one years in East Africa as the region moved from colonialism to independence? "You can't see changes until after they happen," she said.

And what were the small rewards that carry an anthropologist through the long periods of often fruitless searching? "That's a stupid question," she said. "I just do a job that I enjoy."

The steak was good at dinner that evening but the conversation was tough, and Mrs. Leakey soon excused herself, saying perhaps we could talk some more in the morning. But she was up and off before dawn, in pursuit of her two dogs, which had run away during the night, driving across the plains in a Land-Rover, a solitary figure disappearing over the horizon, swallowed up by the African experience.

I had come to Olduvai Gorge expecting to find a sort of heroine and that was the profile I had had in mind to write. Mrs. Leakey had shattered the stereotype—and actually given me a much more interesting angle. "Why don't you just forget all the things you thought she was," Sandy suggested, "and write an article about what all this time alone out here has done to her." It was good advice; the *Times* later put my "noninterview" on page one.

● ● ●

Most people are surprised to learn that, if you exclude Angola and Mozambique, there are more whites living in black-ruled Africa today than there were during the colonial era. In all they number more than half a million, including 20,000 Americans. (Additionally, there are 4.5 million whites in South Africa.) The largest white populations are in Zimbabwe (135,000), Kenya (75,000) and the Ivory Coast (50,000). Some, like Mary Leakey, have lived in Africa for years, and many, I hasten to add, are warm, kind people with whom it is a pleasure to spend an evening. But the majority of white expatriates in Africa today are short-timers who work for Western companies, offering technical or managerial skills in which Africans are not yet trained. They are airline pilots, hotel managers, agricultural experts, oil executives, ministerial advisers, architects, doctors, financiers, and they stay three or four years and move on to other assignments.

Their continued presence is a reminder of how little the colonialists did to prepare Africa for independence. For the most part, Africa has been an accommodating host, although every now and then the size and influence of the expatriate community does become an issue. The complaints voiced against the whites in Africa today fall into four broad areas: the expatriates take jobs that Africans should fill; they try to sabotage the economy to maintain their jobs and perpetuate the myth that Africans are incapable of governing themselves; they live as a privileged class; they are, in some cases, second-rate professionals in their own countries who manage to pass themselves off as "experts" in Africa.

"In the last twenty years," Kenya's vice president Mwai Kibaki said, making a valid point, "Africa and Asia have been invaded with all kinds of social misfits from overseas whose theories and phony products have been rejected in their own countries.

"There are some who propagate theories for the salvation of developing nations. Those we do not need. We need the ones who can accommodate our ideas into a practical approach compatible with our needs, without inviting more foreigners."

Certainly no one would deny that in terms of creature comforts the expatriate lives as well today in countries such as Kenya as he did during colonial times. He has a large home with an acre of gardened grounds and he belongs to the local sports club, where tennis courts cost $1.25 an hour and thirty-year-old ball "boys" get ten cents a set; he does most of his socializing with other expatriates, not Africans; he reads the *International Herald Tribune*, published in Paris, and listens to the BBC on his shortwave radio to keep up with world events; and he finds, at least in places like Nairobi and Abidjan, that life doesn't seem to have changed greatly over the years.

There is a British professional theater, Donavan Maule, in Nairobi where an African is seldom seen. There are restaurants such as Bobbie's Bistro, where the only black faces at dinner are usually those of the waiters. There is Sunday horse racing at Ngong, as pretty as an English country track, where European women in white gloves and wide-brimmed hats place bets with Asian bookmakers. And there is the Muthaiga Club, its library stocked with British newspapers, its men-only bar populated by members who spend many hours musing about how conditions have deteriorated since independence. The high-ceilinged restaurant serves, in the best English tradition, overcooked roast beef and Yorkshire pudding. Coffee is taken in the lounge, where middle-aged and elderly Europeans cling to a vanishing life style, remembering the old days and, for the time being at least, still living them.

One evening an aging Englishman sat dozing in one of the lounge's overstuffed armchairs. *The Times* of London was on his lap and his right hand was wrapped around an empty brandy snifter. A fly buzzed around his nose and he suddenly awoke with a start. "Steward!" he bellowed. A white-jacketed Kenyan hurried over obediently, just as he would have forty years ago, to pour him another brandy.

If Kenya is still one of the last Third World enclaves of the good life, most of Africa offers the expatriate considerably more frustrations. Life is expensive, conveniences few; the shelves of supermarkets are bare, gasoline is rationed; the simplest task becomes an exercise in perseverance.

In Lagos, Nigeria, a three-bedroom house similar to a tract home in the United States leases for $50,000 a year, three years' rent in advance. In Tanzania, items like cheese and butter are as rare as caviar. In Zambia the phones don't work when it rains, and a resident calling the telephone company to inquire if something can be done is told simply: "Wait till the rain stops."

The last time I visited Bob Heisey, an American who was in his fifth year with a U.S. engineering firm in Zaire, he was pushing fifty and tiring fast of the expatriate life. He was trying to save enough of

his salary to buy a boat—$1,000 a foot, he figured it would cost—
and sail away with his wife, Kathy, into the South Pacific sunsets.
There were times, though, when he was ready to forget his dream.

The rent on his little three-bedroom house had just been jacked
up to $1,100 a month. There was no telephone and sometimes no
water. Three of his good friends had been arrested the previous
weekend by Zairian soldiers for taking pictures of the beach. His
own camera had been stolen the week before that. The cook hadn't
shown up for eight days and the gardener wanted another loan. The
temperature peaked at a steady 100 degrees each day and stayed
there throughout much of the night. The air conditioner was broken
and there were no spare parts in Zaire to repair it. The same with his
car.

He decided to forget his misfortunes one evening and take Kathy
out to dinner. The bill was $150. The wine was extra. Driving home
that night, the Heiseys were stopped at a roadblock and the police
shook them down for a few more dollars.

"This isn't living," Bob said to Kathy. "I don't know what you'd
call it. Surviving, I guess. But it isn't living."

When we twice returned to the United States on brief vacations,
friends would ask, "But what is Africa *really* like?" The best answer
was: "Different." The poverty is enormous and yet only by Western
standards would you call the rural African poor. He has all the
things needed to sustain him—food, clothing, a modest shelter,
family love. Health conditions are appalling, but most Africans have
access to better medical facilities than they did thirty years ago. The
phones that don't work and the clocks that are ignored may ruffle an
American visitor but they don't affect the African's life much at all.
The Westerner may have trouble adapting to Third World culture
shock; the African obviously has none at all. He designed the system
and he knows how it works, how to live within its limitations.

Once I spent two fruitless nights at the Inter-Continental Hotel
in Zaire trying to call my Los Angeles office to dictate a story. Over
and over I called the switchboard and each time the operator explained that the lines were very, very busy on the international exchange. But he had a friend in the hotel who had a friend at the exchange and maybe, he explained, he could be of assistance. "Do you
know the system?" he asked. No, I said, and kept waiting for a call
that never came through.

A colleague set me straight the next day. "Dummy," he said, "just tell the operator you want to make the call 'on the system.' You'll be through in five minutes."

Sure enough, that evening I had an immediate connection to Los Angeles. The operator knocked at my door a few minutes after I hung up and I paid him $100. No transaction of the call appeared on my hotel bill or in the Zaire-owned telephone company records. The government had been cheated, the hotel had been cheated, but my call had gone through. The system—as it always does in the long run—had won out.

SOME OF THE NEWS
THAT IS FIT TO PRINT

▲

Truth is whatever promotes your government. If
something is not favorable to your country, then it isn't
true and you should not publish falsehoods.

*—A Somali official, giving his
view of the media's role in Africa*

EVERY TUESDAY MORNING for a good many months I used to drive
over to the Ethiopian embassy in Nairobi to ask, beg and cajole for a
visa. The consular officer, a courteous, noncommittal man, would
receive me warmly. We drank tea together in his office, talked about
African politics in vague terms and eventually got around to my request. Ah, the visa, he would say. No problem. The government in
Addis Ababa was working on it. If I would just be patient a little
longer.

Ethiopia was an important story in those days. The junta that
overthrew Haile Selassie was doing its flip-flop with Moscow and
Washington, and dozens of Western journalists were clamoring for
visas in order to get a first-hand look at the revolution. Finally, at six
o'clock one evening, I received a call from my contact at the embassy. I could pick up my visa the next morning, he said. I was delighted, thinking my persistence had helped me outsmart my colleagues and would lead to an exclusive trip to Ethiopia. No such
luck. Eighty-seven other Western journalists had also received visas,
and two days later, a mini-brigade of reporters from Nairobi, London, Paris and New York descended on Addis Ababa with typewriters and cameras. By any standard, it was an unusual visit, a public relations debacle for Ethiopia, which made us prisoner of
something called "The Program" and tried to deal with us much as
it would with its own dissidents.

The Program is a news-management device used by many African countries. It is a rigid itinerary of people and places to see, designed for a particular visit of journalists and intended to show them only what the government wants them to see. If a journalist tries to deviate from it, such as by talking to a cab driver without authorization, he is told, "You can't do that; it is not on The Program."

From the airport of Addis Ababa we were whisked into the faded old Ghion Hotel and given our instructions by an army major with a revolver in his shoulder holster: we could not leave the hotel without permission, or hire taxis, or go anywhere without an escort, or miss any events on The Program, or eat our meals in other than the hotel restaurant at the appointed hour.

Unfortunately for Ethiopia, Western journalists in a pack are a fairly obstinate, aggressive bunch, so within a day we were sneaking past the corridor guards, slipping away from the dinner table under the guise of going to the bathroom, and making independent contacts in Addis Ababa. Each night gunfire crackled outside the hotel, and in the morning the bodies of five or six "counter revolutionaries" would be stretched out on the sidewalk, left there to rot in the sun until collected by next of kin. No photographs, our escorts said—but the photographers snapped away, anyway.

"I don't understand why you people are so difficult," growled one of the soldiers from the information ministry. "Our journalists do what we tell them. Why don't you?"

One day after we returned from the Ogaden battlefront, where Ethiopian and Cuban troops were repelling the Somali invasion, several local reporters sought us out for interviews, trying to solicit pro-Ethiopian quotes about the war and the revolution. The unmistakable conclusion was that the readers of the *Ethiopian Herald* would put more faith in what we said—even though African officialdom considers Western coverage of Africa stilted—than they would in what their own government-paid Ethiopian journalists wrote. The readers' mistrust of their hometown media was hardly surprising, for in Ethiopia, and in almost every other country in Africa, the prime role of the media is to serve the government, not to inform the people. The press is a propaganda vehicle, used to manipulate and organize and control; any questioning voice is a potential threat and only the government is wise enough to know what the people need to know. Here's how an official communiqué from the Republic of Somalia defines the role of the press: "It is the function of the nation's mass communications media to weld the entire community into a single entity, a people of the same mind and possessed of the same determination to safeguard the national interests."

With only a few exceptions, black Africa's newspapers are government-owned. They are edited and written by civil servants, not independent reporters, and their contents are as unbiased as something a U.S. political party might publish during an election campaign. They contain all of the good news and none of the bad, concentrating on windy speeches made by officials and sometimes printing four or five pictures of the president in a single edition. Readers of the *Ethiopian Herald*, for example, learned nothing about the Ogaden war when the Somali advance was unchecked; the *Herald* simply carried no stories about the war. It was not until Ethiopia took the offensive that the daily paper started covering the conflict, but even then, it made no mention of the Cuban and Russian role, a role that was capturing page-one headlines in the United States and Europe.

Government-controlled media are, of course, more the rule than the exception in the Third World. What is noteworthy, though, is that black Africa inherited a competitive, untethered press at independence and managed to destroy it so effectively that no one asks anymore what the future of the press is in Africa. They ask instead if it has any future at all. Except in Nigeria—where the black press dates back to a paper called *Iwe Irohnin*, first printed in 1859—the early newspapers on the continent were published by colonialists for colonialists. They bequeathed to Africa's young nations an independent press pledged to serving the people and a constitution guaranteeing freedom of expression. But in country after country, the free press was the first of the Western-styled institutions to fall. It was the tool the governments most needed to manipulate the minds of the uneducated masses. News was censored and managed to the point that what got into print was little more than government press releases. Before long there was not a single independent radio station left in all of black Africa. Nigeria's first government needed only one year to forget its proud journalistic history and its independence promises in favor of a more secure course that stifled critical comment. In 1961 the High Court of Lagos found journalist Chike Obi, the "Thomas Paine of Nigeria," guilty of sedition as a result of a pamphlet he had published entitled "The People: Facts That You Must Know." The seditious section read:

> Down with the enemies of the people, the exploiters of the weak and oppressors of the poor! . . . The days of those who have enriched themselves at the expense of the poor are numbered. The common man in Nigeria can today no longer be fooled by sweet talk at election time only to be exploited and treated like dirt after the booty of office has been shared.

The story across the whole continent is not much different. President Hastings Banda of Malawi jailed virtually the whole nongovernmental press corps in the mid-seventies. President Kenneth Kaunda appoints and fires newspaper editors in Zambia; in Uganda and Zaire, journalists shuttle in and out of jail so regularly that their wives don't even ask where they have been when they reappear after an absence of several days. Equatorial Guinea's president Macias Nguema Biyogo went one step further: by the time he was overthrown and killed in 1979, all journalists of note had been executed or were in exile.

South Africa is more subtle, and first-time visitors there are often astonished to pick up English-language newspapers and find editorials critical of the government. Indeed, the country's forty-three daily and weekly newspapers do produce some first-class examples of adversary and investigative journalism. But reporters know precisely how far they can go. South Africa has fifty laws that directly affect the dissemination of information, and another fifty statutes or administrative regulations that indirectly restrict the public's right to know. If a reporter, for instance, wanted to confirm the arrest of a black nationalist, his inquiry would have to include the address and birth date of the person believed jailed. This information is often impossible to provide because the births of many blacks are not registered and not remembered by the family. Thus the authorities have no obligation to say whom they are holding.

Predictably, the role of newspapers in Africa today has declined so much that they have very little significance in society. And not much circulation either. In the mid-sixties, according to the London-based International Press Institute (IPI), there were 299 daily newspapers in Africa. That figure included about forty papers in the Arab states, mostly Egypt, and about thirty in the white-ruled areas of southern Africa. By the early 1980s, only about 150 dailies were left on the continent, and the shrinkage had occurred almost exclusively in black Africa. Nine countries had no newspaper at all.

The combined daily circulation of the papers in Africa fell during that period from well over three million to two million. Thus, the circulation on a continent of 455 million people is only about two thirds of what a single London newspaper, the *Daily Mirror*, sells in a day.

"When you look at the struggle of the press in Africa," said IPI's Frank Barton, "the sad truth is that the press is losing. I can't be optimistic about the press's future in Africa. Everything else on the continent has expanded in the last ten years—roads, education, medical facilities—and newspapers continue to shrink. I'd suspect in another ten years that we may not see more than about fifty dailies in Africa."

Government constraints are not the sole reason for the decline of the African newspaper. Among the others: an illiteracy rate that runs as high as 90 percent in some countries; the emergence of radio as the most powerful communications medium in Africa; the high cost of importing newsprint from Europe; and the absence of daily or weekly newspapers in the rural areas, where the majority of people live. All of this has made newspapers an amenity of the city elite.

If the printed word belongs to the educated few in Africa, the radio belongs to all. It is the voice of authority, though not necessarily truth, and when it speaks, Africa listens. Its importance as a government medium is probably greater than that on any other continent, forming as it does the most direct link between the rulers and the ruled. In 1955 there were half a million radios in Africa; now there are more than twenty-five million. For every 20 people there is one radio, compared to one edition of a daily newspaper for every 210 people and one television set for every 525.

In the Central African Republic, the government uses radio announcements to summon foreign diplomats to the presidential palace. In Nigeria, the government broadcasts to its people in seventeen ethnic languages. In rural Kenya, schoolchildren take "creative writing" courses over static-filled radios set up in small dark classrooms. In Mozambique, the government used to beam its propaganda into white-ruled Rhodesia for an hour a day on 998 kilohertz, and Rhodesia, then in the throes of civil war, used to throw its own right back into Mozambique on 1007 kilohertz. And in most countries, the government radio station is as heavily guarded as the national treasury; get the station and you can take control of the country and the people as well.

Idi Amin regularly used to appear at his 50-kilowatt station, wave the announcer aside and take over the microphone to read what he considered urgent national news. Once he announced that he was setting up a human rights commission. In the next breath he said that since there were no human rights violations in Uganda, he was freeing two policemen charged with beating twelve prisoners to death at Naguru Prison.

Many African countries have both internal and external broadcast services, the former to mold their own people's opinions, the latter to reach dissident groups and other governments outside the country. Somalia, for instance, broadcasts propaganda an hour a day to Ethiopia, a traditional enemy, then turns its transmitter southwestward and broadcasts to Kenya, another none-too-friendly neighbor. The United States and Britain monitor between them every government station in Africa around the clock and exchange the transcripts daily. Despite an abundance of half-truths and outright lies, the African broadcasts often give important clues to government thinking and new policy directions that are helpful to intelligence gatherers and foreign journalists.

"I think we're incorrect and naïve to assume our people swallow everything we dish out on the radio," Kenya's former attorney general, Charles Njonjo, said. "Have you heard the nightly commentary 'That's the Way It Is' on Voice of Kenya? Well, it's nonsense. It's just fodder for the people. It doesn't reflect what that government is thinking or doing at all. We ought to call the program 'That's the Way It Isn't.' "

Where, then, does Africa get its news? Ironically, it turns to the West—namely, the British Broadcasting Corporation (the BBC, affectionately known as the Beeb) and the Voice of America. Both maintain resident Western correspondents in Africa and both cover, say, Tanzania, more accurately than Tanzanian journalists cover their own country. For any African who can afford a shortwave radio, the world is only a kilohertz away.

During the annual Organization of African Unity summit, delegates hurry back to their hotel rooms each evening to see how the BBC and VOA are covering the conference. In Somalia, government offices come to a standstill at five o'clock each weekday when the BBC broadcasts its news and commentary in the Somali language. President Kaunda of Zambia has been known to excuse himself from interviews so he can tune in the BBC six o'clock news from London. And in Zaire, President Mobutu Sese Seko monitors the BBC and VOA so closely that he frequently calls the British and American ambassadors to complain about particular news items, not quite convinced that the envoys are unable to take the correspondent to task.

When the Nigerian head of state, General Yakubu Gowon, was overthrown in 1975 while attending an African summit in Uganda, he learned about his downfall not from a diplomatic note or cable from Lagos, but only after the BBC headquarters in London—which had been monitoring Nigerian radio broadcasts—telexed its correspondent John Osman at the conference, asking for African reaction to the coup. The message was intercepted by the Ugandan secret police and turned over to Gowon. His immediate response was to rush back to his shortwave radio at the hotel and turn on the BBC.

Before being transferred to Moscow, Osman had bounced around Africa for twenty years, and traveling with him was something of a treat. He was as well known in Africa's English-speaking countries as Walter Cronkite was in the United States. Doors would open, presidents would vie for his ear (or more appropriately, for his microphone), surly bodyguards would become gentle and respectful in his presence, knowing that the BBC had more clout than all the stations and newspapers of Africa combined.

Once, a few days after President Amin had been overthrown in Uganda, John and I traveled up a dirt road to St. Teresa's mission outside the town of Bombo. As our Land-Rover went by, villagers dashed inside, to the safety of their huts. Then they would reappear cautiously, look again and break into wild cheers, waving and dancing joyously. For them, the sight of white men driving without a military escort was their first confirmation that Amin had been overthrown.

From the door of the little mission, Father Emanuel Mbogo stepped unsurely, squinting in the sunlight. John introduced himself. The priest threw his arms around him, then stepped back and, star-struck, repeated, "John Osman, John Osman. It is really you?" For three years, the priest said, he had listened to Osman's reports about Uganda on a shortwave radio he kept hidden under his pillow; if Amin's soldiers had caught him listening to the BBC or had found the radio, he surely would have been killed. "All this time," the priest said, "you were the only way I had of knowing what was going on in my own country."

The fact that Africa relies on foreigners for African coverage, not trusting its own journalists to do the job, raises some interesting problems. The flow of communications through the Third World is largely controlled by the West, primarily the so-called Big Four agencies: the Associated Press, United Press International, Reuters and Agence France-Presse. Africa believes, not without some justification, that the Western press portrays the continent in generally unsympathetic terms. The West, so the reasoning goes, seeks out the sensational and the peculiar at the expense of serious analysis of nation-building difficulties. It confirms old stereotypes rather than examining new national directions. It covers Third World stories in the same way it would a four-alarm fire in Brooklyn, as a single isolated event rather than as a slow, integrated developing process based on economic, political and social goals.

Let's set the record straight here. First, the Third World's complaint that it is singled out for special, negative treatment is not true. Africa's coverage, for example, of the United States—which governments receive via the Western wire services—is considerably more sensational than the West's coverage of Africa. The story, say, of a Nebraska farmer who goes berserk and murders his family may, for reasons unknown, get a prominent display in an African newspaper. Stories that reflect positively on the United States, such as one on the advancement of minority groups, generally are ignored.

Second, Western journalists, often to the point of becoming apologists, continually emphasize that the genesis of Africa's problems are imbedded in colonialism and the newness of the independence experiment. But Africa's real grievance, though unspoken, is that it can't control the outgoing flow of news the way it can the news inside the continent. In 1977, for instance, Ethiopia expelled its only resident American journalist, David Ottaway of the *Washington Post*, whose thoughtful analysis of the revolution there represented some of the best Western reporting in Africa; within weeks Ethiopia was complaining that U.S. newspapers were not interested enough in its revolution to keep a full-time correspondent in Addis Ababa. Nigeria once barred all American reporters from entering the country, and six months later lodged an official complaint with the U.S. State Department about the lack of Nigerian coverage in American newspapers.

And third, the contention that American reporters write only about the bizarre side of Africa is erroneous. The most authoritative study I've seen on the subject examined all the stories for a one-week period that moved on the Big Four's Asian wires.* The results, I believe, are fairly typical for any part of the Third World: 62 percent of the stories fell under the headings of foreign relations, economics or domestic governments; 22 percent covered a range of subjects from sports to health and human interest; only 16 percent dealt with military matters, terrorism, violence, disaster, crimes or judicial news.

The countries that have made the most economic progress and are the least repressive—such as Kenya, the Ivory Coast and Senegal—are the ones that are the freest in issuing visas for Western reporters. But most governments still view foreign correspondents with a high degree of hostility, considering them at best a necessary evil, at worst an enemy of the state. The journalist's job becomes a trying one, and at times a dangerous one. He learns quickly to avoid filing all but urgent stories from the country he is writing about, transmitting them instead to his home office from a neighboring country where officials monitoring the telex and telephone wires won't be offended.

Michael Goldsmith, a veteran reporter for the Associated Press, violated that principle once and was lucky he lived to relate his experiences. Writing about the Central African Republic, he filed a report from Bangui that displeased the emperor, Bokassa I. Worse yet, Goldsmith transmitted the article via public telex to the AP bureau in South Africa, asking that it be relayed to the Paris office, which he had been unable to raise on the telex. The report came back garbled so that Bokassa, in addition to being angered about some unflattering remarks in the article, now thought Goldsmith was a South African agent sending coded messages.

Goldsmith was taken from the Rock Hotel late one night to meet Bokassa, who had secluded himself in one of his nine palaces in preparation for his coronation. Bokassa greeted him warmly, raised

---

* The 1977 study was made by the Center for Communications Studies at the Chinese University of Hong Kong. It was commissioned by the Edward R. Murrow Center of the Fletcher School of Law and Diplomacy at Tufts University in Massachusetts.

his club and struck him across the forehead. Bokassa's bodyguards then kicked Goldsmith unconscious and tossed him in prison, where he was kept with unattended wounds. A month later, after intense diplomatic negotiations, Goldsmith was again summoned by the emperor. Bokassa hugged him, kissed him on both cheeks and had his henchmen put him on a plane to Paris.

Almost every country in Africa has a list of Western journalists barred from future entry because of allegedly offensive stories. Stanley Meisler, who covered Africa for the *Los Angeles Times* in the sixties and seventies, ended up after seven years being blacklisted by thirteen countries, even though he was one of the most respected and brightest correspondents on the continent. When he could no longer get visas for any significant African country, the *Times* had to transfer him to its Madrid bureau. The final straw came when he wrote a story about Upper Volta, an impoverished West African country he greatly admired. Meisler said that Upper Volta wore its badge of poverty without shame and suffered from neither the illusion of grandeur nor the expectation of false hopes. Two days after the story appeared in print, he was denounced on the government radio for being hostile to the country.

Nigeria is less subtle in its reaction to outside comment and criticism, still being resentful of what it believes was pro-Biafran Western reporting during its civil war. When the Reuters bureau chief in Lagos filed an incorrect story in 1976, soldiers picked him up, along with his wife and eight-year-old daughter, took them to the river and pushed them off in a dugout canoe without paddles in the direction of neighboring Benin, which they managed to reach safely. The *New York Times* resident correspondent, John Darnton, was expelled the next year on twenty-four hours' notice for writing a story about a poor Nigerian family who could not get proper medical attention for their dying child. It was a very moving story. No one questioned the accuracy of the article, just the choice of subject matter.

Like other African countries, Nigeria contends that all it wants from the Western media is objective reporting, and given that, it will accept exposés along with favorable stories. The argument is not convincing. What Africa really wants is boosterism, a style of advocacy journalism that concentrates on the opening of civic centers and ignores the warts. It wants a new set of guidelines for covering the underdeveloped world, one which, if used in the West, would tell journalists to disregard the Watergates and Charles Mansons and concentrate only on the positive and uplifting. It wants to be covered by historians, not journalists. Africa says it needs this respite from criticism during the early, troubled days of nationhood, but I am not sure who would really benefit if foreign correspondents wrote about Africa as some people wish it were rather than as it is. To write about only what is good does not mean that what is bad will simply evaporate. To contend that truth is only that which promotes national causes is to deny the validity of other causes and the necessity to re-evaluate them. It leaves a people in need of hearing a voice other than their own.

Not surprisingly, most African nations have lined up with the Communist bloc in demanding the endorsement of a UN-sponsored "new world information order." The effect of the Orwellian resolution would be to restrict the free flow of news on the premise that journalism is too important to be left to journalists. One of the draft declarations debated in the United Nations Educational, Scientific and Cultural Organization (UNESCO)—for which the United States pays 25 percent of the budget—would endorse the governmental licensing of journalists and would compel news organizations to print official replies to stories a government considered unfair. "It is the duty of states . . ." one article says, "to ensure that the mass media coming directly under their jurisdiction act in conformity" with the UNESCO declaration. Western critics contend that this is nothing less than giving the United Nations sanction to censorship and government control of the press.

What Africa does not seem to realize is that it can have total control over the news emanating from its countries under the existing ground rules: all a government has to do is deny visas to foreign correspondents and then there is no news to write. Also, Africa seems to have missed the point that government-dictated news is no more credible in the Third World than it is in Europe or the United States. If Africa wants its journalists to write news that is believable to the rest of the world, all it has to do is remove the shackles and let them be journalists.

Two countries, Nigeria and Kenya, deserve special mention in any discussion about the African press. Despite Nigeria's sensitivity toward Western reporters, both countries have produced some distinguished journalists and both have maintained, often against great odds, a perky, pesky press full of critical comment and relatively free of censorship. Even through thirteen years of military rule, Nigeria's fourteen daily and twenty-four weekly papers—including black Africa's largest paper, the *Daily Times* (circulation 300,000)—managed to remain nettlesome and, to a surprising degree, independent-minded. For failing to pay homage to their soldier rulers, journalists risked jail or having their heads shaved by army punishment squads, but it was a price they paid willingly to keep alive one of the last vestiges of a gadfly press in Africa.

In Kenya, the two English-language daily papers combine some intelligent editorial comment with a great deal of sex, crime and scandal. The result is a healthy circulation for each and an X-rated product. The *Daily Nation* (circulation 80,000) offered its readers these page-one stories one morning: "Boy's Body Eaten by Dogs in Hospital Mortuary," "Armed Gang Storms Hotel," "Gangster Shot Dead," "Manager Denies Fraud."

The same day the other tabloid, the *Standard*, led off a lengthy story with this paragraph: "After sleeping with a ten-year-old girl . . . a man pleaded with the child's mother not to report the matter to the police because he was possessed by the devil." Readers were also titillated by a story about a dwarf who turned into a cannibal because of "bad eating habits." And the same readers were no doubt surprised to see John Vorster, the South African prime minister, referred to as a "white friend." The next day the paper ran a correction, saying it had intended to use the word "fiend," not "friend."

Kenya's dailies are unique for more than their unpredictability. For Kenya is the only country in black Africa where the national press is privately owned, one of the few where there is no covert censorship, and probably the only one in the world where the major dailies are owned and controlled by nonresident foreigners. (The *Daily Nation* is owned by Prince Karim Aga Khan IV, the international businessman and spiritual head of the Ismali Moslems, the *Standard* by the powerful British conglomerate Lonrho.)

Even in Kenya, though, freedom of the press is deceptive. It is not so much that journalists have no restrictions as it is that they understand how far they can go. They know which cabinet ministers are out of favor with the president and can be attacked with impunity, which African countries can be criticized without drawing official scorn. They also know that members of the General Service Unit, a state-police force working directly for the president, will come

knocking at their door in the night if they question national policy
or suggest that the government is not working or criticize the president and his family.

"When you talk about freedom of the press, sure, we have it if
you're writing about sports or traffic accidents or the courts," a Kenyan journalist told me. "But I'm not going to write anything that
would embarrass the government and I'm not going to question anyone in high places even if he is a crook. It's all relative. You understand what you can say and what you can't say, and if there is any
question in your mind, you don't say anything."

Self-censorship is often the most restrictive kind of censorship,
but before anyone writes an obituary for journalistic integrity in
Africa, let me introduce you to a remarkable man named Hilary
Ng'weno. He works out of a cluttered, hot second-floor office overlooking Moi Avenue in Nairobi. Now in his forties, he was born in
the Nairobi slums, educated in physics and mathematics at Harvard
University, which he attended on scholarship, and is considered by
those who know him to be a man of great intelligence and little
business sense.

In 1975 he confirmed his friends' doubts about his financial savvy
by starting a weekly news magazine that promised to report critically
on events in Kenya and elsewhere in black Africa. Ng'weno started
with a deficit balance in his bank account, a staff of two and, it
seemed, not much chance of making the *Weekly Review* a success.
Half the original press run on the first edition went unsold, and the
advertising community (which was and still is controlled by Europeans in Kenya) stayed away in droves, unwilling to support any publication that might raise the government's ire.

Ng'weno worked eighteen-hour days. He borrowed and begged
money. He and his wife, Fleur, did the reporting, the writing, the
editing, the bookkeeping, the ad-selling. Ng'weno's political analysis
was so astute that some diplomats in Nairobi based their reports to
their governments almost exclusively on what they read in the
Weekly Review. The publication examined issues usually left untouched in Africa—income distribution, tribal rivalries, rising unemployment, the performance of parliament—and it went to the
brink on challenging the government on some issues, always stopping just short of a dangerous confrontation.

The *Weekly Review* has never turned a profit, primarily because
the advertisers are still gun-shy and ads account for only 20 percent

of the content. But at last count the weekly circulation had risen to 35,000, including 1,000 foreign subscriptions, and the magazine had won local and international recognition as a publication of unmatched editorial excellence in black Africa. By 1980 Ng'weno had increased his staff to eight and was also publishing a Sunday paper, the *Nairobi Times* (circulation 20,000) and a children's magazine (*Rainbow*, 5,000). His modest publishing empire comprised the only African-owned and African-managed independent newspapers and magazines south of the Sahara.

"I've written things that have angered the government and nothing has happened," Ng'weno said one afternoon, his voice rising above the din of traffic and honking horns in the street below his office. "I don't know how much further I could have gone and gotten away with it, but certainly there is a governmental tolerance toward criticism in Kenya that is absent in most African countries."

As Ng'weno sees it, there are three reasons why the Kenyan press has enjoyed a wide degree of freedom. First, any attempt to control the media would throw jitters into the foreign community, which controls a considerable part of the economy. Second, Kenya's *Daily Nation* and *Standard* are part of large foreign-owned businesses with other, extensive investments in East Africa. And most important, Kenyan politicians have learned that there is no such thing as government control; there is only control by a particular faction of government. When that happens, the group that is out of favor loses access to a medium for reaching the public and is cast into the silent exile of the desposed.

When, for example, the radical left was forced out of the Voice of Kenya, the government's broadcasting service, in the 1960s, the first thing its members did was run to the same newspapers they had branded "imperialistic agents" to complain that no one was reporting what they said anymore: it was fine to silence the opposition when the radicals were in power, but not when they were the opposition.

The last time we talked, Ng'weno was cautiously confident that his publishing company, known as Stellascope Limited, could survive financially and could escape government controls. Sadly, he was wrong. In 1981, with advertising dwindling and overhead costs rising, Ng'weno, the majority shareholder in Stellascope, had to turn the company over to a new nonprofit organization, the Press Trust of Kenya.

The patron of the trust was President Daniel arap Moi, and two of the nine trustees were presidential appointees. Ng'weno remained as editor in chief of the publications with "complete autonomy in all editorial matters." But clearly, the realities of Africa had caught up with Stellascope and the future seemed predictable enough: President Moi was not going to have the same news judgment as editor Ng'weno.

SURVIVAL
OF THE FITTEST

▲

People don't live long enough in Africa to worry about cancer or the other diseases that concern us in the Western world. In Africa the big trick is to get to be five years old.

—DR. DAVID FRENCH
of the World Health Organization

DR. MICHAEL WOOD hopped into the pilot's seat of his twin-engine plane. He gave his gauges a quick check and headed down the runway of Nairobi's Wilson Airport, his Cessna 182 climbing slowly into the choppy early-morning breezes, then banking south over the savannah. In the seat next to him, with an aerial map spread out over his khaki shorts, was Dr. Tom Rees of New York City—like Dr. Wood a noted plastic surgeon. Back in the 1950s, over a bottle of Scotch shared in a farmhouse not far from Nairobi, they had tossed around a novel idea: Would it be possible to scrape together enough money to create a flying hospital for Africans living in the bush?

Wood picked his way up through the puffy clouds to nine thousand feet. The high-rise hotels and office buildings of Nairobi faded from sight, and soon the giraffes and zebras on the plains below were only specks. Dead ahead stood Mount Kilimanjaro, snow-capped and solitary, its slopes speckled with small fires set by the villagers to turn timber into charcoal for cooking fuel.

"If you want to be a good doctor in Africa," Wood was saying to his two passengers piled in the rear seats with the medical gear, "you go to your patients. If you wait for them to come to you, they simply die. As it is, we're dealing with people who are half dead—or half alive, depending on how you look at it."

Mike Wood came to East Africa in 1946, a young man just out of medical school. He had intended to stay for six months, assisting a

British surgeon. Instead he fell in love with Kenya, was possessed by its beauty and all that needed to be done, and never returned to England to live. "I knew I just couldn't walk out on the challenge it offered," he said. So Wood learned to fly, saved enough money to buy a secondhand plane, and with Dr. Rees and another plastic surgeon, Sir Archibald McIndoe, established the East African Flying Doctors Service, a Nairobi-based organization supported by donations from throughout the world. Since 1960, the Flying Doctors have covered four million miles and treated half a million patients. They have operated by the light of lanterns alongside bush airstrips, rescued hundreds of people mauled by lions or stomped by elephants, held thousands of clinics to teach the most basic standards of sanitation, hygiene and preventative health care.

By the time Wood swung low over Italal, a collection of mud huts and makeshift cattle corrals 140 miles southeast of Nairobi, the Masai tribesmen—nomadic people not greatly involved with the twentieth century—were lined up at the mobile health unit that had arrived by road a day earlier. Wood landed his Cessna in a nearby field and, speaking in Swahili, told the naked children, who peered at the plane as though it were some kind of strange bird, to cut brush and pack it around the wheels. More than one pilot, Wood knew, had been stranded by forgetting that hyenas love to chew rubber tires.

The Masai had trekked up to thirty miles for this rare opportunity to see a doctor. There were young mothers with their sickly babies wrapped like corpses in red cloths, unblinking children who seemed oblivious of the flies in their eyes, and elders so ill with malaria that they collapsed at the door of the examination tent, and lithe teenage warriors with spears and long braids matted with red ochre who had killed lions as part of their initiation into manhood but who were too timid to accept a smallpox shot.

From the back of the group a pretty, bright-eyed girl of thirteen dragged herself toward Wood. She had suffered a compound fracture of the knee in a village accident. The fracture had been treated at home and the leg was grotesquely twisted. Wood, the first doctor the girl had ever seen, asked when the accident occurred. "Seven years ago," she said.

Many of Wood's operations involve plastic surgery, particularly on people clawed by wild animals and on children burned when they rolled in their sleep into the family campfire. But Wood estimates that 80 percent of the Flying Doctors' patients would never have been sick in the first place if they had cared for themselves properly and had had access to a modern health clinic. "What good does it do to keep dispensing antibiotics if no one ever cleans the water supply?" he asks, pausing for morning tea.

While Wood and Rees treated the long line of patients, one of their Kenyan assistants held court with the Masai women in a clearing a few yards away. There were nearly a hundred of them (for this was something of a social event), and they sat quietly in the heavy heat of summer, holding their suckling children. The paramedic was trying to explain, in the Masai language, that a combination of salt, sugar and water could cure diarrhea. He held up simple charts with drawings that illustrated each step. The women were silent and puzzled; they could not understand the charts, which to them were one-dimensional abstractions. Later, when my wife took a group picture of several women with her Polaroid, the Masai gazed in wonder at the photograph, giggling and blushing. It passed from hand to hand and was always viewed upside down.

"You look at all the work there is to be done," Wood says, "and you know that we are running to catch up. Health standards in Africa today are at about the same stage they were in Europe and the United States during the pre–Industrial Revolution a hundred and fifty years ago. It's already too late to help the present generation. The question now is, What can we do to help the next?"

There is nothing more responsible for shaping the character of Africa than health, or more appropriately, the lack of good health. It is the major obstacle retarding Africa's growth and development, the impartial equalizer that enforces the Africans' casual, fatalistic approach toward life. "*Shauri ya Mungu*," they say—"It's God's will." Whatever will be will be. Life is unchanging, its burdens eternal. The cycles of good and bad are controlled by higher powers, and when death or disease comes unexpectedly in the night, there is always a simple, unemotional explanation: *Shauri ya Mungu.*

Mothers give birth to fifteen or sixteen children in the hope that perhaps half of them will live. "I will lose some but I can always have more," a teen-age mother told me. Parents cannot believe that a drop of liquid (Sabin polio vaccine) on a sugar cube can control the evil spirits that cripple their children or that clean drinking water has anything to do with healthy bodies. So their children fall sick, and the reason, they say, is that the child's father or grandfather stole a cow or his uncle wished misfortune on a neighbor. Perhaps the village witch doctor can exorcise the curse, perhaps not. It is, after all, God's will.

(In traumatic times this casual attitude can change. When a cholera epidemic struck Chad in 1971 and many villages lost 50 percent of their people, the peasants quickly learned to boil their water on the instructions of Western health experts. Once the threat passed, the villagers lapsed back to their old ways.)

Daniel Mwangi, a Kenyan I met one day while researching a story on the physically handicapped, knows the results of Africa's fatalism only too well. His problem started when he was six or seven years old—itchy eyelids, blurred vision, headaches. His father thought the boy had been cursed and took him to his friend, a witch doctor. But the practitioner's herbs and chants did not help, and by the time Daniel was thirteen he was totally blind, the victim of trachoma, a virus disease that could easily have been cured with proper medical attention. Daniel's father went to his grave believing that his son was paying for some evil in the family's past.

Daniel was thirty-seven when I met him. He had been educated by a European missionary, he had a job as a telephone operator and he read his Braille Bible daily. No, he said, he was not bitter. "What could I be bitter about? My father was an old man who believed in traditional things. Modern medicine and Western doctors were things he could not comprehend. I am blind because of ignorance, but I do not blame anyone. In many ways I am lucky. I have a job, a place to live and I have my Bible."

Indeed, he was one of the lucky ones. But for most of Africa's physically handicapped—in Kenya alone one out of every ten persons is handicapped—there is no future, no work, no education and no special governmental concern. They are the forgotten people of the Third World, a huge minority doomed to live as misfits.

The streets of every African city and village are filled with an appalling number of deformed bodies; crippled beggars dragging themselves across intersections; leprosy victims whose limbs are stumps; even well-dressed businessmen and college students with braces and withered arms or legs.

Traditionally the blind, the deaf, the disabled and the insane have been cared for in the rural African society. There was no need for special schools or medical facilities because the extended-family concept embraced all members of a clan. No African was ever alone as long as he had a clan or a tribe to go back to. Only the truly infirm were ever cast out, left behind for the hyenas when the pastoral people moved on in search of better grazing land.

But as Africa became increasingly urbanized, old values changed. The handicapped poured into the cities to lose themselves in anonymity, to collect survival money on street corners, to seek medical attention. For most of them there is little hope of ever getting a wheelchair or a brace, much less a job other than making baskets or carving little statues of elephants and lions to be sold to tourists. They simply are not yet a priority for Africa's financially pressed governments, which are understandably more concerned with the able-bodied who can contribute to society.

The colossal cost of Africa's health problems in terms of blighted lives seems so needless in this day and age, yet the infant mortality rate in black Africa, 137 deaths per 1,000 live births, is eleven times higher than in the United States. Europe has one physician for every 580 persons. Kenya, one of Africa's most developed countries, has one for every 25,600 persons; Upper Volta, one of the least developed, has one for every 92,000.

In several West African countries, children are not even named until they reach the age of two, the assumption being that they probably won't live that long. Lockjaw, polio, sleeping sickness and other ailments all but forgotten or never present in the developed world still kill hundreds of thousands of African children. Diarrheal diseases alone take the lives of 17 million children under the age of five every year in Africa and Southeast Asia—tantamount to wiping out the entire population of Tanzania year after year, generation after generation. Measles has a mortality rate of 30 percent among African children, and in the rural areas of some countries such as Rwanda, the life expectancy at birth is less than thirty-five years. The task of combating these health problems is so immense that Africa literally does not know where to begin: as recently as 1975, it was spending only $1 per person annually on medical care.

Despite the ignorance and the suffering he has endured, the African is astonishingly tough. You will seldom hear an African child cry or an adult complain. The African's patience and stoicism know no limits. Women give birth in the morning and are back working in the fields in the afternoon. Men undergo major surgery and within a day are on their feet again. The postoperative infection rate for the Flying Doctors is only 4 percent, compared to 15 percent in most Western urban hospitals. One possible explanation is that the sun has therapeutic values which are not yet fully understood; a more likely one is simply that the African is a survivor. He is part of a natural selection process, and only the toughest get by childhood.

The African's diet, however, is so inadequate that little resistance can be built up against the continent's killer diseases. Health experts say that more than half of Africa's children are malnourished, and Nairobi's Department of Crop Science estimates that the average East African diet provides only 44 percent of the recommended daily supply of calories, and 18 percent of the protein. Although a well-to-do city dweller may eat an American-style dinner of meat, potatoes and vegetables, the diet of most Africans is dictated by his traditions and what the land will yield.

Some tribes on the shores of Kenya's Lake Victoria survive almost exclusively on sun-dried or smoked fish; others nearby never touch fish, get almost no protein in their diet and do not understand why their children die in infancy of malnutrition or disease. The Kikuyu and Kamba near Nairobi eat a maize porridge every day, 365 days a year. The Masai, who measure their wealth in cattle, live mainly on milk mixed with herbs and on blood extracted from their cows by pricking a vein with an arrow point. In Uganda, bush rats are a delicacy; in Zaire, monkeys are a nutritious treat. People all over the world use a Ghanaian word—*kwashiorkor*—to describe the weakened conditions that result from these imbalanced diets. And without the protein that a child needs for growth and strength, the body has no defense against the parasites or viruses that can kill as stealthily as an assassin.

One of the first Europeans to study tropical diseases in Africa was the explorer and medical missionary David Livingstone, who used to give malingerers among his native porters a powerful laxative pill called a "Livingstone Rouser." In those mid-nineteenth-century days, the west coast of Africa was known as "the white man's grave." Of 225 Methodist missionaries sent to British West Africa between 1835 and 1907, 62 died of diseases. Half the hundred-odd Baptist missionaries sent to the Belgian Congo from 1878 to 1888 succumbed. The white man, of course, was only learning what the black man had always accepted: Africa was a death trap. Even today, after great advances in tropical medicine, the African remains cursed by terrible diseases that are beyond the comprehension of most Westerners.

There is one mysterious viral infection called green monkey disease. Victims develop a high fever and start bleeding from the mouth and rectum; death usually follows within a week. Another disease is known as snail fever (schistosomiasis): the larvae of a parasitic worm penetrate the skin of people wading in streams and grow into inch-long worms within the blood vessels; the liver and spleen become enlarged, blood and eggs are discharged into the digestive or urinary tract, and the resultant internal bleeding leads to death. And there are the tsetse flies that carry sleeping sickness, infecting wild and domestic animals as well as humans. (One epidemic that raged through Uganda from 1900 to 1922 killed 330,000 persons.) The symptoms are fever, weakness, tremors and lethargy, and if the disease is untreated, coma and death follow. There is no preventative and no vaccine for sleeping sickness, and curative drugs are toxic.

In recent years the clearing and draining and spraying with pesticides of areas inhabited by tsetse flies has checked the spread of sleeping sickness, but in Uganda alone, a hundred new cases are still reported every day. There is a district hospital in Iganga, one of the most heavily infected areas, where comatose children lay on filthy mattresses while the district medical officer, Ezra Gashihiri, looked on helplessly. He had no chemicals for doing lab tests, no blood for the blood bank, no intravenous equipment or fluids to nourish the wasted bodies, no one to process the spinal-fluid taps that are essential to determine whether the disease has spread to the brain. Emergency supplies had been shipped into the region by international relief agencies, but Ugandan bandits hijacked them for sale on the black market before they reached the hospital.

Until Idi Amin came to power in 1971, Uganda had sleeping sickness pretty well under control. Consider, though, this tragic scenario: the tsetse flies lay their eggs in the shade of lantana bushes, which grow in Uganda's coffee- and tea-producing regions. The plantations there were owned by Asians. They were smart producers and they cleared the scrub from their land to make more room for their crops and to improve health conditions. But Amin expelled the Asians from Uganda and devoted half his national budget to defense. There was no money left to clear, drain and spray the hazardous areas, nor was there anyone who understood the need for continuing the control procedures. The plantations became overgrown and the bushes spread again like weeds. The Ugandan army started smuggling the reduced coffee crop across Lake Victoria into Kenya. To get to the lake, the smugglers had to pass through the reinfected areas, and in the course of four or five years they picked up the parasite and carried it back to heavily populated areas. Sleeping sickness was again a major health problem in Uganda, and with two thirds of Uganda's 1,650 doctors having fled the country during Amin's reign, there were not enough medical experts available to treat it.

Long ago a terrible scourge struck the people along the Volta River basin in West Africa. It stole their sight, turned their young old, and made their skin as wrinkled and leathery as elephant hide.

Even now, after so many generations of suffering, the old and wise chief of Wayen village in Upper Volta does not understand the source of his people's misery. All he knows with certainty, he explains, is that as long as anyone can remember, the people have fallen sick and blind in great numbers, and he supposes they always will.

Chief Tonsana Ba is a tall, handsome man of simple dignity. He nodded approvingly at my offering of a dozen kola nuts, and finding a comfortable spot on the ground, hunkered amid a group of villagers, dispatching one of the youngsters to fetch a chicken as a gift. The people around him carried wooden hoes. Their legs were thin as twigs and their eyes were flooded with milky whiteness. Perhaps, the chief said, one third of the adults in Wayen were blind, but almost everyone was sick. The children, who act as guides for the sightless adults, sat scratching their arms and legs with rough stones, trying to soothe their cracked skin that burned with the itch of buried worms. At night they rest uneasily and sleep fitfully, tormented like their elders by a mysterious fate they cannot comprehend.

Their disease is called onchocerciasis, or more commonly, river blindness. It is transmitted by tiny black flies known as buffalo gnats, which breed along the banks of fast-moving waters. When the female sucks blood from a human already suffering from onchocerciasis, the fly becomes infected and passes on the disease when it attacks another human and lays eggs on the bitten area. The larvae become worms, which live and breed under the skin of the victims' scalp, ribs and limbs. It takes years to become seriously infected, but eventually a victim may harbor hundreds of worms. They penetrate the eye, causing partial or complete blindness, and destroy the elastic layer of skin, causing itching so constant and painful that suicide is common. The World Health Organization has been trying to control the disease since the mid-1970s—no one talks about eradicating it in West Africa at this point—and if the campaign is successful, the implications will be substantial.

The land near the Red, White and Black Volta rivers is the most fertile in Upper Volta. But because people associate onchocerciasis with the rivers, whole villages were abandoned when tens of thousands of Voltans moved into the plateaus, thus overtaxing the fragile land that has little to give in the first place. Brides, traditionally drawn from villages that have not been stricken, refuse to leave home for fear of becoming infected, and the young men head for the cities of Ouagadougou and Bobo-Dioulasso before they, too, become blind. As the rural population shrinks, the rate of bites per person increases and more people fall sick. The crops are neglected and a listlessness slips over the villages, now inhabited only by the prematurely old and the very young.

In many ways onchocerciasis symbolizes the difficulty man has in finding accommodation with the land of Africa. Though the land may support him and feed him, the African, in the end, remains the slave of his environment. The land owns him and dictates his destiny.

The World Health Organization is spending $10 million a year trying to conquer onchocerciasis (which is also common in the parts of Latin America that imported African slaves). WHO's campaign in Africa involves complex monitoring systems, medical studies, on-site research, clearing and draining land, and spraying the flies' riverside breeding areas with a low-toxic biodegradable compound. In some lesser-infected countries such as Kenya, similar programs have destroyed the flies and eradicated the disease, river by river.

Ending river blindness in East Africa is another reminder that man *is* capable of bringing decent health standards to the world's unhealthiest continent. The most dramatic proof of this came in 1980 when a fourteen-year WHO attack on smallpox succeeded, marking the first time in history that man had totally eradicated a disease. Only a decade earlier, smallpox had been claiming up to two million lives a year in the Third World, and in West Africa had either killed, blinded or left mentally retarded one of every ten children. Travelers in the Ivory Coast had long recognized the meaning of a dead bird hanging from a twig. It warned: "We have smallpox in this village—stay away."

The Smallpox Eradication Program cost $300 million between

1967 and 1980 (about one quarter of what gamblers lose in Las Vegas every year) and entailed the global efforts of 200,000 men and women who dispensed 2.4 billion shots of vaccine. Medical authorities had focused on smallpox for two reasons: the disease is spread only by an afflicted human being, who is contagious for just four weeks; and a vaccine, taken from the skin of a living calf, had already proved to be an effective preventative.

What WHO had to do, then, was to immunize the population in smallpox areas and locate and isolate the remaining cases. Not surprisingly, the world's final cases were tracked down in Africa. To find them, international health officials hired local "surveillance agents" to infiltrate warring tribal groups and look for telltale scabs. Other agents were strung out along the Ethiopian-Somali border to check the nomads who drifted from country to country. Bounties of up to $1,000 were offered to anyone reporting a new case. WHO doctors, aided by army soldiers and college students, traveled through the Horn of Africa on foot and in planes and four-wheel-drive vehicles. They carried with them a powdered vaccine that had been developed specially for the Third World. It did not need refrigeration and it was injected with a simple two-pronged needle that anyone could use merely by lightly jabbing the skin.

The last endemic case in Africa—and the world—was located one October morning by a WHO "search and vaccinate" mission in the ramshackle Somali town of Merka. He was a twenty-three-year-old hospital cook named Ali Maow Maalin. He recovered after treatment, and in 1980 the World Health Assembly meeting in Geneva issued a triumphant statement: "Smallpox is dead."

The smallpox breakthrough showed what a determined international medical effort could do for Africa's physically sick. But for the mentally ill, there is less room for optimism. In many African countries, mental disorders are still treated with aspirin and witchcraft. Psychiatry is a stigmatized or nonexistent profession. Kenya, though far more advanced than its neighbors, has only seven psychiatrists—one for every 2 million persons. In the Swahili language there are no words to describe mental illness and none to express degrees of emotion. A person who wants to say that he is depressed will use the word "unhappy." If he is overjoyed, ecstatic or mildly pleased, he has the choice of only one word—"happy."

"Facilities for the mentally sick are disastrous in black Africa and the general picture is terrible," said one of East Africa's top psychiatrists, Dr. Joseph Muhangi, a British-educated Ugandan. "By the year 2000, mental health is going to be the number one public health problem in Africa. Anyone looking beyond his nose can see that, but no one, it seems, is making any plans for dealing with the inevitable."

I joined Muhangi one Thursday morning at Kenyatta General Hospital in Nairobi. By the time he entered the building at seven-thirty and headed down the long open-air corridor to Clinic No. 17, the rows of steel folding chairs were already filled. On other mornings of the week the plain room with whitewashed walls, adorned only by a black-and-white photograph of Kenya's president, served as a diabetic clinic. But for four hours each Thursday morning it became the psychiatric clinic, the only one in Kenya and one of a mere handful throughout black Africa.

There were perhaps 150 patients waiting for Muhangi and his four colleagues. A receptionist had ascertained that their disorders were mental, not physical, and everyone sat quietly, holding his admission card, neither comprehending his illness nor knowing that he was about to see a psychiatrist. Apparently he understood only that some evil deep inside had twisted his life and brought fears and visions he could not explain.

Although there is a scarcity of reliable research, growing evidence suggests that Africans are no less susceptible to social pressures and resultant mental disorders than people in the developed world. If anything, doctors say, suicide, alcoholism, hysteria and various forms of neurosis are increasing as the competition for jobs, education and financial security becomes greater.

"Old ideas die hard," Muhangi said, arranging the case files on his desk. "It wasn't too long ago that doctors came to Africa from the West and believed the noble savage was free from the pressures of civilization and thus free from psychological pressure. This just wasn't so. Take a man with five wives and twenty children and a little plot of land he's trying to farm with primitive tools. Do you think this man isn't under pressure?

"And how about the pressures exerted when entire societies in Africa are in transition, when social structures are changing, rural populations are shifting to the cities, traditional values are being replaced by Western-oriented values, and young men are competing to get ahead and succeed as never before in Africa?

"Everything considered, there's really far greater pressure on Africans today than there is on a person from the Western world."

None of the outpatients who came to see Muhangi that morning attributed his depression or insomnia or hallucinations or physical pains to mental disorders. When Muhangi asked each what had caused his illness, most replied without elaboration, "I have cholera."

Phillip Ng'eno, a hulking, handsome man of forty-nine, sat down in front of the doctor, his face impassive, his eyes focused on an imaginary spot on the floor. He earned $100 a month as a technician in a medical lab, half of which he spent on school fees for his thirteen children. The heavy rains had spoiled the coffee harvest on his eight-acre plot. The pain in his arms and his general lethargy had grown steadily worse since one of his wives died, but previous medical tests had shown no physical ailment. He feared that soon he would no longer have the strength to father more children or to work his fields.

"Tell me, Phillip," the doctor said, "do you sleep well at night?"

"No, I do not sleep at all. I am up before the roosters. I am always tired but sleep does not come."

"What do you think the problem is?"

"Cholera," Phillip said. "I have been cursed with cholera."

"Ah yes, but how about the things that are frightening you? Let me explain how the mind controls and causes pain. When I was a small boy tending goats in Uganda, sometimes I would cut my leg running through the thickets. I would feel no pain because I was so intent on keeping the goats together. Then when I got home and my mother saw the blood and asked me what happened, the pain would start."

Muhangi glanced at the case file again and scribbled out a prescription for a tranquilizer. "I know your pain is real," he said, "but can you see that the pain is in your mind, not your body?"

"That may be so," Phillip answered in a soft voice, "but have you not some pill that will help my cholera?"

Phillip shuffled out the door. A young girl named Theresa entered with her mother. Theresa was fifteen years old, less than three feet tall and the brightest student in her class. The headaches, cramps and sleepless nights began about the time she learned that she was a midget. Her headmaster refused to advance her to the next class because she was so small, and a Kenyan physician she had seen tried to put her on display in a ward so medical students could see what a midget looked like.

"This headmaster, he is no use, a stupid man," Muhangi muttered as he prescribed an antidepressant and wrote the headmaster saying Theresa should be graduated with her class.

"She is a smart girl," Muhangi said to the mother. Theresa sat nearby, teary-eyed. "If she cannot do some things, at least she should be buying Mercedes-Benzes and writing books someday. After all, people who stammer also become orators. Theresa can still have a full, happy life. Do you understand, Mom?"

The mother said nothing and her face reflected no emotion. She waited for several more moments, but there was little else the doctor could say. She turned as she reached the door and said, "How can Theresa write books if she is so small?"

Muhangi's weekly clinic represents a modest beginning in the treatment of the mentally ill. Yet throughout all of sub-Sahara Africa (excluding South Africa) there are only and estimated 100 psychiatrists serving 342 million people, and in most countries treatment is primitive or nonexistent. Generally only those who act totally made are considered in need of psychiatric help.

In parts of the Sudan, the insane are manacled and beaten twice a day in mental institutions. In at least ten countries there are no mental health specialists and no mental health facilities. Uganda once had the most advanced psychiatric care in black Africa, with twelve European-trained psychiatrists, outpatient clinics in a dozen rural towns, and a modern inpatient hospital at Makerere University in Kampala. President Amin's rule of terror reversed that progress and by the time he was overthrown in 1979, all of Uganda's psychaiatrists were dead or in exile and the mental health facilities were closed.

Kenya has only one in-patient mental health facility, Mathare Hospital. It was built to hold 1,000 patients but has twice that many, and one third of the patients are there on criminal charges. One ward has forty beds and 150 patients, and many patients never see a doctor; they are merely drugged for a few weeks and then released as sort of walking zombies. The admission ward, where all patients spend their first few days or weeks, is similar to a cage in a zoo. It has a cement floor littered with banana peels and human waste, towering bars and no roof. Inside are sixty or seventy patients, glassy-eyed, half-naked, trapped like animals.

Given such conditions, it is not surprising that the primary source of health care for Africans remains, as it has for generations, the practitioner of traditional medicine. Often called a witch doctor or sorcerer, he casts spells, removes curses, treats mental and physical ailments. Anyone who doubts his powers needs only to meet Satigi Soumaouro, as I did one morning in the sleepy West African city of Bamako, capital of Mali.

For three days and three nights Satigi had treated a steady stream of patients, so by the time I appeared at the door of his dark little room at the end of a dirt alleyway, he was weary. He sat barefoot on his mattress, rubbing sleep from his eyes. This was his operating theater and his consultation room, and on the cement floor were his instruments: gourds, rattles, springbok horns, chicken beaks, potions of herbs, several cattle hoofs and a jar of shiny brown beetles.

Satigi was seventy-nine years old. The face beneath his blue fez was lined and drawn, but in his very presence—in the strong, steady gaze, in the soft, melodic voice—there was an aura of power that transcended both his exhaustion and my doubt.

"My mother had these powers too," Satigi said. "From her milk they were passed to me. My knowledge was born with me."

This knowledge had made Satigi one of the most sought-after traditional healers in West Africa. His patients came from as far away as Europe, and many had first gone to Western doctors to seek cures for their illnesses. But in the end they placed their fate in the hands of Satigi, partaking of his herbs, his incantations and rites, his knowledge of the universe's intangible forces.

"There are some things that Western doctors cannot cure," Satigi said, covering his feet with the long red robe that flowed from his shoulders. "There are things that will always be treated best by traditional medicine." And for the time being at least, a major portion of the African medical community agrees with him. In fact, traditional medicine is undergoing a revival of respectability in Africa and is viewed by many competent medical authorities as an important adjunct to Western-style health care.

The traditional practitioners' strength lies in the belief that man is more than a physical entity. His well-being is largely controlled by gods and spirits, and disease is a punishment for wrongdoing. Misfortune is the result of a curse, often uttered in the name of an enemy or a displeased ancestor. Some practitioners will cast evil spells. Others, like Satigi, operate only as the harbingers of good forces; they will remove but not cast evil spells. Both types of practitioners believe that spirits, both good and evil, emanate from one's ancestors and that a precise balance between those conflicting forces guarantees an individual's good health.

The eighteen-year-old girl who now sat at Satigi's feet was barren and gripped by constant stomach cramps. Her father stood behind her and explained that the girl's husband had had her cursed because she had borne him no children. Beetles, he said, now filled her stomach. Satigi listened carefully, questioning the girl about the guilt she felt.

He had the bare-breasted girl put on a white blouse and expose her stomach. She squatted on an upturned urn and watched calmly as Satigi sharpened a small knife on a whetstone. The father pulled a fold of flesh from the girl's stomach. Satigi made a small incision in it, then cut his own right thigh, just enough to draw blood. He mixed the blood with hers, spat on the wounds, rubbed ashes on her stomach, waved a rhinoceros horn over her head and between her legs, closed his eyes and recited a prayer, and had her walk twice over his toes. "In two days she will be well and will bear her husband many children," he said, rising and clapping his hands together. The girl stood. She smiled. The cramps, she said, were gone.

During the colonial era the European administrators condemned these centuries-old beliefs and practices as pagan quackery. Traditional medical techniques were banned and traditional therapists were driven underground, although each was—and often still is—the most influential figure after the chief in his village. Many countries today still prohibit the casting of evil spells. In Kenya not long ago, two men went to jail for killing chickens in an attempt to put a hex on an opposing soccer team, and it is common for a candidate seeking office to have a spell cast on his opponent. But at least nineteen African countries have established institutes of traditional medicine for research and treatment. They are not involved with sorcery or quackery, and their techniques are respectably scientific.

"Remember, the African was being treated for his sickness long, long before any European doctor ever set foot on the continent," said Dr. Adama Kone, the director of Mali's Institute of Traditional Medicine, which was cleaner and more modern than most hospitals I saw in Africa. "Only fifteen percent of the people in Mali have access to modern health care. The others have to rely entirely on traditional practitioners. In some cases, as with hepatitis, their cures are faster and better than anything offered by modern medicine."

For hepatitis, the seven-day cure involves grinding the living layer of bark from a gardenia micranthum tree into a fine yellow powder.

The first day the patient takes five grams of the powder, which has been mixed with one-quarter liter of fresh milk and allowed to stand for twelve hours. On each of the following six days he takes five grams mixed with water that has stood for thirty minutes.

The leaf of the same tree is used as a laxative, and its chopped root is used to treat diabetes. Asthma is treated with the carbonized nutlike fruit of the tree.

Traditional medicine does not ignore the organic and physical aspects of disease, although its approach stresses social and psychological factors as well. Satigi, for instance, started each diagnosis by taking the patient's history: Have there been financial or marital problems that would cause stress or other conditions? Have there been hostilities in relations with others? Has an evil spirit intervened? Have there been strains on the family as a unit?

Satigi rose from his mattress. "Now I must sleep," he said. "I am growing old, but there are so many who want to see me that there is not much time for sleep. You go now and when you write your story, do not write that I carry the forces of evil. It is I who confront the evil with my powers of good.

"Now go. Allah will protect you and love you. Your spirit will never be broken or cut. Your name is good as mother's milk."

He bowed and disappeared into a little cubicle off his consulting room to find rest at last. Four days later he died in his sleep.

In colonial times traditional healers like Satigi were often jailed by the authorities. They were considered part of the primitive un-Christian past which Europeans thought Africa needed to bury in order to take its place in the modern world. But there has been a dramatic shift in such thinking in recent years, and today the World Health Organization is trying to revolutionize the way health needs are handled in Africa and other parts of the Third World. The organization now defines health as "a complete state of physical, mental and social well-being and not merely the absence of disease and infirmity." To achieve this, Africa's primary emphasis must be on primary health care. Clean drinking water, improved sanitation, better birth-control programs, a balanced diet and increased food supplies are more important for Africa today than more drugs and doctors. Medical facilities such as the open-heart surgery unit built in Nairobi in the late 1970s can wait for another decade. Africa can no longer afford to concentrate all its medical services in the cities while ignoring the huge majority of people who live in the country.

As part of this realization, WHO now endorses the integration of traditional and modern medicine and recommends increased research into herbal as well as magical-religious cures attributed to thousands of practitioners such as Satigi. There is, the organization says, "an absolute need to establish national associations of traditional healers recognized by the authorities, members of which . . . would gradually come to realize their strength."

The health problem, like so many others in Africa, is one of education. Even if Africa can shift its medical emphasis from the cities to the villages, even if it can train the medical assistants willing to work in the rural areas, even if traditional and modern medicine can be integrated, it still will not be easy to convince an African mother that her children should not drink with the cattle from the same polluted waterhole or that dogs and humans should not share the same plate. After all, she will tell you, that's what her parents did and they lived to be forty or forty-five years old, so what can be wrong with the practices? But until public health becomes the concern of every village, the general standards of health will remain abysmal. Every developed country, including the United States, had to make this same transition.

In 1981, members of WHO meeting in Geneva voted 118–1 to restrict marketing practices of the $2 billion-a-year international baby-formula industry.* WHO estimated that the formula caused as many as ten million serious cases of malnutrition or diarrhea each year in the Third World, and one million deaths. Almost overlooked in the debate was the fact that there is nothing harmful about the formula itself; the danger occurs because illiterate mothers cannot read the instructions for preparing the formula and mix the powder with polluted water in unsterilized bottles.

But the Third World's suspicion that Western food and drug companies don't care how their products are used abroad is easy to understand. Foreign drug companies, in fact, have discovered a bonanza in black Africa, which they have turned into a dumping ground for their pills by capitalizing on the absence of consumer-protection laws and of regulations against false advertising.

---

* The United States cast the lone dissenting vote, contending that WHO should not act as an international Federal Trade Commission. Lobbyists for the baby-food industry pointed out that the formula was better for babies than the homemade concoctions many Third World mothers brew: paps, gruels, sugar water or herbal teas.

In movie theaters and on billboards across the continent, Africans are bombarded with messages that various drugs can restore youthful vigor, sexual potency, even mental alertness. Most of the advertisements are outright lies—they never could be published in the United States in the first place—yet Africans in huge numbers turn to these "miracle drugs" to cure everything from ankle sprains to polio. The practice is reminiscent of the quick-tongued salesmen who used to travel the Western frontier a century ago, peddling their cure-all potions from the back of horse-drawn carts; the results, though, are far more lethal in Africa than they ever were in Montana or Wyoming.

The most damning study I found on the role of drug companies in Africa was in a recent report published by Dr. John Yudkin of the London Hospital Medical College. His study dealt with the purchase, use and promotion of drugs in Tanzania, a country where there are 147 drug-company representatives (most of them Tanzanians working for firms with ties abroad) and only 600 doctors. The report said, in part:

> Aminopyrine and Ipyrone are analgesics [pain relievers] which may produce agranulocytosis—where, due to an allergenic reaction, the marrow stops producing white cells—with a mortality rate of about 1 in 200. In Britain and America these drugs have been virtually withdrawn from the market.
>
> They are licensed for use (in the West) only in patients with terminal malignant disease in whom safer fever-relieving drugs have been unsuccessful. In the African Monthly Index Medical Specialities [MIMS, a handbook published by the drug industry] thirty-one preparations containing these drugs are recommended as analgesics for minor conditions.
>
> Anabolic steroids may produce stunting of growth, irreversible virilization—changes of external genitalia and hair growth—in girls, and liver tumors. They are used in Britain to treat renal failure, terminal malignant disease and aplastic anemia. They are not recommended for use by children before puberty. In African MIMS, however, they are promoted as treatment for malnutrition, weight loss, exhaustion, "excessive fatiguability" in schoolchildren, and as appetite stimulants.
>
> Methadone is included in African MIMS as a cough repressant.

The West has poured billions of dollars into Africa in the past twenty years, attempting to elevate living standards. Most of the money has been wasted and many of the projects have been counterproductive. First, Africa cannot possibly afford the Western-style medical technology that has been forced on it by foreign governments and private donor agencies. (The health budgets of most African countries range from $1 to $10 per person; the United States spends about $800 per person.) Second, many of the development projects actually have *lowered* health standards instead of increasing them. For example, irrigation schemes and dams are intended to improve food production, but what they usually end up increasing is snail fever, the parasitic disease that drains the energy of 200 million people in the Third World.

Fortunately almost everyone now agrees that Africa must get back to basics in health care. Efforts to make Africa economically stable will fail until attempts to make Africa tolerably healthy succeed. There is no middle ground. In many ways the problem is more educational than medical and its genesis is at the lowest grass-roots level. Increasingly Africa itself recognizes this and is taking steps to change the emphasis of health care.

Nigeria plans to build 285 rural health clinics and has boosted its national health expenditures over a five-year period from $350 million to $2 billion. Mozambique inoculated more than half of its 10 million people against cholera and smallpox in one impressive nine-month campaign. Liberia has installed clean, piped water in six of its cities and now has ten hospitals and 220 clinics operating through the Ohio-sized country. In Kenya alone, more than 700 young Africans are studying medicine at the university level.

But Africa cannot do the job alone. The foreign powers which enslaved Africa, which colonized it and sent countries such as Chad and Guinea-Bissau reeling into independence without a single indigenous doctor, which exploit its minerals today and supply guns for its wars—all of them have a moral obligation to provide the personnel and monetary assistance the continent needs to escape the bondage of medieval health conditions. I remember touring a hospital in rural Zaire one day. Two and three patients shared the same bed. There was no air conditioning and most lay perspiring heavily, too weak to brush away the buzzing flies. Entire families camped around the bed of their sickly relatives. What, I thought, if the West never built another airport for an African government, never bought another gun, never underwrote another foolish project to pad the personal coffers of some soldier-president? What if the West—and even the East—concentrated instead on waging war on the conditions that cripple the bodies and spirits of Africa. A naïvely idealistic thought perhaps, but how exciting the results could be!

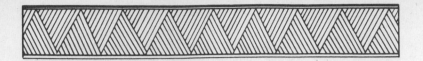

SYLIS AND CEDIS

▲

If we are to remain free, if we are to enjoy the full benefits of Africa's enormous wealth, we must unite to plan for the full exploitation of our human and material resources, in the interest of all our people.

—KWAME NKRUMAH,
president of Ghana (1957–1966)

THE CHARTERED CARGO JET from London arrived in the dead of night, taxiing past the deserted passenger terminal and whining to a stop at the far end of Ghana's Kotoka International Airport. A platoon of heavily armed soldiers moved quickly to take up their positions around the Boeing 707. Within seconds, word of the plane's arrival was flashed to a command post in nearby Accra, the capital, and the government broadcast an urgent message over the state radio station: the airport, all seaports and the international borders were closed until further notice.

Was this another coup d'état? Was the head of state returning from some secret mission or an unannounced vacation at his European estate? Not at all. In this hush-hush operation in 1979, Ghana was changing money, not governments. Its currency—the cedi—had been battered beyond value and would in the days ahead be banned, bundled and burned. In the plane was $690 million worth of new, redesigned cedis to replace the old money.

The Ghanaian cedi is among the frailest of Africa's currencies, but it has lots of company in the financial sick bay. From the birr of Ethiopia to the kwanza of Angola, currencies in black Africa are under siege, the victims of inflation, mismanagement, rising import costs and unsteady export prices. Most are as worthless as yesterday's newspaper and are neither accepted in neighboring countries nor exchanged for convertible currency at any foreign bank in the world. Just imagine that the dollars you used in California were useless in Nevada, New York and Washington, D.C., and converting California dollars to, say, Nevada dollars was a process that required several levels of governmental approval. You probably would not trade with Nevada, you would not travel to Nevada, you might not even communicate with Nevada. That is precisely what has happened in Africa where Monopoly-money currencies isolate countries economically and socially as surely as a border strewn with land mines.

Africa's general response to the weakening of its overvalued currencies has been to print more money. Nigeria increased its money supply between 1975 and 1977 by 180 percent. Ghana increased its supply 80 percent in 1976 alone and in one fourteen-year period (1965–1979) devalued its cedi seven times. And when the Ugandan finance minister told President Idi Amin that his treasury was out of money, Amin replied, "Well, print more."

With more money suddenly chasing fewer available goods, the annual inflation rate soars—it is regularly over 100 percent in countries such as Zaire and Uganda—and a dizzying rise in the cost of living destroys any sensible relationship between wages and prices; the poor became even poorer. The price of food in Ghana increased twenty-three-fold between 1963 and 1977, and in 1981 a single car tire cost the equivalent of $360, a tube of toothpaste $6.50. In Zaire a copy of *Time* magazine sells for $10, a loaf of bread for $2. In Zambia a laborer must spend seven days' wages to buy a crude cooking pot. Ghanaian laborers earn an average of $1.50 a day, but according to one Western study, it costs them $11 to buy a decent meal for a family of four.

"How do people survive?" asks Yaw Saffu, a University of Ghana professor, who served me a glass of water in his home, apologizing that he could not afford coffee. "With difficulty. They cut back to one meal a day. They get a second job. Their children get milk less often. They go to the countryside on weekends and pick bananas. Some go back to a barter economy. They buy nothing but absolute essentials in the stores.

"Of course, there's almost nothing available in the stores, anyway. And when something does show up—say a luxury, like a can of dried fish—it's so expensive you can't afford it. These cedis in my pocket don't mean anything, because they can't buy anything."

One survival technique is a lack of wastefulness; the African puts everything to use. Discarded wax-coated milk containers make far better starters for a charcoal fire than the fluids American supermarkets sell for $2 a can. Plastic sandwich bags brought to Africa by expatriates are washed over and over and seem to last forever. Old rubber tires are turned into sandals. Empty whiskey bottles are sold for a penny and filled with kerosene. Newspapers are recycled. Clothes are stitched again and again. Kitchen sponges are used until they disintegrate. Tin cans become patches for car fenders. Human waste is collected to fertilize the garden. Cardboard boxes become the walls of shanty homes. In many countries you cannot buy a beer to take out of a grocery store unless you first turn in an empty bottle.

The strength of any currency, in the developed or underdeveloped world, is dependent on the power of the local economy to produce goods and services. Thus South Africa's rand remains strong because that country's economy is bullish. And Liberia has a built-in cushion because it uses U.S. paper notes as its official currency. But in most African countries, production is declining at the same time that the money supply is increasing, and in twenty of them, according to the World Bank, the per capita income actually decreased during the decade of the 1970s. So with nothing to back the face value of its currencies—such as gold reserves, an accepted international currency, or the ability to produce goods and services—Africa's money has no more buying power than a barrel of penny postage stamps. When Pan American World Airways ended its service to Zaire in 1978, it had $3 million in local currency in its Zairian bank accounts. Pan Am could no nothing with the money other than pay a few bills in Kinshasa.

At independence, most African countries inherited a monetary system based on the English pound, the French franc, the Portuguese escudo or the Belgain franc. Nationalistic pride, however, got in the way of financial practicalities, and one country after another cut itself adrift from the backing of European currencies and began turning out a mind-boggling array of nonconvertible local currencies: the pula in Botswana, the dalasi in Gambia, the ekuele in Equatorial Guinea, the lilangeni in Swaziland, the naira in Nigeria, the ouguiya in Mauritania, the zaire in Zaire. If nothing else, the new presidents got a chance to put their picture on a paper bill, but most were overthrown before long and the notes had to be redesigned with a portrait of some other head of state.

Then came the inevitable coup de grâce to economic stability, the black market. The inflated prices for goods created an artificial economy for the local currency. The real economy came to be based on the illegal transactions of foreign currency and on smuggling. But to gain access to this economy, one needed "hard" money such as British pounds or American dollars, something only the privileged few and the foreigners possessed. So the average African had to live on the inflated economy—and pay its sky-high prices—while the elite converted its foreign exchange at illegal rates and paid realistic prices.

These money markets are controlled by the Lebanese in West Africa and the Indians in East Africa, who usually own legitimate businesses in addition to their moonlighting venture. They will exchange their local currency at a discount rate for your hard currency—cash, traveler's checks or personal checks—which they then smuggle to European banks.

Consider Uganda as an illustration. In 1980, before the International Monetary Fund ordered a devaluation as part of an unsuccessful economic recovery package, seven Ugandan shillings equalled one American dollar at the legal rate. But the black-market merchants gave you 140 shillings for that dollar, or twenty times what the bank offered. At the time a room in Kampala's International Hotel cost about 1,000 shillings a night. So if you were an African who only had shillings, the room cost the equivalent of $142. But if you had a convertible currency and changed it with the Indian importer who slipped through the hotel each morning with a suitcase full of Ugandan shillings, the cost became $7. Thus two economies operated in tandem—one for the unlucky majority that was based on Ugandan shillings, the other for the fortunate few who had access to foreign currency.

The struggle for foreign currency is so intense in countries such as Tanzania and Ghana that hotels insist guests pay their bills in something other than African currency. Kenya Airways, the national carrier, will not accept Kenyan shillings on its flight for the purchase of a cocktail—foreign currency, only, please. In Guinea, departing nonresidents must pay the $8 airport departure tax in currency other than the local syli (pronounced "silly"). In almost every country, airline tickets can only be purchased with foreign currency.

Africa's funny-money underscores the desperate condition of the continental economy. In absolute terms, the average African's standard of living is declining, particularly in relation to that of the ruling soldiers and the bureaucracy. The per capita income of $365 in Africa—or $1 a day—buys less than it did a decade ago. The food supply is dropping, while agricultural production declined an average of 1 percent each year through the 1970s, the population grew at an annual rate of 2.9 percent. In Zambia (where 280 white settler farmers produce more than half the food grown in the country) the per capita income has dropped 14 percent since 1970, exports have fallen 25 percent and consumer prices have risen 70 percent. A French agronomist, René Dumont, concluded after a lengthy study that what Zambia needed to revive its agricultural sector was not more expensive tractors or sophisticated techniques, but rather, he said, more reliance on oxen and carts, organic manure and more crop rotation with legumes to obtain higher yields and to save foreign exchange. His advice was ignored and the minister of agriculture, Alexander Chikwanda, denounced him as a "sham radical from Europe who wants us to be perpetual drawers of water and hewers of wood."

The response was an unfortunate one—and one that was very reflective of both the problems and the mood of Africa. The scars of slavery and colonialism run so deep, the suspicions of white motives are so great, the sensitivity toward any primitive part of the past is so numbing that black Africa is willing to stumble blindly into the future, oblivious of the consequences, finding almost masochistic pleasure in making its own mistakes.

The greater the public discontent becomes over economic conditions, the greater the social control that Africa's leaders exercise to retain power. The greater the national debt becomes, the greater Africa's reliance grows on foreign governments whose grants and loans—currently running about $10 billion a year—keep regimes in power. It is a destructive cycle that discourages the emergence of fresh faces and competent minds in the leadership hierarchy, leaving Africa's new generation of restless, educated youths with little role to play in their countries. When one of Liberia's top financial advisers tried to explain to the sergeant who ran the country, Samuel Doe, why a rise in gasoline prices was necessary, Doe balked. Finally the adviser said, "You don't sign this paper, country go blooey." Doe understood and signed.* (The adviser, a bright young man with a business degree from an Ivy League college, did not relish communicating with Doe in pidgin indefinitely and soon found an exile home in the United States.)

Some African countries are so inherently poor that there seems

---

* Quoted from the *New York Times* (January 20, 1981).

little hope they can ever survive without a tin cup extended. The gross national product for, say, Cape Verde (population: 350,000) is only $50 million a year. But what of the other countries? How did a continent of such great potential wealth, including 30 percent of the world's known mineral reserves, end up being the most economically depressed cluster of beggar states on earth? The answer lies in both the legacy of colonialism and the conduct of independence.

When Europe ran the continent, African peasants were forced to produce export crops to satisfy the import needs of Europe and to help pay the colony's bills. The colonial economy—and later the national economy of individual African countries—was more often than not based on a single commodity such as cashew nuts or cocoa and was deprived of the cushion that diversification provides. Each country, in effect, had all its eggs in one basket. If disaster struck, in the form of drought, famine, crop failure or mismanagement, the fragile economy shattered.

Kenya, for example, gets most of its foreign currency from coffee and tea, but in just one ten-month period, between 1976 and 1977, the price for a ton of coffee ranged from $1,636 to $3,958, and what may be a boom for Kenya one day is a bust the next. Nigeria gets 85 percent of its government revenue from oil. Zambia gets 96 percent of its export earnings from copper and cobalt. Guinea-Bissau doesn't produce much of anything besides groundnuts.

Africa, then, suffers twice in any international recession: first when its export earnings fall because of depressed world prices over which it has no control, and again when inflation forces up import bills for oil, food, spare parts and other commodities it needs to sputter along economically. The industrialized West can adjust for inflation and higher oil bills by charging more for goods; Africa, which produces so little, has no such luxury. It just grows poorer. In 1970, only 10 percent of Africa's export earnings went to pay for oil imports. By 1980 the figure was 22 percent. Uganda earns $10 million a month in government revenues (mostly from coffee) and spends precisely the same amount for oil. Tanzania has cut back its oil imports to 700,000 tons a year, less than it used in 1972, but is paying ten times more than it did a decade ago. National development becomes virtually irrelevant in such circumstances. Only survival counts. When Africa goes shopping it has the diminished buying power of a man who takes a wage cut year after year.

• • •

Ghana is a case in point. Black Africa's dreams were born in that West African country; they are also buried there, temporarily at least, in the folly and greed of soldier chiefs whose misrule spanned a decade. The Ghanaians, a proud, extroverted and educated people, shake their heads in wonderment today over what their country has become. Can this destitute, demoralized place, they ask, be the once thriving "Black Star of Africa," which in 1957 became the first black African nation to win its independence?

Known as the Gold Coast when it was a British colony, Ghana is shaped roughly like a shoe box and covers an area about the size of the United Kingdom. It is located on the Gulf of Guinea, just a few degrees north of the equator. Half the country is less than five hundred feet above sea level. The scrub-covered plains are criss-crossed by the mighty Volta River and numerous streams, most of which are navigable only by canoe. A tropical rain forest extends northward from the shore to the heavily forested northern hills, where the climate is so steamy-hot that it feels as though it were drizzling even when the sky is a cloudless, crystal blue. This area, once part of the Ashanti kingdom, produces most of Ghana's cocoa, timber and minerals.

There is no great treasure chest of gold in Ghana (the term "Gold Coast" actually refers to the money that slave traders made raiding the population) but the country *is* blessed with immense natural wealth. At independence Ghana was the world's largest producer of cocoa and the world's largest exporter of manganese. The British wanted Ghana to be an *African* country, and it was. No Europeans were allowed to settle there, or even to seek employment without specific government approval. British administrators in the colony numbered fewer than four thousand, and the people were left pretty much alone to "enstool" and "destool" (elect and dethrone) their own chiefs. This was done by popular vote in a state council.

But Ghana was brought to its knees after independence by its own leaders, men who pillaged with unabashed thoroughness. For many, what mattered was not that Ghana prospered and grew, but that they got their cut, deposited in European bank accounts. One head of state alone, General Ignatius Kutu Acheampong, was accused of—and later executed for—amassing an overseas fortune of $100 million. The Cocoa Marketing Board was unable to account for half of its foreign exchange earnings between 1975 and 1979. The ruling soldiers flew scores of Mercedes-Benzes into Ghana for personal use (cost $110,000 each, plus shipping charges) and squandered so much money that soon there was no more foreign exchange. The transportation system broke down, the stores displayed little but empty shelves, the legitimate economy was replaced by a black-market system known as *kalabule**** (cheating and smuggling), and when the inflation rate fell to 70 percent one year, the government declared an economic victory. Twenty-five years earlier, the people in Ghana had talked about their ability to achieve; now they speak only of their capacity to endure.

"The great thing about us," said Essilfie Conduah, a Ghanaian journalist, "is that we're never violent, even if the situation seems to call for violence. We keep our cool. There's a resiliency in the people, an ability to get clobbered and still survive. The Nigerians call us the eleven million magicians."

The irony of Ghana's economic collapse is that like so many African countries, it is not inherently poor. Its exports (mainly cocoa) still top $1 billion a year. Its overgrown farmland is potentially productive. Its waters are rich with fish, its forested interior holds diamonds, bauxite, gold and manganese.

But by the late 1970s, Ghana had been stripped bare, cannibalized like a car whose working parts had been stolen by thieves. As the economic situation worsened, the country produced its own version of boat people, peasants fleeing not repression but poverty, moving north in little homemade boats to the Ivory Coast and Liberia. When the Accra government offered free transportation home to the 50,000 Ghanaians living and working in Nigeria, no more than a handful accepted. And each day an average of fifty Ghanaians, the majority students, lined up at the American embassy in Accra to seek permission to enter the United States. Nearly half the applicants were rejected out of hand for submitting fraudulent educational documents. (Two firms in Accra supply, for a fee of $180, professional test-takers to ensure a passing mark on the government-administered education examination.) Nevertheless, more than 2,000 Ghanaians entered the United States in 1979 to study at American universities, and another 828 immigrated for noneducational reasons. Many of the students try to drag out their studies as long as possible, and if you spend a day riding taxi cabs in Washing-

---

* *Kalabule* is a Hausa tribal word, brought to Ghana by the traders from the north. It means "to take away without looking."

ton, D.C., I guarantee that at least a dozen of your drivers will be from Ghana, Nigeria or Ethiopia.*

It is a grievous state of affairs compared with what President Kwame Nkrumah had promised for Ghana in 1957. A man of extraordinary energy, idealism and patriotism, Nkrumah had spent a decade in the United States traveling and studying during the thirties and forties, and after leaving at the end of World War II, he wrote: "I saw the Statue of Liberty with her arm raised as if in personal farewell to me. (I said silently) 'You have opened my eyes to the true meaning of liberty. I shall never rest until I have carried your message to Africa.' " And carry it he did. Campaigning on the slogan "Self-Government Now," he quickly became a national hero—and nearly as quickly was jailed by the British on sedition charges. Later freed on orders of the British governor, Nkrumah was hailed as another Nehru, even a "Modern Moses." He was a handsome, charismatic figure whose jubilant people were spearheading political advancement in colonial Africa. His vision of black consciousness was instrumental in independence movements throughout the continent and in influencing civil rights initiatives as far away as the United States.

Nkrumah, who referred to himself as The Redeemer, believed that black people would never escape the bondage of servitude until they ended their dependence on agriculture and moved toward a manufacturing economy based on finished products. It was, in retrospect, the first of many Nkrumah decisions that transformed Ghana from the African model of freedom and prosperity to the African prototype of repression and poverty.

Great sums, much of it in foreign aid, were lavished with remarkable speed to fulfill Nkrumah's dreams of personal and national greatness. More than $16 million was spent on a conference hall to host a single meeting of the Organization of African Unity. Another $9 million went for a showcase highway that was only a few miles long and usually deserted, $8 million for a state house, $17 million for a drydock. Within seven years (1958–1965), foreign-exchange reserves of $481 million had turned into a $1 billion national debt, and as the people grew restive and angry, Nkrumah became ruthless and suspicious. He jailed his opponents, made himself president-for-life, reduced the parliament to a single-party rubber stamp,

* More than 40,000 Africans, half of them from Nigeria, are studying in the United States, and nearly 13,000 other Africans immigrate to the United States annually for reasons not related to education. In 1979, 2,667 Africans became naturalized American citizens.

passed a law permitting the imprisonment of dissidents for five years without trial and moved closer to the Communist world. When he was overthrown in 1966 while headed for China—where, he said, he intended to find a solution to the Vietnam war—his people shed few tears. They tore down his statue and sent his portrait to the sixty member countries of Interpol (the international police agency), charging him with extortion and corruption. It was indeed an inglorious ending for a man who once held such hope as a leader of global stature, a man whose gravest error may have been that in the final years he began believing he really was all the things he said he was.

Nkrumah lived in exile until he died of cancer in Guinea, where President Sékou Touré had taken the unusual step of making him a "co-president." His obituary read like that of so many other African presidents. "Nkrumah could have been a great man," wrote Colonel Akwasi Amankwa, one of the leaders of the 1966 coup. "He started well, led the independence movement and became, on behalf of Ghana, the symbol of emergent Africa. Somewhere down the line, however, he became ambitious, built a cult of personality and ruthlessly used the powers invested in him by his own constitution. He developed a strange love for absolute power."

The removal of Nkrumah, though, did not solve Ghana's problems; in an African country the first coup is seldom the last. The soldiers who toppled him surrendered power to a democratically elected civilian government three years later. But in 1972 the civilians were overthrown by General Acheampong, a devout Roman Catholic who frequently appeared at morning meetings sweating profusely, chain-smoking and drinking whiskey. Acheampong was ousted by his chief of staff, Lieutenant General Frederick W. K. Akuffo, in 1978. The next year Akuffo was overthrown by a thirty-two-year-old air force lieutenant, Jerry Rawlings, who had Acheampong and Akuffo executed after a secret trial as part of his "coup of conscience" to clean up Ghana. "Action, action, finish them all!" yelled the crowd as the former heads of state and several other top officials were blindfolded and bound to execution posts. Three months later, in September 1979, Rawlings surprised a good many people by handing over power, as he had promised to do, to an elected civilian government headed by President Hilla Limann, a career diplomat who had once served with the overseas arm of Ghana's secret police.

Shortly before Limann took office, an American diplomat asked the president-elect what he was going to do to encourage the foreign investment Ghana so desperately needed. "Encourage it?" Limann asked. "We won't have to. As soon as we have a civilian government, foreign investment will pour into Ghana."

It didn't. Admirable as Ghana's return to civilian rule was, by 1982 the country had slipped so far backward that no one, least of all the Ghanaians, had any faith left in its future. Ghana's national debt at the time was nearly $2 billion; it was eighty-nine months behind on its loan repayments; its inflation rate topped 100 percent a year. Shortages of essential commodities were so severe that, as a Christmas present, nearby Nigeria sent Ghana twenty-three truckloads of food and medicine. Even Limann was not sure that he could hold the place together. "I am sitting on a time bomb," he said.

On New Year's Eve 1981, the bomb went off. Jerry Rawlings, who had been scuttled into retirement by Limann's civilian government, stepped from the shadows with gun in hand and the support of the army. Within six hours Limann had been placed under house arrest, accused of corruption and mismanagement, and Rawlings had taken power for the second time in twenty-seven months. Ghana's overjoyed soldiers promptly went on a looting rampage in Accra, cleaning out the shops of anything that wasn't nailed down. "We are asking for nothing more than proper democracy," Rawlings said somewhat inexplicably in a broadcast to the nation.

Like every African country, Ghana pays a stiff price today because it still trades principally with the developed world, not with its neighbors. This is another legacy of the one-commodity economies introduced by the colonialists and another retardant to Africa's economic growth. Only 4 percent of Africa's total trade is with Africa, the smallest intracontinental trade in the world. To understand the obstacles this creates, imagine what would happen to the American economy if each of the fifty states traded with the world but hardly ever with one another. California and Nevada might not do business, so Nevada would buy its lettuce from Mexico and its beef from Australia. Maine would sell fish to Italy and canoes to Brazil and nothing to Massachusetts. New York and North Carolina would buy all their manufactured goods from Europe and Asia. If the New York apple crop failed one season, the state would have to borrow money from England because it would have no other commodities to cushion the loss of revenue.

To break this dependence on foreign markets, each U.S. state would then try to develop its own light industries, but with no regional coordination, would never know what its neighbor was doing. Soon every state would have its own brewery, cement plant, tobacco industry. Most would be too small to turn a profit and would have to be subsidized by state governments and protected by high interstate tariffs. Recognizing the absurdity of the situation, the New England states—each with its own international airline—would establish a regional economic community. They would merge their six airlines into a single carrier, remove trade barriers and eliminate immigration formalities at the borders. A single tobacco factory in Vermont would supply cigarettes to the entire region, New Hampshire would produce beer for its five neighbors. But there would be problems right from the start. The states would speak different languages and use different currencies, which would not be honored next door. To complete the scenario, let's say that Vermont and New Hampshire were fighting a border war; Maine was governed by the national guard and had decided to pursue a Marxist philosophy; Connecticut had a new civilian government oriented toward capitalism; Rhode Island was ruled by a former police chief who had declared himself governor-for-life; and Massachusetts had foiled an attempted coup and asked Canada to send troops to protect its territorial integrity.

Ludicrous as all this sounds for the United States (which did, in fact, have interstate economic rivalries early in its history), it is the reality of trade and regional relations in Africa. Trapped by its colonial past, divided by political and cultural differences, isolated by the absence of an intra-Africa highway or an intra-Africa communications system, each country is little more than a haphazardly placed economic pocket, neither related to nor dependent on its neighbors. As a group of three or four major regional communities, Africa could have great economic strength. As fifty-one separate entities, it has virtually none.

The colonialists' introduction of export-crop farming had moved the African peasant from a barter to a cash economy. But the countryside could not provide the wages and jobs families needed, so men left their farms—and their wives and mothers—and drifted into the cities where the money and the work were. There they found that the promises of the cities were mostly an illusion. Governments nationalized private enterprises, resulting in economic stagnation, and presidents preached a doctrine of economic socialism without understanding socialistic theory or daring to give workers control of state power. Economies could not expand fast enough to absorb the job seekers and many young, talented Africans went off to Europe and the United States to study and work, depriving Africa of some of its brightest minds. Factories were set up, but they chugged along in the red because, although African wages are low, African labor is expensive. The high cost stems from inefficiency that is related to lack of discipline, absenteeism and lack of skills. Production declined and population soared. Everything was run by trial and error, and no one seemed to worry that Africa was producing less and less food.

"Twenty years ago, the farmer had real status in the community," said B. N. Okigbo, deputy director of the International Institute of Tropical Agriculture in Nigeria, where 90 percent of the farmers work no more than five-acre plots. "Today farming is an old person's profession and farmers don't have much status unless they have material possessions to show for their work."

Africa has one other great natural resource that has not been mentioned—its wildlife. And that wildlife translates into big money because wherever there are well-maintained national parks there are tourists, and tourists leave behind precious foreign currency. In Kenya alone, tourism brings $150 million a year into the country, making the industry nearly as valuable as Kenya's coffee crop. But the wondrous herds that once roamed free across the continent are today part of a drama for survival that is unfolding on the dust-red, powder-dry plains. The drama pits the cunning and endurance of the beast against the greed of man and the ravages of nature; in the nearly unanimous view of conservationists, the wildlife is losing, its very existence threatened. "Simply put, one of the real treasures of Africa is disappearing," said Sydney Downey, a white Kenyan and retired professional hunter.

Many conservationists believe that Africa is destined to become a graveyard of wildlife. Theodore Roosevelt rode a train through Kenya's Athi Plain in 1909 and wrote: "As we sat over the train's cowcatchers it was literally like passing through a vast zoological garden." Today a traveler on the same route would be lucky to see a score of zebra or wildebeests, and game lodges along the way have been forced to install waterholes, salt licks and floodlights to lure animals within camera range of cocktail-sipping guests. The herds of elephant and rhinoceros that once moved across the continent have all but vanished, and only within the sanctuary of national parks do they wander with any degree of safety.

The reason is money, for a new currency has been introduced to Africa that is far more valuable than all the sylis and cedis combined. It is ivory. In 1970, ivory was bringing $2.30 a pound on world markets in Brussels, Hong Kong and Tokyo. A decade later it was fetching $70. The rhino horn—made of compressed hair and gelatin—is even more valuable.* It sells for up to $300 a pound in the Middle East, where it is carved into handles for traditional Arab daggers, or in Asia, where it is ground into a fine powder for use as an aphrodisiac. Thus enter a new predator, the poacher. Using poisoned arrows, machine guns and Soviet AK-47 assault rifles and operating in well-organized groups, the poacher can kill an elephant, cut off its trunk, gouge away the mouth and hack off a pair of six-foot-long ivory tusks in a matter of hours. The booty he receives is more than he could make in five or six years of honest labor.

Iain Douglas-Hamilton, a Nairobi-based British scientist who in 1980 completed the first continental study ever done on elephants, concluded that there were about 1.3 million elephants left in thirty-five African countries. But they are being killed at the rate of 50,000 to 150,000 a year, far faster than they can reproduce. Kenya had 70,-000 elephants in 1973 and probably has half that number today. Its rhino population has fallen from 10,000 to 2,000 in the same period—and in some parks rangers are assigned to guard individual rhinos twenty-four hours a day. The southern district of Uganda's Kabalega Falls National Park had 8,000 elephants in 1966. Systemic slaughters carried out by president Idi Amin's soldiers reduced them to a panicked herd of 160, which since has been exterminated. For the Europeans and Americans preaching wildlife conservation—the missionary-style campaign, unfortunately, is handled almost exclusively by whites—the message seemed clear enough: in another generation or two, the African elephant may be as rare as the American buffalo.

With international pressure mounting, Kenya banned hunting in

---

* Each rhinoceros has two horns, which combined weigh about eight pounds. Despite their belligerent appearance, the 1.5-ton adult rhinos are generally placid, inoffensive vegetarians. They fear no predators except man and are easy prey for poachers. Rhinos once inhabited widespread areas of the eastern and western hemispheres but are now restricted to tropical Asia and Africa.

1977 to protect its wildlife and tourist industry and formed an anti-poaching unit (whose seventy rangers "patrol" an area twice the size of Great Britain).* It was a good public relations gesture but had little practical effect because, as in most African countries, the people who hired the poachers, bought the ivory and used bogus documents to export it were top government officials and senior game wardens. For years, the biggest illegal ivory exporter in Kenya was the United African Corporation (UAC), which operated out of a posh suite on Kimathi Street, a downtown Nairobi boulevard named for a Mau Mau general. The chairman of UAC and the holder of 49 percent of its capital was the mayor of Nairobi, Margaret Kenyatta, none other than the daughter of President Jomo Kenyatta. In 1975, according to government figures, Kenya exported to Hong Kong 106 tons of ivory (which meant the killing of about 1,010 elephants). Hong Kong figures, however, show that it *imported* 148 tons from Kenya that year. The difference—46 tons, then worth approximately $2 million—was presumably smuggled out of Kenya. In the late 1970s, the World Bank gave Kenya $3 million to train and equip an antipoaching unit. Kenya instead used most of the money to form a paramilitary force that was stationed along its border with hostile Somalia, a desert area where there is no wildlife.

Prince Bernhard of the Netherlands—president of the World Wildlife Fund, the influential conservationist group—flew to Kenya in 1973 and gave President Kenyatta a check for $40,000 to enlarge the great bird sanctuary around Lake Nakuru in the Rift Valley. When Bernhard urged in private talks that Kenya take firm steps to halt elephant poaching, Kenyatta responded by promising to ban all ivory dealings. He set up a study group to assess the problem, then promptly fired the author of the resultant report, who implied that the problem was close to home. Poaching continued unabated and the Kenyatta Royal Family, as it became known, continued to prosper. Nonetheless, Bernhard returned to Kenya the next summer to bestow on Kenyatta—patriarch of the world's most important ivory-dealing family—the "Order of the Golden Ark" for services to wild-

---

* Kenya's 106 professional hunters—90 whites and 16 Africans—argued convincingly that their presence in the bush was actually a deterrent to poaching and represented no threat to the well-being of wildlife. Their livelihood, they said, depended on observing conservation regulations and avoiding reckless shooting. In the last year that hunting was legal, the professionals and their clients took only 6,000 trophies, a fraction of what poachers killed.

life. Conservationists were so aghast that Bernhard, after receiving a series of eleventh-hour long-distance phone calls, agreed to rewrite his presentation speech and ended up thanking Kenyatta for little more than his donation of some animals to West Africa.

It would, of course, be a noble accomplishment if Africa could protect and save its wildlife. But to condemn the Africans for not doing so is to impose Western standards on a situation in which they are irrelevant. The African sees no more beauty or mystique in an elephant than an American does in a porcupine. For those with guns and connections, all wildlife is a source of instant wealth. For those of meager means, it is competition for the land, a marauding army that can wipe out a season's harvest in an overnight rampage. A Kenyan friend remembers seeing his school and home destroyed by a herd of elephants and spending the night perched in a tree with his family to escape the beasts below. "And you tell me I should *love* the elephants?"he asks. One elephant alone eats six hundred pounds of food a day. Turn a herd loose for a week and it can uproot enough trees, tear down enough fences, trample enough acreage and eat enough foliage to transform a lush green valley into an arid wasteland fit for neither man nor animal. In countries such as Kenya, where every inch of usable land is already under cultivation, the wildlife that the tourists marvel over is a luxury the peasants can ill afford.

When two herds of elephants moved into Rwanda's overcrowded farmland in 1975, the government commissioned several white hunters to reclaim the land for the people. On foot and in an airplane, they shot and killed 106 of the elephants and "darted" the remaining twenty-six young ones with tranquilizer guns, moving them into a national park. The conservationists howled. But the Rwandan government had had a simple choice: either the people or the animals survived.

Kenya's response to a similar dilemma also seems a sensible one. Relying on tranquilizer guns and huge nets, Land-Rovers and airplanes, the government is moving great numbers of elephants, rhinos, zebras and giraffes back into the national parks (one of which, Tsavo, is as large as the state of New Jersey) where, for the time being at least, they will not compete with man for the country's diminishing farmland. Over several years in the late 1970s, drought and poachers forced thousands of elephants to migrate from Kenya's barren north to seek safety and food in the highlands, the country's most fertile and productive region. I joined the rangers one day as they tried to move a herd of two hundred elephants into Aberdare National Park.

The herd, frightened and enraged, thundered across the highlands' plateau like a fleet of tanks, crashing through trees, fences, even villages. They gathered in a great milling mass, trunks raised in trumpet, then spun and rushed again. The earth trembled and entire villages fled the advance. Dust clouds swirled into the early-morning mist and the herd turned up the wooded valley, the calves struggling to keep up, the bulls and cows scrambling just ahead of the helicopter that hovered at treetop level with police siren screaming.

Darting to and fro overhead, the British-born warden Tedd Goss used the helicopter as a trail boss used his horse in an Old West cattle drive. He nudged the herd along, heading strays back into the group, picked out suitable terrain ahead and gave commands to the African elephant drovers who slogged along on foot.

"There's a mob trying to break off to the south, chaps," he radioed. "I don't want that. Get some men over there ... Okay, Bongo One, that's far enough with the vehicles. Leave them there to block ... Phil, what have you got up there?"

In his command post two thousand feet above, Phil Snyder, a warden from Berkeley, California, peered from the window of his single-engine plane, a floppy brown hat on his head, his long brown hair tied in a bun, a roll of toilet paper on the control panel to cope with a nagging cold.

"What you see down there," Snyder shouted to me over the roar of his engine, "is the cutting edge of a conservation conflict that's just beginning. You've got Kenya saying it wants to preserve its wildlife and, at the same time, committing itself to becoming self-sufficient in food production.

"They're ambitious goals. But are they compatible? As the marginal land gets settled and farmers and wildlife compete for what little land is left, Kenya is going to have to make a national choice. The question is, Can Kenya accommodate both?"

History would seem to make the answer evident. The epitaph for Africa's wildlife may, in fact, already have been written; from the frontier of America to the plains of Africa, there has always been only one winner when the needs of man and animal collide. As I write this, Phil Snyder is preparing to leave for a new job in the

Sudan, his position in Kenya having been "Africanized."* The European wardens in Kenya are being eased out of their jobs too, and soon the Kenyan Tourism and Wildlife Ministry will be entirely in the hands of the men who control the country's poaching operations. Another chapter of white influence in Africa is ending and the result will be that the continent's wildlife cannot hope to survive outside the national parks. It is sad, but that is the future.

Thus far I have spoken only of Africa's economic problems. But what of the solutions? Are there even solutions? The answer, I believe, is an unqualified yes—if the West is willing to help and Africa is able to capitalize on its tremendous assets by mounting a serious campaign to promote national instead of individual advancement. Just think how much has been written about Saudi Arabia's flashy future. Yet that country has just one limited resource. Africa has oil too, but it also has great quantities of other minerals and the endless farmland a continent needs to be self-sufficient. Saudi Arabia is only now establishing the infrastructure—ports, highways, communications, government services—that a country must have to develop. Africa has an infrasructure, however shaky, established nearly a hundred years ago by Europe. Saudi Arabia was isolated from the outside world for centuries. Africa has been exposed to it for generations. And while Saudi Arabia is painfully hot and full of sand, most of sub-Sahara Africa is blessed with a favorable climate and great beauty and could become a multibillion-dollar vacationland for tourists from around the world.

If you look at the handful of African countries that have combined economic progress with political stability since independence—the Ivory coast, Kenya, Malawi and Cameroon—four common denominators are apparent. First, all four countries were ruled for at least the first fifteen years of nationhood by their founding presidents, each of whom was authoritarian bt not wildly repressive. (Malwai's Hastings Banda fell just short of being a tyrant, though.) Their governments had a continuity that enabled national

*Synder was hired by the Frankfurt Zoological Society to set up Sudan's first wildlife preserve—the Boma National Park, a day's drive from Juba. In June, 1983, while Snyder was in Khartoum on business, rebel guerrillas took five Western relief workers hostage at the Boma airstrip. The rebels' demands included $189,000 in cash, 150 pairs of shoes, some pants and air time on the Voice of America. Government troops attacked a few days later, killing eighteen of the guerrillas and freeing the hostages unharmed. The project to establish the park was scrapped.

politics to be formed and pursued, and obviated the need for major expenditures on defense and internal security. Second, all four continue to use a large number of Europeans in the private and public sectors. By moving cautiously in the "Africanization" of their economies, the countries maintained a level of expertise in key positions and were less apt to be run on a trial-and-error basis by untrained Africans. Third, all placed a higher priority on economic pragmatism than on political ideology, and none had an alliance with the Soviet Union or even a dalliance with Marxism. There were economic incentives for people who produced, and individual achievement was encouraged, not stifled. Fourth, all made agriculture the backbone of their economies, and only when their farmlands were productive did they turn their attention to developing a light-industrial base.

The United Nations' Economic Commission for Africa has set a goal of Africa having one fiftieth of the world's industrial output by the year 2000. That modest accomplishment would represent four times more productivity than Africa had in 1980 and would require an investment of $250 billion to build the necessary highways, ports, factories and vocational training facilities. That is an unlikely sum for Africa to muster, but the continent can still take important steps toward fulfilling its economic potential if three objectives are established and met: (1) increase farm production and decrease baby production; (2) allow a new generation of national leaders with the integrity, wisdom and courage to act on behalf of the majority; (3) form regional economic communities that would absorb the weak states and give strength to the unit as a whole.

The idea of regional groupings is not new. Kenya, Tanzania and Uganda were linked at independence in the East African Community, which many economists viewed as one of the world's best models of regional cooperation. The three countries shared a common airline as well as postal, transportation and customs facilities. Their currencies were convertible within the community, and residents of one country could move freely throughout—and work in— the member states. In West Africa, fifteen states of varying linguistic and political backgrounds have been loosely joined since 1975 in the Economic Community of West African States (ECOWAS). Liberia, Sierra Leone and Guinea have formed what is known as the Mano River Union. And in 1981 Senegal and The Gambia established a union called Senegambia.

What sounds good in theory, however, is difficult to promote in practice. The communities have not worked out, for the same reason that a Cairo–Cape Town transcontinental highway has never been built: cross-border rivalries are stronger than the desire for neighborly cooperation. The East Africa Community was dissolved in 1977 due to political differences between capitalistic Kenya and socialistic Tanzania and militaristic Uganda. President Julius Nyerere closed his border with Kenya—it was still sealed in 1982—in a futile attempt to get European tourists to fly directly to Tanzania instead of transiting through Kenya. But all he managed to accomplish was the loss of valuable trade routes into Central Africa for both countries and the reduction of tourism in all East Africa. For just that reason, the oft-discussed idea of a transcontinental highway—similar to, say, the Pan American highway in South America—is an idea whose time has not yet come. Presidents would close it down out of petty jealousies, soldiers would blockade it to collect duties, governments could not afford to maintain it. Until Africa can develop continental transportation and communication networks, and can achieve regional harmony, most states will continue to find that it is cheaper to trade with Europe than with one another.

As for Africa's failing currencies, the solution seems fairly straightforward. Individual national currencies should be discarded in favor of four or five regional ones that are closely linked with a European monetary system. This, in fact, has already proved effective. Thirteen French-speaking countries in Africa use the Communauté Financière Africaine (CFA) franc, a currency backed by France which is as convertible at a Paris bank as an American dollar or a British pound. There is an interesting historical aside here that shows that the system benefited both Africa and Europe. In the fifties and sixties, when France needed hard currency for its own development, all foreign exchange flowing through the thirteen countries or colonies eventually ended up in the central bank in Paris. Theoretically, the African governments could draw foreign exchange freely to meet their own needs, but the system and the issuance of import licenses was controlled by Frenchmen and little hard currency found its way back to Africa. Thus, the Ivory Coast sold its coffee to the United States for American dollars, which went to Paris and were used for France's development. CFA francs, in turn, went to the Ivory Coast and were used to buy French goods.

Neither party lost: Africa had a convertible currency to buy the goods it required, and France had $300 million a year that it otherwise would not have had access to.

Today much of the foreign currency goes directly to Africa. But because the CFA franc is convertible in France—and not in the United States or most other European countries—the thirteen African nations are obligated to buy mostly French goods. If the transaction sounds one-sided, just remember that countries like Guinea and Ghana can't buy anything at all abroad with their sylis and cedis.

Undeniably, though, the West's post-independence contributions to Africa have been paltry and often misdirected. The billions of dollars in aid money thrown haphazardly into Africa have accomplished no more than President Lyndon B. Johnson's War on Poverty did in America. They have created a welfare-state mentality, and governments have come to realize that there is no need to do anything for themselves because someone in Stockholm or Paris or Washington will do it for them at no cost. Poverty has become the engine that drives the African economy.

Why should Africa worry about producing more food when a Western government will ship in all the grain it needs as soon as some president hollers "Emergency!"? What the West should do is formulate a Marshall Plan for the Third World that places the emphasis on producing more and wasting less. It should help every country, regardless of its ideological persuasion, because to isolate the radical states only drains the cohesiveness and potential growth of the region as a whole. To use aid—as the United States does—primarily to reward those who share Washington's political views serves to heighten cross-border rivalries and retards Africa's development as a unit.

The West holds the key to Africa's development. But for Africa to seek a closer economic alliance with Europe, for presidents to throw away the paper notes bearing their portraits in favor of a regional currency, would require a few people to swallow some national and personal pride. It would, though, be a significant move toward economic stability and regional collaboration. It would strengthen the weaker states and enrich the already buoyant ones, such as Nigeria. Some critics undoubtedly would say the suggestion is a neocolonial one. But if it helped the continent realize its awesome economic potential, wouldn't Africa really be stepping into the future instead of slipping into the past, as it is doing today?

NIGERIA:
THE FUTURE IS NOW

▲

Nigeria marches on. Every day is a new day in this
march forward. Where do you belong? To yesterday,
today or tomorrow? Nigeria needs your contribution, a
positive, meaningful contribution.

—Background voice on Nigerian
TV each evening at 9 P.M.

NIGERIA IS NAMED for the river Niger, which means black, and
there is no place else in Africa quite like it. The contrasts are greater,
the beat is faster, the dreams bigger. Every time I entered Lagos, the
capital that seems a combination of Calcutta and Harlem, I shuddered, wondering if there wasn't an easier way to earn a living than
journalism; every time I left I felt exhilarated, my belief in Africa's
future rejuvenated, for I knew that I had been in the most exciting
country in all of the Third World.

Nigeria is as large as California, Arizona and New Mexico combined. It has 250 ethnic groups, which speak a hundred different
languages. Its coastal mangrove swamps extend to the wooded savannah of the central plateau and finally give way to the northern
deserts, as barren and God-forsaken as the Sahara. Its cities are
overcrowded and unmanageable, with slums and suburbs competing
for the same turf, and Oxford-educated millionaires and unemployed illiterates sharing the same block. Contrasts and contradic-
tions are everywhere. And everywhere there is a reminder that Nigeria moves to the rhythm of money, big money that springs from its
plentiful oil wells. Nigeria is the Brazil of Africa. It is a country that
has come alive and made things happen, even though it is far from
immune to the problems that haunt every African nation.

Part of what makes Nigeria different from the rest of black Africa
is its history, for it is no cultural upstart. The Noks were casting iron
and producing terra-cotta sculpture before the birth of Christ. The

northern cities of Kano and Katsina were cosmopolitan terminals on the trans-Sahara caravan routes when William the Conqueror ruled England. And when the first Europeans reached Benin in the fifteenth century—a good many years before Columbus set off for the Americas—they found a highly organized kingdom with a disciplined army, an elaborate ceremonial court, and artisans whose work in ivory, bronze, wood and brass is prized throughout the world today for its craftsmanship and beauty.

The first whites to reach Nigeria were Portuguese explorers. Then came the traders, who bought strong young Nigerians for $4 each from local chiefs—the slaves sold for up to $130 apiece at auctions in the Americas—and the missionaries. The European powers recognized Britain's claim to Nigeria at the Berlin Conference and the London-based Royal Niger Company was chartered to develop commercial ties. The British government took over the company's territory in 1900, and fourteen years later the area was formally united as the Colony and Protectorate of Nigeria. (Administratively Nigeria remained divided into the Northern and Southern provinces and Lagos Colony.)

By African standards Nigeria was an advanced society, and the British, realizing its economic potential, tried to make sure that it would develop as a truly *black* colony. There were fewer than 12,-000 Europeans in Nigeria's pre-independence population of 32 million, and no white man was allowed to enter Nigeria, much less work there, unless he could prove that his presence was necessary. Whites were not allowed to settle or buy businesses, and everyone who did enter had to post a sizable bond. Interestingly, the British seldom referred to the local population as "natives." They called the people what they were, "Nigerians," a mark of respect seen in almost no other colony. As far back as 1922, the British permitted African legislators to be included in a council for Lagos Colony and the Southern Province. In 1943 the British appointed three Africans to the Nigerian Executive Council, which was under the jurisdiction of the British Governor's Cabinet. By the end of World War II, Britain was moving Nigeria toward self-government on a representative, federal basis. The reason was more self-serving than altruistic: London did not want to risk losing Nigeria as a member of the Commonwealth when independence inevitably came.

In October 1960 Nigeria passed, peacefully and uneventfully, from colonialism to nationhood. The enterprise of black traders and businessmen, based on cocoa and palm-oil exports, was well established by then. There was, however small, an educated African middle class, a lively black press that had been functioning for more than a hundred years, an active parliament, a sturdy economy and an agricultural sector that produced enough food to feed the nation. Nigeria even had five hundred black doctors, a remarkable number considering that many new countries started off with none. On top of that, four years earlier, drillers had discovered deep pools of oil in the Niger delta. Even nature, it seemed, had smiled on Nigeria.

But black Africa's biggest hope soon became its greatest disappointment. In the first sixteen years of independence there were three coups d'état, the assassinations of two heads of state, and one civil war that claimed a million lives. The country's oil revenues were squandered in the biggest spending binge any African country ever went on. The soldiers came to power and proved themselves more corrupt and less efficient than the civilians they had overthrown for their corruption and inefficiency. The cities filled up and broke down. The farmlands emptied and stopped producing. The parliament dissolved, the economy deteriorated, the dreams disintegrated.

With many African countries, you could end the story right there. But not with Nigeria. It did what no other African country had been able to do: reverse the downward skid, revert from military to civilian rule and recapture some of the promises that independence was all about. For Nigeria, the 1980s brought membership in an exclusive club of one. It was emerging as black Africa's first minipower, a nation with enough clout to influence policy in capitals from Washington to Moscow. It is the one black country in Africa whose future really matters to the outside world, and the one country whose present is described in superlatives.

▶ Nigeria (which retains its membership in the Commonwealth) is the most populous nation in Africa, and with more than 80 million people, it has a larger population than any country in Western Europe. Nearly one of every five Africans is a Nigerian.

▶ Nigeria is black Africa's wealthiest nation. Its gross national product is more than half that of the other forty-five black African nations combined (and is larger than South Africa's).

▶ Nigeria is the world's fourth largest democracy (ranking behind India, the United States and Japan). The soldiers ended thirteen years of military rule in 1979 and handed over power to civilian leaders whose new political system was modeled after that of the United States. It marked the first time any Third World country had chosen and implemented an American-style form of democracy.

▶ Nigeria is the world's sixth largest exporter of crude oil, about half of which goes to the United States. Only Saudi Arabia sells more oil to the United States. Nigeria's oil revenues plunged from $26 billion in 1980 to $10 billion in 1983, but even with the decline, Nigeria was still earning more from its petroleum in a single year than a country such as Equatorial Guinea would earn from all sources in thirty-three years. (Nigeria's revenues were cut by more than half by the oil glut of 1982, a setback that is no doubt temporary.)

In the 1960s, before world oil prices went crazy, Nigeria was banking a modest $400 million a year from its petroleum production. Then, almost overnight, that income soared to $9 billion a year, and by 1975 Nigeria was facing the prospect of a $5 billion annual surplus. Suddenly no dream was too distant, no vision too expensive.

Cocky as a teen-ager, Nigeria started walking with a swagger. Millionaires emerged; a privileged, middle-upper class was born. The able-bodied left their farms and poured into the cities in search of spoils. The government drew up a $100 billion development plan (1975–1980), the most ambitious ever underwritten by a black African government. It was designed to transform an ancient, heterogeneous society into a modern, unified state in five years.

While soldier politicians and businessmen collected millions of dollars in illegal kickbacks on each new project, plans were made or ground was broken for seven new universities, thirteen new television stations, thirty-four new prisons, three new international airports and a new federal capital at Abuja. With hardly a glance at the national checkbook balance, the minimum wage was doubled and the government granted all civil servants a 60 percent pay raise, backdated tax-free for ten months. Similar increases for the trade unions followed.

More than $3 billion was earmarked to overhaul the communications system, another $3 billion to build 13,000 miles of paved roads, and $2 billion more for a petrochemical plant. An international black arts festival was staged for $200 million, an international trade fair for $100 million. The vanguard of 50,000 young Nigerians was sent to the United States and Europe to learn the technical and professional skills necessary to run the New Nigeria.

Predictably, the world took quick notice of Nigeria. Suitors arrived from everywhere, and both Washington and Moscow elbowed for influence. Nearly a hundred foreign embassies were set up in Lagos, and the sauna-hot, jam-packed capital took on all the trappings of a frontier boom town. Diplomats and businessmen filled the hotels, stoically ignoring broken air conditioners, stalled elevators, power failures, water rationing, dead telephones and nightmarish traffic jams (known as "go-slows"). Lagos was suffocating in its own growth, but no one seemed to care. Everyone wanted a slice of the action, and in 1978 President Jimmy Carter made a state visit to Nigeria, telling gathered officials and journalists somewhat inexplicably, how much Nigeria and the United States had in common (even though Nigeria was then under military dictatorship).

But by the time Carter arrived a traumatic thing had happened: Nigeria had awakened one morning with a spending hangover. The party was over. Nigeria had priced itself out of the world oil market at a time when demand was falling. Its commitment to ongoing projects was four times the funding available. Frugality became the new order of the day. The government auctioned off two thousand official limousines, froze wages and prices to stem a 30 percent inflation rate, put most of its flashy development plans on ice and banned a long list of nonessential imports ranging from toothpicks to macaroni.

No one, to be sure, is crying poverty these days. Nigeria, which owns 55 percent of its nationalized oil industry, still has known reserves for about forty years at the extraction rate of 2 million barrels a day. It also has vast untapped quantities of natural gas. But Nigeria learned that petrodollars alone will not bring prosperity. It paid the price for having a one-commodity economy and discovered the dangers of trying to go too far too fast. The oil that was Nigeria's blessing had provided as many curses as it had cures.

Like every African country endowed with mineral wealth, Nigeria forgot its farms—and the fact that a nation unable to feed itself cannot be truly free. As people flocked into the cities, food production tumbled and imports soared. The country that was once self-sufficient in agricultural produce now imports four times more food than it did a decade ago at an annual cost of $1 billion. Before the boom faded, Nigeria was spending $5 million a month just to fly frozen meat into Lagos, a luxury best left for Third World countries like Saudi Arabia. The rural exodus also strained the already meager urban services to the breaking point and beyond. Nigeria had become a prisoner of its own wealth, and Lagos was a capital that tourists avoided and numerous Western diplomats refused to be posted in.

Government offices in Lagos are so overstaffed and underequipped that hundreds of civil servants work at desks lined up in stuffy, dimly lit corridors. Most telephones don't work, so businessmen must make appointments in person, a Herculean feat in a city where it can take an hour to travel a few blocks by car. One U.S. bank, Morgan Guaranty Trust, operated for more than a year in Lagos without a telephone or telex, not bad for an institution dealing in millions of dollars every day. Guests are lucky to have water two hours a day in their $90-a-day hotel rooms, and diners in downtown restaurants merely shrug and light candles when the electricity flickers, then gives way to darkness. What had happened was no mystery. Lagos' population had exploded from 300,000 to 3 million in a decade, and the city was sinking under its own weight.

Traffic congestion became intolerable—the thirteen-mile trip from the airport to Lagos used to take five hours. Policemen routinely pulled errant drivers from their cars and beat them senseless. After one Nigerian head of state, General Murtala Rufai Mohammed, was ambushed and assassinated in 1976 while his limousine was stuck in a "go-slow," the government decided some tough measures were in order. It decreed that on alternate days cars whose license plates ended in an even digit were banned from the road. Wealthy Nigerians circumvented the restriction by buying another car whose license plates ended in an odd digit.

Big money was everywhere. The rich grew richer, the poor poorer, and Lagos became one of the world's most expensive cities. The last time I was there a Christmas ham cost $88, a head of cabbage $5, and lettuce was sold by the leaf. Modest three-bedroom homes rented for $50,000 a year—three years' rent in advance, please—and the London-based Executive Resources International reported in 1980 that the cost of food and drink in Lagos was two and a half times more than in London, and three times more than in New York.

The distribution of national wealth under a capitalistic system in most Third World countries, however, is far more inequitable than in the developed world—the money just keeps circulating around at the top—and Nigeria proved no exception. While 1 percent of the Nigerians control 75 percent of the country's wealth, and elegant suburbs reach to the doorstep of ghastly slums, the average Nigerian earns less than $600 a year and one in ten children dies before the age of five because of inadequate medical care. Outside the cities much of the countryside remains woefully undeveloped, and despite large governmental expenditures on education, only one fifth of Nigeria's 25 million children attend school. To survive one has to hustle, and to hustle one has to move through a labyrinth of corruption and bribery known as "dash."

Generals and civil servants grow rich on meager salaries and almost everyone has his price. You have to "dash" the receptionist to get a hotel room, the immigration official to get an entry permit at the airport, the doctor to get a bed in his hospital. Fifteen percent kickbacks on construction contracts are standard practice, and one British medical-supply company set aside $50,000 in its budget to cover annual "dash" costs. In 1976 alone, smuggling of Nigerian goods to neighboring countries cost the government $480 million in lost revenue. By 1978 the government had ordered the firing squad for smugglers, but the edict had little effect. Nor did the public executions of young thieves have much impact on Lagos' burgeoning crime rate. Each Saturday on Bar Beach, a five-minute walk from the Eko Holiday Inn, three or four youths would be tied to oil drums while enthusiastic crowds cheered and clapped. The government executioners were not good shots and they banged away as though they were taking target practice, often needing two or three minutes and dozens of bullets to kill the suspected criminals. The spectators roared approvingly as errant bullets thudded into an arm or a shoulder or a leg. At last count, six hundred Nigerians were in prison awaiting execution—which now takes place behind the prison walls instead of on the bathers' beach.

"Before you criticize such behavior, please remember that this is Nigeria, not England or the United States, and you cannot judge all the world by your own standards." The speaker was Chief Godfrey Amachree, a British-educated, millionaire businessman and attorney with whom I lunched one day. His financial interests ranged from oil to imported furniture and a local Schweppes bottling plant, and he is as at home in New York or London (he has apartments in both cities) as he is in Lagos. His wife, Wylda, was born in Arkansas and attended the University of California, and Amachree wants nothing less for his four children than what his father gave him: "The best education money can buy." Amachree is a big man, articulate in

tone and distinguished in demeanor. His graying temples and tor-
toise-shell glasses give him the look of a college professor.

Like Nigeria itself, his world is a medley of the old and new. In
Lagos he wears three-piece Western business suits, speaks impeccable English and carries an attaché case. But on the Friday after our
luncheon he was to travel to his native village, forty miles upriver
from Port Harcourt. There, dressed in traditional robes, he would
address his gathered clan in his native tongue, Kalabari. At stake was
the distribution of a deceased cousin's property, and in his role as
chief, Amachree would be both judge and jury. "I'll listen to what
everyone has to say," he remarked, "and then I'll tell them what to
do."

At other tables around us in the rooftop Quo Vadis restaurant,
Nigerian businessmen, government officials and a handful of Europeans huddled over bottles of French wine and $40 entrées. Waiters
in tuxedos hovered about, moving unobtrusively through the bright
air-conditioned restaurant, dusting crumbs from the checkered table
cloths, filling long-stemmed wine glasses to just the proper level.
This was a quiet, comfortable world populated by men who had
succeeded, isolated from the city of Lagos, which spread out eighteen floors below us, an incubus of uncontrolled growth. Down
there the open sewers ooze odors of the foulest sort, slums languish
in the shadows of high-rise office buildings, filthy streets teem with
traffic and people. But unlike most African capitals, there is no idleness in those streets. Nigerians and foreigners jostle and hustle
through the crowds, sweat dripping from their brows, dodging
honking cabs, hurrying at a New York–style pace to their next appointment. A din of voices engulfs the streets, arguing, bartering,
insulting, challenging. "It may sound like we are quarreling all the
time, but it's actually just affectionate banter," a Nigerian newspaper editor told me. "We tend to say harsh things to each other. My
father used to say, 'If you are a rich man, Nigerians will abuse you
for being rich. If you are a poor man, they will abuse you for being
poor.' " The Nigerians are a people in a hurry, and to understand
Nigeria, you have to understand their language of abuse.

"There's so much opportunity down there for anyone willing to
work," Amachree said, finishing his chef's salad and glass of
Schweppes tonic water. "But my biggest worry is that our young
people today aren't willing to work the way we had to. They have
had it too easy. They want the money handed to them. They want
to become millionaires overnight.

"You know, we've got such great potential in this country if we can truly pull together as one people, one nation. But there are these deep divisions that have torn us apart before. I can only hope we've learned our lesson. Have we? I don't know. I'd only be guessing. It all depends on whether we're ready to start thinking in terms of nation instead of tribe."

Indeed, with its Moslem north and Christian south, its tribal divisions and its boisterous, argumentative people, Nigeria traditionally has been one of Africa's most ungovernable, undisciplined countries. When the British arrived in the mid-nineteenth century, they found not a single entity but several regional mini-nations representing the major tribes: the Arab-like Hausa and Fulani of the north, whose feudal emirs built empires and huge palaces of baked mud that was carved into crenellations and parapets; the Yoruba of the west, self-assertive and capitalistic people who worshiped more than four hundred gods and who today make up the majority of Lagos' population; and the pastoral, primitive Ibos of the east, who occasionally supplemented their low-protein yam diet with human flesh. Intertribal warfare and the slave trade of the seventeenth and eighteenth centuries had begun the deterioration of Nigeria's cultures before the colonialists' arrival. The British completed the process by forcing the major tribes to meld into a single colonial boundary. But true to their divide-and-rule policy, the British did not treat each ethnic group equally, and the people they chose to favor with privilege were the Ibos.

Backward as they appeared, the Ibos had a unique culture that was compatible with the concepts of Western-style advancement. They were ruled not by autocratic village chiefs, but by high achievers—successful yam farmers, warriors and public speakers. The titles and achievements of a man were buried with him, and his sons, unlike most young men in Africa, were required to earn their own reputation. The Ibos were eager to learn, and they welcomed the missionaries who brought books and schools. Soon each village was collecting money to send its brightest youths off to Europe to be educated. Those who remained behind eagerly accepted the mechanics of capitalism and administration that the colonials brought, and the British came to rely on the willing Ibos as the backbone of Nigeria's bureaucracy and commerce. The Ibos spread out from their homeland in the eastern region and became Nigeria's most successful and capable entrepreneurs, administrators and educators. They were proud, arrogant and given to self-praise. And because they had become the dominant tribe of the emerging nation, they were resented by other Nigerians. They valued what other tribes decried: high personal achievement. When the British left Nigeria in 1960, the Ibos inherited the controls of an infant country.

Within months of independence, the major tribes began struggling for power and control of natural resources. (Iboland included Nigeria's biggest oil fields and the only refinery, at Bonny.) The Ibos and Hausas formed a coalition against the Yoruba, causing the civilian government to break down. In 1966, five young Ibo officers overthrew the government, killing the prime minister and murdering or kidnapping several other prominent northerners. Six months later the northerners regained power by toppling the Ibos.

Northern soldiers chased Ibo troops from their barracks and murdered scores with bayonets. Screaming Moslem mobs descended on the Ibo quarters of every northern city, killing their victims with clubs, poison arrows and shotguns. Tens of thousands of Ibos were murdered in the systematic massacres that followed. Finally the Ibo elders in the east, fearing that reconciliation with the federal government was impossible and annihilation likely, invoked the call of Ibo brotherhood and issued a simple message to their people: Come home. From desert villages in the north, from government offices in the south, from every distant corner the Ibos came, on foot and bicycle, in wagons and railroad cars. They were burdened down with everything they could lug, and a few parents arrived carrying the severed heads of their children in baskets. On May 30, 1967, at a champagne reception in the regional capital of Enugu, the leader of the 10 million Ibos, an Oxford-educated lieutenant colonel named Chukweumeka Odumegwu Ojukwu, proclaimed the independent Republic of Biafra (named for the Bight of Biafra off the Atlantic Coast).

For thirty months the Ibos fought for their republic, receiving little sympathy at first from the outside world and getting no substantial support from any European country except France, whose policy was dictated not by sentiment but by the need for oil.* The rest of Europe, the United States and the Soviet Union saw an opportunity to gain a foothold in Africa by backing the likely winner (the Nigerian government), and for the first time an African country was

---

* Only four African countries—Tanzania, Gabon, the Ivory Coast and Zambia—recognized the Ibos' independence. The others believed that to violate the borders inherited at independence and to legitimize any secessionist movement would set a dangerous precedent.

able to fight a war using the modern weaponry of outside powers—
heavy artillery, automatic rifles, Russian MiGs and Czechoslovak
Delfin jets. The Ibos were forced out of Enugu by the federal advance and set up other capitals, from which they were also soon
driven. Packed into forests and swamps that could not support
them, the Ibos began starving to death at the rate of a thousand a
day. A shocked world saw pictures of swollen-bellied, hollow-eyed
children whose survival depended on the daring nighttime runs
free-lance Western pilots made into jungle airstrips with food and
medical supplies. Finally, in January 1970, the Ibos—denied access
to the major cities, low on ammunition and virtually without
food—surrendered. Lieutenant Colonel Ojukwu went into exile.*

"It was a very strange thing," a Nigerian colonel who fought the
Ibos recalled one evening over a drink, "but when the war ended, it
was like a referee blowing a whistle in a football game. People just
put down their guns and went back to the business of living. You
wonder now why the war was ever fought in the first place."

The man who led the federal forces to victory as Nigeria's head of
state, General Yakubu Gowon, the thirty-three-year-old son of a
Methodist missionary and a Sandhurst graduate, displayed both
skill and style in his postwar conduct of national affairs. Although
fellow soldiers criticized his handling of the economy, Gowon pursued a popular policy of reconciliation instead of retribution in dealing with the Ibos, decreeing that there were to be no witch hunts.
And there weren't. When you fly today into Enugu, you find no re-
minders of the war other than an occasional bullet hole that no one
got around to patching. The same people who nearly destroyed Nigeria have re-entered the mainstream of society. They have rebuilt
their towns and again become a prosperous, industrious community.
Ibos serve today as ambassadors and executives in large companies,
as state administrators and army officers. The University of Nsukka
in Enugu, leveled in bombing attacks during the war, flourishes
once more, this time with a student population reflecting the nation's ethnic diversity.

Enugu, like many towns a visitor sees after escaping from Nigeria's cities, is a lovely place. The trees along the tidy main street

---

* Ojukwu set up a trucking business in the Ivory Coast and became a millionaire. The Nigerian government refused to allow him to return home to contest the national elections of
1979, as he said he wanted to do. The government finally lifted the travel restrictions in
1982 and granted Ojukwu a pardon. He returned to his homeland and proclaimed, "The
Ibos first responsibility is to think of themselves as being Nigerians above all else."

provide welcome shade, the little houses are whitewashed and tidy, their grassy backyards clipped and ablaze with flowers. Life moves slower here than in the cities, and people are more at peace with their surroundings, less the victims of change. The green hills roll through little-used pastureland, dripping with mist in the first light of dawn, and barefoot women in colorful print dresses walk single file along the dirt shoulders of the roads, balancing atop their heads produce they will sell at the market. At night the air is crisp and cool and the town falls quiet very early, almost as soon as the darkness creeps in from the east. In the distance, charcoal embers glow like fireflies from dozens of backyard cooking pits. A dog barks and ever so briefly the crickets are still. Sitting alone one night, beside the empty swimming pool of a hotel on the outskirts of Enugu, I tried to imagine, but could not, what the sound of gunfire and the sight of starving children was like in this soft, silent setting. It was an alien thought and I soon put it out of my mind.

"Europe still discusses its war after thirty-five years, so you can't expect us to forget ours entirely in just a decade," said C. O. D. Ekwensi, a noted Ibo novelist. "There is still work to be done for true reconciliation, but we have gone a long way, probably further than any people in Africa. It is more than just a beginning."

The lesson of the terrible Biafran war seems to be that nationhood *is* possible in Nigeria—and perhaps in Africa as a whole—if there is a strong central government, a willingness to put nationalism ahead of tribalism, a united leadership capable of establishing priorities for the population as a whole, and a people with something to gain, materially and spiritually, by fulfilling their national potential. In pursuit of these goals, the soldiers who in 1975 replaced General Gowon's administration (he was overthrown in a bloodless coup while attending an African summit in Uganda) began the long and arduous task of returning the country to a civilian government. It was a promise often made and seldom kept in Africa. But most of Nigeria's senior officers were trained at Sandhurst, the British military academy, and they understood that a soldier's place was to serve, not to govern. They were keenly aware of Nigeria's rich ancient history and chagrined by how low Nigeria had sunk since independence. Most important, they knew that Nigeria could neither win international legitimacy nor earn the leadership role it sought in black Africa with a military government that had come to power in a coup d'état.

So the soldiers set off on the unusual mission of working themselves out of office. Planning was meticulous and every deadline was met. The army was reduced from 250,000 to 138,000 men; study groups flew off to the United States, Australia and Western Europe to examine various forms of democracy. A constitution was adopted after much debate. To diminish tribalism the constitution stipulated that there would be nineteen states with boundaries that *overlapped*, thus parceling out monolithic ethnic groups into different political entities;* a cabinet with at least one minister from every state; and political parties that needed a national, not just regional base of support to gain federal recognition.

Significantly, the political system Nigeria chose was modeled after that of the United States, with a president and vice president serving four-year terms, a supreme court, a senate and a house of representatives. In rejecting Britain's form of parliamentary democracy (because governments are easy to topple through a no-confidence vote) the Nigerians were, in effect, telling the United States that its form of democracy—and capitalism—were the best hope for black Africa's most important country. It was hardly the kind of praise Washington was used to hearing from the Third World.

Within two weeks after the ban on political parties was lifted in September 1978, no fewer than fifty-two parties had been formed to contest the elections. (Forty-seven of them were eventually banned for failing to gain a national base of support.) The parties' platforms ranged from socialistic to capitalistic, and as in any election in the West, were full of more idle promises than obtainable pledges: when, for instance, farmers complained that wildlife was trampling their crops, the eventual president-elect promised to shoot all the elephants in Nigeria. (He didn't.) There was, though, no disagreement on one major theme: Nigeria needed a strong government that would put national interests ahead of self-interests and would implement realistic, cost-conscious plans for the country's growth.

---

* Tribalism remains such a sensitive issue that Nigeria—like seven other black African countries—has never taken a nationally accepted census since independence. A 1963 head count collapsed in confusion when it showed that the Moslem north, the early seat of national political power, held only a slim population lead over the Christian south. A 1973 census was thrown out when it reported that the north had nearly twice as many people as the south. (The accuracy and integrity of both counts were highly suspect.) Nigeria accordingly bases its population information on projections from a pre-independence census in 1960, which makes it all but impossible to establish realistic development plans. Estimates of Nigeria's population vary from 80 million to 120 million.

Nigeria went to the polls in 1979—a rare event in itself in Africa—and elected as its president Alhaji Shehu Shagari, a wealthy businessman and former headmaster of a primary school. He is a northern Moslem, one of the Hausa-Fulani people, and in accordance with a constitutional requirement that the vice president be from a different tribe, he picked an Ibo as his running mate. With a capitalistic economy and a foreign policy favoring the West, Shargari built a solid foundation for democracy. He was reelected in 1983 by more than four million votes in an election carried off as smoothly as anyone had dared hope. It was a mark of how far Nigeria had progressed that in the 1983 election, there were more polling places in the country (166,000) than there were soldiers in the army (138,000).

Many formidable challenges lie ahead for Nigeria. Will the soldiers stay in the barracks if the civilians falter? Can oil really be put to work to benefit the majority instead of a chosen few? Will tribalism again surface as the most powerful force? Can corruption and greed be contained and national energies channeled toward common goals? These may remain unanswered questions for years to come, but the most encouraging sign, I think, that the Nigerian experiment will succeed is the presence of a growing middle and upper class. It is the largest, most substantial one in black Africa, and it is certainly worth remembering that it was the birth of an English middle class in the sixteenth and seventeenth centuries that enabled Britain to become stable and powerful. If Nigeria can hold together the pieces of nationhood, its return to civilian government is perhaps the single most significant event to have happened in postcolonial Africa. If Nigeria can succeed, other struggling black African nations will surely try to follow.

Postscript: Every update I have had to make since the first edition of *The Africans* appeared in print has been the result of unfortunate news, and Nigeria is no exception. On New Year's Eve, 1983, Nigeria's civilian government was overthrown in a bloodless *coup d'état*. Sharagi and scores of his officials were jailed for corruption. Nigeria's exciting experiment with democracy was over and the soldiers were back in power. The general who led the *coup*, forty-one-year-old Mohammed Buhari, promised to end graft and straighten out the economy. It was a promise the Nigerians had heard made many times before.

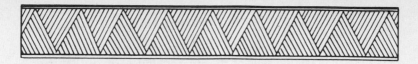

ALONE AGAINST
THE WORLD

▲

All other African black nations govern themselves. We
have been in Africa three hundred years and have the
same right to govern ourselves as they. This right we
cannot and will not forfeit.

JOHN VORSTER,
former South African prime minister

Right from my days as a young military officer, I always
felt that I would achieve a life ambition if I could fight
for liberation in southern Africa.

—LIEUTENANT GENERAL OLUSEGUN OBASANJO,
former Nigerian head of state

NOW WE COME TO THE PAYOFF, South Africa, the continent's only
developed, First World nation. Were it not for its institutionalized
racism, South Africa is what every African country would aspire to
become. Built with cheap black labor, white ingenuity and a seemingly endless supply of gold and diamonds, South Africa is advanced
enough to have the capability to make an atomic bomb, powerful
enough to withstand the condemnation of the entire world, prosperous enough to make any government in Europe, not to mention
Africa, full of envy. The great irony of all this is that South Africa's
resources are no greater, its farmland no more fertile, its people no
more inherently intelligent than those of other countries whose economic and social infrastructures have collapsed.

But to understand South Africa, we need a new frame of reference. Little of what I have written thus far applies to South Africa,
for everything about the place is different. Its economy is as solid as
a cement foundation, its leadership united, its army disciplined and
skilled. Even its physical characteristics often stand in contrast to
the rest of equatorial Africa. There are little towns that seem to be-

long in England's Cotswolds, beach resorts along the 2,700-mile coastline that remind you of the Riviera, and perhaps the world's most magnificent city, Cape Town, overlooking the "Tavern of the Seas"—the confluence of the Indian and Atlantic oceans. The moderate climate, with warm sunny days and cool nights, provides excellent growing conditions for everything from grapes to grain. On Table Mountain in Cape Town there are more varieties of wild flowers than can be found in all the British Isles.

If you asked an Afrikaner why his country had fared so much better than the rest of Africa, he would give you a simple explanation: South Africa is run by whites, the rest of sub-Sahara Africa by blacks. "Let a black man be trained as an airplane mechanic; let him overhaul a Boeing 747 from nose to tail and let [Prime Minister] P. W. Botha and his cabinet go for a ride in it," says Jaap Marais, a conservative former member of parliament.

Marais did not, of course, mention that black Africans pilot and provide maintenance for most national carriers on the continent (and I've never known one to crash with a load of government officials). But white South Africans look at the world—and their own country—with tainted glasses, and everything they have accomplished has been achieved at a terrible cost. The fact that what they have done to their black population is no worse than what some black governments have done to their own people is not a viable argument on the continent. To most Africans, the world's ultimate crime is the racism of whites toward blacks. In its shadow the threats posed by poverty, disease, warfare or Communism all pale. There is only one place left in Africa where that racism is both overt and legal, and until it ends, however violent that ending may be, Africa can never be at peace with itself.

Before we take a close look at this country, which is really the linchpin of the continent's future, let me recite two telling statistics: (1) With 125,400 people in jail, South Africa has the highest per capita prison population in the Western world.* The government provides no racial breakdown, but diplomatic sources estimate that less than 3 percent are white. (2) Ninety-five percent of the Western world's executions are carried out in South Africa. In 1980, the hangings totaled 130. Only one of the victims was white.

* The prison population figures were provided by the National Institute for Crime Prevention and Rehabilitation in Johannesburg. Although many people might not consider South Africa part of the "Western world," the term refers broadly to all non-Communist, industrialized countries.

Today it seems impossible to think of South Africa without re-membering a haunting phrase from Alan Paton's *Cry, the Beloved Country.* "I have one great fear in my heart," says a black minister, "that one day when they [the whites] turn to loving, they will find we are turned to hating."

Every evening at five-twenty a South African Railways passenger train pulls out of Maputo, the Mozambican capital, bound for Jo-hannesburg, 376 miles away. It is a journey between two universes, between two mutually dependent enemies separated by seventeen hours in travel and light-years in mentality.

All seven cars—like the toilets inside—are marked NONWHITES and in them are packed five or six hundred Mozambicans, men heading for the South African gold mines, women clutching chickens and vegetables to be sold at the markets along the way, ev-eryone squeezed together like matchsticks, two and sometimes three people sharing the same seat. I checked my ticket again. Sure enough, it said "First Class." The coal-black Mozambicans around me, the only non-African on the train, chuckled good-naturedly as I sucked in my breath and wiggled my buttocks, hoping to salvage an extra inch or two on the wooden seat. For three hours our train poked along, its whistle clearing cows and errant children from the tracks, moving ever so slowly through the sleepy, primitive villages between Maputo and Ressano García on the border.

The town of Ressano García is all but invisible in the blackness of night. The train grinds to a halt there with squeals and hisses, and an amiable Mozambican soldier dressed in sandals and baggy old fatigues ambles onboard. While checking everyone's ticket he bor-rows a few cigarettes from the passengers and waves his rifle around casually as though it were only a plaything. Then we all file into the dark, dingy terminal. The kiosk is dust-covered and closed, ap-parently abandoned long ago. The overhead light fixtures are with-out bulbs and hang from frayed electrical cords. In the far corner an immigration official, holding a flashlight over the top of his little wooden table, riffles through the passports of the people queued in front of him, stamping an exit visa in each. One by one the travelers saunter back onto the train for the final leg of the journey, which will carry them into the strange land of South Africa.

Komatipoort, the South African border town, is only a few miles down the track, but its bright lights can be seen for quite a distance. The terminal is clean and freshly painted; the white-owned homes nearby have small tidy yards and windows ablaze with lights. The train stops briefly in Komatipoort so that a white crew can take over and two cars designated WHITE ONLY can be added. Now, I'm told, I will have my first-class seat. The black passengers file off the train again, standing this time silently and rigidly before an Afrikaner immigration officer in a crisply pressed uniform. They shuffle their feet uneasily. The white man eyes them wordlessly, as though seeing through them rather than looking at them. He examines each travel document with deliberate thoroughness. His rubber stamp falls with a thud. Permission to enter South Africa granted.

To cross that border is almost like landing on an alien planet, for no two countries in Africa represent greater extremes, ideologically and politically. Mozambique, a revolutionary Marxist state, which defeated the Portuguese colonials in a war of independence, is dedicated to the downfall of the white government in Pretoria; South Africa, a quasi-fascist state, which has borrowed philosophical elements from the Nazi doctrine, is committed to the supremacy of the white race. Understandably enough, black Africa is obsessed with the injustices of the racist giant at its southern doorstep, yet it needs South Africa economically, and its calls for boycotts and sanctions and wars amount to little more than idle threats it cannot back with action. When your grain silos are empty—and your enemy's are full—you do not have much bargaining power.

Indeed, black Africa depends on South Africa. Without it, national economies in the southern third of the continent would fall like dominoes. Because of its economic self-sufficiency and military strength, South Africa—governed by the continent's only white tribe, the Afrikaner—has managed to do pretty much as it pleases to its black majority while remaining immune to mild pressures exerted by the international community. As long as black Africa remains economically weak it can do nothing to influence change within its southern neighbor, and South Africa will continue to stand out like a millionaire general in a room of penniless privates. It is one of only eleven countries in the world that feeds itself and has food left over to export. It is the only industrialized country on a continent otherwise populated exclusively by Third World nations. It is the world's richest nation in terms of white-per-capita, non-petroleum wealth. And its military could take on any dozen black African armies in conventional warfare and still punch through to the northern Sahara in a month or so.

The government can afford to spend nearly 20 percent of its budget, or $3 billion a year, on defense. Its armed forces are comprised of 86,000 regulars and 260,000 reservists—blacks and whites, though 90 percent of the officers are white and military facilities at the camps are segregated. The South African army is one of the most mobile and self-sufficient in the world, needing only one man in the rear to support one soldier on the front lines. (In Vietnam the United States has seven support troops in the rear for each combat soldier.)

Only one black African nation, Malawi, has diplomatic relations with South Africa, and virtually none admits to doing business with South Africa. But what goes through back doors is another matter. Each year at least twenty African countries indirectly support apartheid by purchasing more than $1 billion worth of South African goods and services. Kenya buys South African maize, which it says comes from Mozambique. Zambia buys South African beef, which it says comes from Botswana. Gabon buys South African construction equipment, which it says comes from Europe. Zaire gets 50 percent of its food from South Africa; eighty percent of Zimbabwe's trade goes through South Africa; Malawi built its new capital at Lilongwe with the help of a $12 million South African loan; Mozambique keeps its ports and railroads running with South African technicians and administrators; six neighboring countries supply 182,000 laborers for the South African mines; the Republic of Cape Verde gets 20 percent of its foreign earnings from landing fees and refueling charges at the South African–built airport on Ilha do Sal. (Denied landing rights at almost every other airport in Africa, South African Airways could not make its long-haul flights to New York and Europe unless its planes stopped at Ilha do Sal.)

Make no mistake, though. South Africa *is* the enemy. Fewer than 4.5 million whites there hold 24 million blacks, colored and Indians* in a form of bondage unique to the modern world, and if there is one thing that unites black Africa, it is a shared hatred of the Afrikaner and his system. But in business, pragmatism takes

---

* The 20 million blacks are African descendants of the Sotho and Nguni people who migrated southward centuries ago. The 3 million "coloureds" are the progeny of the earliest white settlers and the indigenous people or Malay slaves from Dutch West India. The 1 million Asians, mostly from India, were first imported in 1860 as contract laborers for the sugar plantations. These three groups are officially lumped together and classified as "nonwhite."

over where morality and ideology leave off. Apartheid in another country is one thing; economic suicide at home is quite another. As President Nyerere once said, "If I didn't have shoes and South Africa was the only place to get shoes, then I would do without them. But if I didn't have corn and South Africa was the only place to get corn, then I would go to South Africa."

I had been traveling throughout black Africa for nine months before I got to South Africa for the first time. By then I had grown used to hearing how beautiful cities such as Luanda and Maputo had once been. I had become accustomed to visiting dirty, under-staffed hospitals, government offices full of broken typewriters and telephones, and schools without chalk for the blackboards or seats for the toilets. Nothing, I thought, could faze me anymore, but when I reached South Africa, I was dumfounded. *It works.* You pick up the phone and get a dial tone. You summon a waiter and are handed a menu. You get on an airplane and it departs on schedule. Modern highways carry you through the country, which is twice the size of Texas, and the stores are stocked with goods (radios, cotton shirts, hardcover books, tennis rackets) that I hadn't seen since my last trip to Europe. Arriving in Johannesburg is like being back in Cleveland or St. Louis.

Johannesburg, built on a mile-high plateau, did not exist until gold was discovered there in 1886. The city is neither pretty nor exciting but it has a sense of vitality, a feeling of substance and permanence, unlike so many African cities that seem ready to blow away in a strong wind. It has high-rise office buildings, more than a hundred carefully tended parks, and Beverly Hills–like suburbs that contain more swimming pools and tennis courts than I've ever seen in one place. Johannesburg (population 1.5 million, about the same as Houston) is also the starting point for the world's most elegant passenger train, the Blue Train, which makes the twenty-four-hour trip to Cape Town three times a week, usually arriving within the appointed minute.

But the spooky thing about South Africa is that—if you are white—you don't sense initially that anything is wrong. You can't sense the tension or feel the oppression. There is, in fact, often no awareness that you are in a *black* country. In the heat of downtown Johannesburg, you don't even see many blacks around. You go through the department stores, which are staffed with white clerks and filled with white customers. You sit in a restaurant and find only white patrons. But where are the blacks? If this is their country, where is their world? Poking through Johannesburg after dark is like visiting Iowa and finding no farmers.

What you don't see—and what you can't see without government permission—is Soweto (short for South-West Township), thirty minutes from Johannesburg on the black-only commuter train. It is a teeming, clamorous township of 2 million blacks, an enclave where horse-drawn coal carts creak along the dirt roads between box-shaped houses with outhouses and no electricity, where men confront their defeats with half-jacks (half-quart bottles) of brandy in more than 1,400 illegal *shebeens* (speakeasies), where gangs of young toughs calling themselves "Wild Geese" or "Russians" roam the dark streets with pistols stolen from whites' homes, where on any given day there are three murders.

"If you take a million whites," says Shimane Kumalo, a black social worker in Soweto, "and you subject them to the same process of uninterrupted poverty, the same poor schooling facilities, the same school dropout rate, the lack of occupational skills and the unemployment rate, you will certainly have a murder rate just as high."

The irony of all that is sad and wrong in South Africa is that the South African black is, on the whole, the best educated, best dressed, most prosperous, most literate black on the African continent. He has access to the best medical care—the 2,700-bed Baragwanath Hospital in Soweto is the largest in Africa—and to the steadiest employment. But such superlatives are both relative and irrelevant. The South African black does not want to be compared with other blacks in Africa. He compares himself, and his opportunities, to white South Africa, and on that score he comes up miserably short. He is not a citizen of his land. He is its hostge. In Soweto and other townships adjoining white cities, he is not allowed to buy property. He cannot enter Johannesburg without a pass and cannot stay in the city after nightfall without permission. He has no vote for or say in the all-white parliament. If he is over sixteen years of age, he must carry a pass book listing his tribe, his employer and his tax payments. If he wants to use a restroom in Johannesburg, he has a choice of 161 public toilets. All the others are reserved for whites.

His is the only country in the world where racism is institutionalized—the government operates one television channel for whites, another for blacks—and every aspect of his life is dictated by South

Africa's 300-plus discriminatory laws. They determine whom he can love, kiss, marry and have sex with, where he can live, eat, travel and go to school, what he can do for his vocation and avocation. South Africa's "Heartbreak Laws" maintain racial separateness at all significant levels of society. A 1949 act outlaws mixed marriages. "A marriage," it says, "between a European and a non-European may not be solemnized and any such marriage solemnized in contravention of the provisions of the section shall be void and of no effect . . ." A 1953 act bars interracial sex. Persons violating the sex law are arrested, tried and usually sentenced to six to nine months in prison. The sentence is frequently suspended if the couple agrees "not to carry on."

Although the government in recent years has made cosmetic changes to reduce petty discrimination—some public parks and sport teams, for instance, are now integrated, and about 650 blacks attend white universities—the bottom line of South African society is that a man's color establishes his identity. And the basis of that policy is fear, the whites' fear that without apartheid the Afrikaner culture and economic superiority would wither and die like the green grass of summer. "If the European loses his color sense, he can not remain a white man," former South African prime minister J. G. Strijdom once said. The Afrikaner believes that if the blacks gain, the whites lose. He views minor changes such as the integration of city parks as revolutionary. The black sees them as meaningless. Both groups have entirely different concepts of what constitutes change, and the blacks, at least the more militant ones, want nothing less than the same rights other Africans have won throughout the rest of the continent. They are not eager to destroy Africa's only technologically advanced country, but eventually they will if that is what it takes to win their political rights.

The ultimate authority in deciding to what caste a person belongs is the little-publicized Population Registration Board, a group of white social workers who meet privately and classify all South Africans according to race. The board is the final appeal for people who think they have been wrongly classified and for people who want to "pass" from colored to white or vice versa in order to legalize a relationship. (Whites and nonwhites cannot legally stay under the same roof overnight.) Deliberations take months, sometimes years, with the board paying careful attention to skin tint, facial features and hair texture. In one typical twelve-month period, 150 coloreds were reclassified as white; ten whites became colored, six Indians became Malay; two Malay became Indians; two coloreds became Chinese; ten Indians became coloreds; one Indian became white; one white became Malay; four blacks became Indians; three whites became Chinese.

The Chinese are officially classified as a white subgroup. The Japanese, most of whom are visiting businessmen, are given the status of "honorary whites." Absurd? Yes, if all this were part of an anti-utopian novel. But in real life it is a chilling part of the most complex system of human control in the world (the Soviet Union notwithstanding). When Mymoena Salie became the first black woman to win a multiracial beauty contest in South Africa several years ago, she found herself unable to accept the prize—a two-week seaside vacation—because the hotel did not admit blacks. An American tourist at the hotel that offered the prize was gazing out one day at the beach and the sea beyond. "Is that the Indian Ocean?" he asked the waiter who brought him a drink. "Oh no, sir," the waiter replied. "That's the European ocean. The Indians use the next beach over."

Cape Town is the home of South Africa's oldest white settlement and a beautiful city it is, full of manicured gardens and sheltered bays, overlooking the Cape of Good Hope and the shipping routes for supertankers that make South Africa one of the continent's most strategically important countries. "This cape is a most stately thing and the fairest cape we saw in the whole circumference of the earth," Sir Francis Drake wrote after rounding the cape in 1580 on the *Golden Hind*.

On a clear night, which most nights are in Cape Town, you can see the lights of Robben Island a few miles off the coast. It is a low, flat, scrub-covered islet where the U.S. ambassador, John Heard, used to hunt birds in the early 1970s. But Robben Island is no more a recreation facility than Alcatraz was, for that is where the government keeps the blacks who would be the leaders of a South Africa ruled by the majority. The currents are treacherous there and no one has ever escaped, even though the mainland is so tantalizingly close.

The large picture windows of the seaside restaurants in Cape Town look directly out at the island, and one evening, over a dinner of fresh lobster and a bottle of local wine, the conversation turned, as almost every one eventually does in South Africa, to race. Sandy and I were with another couple we had met earlier in the day.

Martha and George were both divorced and in their fifties. She worked as a secretary for a European embassy; he owned a small hotel.

"See that blinking light out there?" George volunteered, as though the subject could not be ignored. "That's Robben Island, where they've got the political prisoners. You've heard of Nelson Mandela? He's out there. Walter Sisulu? Govan Mbeke? They're there too. There are one hundred and sixteen of them."

"Only one hundred and sixteen?" said Martha. "If I had my way, there'd be two hundred and sixteen. I don't like subversives, and it's as simple as that. I'm conservative. I don't apologize for it."

"Well, I don't think it's right myself," George said. "I don't think they should be locked up for not going along with the government. And I don't think the government should tell a man where he can go. Like if I want to invite a black person into my house, I need a permit."

"That's rubbish," Martha said. "You don't need any permit. I've been to lots of parties with blacks, whites, coloreds. I've got black and colored friends, and I never needed any permit."

"Have you ever had one of them in your house?"

"Of course."

"When?"

"I have, that's all," said Martha, an Afrikaner, and the conversation quickly shifted to how tasty the lobster was.

The next morning as I was checking out of the hotel, I was paged for a telephone call. It was Martha. "You deserve an apology for the way George was talking," she said. "I really don't know him very well, and I didn't want you to think that all South Africans feel that way. He wasn't speaking for me, I can promise you."

Most impartial observers would refer to the prisoners on Robben Island as nationalists. The South African government calls them subversives, Communists and terrorists—which, indeed, they may well be if they ever get their freedom.* To deal with these dissidents South Africa, like most police states, has a myriad of laws to legalize its mistreatment. A 1950 act outlaws the South African Communist

* The most significant antigovernment group is the outlawed African National Congress, founded in 1912 to seek peaceful change through reform. Its philosophy became revolutionary only when the whites' intransigence made reform impossible. The ANC's titular head is Nelson Mandela, who has been in prison on terrorist charges since 1964 (when he was 46 years old). The ANC, with 6,000 guerrillas based in neighboring black African countries and thousands of clandestine supporters inside South Africa, is credited with eighty acts of sabotage that killed eight persons between 1981 and mid-1983.

Party and any other organization that furthers the aims of Communism. A 1962 act makes sabotage a capital crime and presumes the accused guilty unless he can prove his innocence. A 1967 act provides for indefinite detention in solitary confinement without access to a lawyer for suspected terrorists. The most bizarre tool the government uses to silence dissent is called "banning," which in effect turns a person into a nonperson. The 150 or so banned people in South Africa are not allowed to leave the city where they live, to talk with more than two people (including relatives) at one time, to publish, teach or entertain visitors at home. The local press is not allowed to quote anything they say or anything they have ever said or written. For all practical purposes, they cease to exist.

So when Martha called, I said she did not need to apologize and let the subject drop. Talking race with an Afrikaner is like discussing mathematics with a stone wall. Unlike other whites in Africa, the Afrikaner has no ties to Europe. He has no home other than Africa, no passport other than South Africa's. He is the descendant of the stern, hard-working Dutch, French and German pioneers who came to Cape Town in the seventeenth century and who stayed on to confront first the British, then the black Africans and now the world. His perspective is introverted and fiercely nationalistic, his society rigid and so puritanical that bars and movie theaters are closed on Sunday. He speaks a unique Dutch-based language called Afrikaans, follows a fundamentalist form of Calvinism and has a sense of special mission created by his own history of suffering. But the very history that gives him strength is also the source of his isolation and imprisonment, the burial ground into which the seeds of his own self-destruction have been sown

Afrikaner history dates back to April 1652, when, after nearly four months at sea, the Dutch ship *Dommedaris* brought the first whites—Captain Jan van Riebeeck and a crew of 125 men—to Cape Town. They came to establish a station for the Dutch East India Company where vessels on the route to India could stop for provisions and medical facilities, and they met no resistance from the indigenous Hottentots and Bushmen who then inhabited the cape. The company had not intended to set up anything more than a way station, but gradually, almost imperceptibly, a colony of settlement began to emerge. In 1657 the company released some of its servants as free burghers to cultivate land and raise cattle. That same year slaves from Angola and the East Indies were imported as laborers. Dutch settlers began to arrive, along with French Protes-

tant Huguenots seeking religious freedom. Later came German immigrants. Interracial marriage was common—and legal—and the
Cape colored became a new ethnic group. The way station grew and
became a regular port of call for European vessels. Cape Town was
no longer a mere outpost. It was the birthplace of a nation—and of
a new, white tribe.

Britain seized the cape in 1795 and soon missionaries, traders,
administrators and settlers were arriving by the shipload. They considered the original white settlers inferior and obdurate and treated
them with disdain. The Afrikaner was denied land rights and fined
for such minor offenses as allowing his cattle to stray. He was ex-
cluded from jury duty because of his language and forced to accept
English-speaking ministers for his churches. If his children spoke
Afrikaans at school, they were punished by having to put a placard
around their necks that read: "I am a donkey. I speak Afrikaans."

The British returned the cape to the Dutch in 1803, then took it
back again in 1806 because of the need to protect their sea routes to
India during the renewed Napoleonic Wars. The Dutch settlers,
who called themselves Boers (farmers), felt threatened. And in
1835, rifle and Bible in hand, they began moving north in small
groups to escape the British and to secure a land of their own. Over
the next eight years more than 12,000 *voortrekkers** rolled across
the plains in ox wagons, headed on an uncharted course for the high
veld of Natal and Transvaal provinces, firmly convinced that God
had chosen them to implant a new nation in Africa. On their odys-
sey, which became known as the Great Trek, they carried with them
much bitterness and a sense of purpose forged on the anvil of oppression.

The trek was a perilous one, and in times of danger the Boers took
up positions in the *laager*—a protective circle of wagons with locked
wheels. In the bloodiest battle of the trek, 12,000 Zulu warriors attacked a *laager* in 1838 along the banks of the Ncome River. The
500 Boer defenders annihilated them, and keeping the vow they had
made to God during the fight, built a church to commemorate the
victory. The day of that victory, December 16, is celebrated today as
a national holiday, the Day of the Covenant, and the Ncome in
Natal province is now known as Blood River. (The Zulus, however,
remained a formidable force in northern Natal until 1879, when the
British destroyed them militarily and occupied Zululand.)

In the early 1850s the Boers established two independent repub-

---

* Voor means "forward" in Afrikaans, thus *voortrekkers* translates as the forward trekkers,
or pioneers. The trekkers and their descendants are known today as Boers.

lics, one known as the South African Republic in the Transvaal, the other as the Orange Free State. They made alliances with the local chiefdoms, but the peace and isolation that they sought still eluded them. Britain was uneasy with this maverick white tribe and it annexed both the Transvaal and Natal. In 1886 one of the world's richest gold deposits was found in the Witwatersrand (the "Ridge of White Waters") region of the Transvaal, where Johannesburg is now located. English-speaking immigrants and British investment poured into South Africa. Again the Boers felt threatened. Only this time, instead of trekking north, they stood and fought. It was Africa's first war of independence and the only one that pitted whites against whites.

The two Anglo-Boer wars (1880–1881 and 1899–1902) were among the bloodiest Africa has ever witnessed, and they divided the British population much as the Vietnam war would divide the United States in the 1970s. Britain committed 500,000 troops to the Second War of Freedom, as the Afrikaners called it, against a force of 88,000 Boers. The campaign cost Britain 22,000 dead and 150,000 wounded. The Boers, using the same guerrilla tactics that black nationalists would rely on in liberation wars against colonial authorities nearly a century later, attacked on two fronts, into the northern Cape from the Orange Free State and into Natal from the Transvaal. Their commandos harried British supply lines and communications facilities, and for awhile the Boers held the British to a stand-off.

But Lord Herbert Kitchener, the British commander in chief, responded with a scorched-earth policy, protecting railway installations and government facilities with barbed wire and destroying the farms of both the Afrikaners and the black Africans. The wives and children of Boer farmers were rounded up and put in concentration camps, where more than 20,000 died because of neglect and unsanitary conditions. As brutal as they were, Kitchener's tactics paid off. In May 1902 the defeated Boers accepted the loss of their independence and signed the Peace of Vereeniging treaty. (Later, in 1910, the former Boer republics and the two British colonies, Natal and the Cape, were joined to form the Union of South Africa, a dominion of the British Empire. The union became a sovereign state within the empire in 1934. South Africa left the British Commonwealth in 1961 and became a republic.)

The Boer wars helped fashion a new sense of Afrikaner nationalism. His language, his culture, his claim to the African land made him unique, and everyone, white or black, was seen as a potential enemy. In defeat he had become a second-class citizen in what he considered his own country. New Dutch immigrants had long since stopped coming to South Africa and, isolated and alone, he knew that Afrikanerdom could survive only as a unified entity if it were uncorrupted by outside influence. He took a refuge in his church and his secret societies such as the Broederbond (literally, association of brothers), and he waited for the political power which would enable him to build a nation, where everyone was of the same mind, the same color, the same faith.

That opportunity came in 1948 when the Afrikaner-led National Party upset Jan Smut's United Party and began the longest uninterrupted reign of any political party still in power in the Western world. Believing that integration would lead to the ultimate destruction of the whites, the Afrikaner government moved quickly to enact a web of racial laws and to strengthen its system of self-preservation known as apartheid. It is worth noting here that apartheid did not create racial discrimination; it only institutionalized it. Back in 1909, for instance, the British withdrew the rights of nonwhites to sit in the South African parliament. The next year coloreds staged a nonviolent protest demonstration in Cape Town led by Mohandas Gandhi.

In Afrikaans, *apartheid* means "apartness" or "separateness," although the word has become so stigmatized internationally that South Africans no longer use it officially, preferring instead euphemisms such as "plural democracy" or "separate development." According to the doctrine, every race has a unique destiny and a unique cultural contribution to make; therefore the races must be kept separate to develop along their own lines. But however one rationalizes it, the real intent of the system is the retention of *baaskap* (white supremacy). Apartheid still means racial purity, the subjugation of the nonwhite majority for the benefit of the all-white minority. It is the instrument that officially transformed the oppressed into the oppressor.

Although there are some black lawyers and doctors and millionaire businessmen in South Africa (and, unlike anywhere else in Africa, even a few poor whites), it goes without saying that the whiter a person's skin, the better his fortunes. The government spends $677 a year to educate each white child, $277 for a colored, and $66 for a black. White miners earn $16,630 a year and get a house virtually rent-free; black miners average $2,546 and sleep in crowded dormitories. In the construction industry, a white makes twice the salary of an Asian, three times that of a colored, and five times that of a black. Ignoring the almost insurmountable barriers that these educational and monetary inequities create, the Afrikaner then dismisses the black as being incompetent, unmotivated and inarticulate. "It's the K factor," he will say with a shrug, meaning that blacks are inherently inferior. The K stands for "kaffir" (the Kaffirs being one of the South African aboriginals), a pejorative whose meaning and use is similar to the word "nigger."

The centerpiece of apartheid is the Land Resettlement Act of 1936, which, paradoxically, was the result of international pressure on South Africa, exerted by the League of Nations in an attempt to improve the blacks' lot. The plan called for resettling of the blacks, who comprise 67 percent of the population, into ten separate *Bantustans*, or "homelands," that represent 13.7 percent of the country's total area—and hold almost none of its natural wealth. Only four of the homelands are composed of a single piece of land—the others are broken into two or more parts surrounded by South Africa—and most are not even identified by any sign at their borders to inform a traveler that he is leaving South Africa and allegedly entering a new country. By 1982 four homelands, each representing a particular tribe, had been declared independent states by Pretoria.* Each has a president, a parliament and some political autonomy. But their "independence" is only a sham, an event staged by Pretoria, and no government in the world other than South Africa's extends them diplomatic recognition.

South Africa claims that the Bantustans are designed to give all peoples equal opportunities, but the obvious purpose is simply to segregate the four main racial groups—white, colored, Asian and Bantu—into separate national communities, thus maintaining the whiteness of the Afrikaners without disturbing their access to cheap labor. The scheme is like a giant United States' school busing project in reverse. (No rural land is set aside for the coloreds and Asians; instead they are allocated residential areas in the urban centers.) The only ones who benefit are the whites.†

* In 1976 Transkei became the first "independent" homeland. It was followed by Bophuthatswana in 1977, Venda in 1979 and Ciskei in 1981. The other six homelands are Kwa-Zulu (the eight splintered parts of the once powerful Zulu nation), Qwa Qwa, Lebowa, Gazankulu, Kangwane and South Ndebele.
† Western entertainers and athletes had refused to perform in the homelands on the premise that to do so would give them—and South Africa's scheme—credibility. But in 1981 Frank Sinatra provided Bophuthatswana with a much needed sense of legitimacy by giving nine concerts at the Sun City, a Las Vegas–style gambling resort, for a reported fee of $1.6 million. The $85 top ticket price ascertained that the audience would be mostly white,

What apartheid does, then, is to sever the links of contact and communication that people have in a normal society. The whites meet only black garbage collectors and janitors, not their counterparts who are teachers, doctors and social workers. The blacks deal mostly with white Afrikaans-speaking policemen and civil servants. By day the black works in the shadow of the white preserve, in the clean, sparkling cities and the expansive suburbs. By night he returns to his smoky slum where, by law, he must remain until dawn. The discontent builds, and the envy and resentment take firm hold.

To be sure, there are some moderates in the white community who see what the inevitable result of apartheid has to be. But they can be found mainly among the people of English stock, who make up 40 percent of the white population. The Afrikaner remains intransigent. Contrary to what he believes, though, his intransigence is endangering the whites' long-range interests in South Africa. It will create the very conditions that the Soviet Union can best exploit—racial unrest and political instability. It will make Communism a far more real threat to South Africa than it is to the rest of the continent. For no matter how alien the tenets of Communism may be to Africa, there comes a point, when the unhappiness of the general population runs deep enough, that the propaganda of the left sounds like a hopeful panacea.

President Jimmy Carter recognized this and put some distance between his Administration and the Pretoria government. Not so with President Ronald Reagan. He moved quickly to repair the damaged relationship, asking: "Can we abandon this country that has stood by us in every war we've ever fought?" It is true that South Africa did fight with the Allies in the two world wars, took part in the Berlin Airlift, participated in the postwar United Nations' force in Korea and maintains a foreign policy that is staunchly anti-Communist. But Reagan's statement seriously distorted the historical record.

The South Africans who twice stood by the Allies at the start of global hostilities were largely the English-speaking white minority. The Afrikaners argued against declaring war on Germany in 1914. They held demonstrations throughout South Africa to protest the

---

though Sinatra insisted he was in no way supporting segregation. "I play to all—any color, any creed, drunk or sober," he said. President Lucas Mangope was so delighted that he awarded Sinatra the "nation's" highest decoration, the Order of the Leopard, and made him an honorary tribal chief.

United Party's decision to enter the war, and in 1939 the National-ist leader, J. B. M. Hertzog, defended Hitler in the South African parliament and contended that Germany had annexed Czechoslova-kia in self-defense. South Africa joined the Allies only after a close parliamentary vote, 80–67.

The end of World War II saw the political emergence of the Afrikaner and the introduction of apartheid. The international com-munity gradually cut South Africa adrift. In 1974 the United Na-tions revoked its General Assembly seat. In 1977 an embargo on the shipment of weapons to South Africa, which the UN had made "voluntary" fourteen years earlier, became mandatory. South Afri-can sports teams were barred from the Olympics and most interna-tional competition. South African airplanes were banned from land-ing at almost every airport in Africa, and South African resident diplomats were welcome nowhere on the continent except in Ma-lawi. Telephone operators in most black-run countries won't even connect a caller to a South African number. By 1982 South Africa had only one unquestioning friend left, Israel, another outcast of the world community. There are 120,000 Jews in South Africa, but the relationship seemed to be based more than anything on the premise that my enemy's enemy must be my friend.

South Africa has not only survived in the face of global condem-nation, it has prospered. A century ago it exported little more than some wine from Cape province. Today it mines nearly three quar-ters of the West's gold, manufactures everything from refrigerators to automobiles, exports vast quantities of food, textiles and ma-chinery, and is the tenth largest weapons producer in the world. Some of those armaments are both indigenous and innovative, nota-bly the Ratel, a high-speed armored personnel carrier that has a range of 900 miles and is built for rugged conditions. The weapons and munitions are assembled by black laborers and are a major fac-tor in the continuation of white rule.

Two aspects of South Africa seem abundantly clear: the country must make a dramatic change to transform itself into an integrated multiracial society; and if that change is initiated by violence, per-haps in the form of Africa's first race war, the effects on the conti-nent and the world would be cataclysmic. What can the United States do to effect a peaceful change? One popular line of reasoning says that the 350 U.S. companies in South Africa should close down and the United States should divest itself of all investments there and should terminate its trade with the Pretoria government, which runs in excess of $5 billion a year.

The gesture would, I believe, be futile. First, embargoes and sanctions have never been effective because, whether the culprit is Communist Cuba or capitalistic Rhodesia, someone is always willing to break them. Second, if the South African economy deteriorates and jobs are lost, the first to suffer will be the blacks, not the whites. Third, if Washington ordered U.S. companies to pull their money out of South Africa, the Pretoria government would undoubtedly freeze the funds, and another country such as France or Japan would step in to pick up the United States' share of the trade market. Fourth, if the United States cut its commercial ties, it loses whatever leverage it has to pressure South Africa to make changes. Fifth, any action taken by the West is meaningless as long as black Africa demands that others do what it is unable or unwilling to do itself.

That leaves Washington with only one sensible policy to follow, other than the use of diplomatic pressure: make sure that American companies in South Africa provide equal pay for equal work to all races, formulate training programs to elevate blacks into positions of authority, end all segregation in their plants. The results will not topple the pillars of Afrikanerdom, but they will make them quiver, for anything that gives the South African black a fair share of wages and increased authority gives the South African white reason to worry that what he has created cannot last forever.

In the end, the apartheid that gave the Afrikaner his strength may be the very system that will destroy him. He has relentlessly denied the blacks opportunity, and now the white population is no longer large enough to supply all the skills and services an industrialized country of 28.5 milion people needs. He has built a powerful military and developed nuclear capabilities to protect this system. But the threat is at home, not abroad, so what are his choices? To rain bombs on his own country in a frenzy of self-destruction? He has enjoyed one of the highest standards of living in the world while holding 85 percent of the people in a form of serfdom. The prison on Robben Island is already full. What does the Afrikaner do with the young, educated, unemployed blacks who surely will not be as tolerant as their parents were?

I can think of no single event that would bring more benefit to all of Africa than the peaceful advent of an integrated multiracial society in South Africa. And indeed, by the spring of 1984, there were encouraging stirrings underway, with South Africa and Mozambique signing a nonagression pact and South Africa and Angola holding secret negotiations to find a formula for peace. If South Africa could trade freely with the rest of the continent, its political and economic influence would be gigantic. It would dominate Africa as no single country dominates Europe or South America. It could take the leadership role in the Organization of African Unity (of which it is not even a member now). Its technicians and experts could travel without restriction and help other governments develop their countries the way the Afrikaner has developed his own. They could make the ports and railroads and telephones of Africa work again. The resultant economic stimulation to the continent would be nothing short of revolutionary. The Russians would have to pack their bags and go home, for without poverty, instability and discontent they have little hope of gaining the foothold they seek in southern Africa.

And what of the comfortable life style the white man in South Africa cherishes so dearly? It probably would not change much if the transition occurred before, as Alan Paton wrote, the blacks "are turned to hating." The Afrikaner would still control the commercial and professional world. He would still belong to the same country club (with, to be sure, a few black members). He would still live in a comfortable suburban home and have a domestic staff. He would learn, as others in Kenya and Zimbabwe already have, that there is no reason why blacks and whites cannot work together to build a nation and a continent, especially when both races are African.

On a map, Zimbabwe looks like a big rock balancing on the toe of South Africa. The illusion is a symbolic one, because in 1980 Zimbabwe began an experiment in black-white peacemaking that, in its infancy at least, showed promise of offering the South Africans an enlightened alternative to apartheid.

But comparing South Africa with Zimbabwe—formerly the outlaw state of Rhodesia—has some limitations, for the whites in the two countries are of different character. The Afrikaner tends to be humorless, stern and pious. He would not, I suspect, look misdressed in a Nazi storm-trooper uniform. The white Zimbabweans, on the other hand, have the earthy manner and breezy informality of Australians. They have a pioneer spirit and a colonial temperament. Laughter comes easily to them, and they rather enjoy a Saturday night "punch-up" at the local pub. They wear shorts with knee socks in the countryside, and their faces are as lined and browned as the basin of a dry riverbed. Unlike the Afrikaner, they never severed their sentimental or family ties to Europe. They had a place to go—if they wanted one—when their white homeland collapsed and, slipped across the border to Botswana one night, making his way outnumbered by blacks 28–1, they had the sense to realize that their only hope for survival lay in integration.

I first arrived in Rhodesia (as it was then called) on Pioneers Day in 1978, a national holiday that celebrated the hoisting of the Union Jack over Salisbury eighty-eight years earlier. At that time the flag was raised by 180 pioneers who had traveled in ox carts from South Africa, moving through country unknown except to a handful of traders and missionaries. Most were "British" South Africans, not "Dutch" South Africans, and they came, like frontiersmen settling the Old West, in search of land and a better life. Their trek, led by Frederick Selous and organized by Cecil Rhodes, a Briton who had made a fortune in South African gold and diamonds, was made under the auspices of the British South Africa Company.

Now the whites, including six surviving daughters of the founding pioneers, gathered in Cecil Square on that September morning in 1978. The women wore broad-brimmed hats, spring dresses and white gloves. In the parks of Salisbury there was a profusion of purple jacaranda in bloom, and the broad boulevards—designed by Rhodes to be wide enough for an eight-team ox wagon to make a U-turn—ran along rows of low white shops with overhanging steel awnings that shaded the spotlessly clean sidewalks. Whereas Johannesburg is a real city, Salisbury (now called Harare in honor of a Shona Chief) is really a large country town. It feels very British, reminding me of what York would look like if it were stuck in the middle of the Montana plains. The soft spring sun beat down on the whites in Cecil Square and on a small group of blacks, watching impassively from across the street. There was a roll of drums and a bugle call as the great-grandson of a founding pioneer raised the Union Jack—a ceremony that would be repeated in 1979 but never again. White heads bowed. The words were brave, even defiant, but everyone knew the end was near. The whites had overcome great odds and built an amazing country. Now the lessons of Africa had caught up with them, and Rhodesia, racked by a liberation war that would claim 27,000 lives between 1972 and 1979, was in the throes of transition.

"Our hearts are heavy," said the Reverend C. W. A. Blakeley, "for there is sadness and pain and fear and war in our land, and a terrible desire for destruction has been thrust upon us. God, give us all the courage to be part of the solution to our problems and not part of the problem itself."

Prime Minister Ian Smith—accused by the liberal whites of attempting to maintain white supremacy and by the conservatives of trying to turn Rhodesia over to "Marxist thugs"—moved among the descendants of the pioneers. "How nice to have you here, to see you looking so well," he said, and ninety-eight-year-old Maria Mooman smiled back and patted his hand. Then Smith, a farmer-turned-politician, walked to his limousine, one hand clutching his hat, the other on the shoulder of his wife, Janet, and sped away without looking back.

Rhodesia had done well under the early settler farmers; there was at the time only one country in sub-Sahara Africa more prosperous than Rhodesia—South Africa. In 1923, when the charter of the British South Africa Company was abrogated, the whites in Rhodesia were given the choice of being incorporated into the Union of South Africa or becoming a self-governing entity within the British Empire. They chose the latter. The whites never institutionalized racism the way the South Africans did, but the blacks in Rhodesia didn't fare much better than their counterparts in the country next door. The best farmland was reserved for whites. All the top jobs and every seat in parliament were held by whites. The whites' per capita income in 1975 was $7,800, the blacks' was $716. The whites' literacy rate was 100 percent, the blacks' 30 percent.

"These Africans in Salisbury don't have anything to do with the terrorists in the rest of the country," a white housewife told me. "To my mind, they're terribly lazy and inefficient—much too inefficient to be terrorists—and sometimes difficult to handle, but they're good people. They're part of our family, even when they're working as servants. We tend to their aches and pains and we treat them like we do our own children."

After World War II, thousands of immigrants from England moved to Rhodesia, attracted by one of the world's most pleasant life styles, and in 1963 Rhodesia began negotiating with London for its independence. In 1964 the United Kingdom granted independence to Northern Rhodesia (now Zambia) and Nyasaland (Malawi) but demanded that the whites in Southern Rhodesia first demonstrate their intention to move toward eventual majority rule. They refused, and on November 11, 1965, Ian Smith and his Rhodesian Front Party unilaterally declared independence. In March 1970 Smith proclaimed a State of Rhodesia.

The world responded by isolating Rhodesia with political and trade boycotts. But Rhodesia, with the help of South Africa and some Western oil companies willing to ignore sanctions, continued to prosper. Its 6,000 white farmers—who produced 80 percent of the country's food—were as industrious and ingenious as any in America's Corn Belt. They fed the California-sized country and had plenty of food left over to export. Agriculture became a $500 million industry as the farmers moved away from their one-crop economy (tobacco) and diversified. By the late 1970s Rhodesia ranked first in the world in per-hectare yield of groundnuts, second in maize and soybeans, and fourth in wheat. Denied legal trade with the developed world, Rhodesia started making its own wine (not bad) and whiskey (terrible, but the Rhodesians drank it with pride) and producing everything from air conditioners to radios. Despite the international sanctions, a young married couple setting up a home could meet 85 percent of its needs with Rhodesian-made products. (There was even a locally produced version of Monopoly, but since that name was patented, the Rhodesians called their game Around The Boardwalk.) The Rhodesian economy was further buoyed by important supplies of chrome, coal, copper and nickel.

Nevertheless, Rhodesia reverted to the status of a British colony in 1979 and became the independent, black-ruled nation of Zimbabwe in April 1980. What forced the whites to reluctantly surrender power was not sanctions but a guerrilla war that ended up costing the country thirty lives and $1.5 million—or 40 percent of the national budget—each day. The black nationalist forces of the Patriotic Front just wore the country down, economically and spiritually. One faction of the front was headquartered in Zambia, armed by the Soviet Union and led by Joshua Nkomo, a 300-pound former railway worker whose high living raised some eyebrows; the other was in Mozambique, equipped to a large extent by China and led by Robert Mugabe, a Marxist who once said, "Genuine independence can only come out of the barrel of a gun."

Mugabe, a disciplined scholar and nonpracticing Catholic, spent ten years in detention or under restriction until 1974 in Rhodesia, and the whites' greatest fear was that he would persecute his former tormentors, turn Zimbabwe into a Communist state aligned with Moscow and preside over the disintegration of another African economy. None of those things have happened, and Mugabe has shown far more respect for the due process of law than Ian Smith ever did. As the elected prime minister, Mugabe deftly juggled black hopes and white fears, and in the process proved himself to be perhaps the most capable leader in black Africa. His brand of Marxism thus far has been no more radical than social democracy in Europe and appears no more revolutionary than the demand that the exploitation of blacks must end. He has taken a page from Jomo Kenyatta's scenario in Kenya and attempted to accommodate the whites, knowing that their presence is essential if Zimbabwe is to prosper. He has remained aloof from the Soviet Union, not even allowing Moscow to set up an embassy in Salisbury until more than a year after independence. In short, this former teacher whom the West called a Marxist terrorist is no more than a socialist and nationalist trying to serve the entire country on a basis of equality.

One of his early moves, after relegating Nkomo to a minor cabinet post, was to convene a conference of thirty-six nations in Zimbabwe to raise money. The scene was similar to a TV telethon in the United States in which viewers make pledges to combat various diseases or to finance political parties. But this one was a bonanza and Mugabe netted $1.4 billion for Zimbabwe. The United States, recognizing that a successful multiracial Zimbabwe could influence the future of South Africa and diminish Soviet pressure in all of southern Africa, pledged $225 million over three years. Even the impoverished West African nation of Sierra Leone kicked in $90,-000. No Communist countries were invited, although a Soviet delegation flew into Salisbury and cooled its heels for two days at a local hotel, waiting for an invitation that never came.

The creation of Zimbabwe was in itself a rare achievement and the government's accomplishments have not been insignificant. It has paid fair-market prices to whites who sold their farms and left the country, unable to tolerate a place where black cabinet ministers called each other "comrade." Majority rule has seen the school enrollment more than double, from 800,000 to 1,760,000, and the reopening of 2,000 schools closed by the war. The minimum wage has risen 50 percent, and health care is now free for anyone earning less than $235 a month, which covers the majority of the 6.8 million blacks. The government has subsidized food prices by $385 million to make staples cheaper for the poor. Black employment has increased by 100,000.

Under the constitution, whites are guaranteed twenty of the hundred seats in parliament until 1987. No other African colony has entered independence with similar assurances for the minority race. About half of the original 270,000 whites chose to stay in Zimbabwe, but by the summer of 1983 events had taken a decided turn for the worse in Africa's youngest country, and Mugabe's dream for a prosperous, multi-racial society had been derailed by tribalism and was in jeopardy.

Joshua Nkomo, the father of independence who had been cheered by thousands when he made a triumphal return to Rhodesia in January, 1980, had been thrown out of the cabinet and had slipped across the border to Botswana one night, making his way back to London—and another home in exile.* What he left behind was an army from the Ndebele-speaking minority, which represents 17 percent of Zimbabwe's people.

Nkomo had fallen from favor after arms caches were discovered in his tribal district of Matabeleland, where there had been much banditry and terrorism, including the killing of white farmers. Mugabe dispatched the government's North-Korean-trained elite unit, known as the Fifth Brigade, there with vague instructions to restore order and apprehend deserters who had fought in Nkomo's liberation army. The Fifth Brigade undertook its assignment with enthusiasm, killing several hundred unarmed civilians in a matter of weeks.

The fragile fiber of society seemed to be unraveling around Mugabe, a member of the Shona-speaking majority that comprises about 80 percent of all Zimbabweans. The economy had been scorched by drought and the world recession, and the departure of whites had reduced productivity. South Africa appeared intent on doing what it could to ensure that there would be no black success stories in next-door Zimbabwe. Mugabe, however, did not overreact as most African presidents do in time of crisis and personal challenge. He continued to preach that blacks and whites, if they worked together, could still create the Zimbabwe that was promised during the war of liberation.

Zimbabwe's future is far from settled, but a nation of great economic potential has emerged from the ashes of war and racial inequality—a feat that seemed impossible just a few years ago. I would like to think that South Africans will learn from the lessons of what Mugabe has tried to do in Zimbabwe—and what other leaders have done in Kenya, the Ivory Coast and a handful of former colonies. The Afrikaner has only to look across his borders to see the advance of history's tide. The black nationalism that led to the birth of Ghana in 1957 and the death of Rhodesia in 1980—and in between the freeing of an entire continent—is now at South Africa's doorstep. There is no buffer zone left. The Afrikaner stands alone, and in

*Nkomo returned to Zimbabwe after 160 days in exile when Mugabe assured him that his life would not be in danger.

doing so, he has made his country a destabilizing, isolated force on a continent that South Africa ought to dominate politically and economically.

But however shameful his system is, one cannot ignore the fact that the Afrikaner has built the most remarkable country in Africa. "Everyone knows that if you took away apartheid, South Africa would be the best place around," a black Kenyan friend told me. I suspect most Africans would agree, and perhaps it is time for other African governments to take a fresh look at their southern neighbor. They already know what South Africa has done wrong. Now they ought to start considering what it has done right. The farms, industries and mines that produce so bountifully, the cities that function so smoothly and efficiently, the government officials who work without the incentive of bribes and thievery—these are achievements that should be examined, not dismissed out of hand. If the Organization of African Unity spent as much time studying South Africa's agricultural sector as it did drafting resolutions to condemn apartheid, the fifty member states might eventually grow strong enough to pressure Pretoria into changing its internal policies.

In 1978 a poll taken at the University of Stellenbosch showed that 54 percent of the students "would die if necessary" to uphold white rule. They may have that chance unless meaningful reform starts dismantling the structures of apartheid. But the Afrikaner is not going to change voluntarily for the sake of being a humanitarian. Black urban terrorism will probably come first. The whites will respond with increased repression. Blood will be shed. The whites of English origin will start leaving South Africa (as, in fact, they already are in small numbers). The blacks' strength will grow, and so will their population, to a projected 35 million by the year 2000.

It is not a cheery scenario, and the sane world should pray that the inevitable violence can be kept limited and controlled until the South African whites come to understand—as did the Rhodesians—the futility of fighting. Given a choice between relenting or perishing, the white man in Africa has always relented. The Afrikaner is now confronted with that same choice. He must soon make his decision because for South Africa, time is running out.

SUMMING UP
AND LOOKING AHEAD

▲

The inherent vice of capitalism is the unequal sharing
of blessings; the inherent virtue of socialism is the
equal sharing of miseries.

—WINSTON CHURCHILL

WE LEFT AFRICA on a midnight flight to Rome, not quite believing
that four years could have passed so quickly. I do not like goodbyes,
thinking that partings are only temporary when you leave people
and places you care about, so Sandy and I slipped out of Nairobi
rather quietly, without farewell parties or airport send-offs. The
packers had cleared out our home on Riverside Drive, and I stood
briefly in the living room, near the empty bookcases by the fireplace,
remembering all the friends who had gathered there, hearing the
voices that at some point each evening always seemed to turn to a
discussion of Africa, about how it was doing and where it was going.
It was, we had found, impossible to live in Africa and consider it as
just a place to work. Africa had become an obsession, a state of
mind. You can love it or hate it but you cannot be indifferent to it.

Lloyd's of London had, at my request, insured the huge carton of
research material I had collected in my travels through Africa for
$20,000. It was, of course, unlikely that anyone would want to steal
a cardboard box full of notebooks and maps and articles and photographs, but I did not rest easy until I saw the container being un-
loaded in Los Angeles. The other day I dug out the first notes I had
taken in Africa. They were of Kenya's president, Jomo Kenyatta, addressing a crowd on Kenyatta Day, a holiday that marked his imprisonment in 1952 by British colonial authorities. I had jotted down:
"Crowd silent, mesmerized . . . JK in leather jacket . . . fly whisk in
right hand . . . penetrating eyes, powerful voice . . . great presence,
sort of magical." And I noted him saying, " 'Throughout history

there has been no stronger weapon to fight for the equality of human rights than unity.' "

Kenyatta is dead now, as are most of the other men who led Africa out of colonialism and into independence, representing what surely was one of man's greatest triumphs over human injustice. But the unity of which Kenyatta spoke remains an elusive dream on a wounded continent, and the equality of human rights has proved easy to preach and difficult to practice. So much remains to be done. Three decades ago, when Kenyatta was in prison as the alleged Mau Mau leader and the colonial empires were first showing signs of cracking, John Gunther wrote in *Inside Africa:* "The two things Africa needs most are development and education." The same is still distressingly true today. Coming back to the United States, back to the affluence and abundance that Americans accept so unquestioningly, one is overwhelmed by the widening chasm that separates the industrialized nations of the First World and the hoe-farming nations of the Third World. Here in the United States I have become more convinced than ever that the West must close this gap, that the one global competition that really matters is the race to develop all men's abilities. To ignore black African countries, instead of aiding them, is to let them slide into the Soviet camp. To be oblivious to the problems of Africa is to promote more international misery, hunger, instability—and to increase the threats to peace in the world.

I have written at length during this long journey about the obstacles Africa must overcome if it is to develop and realize its almost unlimited potential: an out-of-control birth rate, declining food production and primitive health conditions; inadequate leadership whose prime concern is the perpetuation of its own power; a rural exodus that strains urban social services to the point of collapse, and sometimes beyond; an untrained, unskilled population and a lack of opportunities for the educated; political instability, official corruption and an unequal distribution of national wealth, jobs and authority, all of which take root in tribalism.

Some countries, notably Kenya and the Ivory Coast, have been able to cope with these problems and have at the same time provided their people with political stability and growing economies. It is no coincidence that both nations had strong central leadership in Kenyatta and Félix Houphouët-Boigny, both relied heavily on expatriate assistance and both adopted a free-enterprise system. They are among the few luminaries on a continent that will, as the World Bank has noted, require a great deal of effort "simply to stand still" in the 1980s.

One reason that so many countries—and again, Kenya and the Ivory Coast are exceptions—have been unable to meet the economic challenge of nationhood is that there are no incentives for the individual to produce. Trying to separate themselves from everything left behind by the European colonialists, government after government embraced socialism, and sometimes Marxism, believing that people were willing to work for the community rather than for themselves. Economies were nationalized and individual incentives were eliminated.

Tanzania's president, Julius Nyerere, once put it this way: If underdeveloped countries "do not choose socialism, they will continue in a state of weakness, they will be maltreated, oppressed, exploited. We are fighting against capitalism."

Though he still clings to his doctrine, Nyerere's experiment has been one of the great failures in independent Africa, and one that should be a lesson for other countries. Half the 330 companies he nationalized went bankrupt within a decade. Worker productivity, the Tanzania Investment Board admitted, dropped by 50 percent between 1969 and 1979. The government's bureaucracy grew at the rate of 14 percent a year, and government expenditures increased twice as fast as the gross national product. What Nyerere overlooked was that people in Africa do not have to work to feed themselves, and in that setting socialism is a bad alternative. The rich soil and tropical climate provide ample food for subsistence. Take away the monetary rewards for increased production and people are perfectly content to live as they always have, growing just enough food for themselves and their families.

Each of the United States' 5.5 million farm workers produce enough food and fiber to care for 68 people (compared to 45 people a decade ago), according to the U.S. Department of Agriculture. Africa has an estimated 200 million farmers, and they produce, in the best of times, barely enough to fill their own stomachs. I am not suggesting that Africa rush out and abandon socialism in favor of American-style capitalism. But I do think that Africa must improve its economic health before it can restructure its political and social systems, and a first step in this direction would be the creation of mixed economies that offer inducements for working harder and producing more.

The West needs to play a major role in altering the self-destructive course on which Africa seems headed. And not just for humanitarian reasons. Africa's mineral wealth, its agricultural potential and strategic location thrust the continent into the likely position of influencing the events of tomorrow. For self-serving reasons alone, it is to the West's advantage to share its knowledge and monetary resources with the poorest of the poor in order that Africa can become a contributor to, rather than a drain on, the global community.

Western aid should focus on vocational training in the cities—Africa needs mechanics and medical technicians at this point, not architects and open-heart surgeons—and on rural development. It is nothing less than a crime for the West and East to "assist" Africa by building airports and donating weapons when 30 percent of the food grown on the continent is lost because of faulty storage facilities and inadequate transportation systems. Granted, most of the aid that pours into Africa today is wasted or stolen and accomplishes little other than massaging the consciences of the donors. The United States, for instance, spent $4.6 million for a cereal-production project in Senegal that did not increase grain output by a single bag. It spent another $13 million on a livestock scheme in Mali and later admitted that nothing whatsoever had been achieved. Somalia once refused to accept a $12 million crane from West Germany until the donors paid the importation customs duties. "But this is a *gift*," said Bonn's representative. "That has nothing to do with it; you haven't paid the duty," replied the Somali. West Germany paid up. I could cite dozens of similar examples, but nevertheless, the concept of international aid remains a good one. Aid is both worthwhile and essential for Africa's development. Its failure is that the money is often dispensed and used in the most senseless manner.

In looking at all the troubles that have haunted Africa over two decades of independence, one tends to forget how young Africa is as a group of nations. Probably the world expected too much too quickly. We got swept up in Africa's early enthusiasm and rhetoric. "Be like us and you will succeed as we have," the West told Africa, ignoring the fact that Africa did not want to be like us. And when we criticized Africa for stumbling we never mentioned that the United States in, say, 1796 was a country where corruption was rampant, political unity and national prosperity were distant goals and a civil war lay half a century down the road.

For now, the key to the continent's future is South Africa. There can be no lasting solution for Africa as a whole until a multiracial society in South Africa has been created. If South Africa had normal relations with its neighbors, and if those neighbors could draw freely upon South Africa's surplus food, industry, expertise and efficiency, the economic character of all southern Africa would be dramatically altered. Then everything else would follow, for economic self-reliance is the forerunner of political stability, the birth of a middle class, improved health conditions and a controlled birth rate.

When white rule ends in South Africa—it will; the only question is how violent the ending will be—there seems to be no earthly reason why black Africa cannnot come to grips with its problems. Tribalism will become less important as Africa becomes more urbanized. The leadership will become more competent as an increasing number of young, educated Africans demand a share of authority in setting national destinies. The thin elite class that has established itself largely through corruption and nepotism will give way to a growing middle class that is legitimately founded on individual merit, education and honestly earned money. A new nationalism may even evolve, one that is based not on the flush of victory over colonialism but on the pride of national achievement.

As our Kenya Airways Boeing 707 lifted off from Jomo Kenyatta International Airport (recently built for $60 million by West Germany), heading through the darkened skies past Mount Kenya and over the Kenyan Highlands, where whites and blacks who had fought one another in the Mau Mau war now farmed side by side, I thought about how many times in so many countries I had heard Africans say to me, "Give us time. We are young."

It seemed a reasonable request.

EPILOGUE:
AFRICA RECONSIDERED

▲

What has happened to Africa in the past two decades can be compared to the effects of a world war. Its crisis is different from anything else found anywhere in the world: No other continent is suffering such acute famine and environmental loss, and nowhere else do institutions and skills lag so far behind the problems. No other region of the developing world finds itself in such a steep and steady decline as Africa.

—COMMITTEE ON AFRICAN DEVELOPMENT
STRATEGIES, *a group of
forty Americans who met in 1985 to assess
Africa's future*

LATE IN 1984 my editors in Los Angeles asked me to return to Ethiopia to cover the famine that was carving a swath of death across Africa. *The Africans* had been banned in Ethiopia—and denounced as a "Communist book" in the parliament of neighboring Kenya—and I doubted whether government authorities in Addis Ababa would grant me a visa. They dawdled over my request for a month, finally granting me entry only after my friend Mohammed Amin, a noted African filmmaker, told the man in charge of issuing visas, "Come on. Let him in. You know what he wrote is true. The disaster is all around you."

I flew from Cairo to Addis Ababa. Nothing seemed to have changed in the five years I had been gone, except that the Ethiopian capital looked shabbier. I checked into the Hilton Hotel, which had been virtually empty on my last visit. Now it teemed with relief workers from around the globe. Among them was a sprinkling of American movie stars, politicians, coiffured television notables and college-age disaster junkies. The famine that threatened the lives of 7 million Ethiopians had become a celebrity event, and Ethiopia had caught the fancy and stirred the guilt of the outside world, as African emergencies always do briefly before compassion burnout sets in. On the elevator going up to my room, I met a gaunt gentleman some journalists still identified as a comedian. He was the social activist Dick Gregory, and he said he was going on another fast to call attention to the famine. He had fasted so often during the last twenty years that I couldn't figure out how he had managed to stay alive.

The head of the Ethiopian relief effort, Dawit Wolde Giogis, was an articulate soldier-spokesman for the Marxist government, who railed against the West in his speeches—and who would flee Ethiopia the next year and take up residency in the United States. He wasn't in his office when I called, so I made an appointment to see his assistant. He and I chatted amiably for a while, then he reached into the bottom drawer of his desk, took out a copy of *The Africans* and asked me to sign it. "I shouldn't have this, you know," he said, "but I think it's pretty good. We need to be reminded just how bad things have gotten and why . . . even though it hurts when a non-African says it."

Indeed, I am not sure I initially fathomed just how ominous and imminent was the specter of disaster that hovered over the continent. By any yardstick, the forces of man and nature buffeting Africa have extracted a toll in suffering more severe than I had dared imagine. Millions of people have been relegated to surviving at the mercy of pop charity events and international donors. Sub-Sahara Africa's indebtedness has grown to $130 billion, representing more than 200 percent of its total exports. AIDS, an unknown disease when I left Kenya in 1980, has struck 50,000 Africans, and the World Health Organization estimates that as many as 2 million other Africans may be symptomless carriers of the virus. Malnutrition and hunger is killing 5 million children a year and permanently crippling another 5 million. Sixty percent of all Africans, according to the World Bank, are consuming fewer calories each day than thought to be necessary for a fairly normal life. The continent's population continues its unimpeded rise toward the frightening figure of 1.6 billion by the year 2025. Of the forty-six countries south of the Sahara, only giant Nigeria has a gross domestic product larger than that of the city of Hong Kong. As Tanzania's former President, Julius Nyerere, put it after touring his country's state-controlled sisal industry, "If I called back the British today to look at their former estates, I am sure they would laugh at us because we have ruined their estates."

Many of the changes in Africa since *The Africans* was first published have been cosmetic. Upper Volta changed its name to Burkina Faso. Nyerere retired as president but maintained ultimate control by retaining his leadership position in the sole political party, and thus still presided over a country that had become one of Africa's most unfortunate shambles. President Samuel Doe of Liberia learned to appreciate the perks of office and started driving around dirt-poor Monrovia in a $134,000 silver Mercedes-Benz limousine while espousing fiscal responsibility for all others. And exiled Idi Amin, whom I reached on the phone one day at his home in Saudi Arabia, told me, "What Uganda needs is democracy. Of course, I can see that democracy would not work immediately in Uganda. Security is very bad there now, and there are many problems. Democracy takes discipline. But a tough person with military knowledge like me could teach the people discipline and prepare them for democracy."

Other more substantive changes caught me by surprise. Sudanese President Jaafar Numeiri, whom I had respected as a statesman of real stature, surrounded himself with mystics, became a fundamentalist Moslem, seemed to go daffy, let the country slip back into civil war and was overthrown. President Sekou Toure of Guinea died, and within days his people destroyed every statue and every memory of that tough socialist who had been at the forefront of Africa's independence movement. The experiment with democracy and civilian government in Nigeria ended abruptly with two military coups d'état. Mozambique signed a treaty of nonaggression and good neighborliness with South Africa. Libyan troops invaded Chad and were driven back by the French.

It was the famine, though, more than any single event, that symbolized Africa's "Decade of Decline." It spoke of an unbearable future and of the need to alter course dramatically. And it left me with an indelible portrait of suffering when I awoke in a tent one December morning in Alamata, 375 miles north of Addis Ababa, and knew I was part of a nightmare. I listened and I shuddered. In the last moments of that chilly, windy night, when all the valley was as still as death and the foreboding darkness seemed eternal, the wailing began, softly at first, like the distant chant of ghosts. It was a high-pitched, eerie howl that sliced through the night, gathering strength until it lingered and echoed over the mile-high valley—thousands of voices united in prayerful pleas for mercy and forgiveness, voices that mourned the dead and begged the privilege of living another wretched day.

When the half-light of dawn reached over the stone-faced mountains that surrounded the valley, the wailing passed, giving way to the husky coughs of children. As far as I could see stretched a scene resembling a medieval battlefield—legions of peasants, barefooted and rag-wrapped, a vast civilian army conquered by famine awaiting its daily ration of porridge.

The word had spread quickly. There was food in this feeding center run by World Vision International, a Christian humanitarian organization. There were doctors. Sometimes there were blankets. The people had come, first by the hundreds, then by the thousands, from their mud homes deep in the mountains, crossing parched earth that once bore bountiful harvests of grain, trudging past corpses and carcasses, and finally, after many days, settling on this hillside where the morning dew was heavy with the smell of sickness. "Their suffering brings out a certain grace in them," said Sister Bertilla, of Mother Teresa's Missionaries of Charity, as she stirred a huge cauldron of porridge."They do not complain. They do not ask why. They do not try to take more food than they are entitled to. These are beautiful people."

About 200,000 Ethiopians had died of hunger by the time I reached Alamata. I walked over to a wooden medical shack where 800 or so people squatted and sprawled in an orderly, patient line, knowing that a Western doctor would soon appear. A frail old man, carrying his wife on his back, moved unsteadily toward the group. His legs wobbled and gave out twenty yards short and they both tumbled to the ground, remaining there for several seconds until he, summoning all his strength, began crawling. He pulled his wife behind him.

The political irony of Ethiopia's disaster was that Haile Selassie had been deposed in 1974, at the age of eighty-one, after trying to cover up a famine that had swept through his ancient land. Now the uncompromising Marxist soldiers who had overthrown him were faced with a similar dilemma, and they, too, were culpable. They had tried for months to hide the famine from the world while the death toll mounted. They devoted 45 percent of their national budget to defense and security, and they had spent millions of birrs staging an extravaganza to celebrate the "accomplishments" of their ten years in power. What's more, they had long since severed their links to the industrialized West that had the resources to help and had tied their fortunes to the Soviet Union, which had little to offer except guns and ideology. They had abrogated the first obligation of any government—the responsibility of feeding its people.

Despite Addis Ababa's infatuation with Marxism, the West mounted a $3 billion rescue package for Ethiopia and Africa's other drought-ravaged countries. Moscow managed to send not much more than a couple of planeloads of rice. The relief effort averted what could have been the worst peacetime disaster of modern times, but no sooner had the rains returned and renewed crops begun to grow than a plague of billions of locusts—described as potentially the most serious infestation in half a century—cut through Africa from Ethiopia to Senegal, devastating the harvest. Relief specialists estimated that it would take three years to eradicate the ravenous locust swarms, which were so thick they turned the daytime skies black. Each of these swarms could eat enough crops in a day to feed 50,000 people for a year.

"Sometimes I think we are cursed," an African doctor told me, and there were moments when I thought the same thing. But I think that Africa's "Great Famine" of the 1980s may be a watershed, the event that future African generations will look back to as the turning point. It jolted Africa into a new realism, and the world into an awareness that we cannot pay attention to Africa only in times of catastrophe. For the first time, really, African leaders met to examine—and admit—the failure of Africa and the bankruptcy of some of their policies. What they addressed were the fundamental problems underlying poverty and stagnation. And that may be the most significant step toward eventual self-sufficiency that Africa has taken collectively since independence.

In Addis Ababa, Africa's heads of state summed up their shared dismay during an Organization of African Unity summit in 1985.

"We are most gravely concerned," they said, "by the continued deterioration of our economies, which have been severely affected by the deep world economic recession and penalized by an unjust and inequitable international economic system. This situation has been aggravated by unprecedented severe, persistent drought and famine and other natural calamities, such as cyclones and floods. These developments, added to some domestic political shortcomings, have brought most of our countries near to economic collapse."

In Zimbabwe, representatives from twenty-nine countries gathered to discuss ways of curtailing Africa's uncontrolled population growth. It is hard to imagine that happening a decade ago. In Tanzania, Madagascar and Somalia, government leaders accepted the failure of nationalization policies that had stifled individual incentive with artificially low price controls. Nigeria announced an austerity budget, and Ghana, still under the stern leadership of Jerry Rawlings, adopted Western-inspired economic reforms that cut inflation from 123 percent to 10 percent and helped the gross domestic product grow by 5 to 7 percent a year. The Ivory Coast and Cameroon continued to enjoy political stability and economic expansion. A soldier by the name of Yoweri Museveni took over in Uganda, and Ugandans were amazed that his disciplined young troops did not rape, loot and go on drunken rampages. For the first time in a decade, a measure of stability returned to that ravaged nation.

These were good omens. And there were others. Across the continent a consensus was evolving that the private sector had to play a major role in economic recovery, that prosperity had to rest on the pillars of agriculture, that Marxism and heavy-handed socialistic policies had led to social and economic retardation.

Zimbabwe offered particularly illuminating evidence that Africa does not have to fail simply because it is Africa. Prime Minister Robert Mugabe, perhaps the most competent leader in sub-Sahara Africa, had turned Zimbabwe into a one-party, multiracial, socialistic state that rewarded individual incentive and respected freedom of expression. He embarked on an aggressive program to reduce the birth rate and focused not on grandiose building projects but on modest industries that would reduce the country's reliance on expensive imports. Zimbabwe had a grain surplus in 1986 (six years after the death of white-ruled Rhodesia), and 30,000 white farmers who had left Zimbabwe around the time of independence had returned to work the land and to make it as productive as any in black Africa.

One great change still awaits the continent—the end of apartheid in South Africa. The mechanism to bring about that end—international pressure, increasing black violence, a declining economy that has forced some white moderates to reconsider national policies—is now in place, and it saddens me that the end of white rule may come with the United States being on the wrong side. The Reagan Administration still clings to some peculiar, unspoken moral commitment to the white minority, ignoring the inevitable and seemingly unaware of the need to initiate "constructive dialogue" with tomorrow's leaders in the black majority. Confusing nationalism with radicalism, we have lost opportunities to earn understanding from the African National Congress, and I can only wonder how much our ignorance must delight Moscow.

Since *The Africans* was first published, 2,000 people, mostly black, have died violently in South Africa, and that total surely represents only a hint of the bloody horrors that could loom ahead. The white government in Pretoria has made some superficial changes to quiet the outcries against apartheid, abolishing, for instance, the pass laws and the laws against marriage between whites and nonwhites. But it remains committed to keeping the system intact, and the repression it uses to enforce the country's state of emergency is reminiscent of the most repugnant behavior exhibited by former black African regimes the West used to denounce as barbaric.

Many Afrikaners believe the West will not abandon them because we need their gold and platinum, their guardianship of the sea lanes around the Cape of Good Hope, their strategic presence as a bastion of anti-Communism. Granted, all those things are important. But they are no more important in the hands of whites than they will be in the hands of blacks. Already, fifty-five American companies have pulled out of South Africa and others will follow. White South African professionals are leaving their country in substantial numbers for Australia, Great Britain and the United States—at last count the Australian Embassy in Pretoria was processing 15,000 applications to immigrate—and with each passing day, with each new demand for racial reform, the South African *laager* is drawn tighter. "We are not jellyfish," President P. W. Botha reminds his critics.

Botha, though, is a captive of both extremes. He risks a racial civil war if he does not dismantle apartheid, and he risks a *white* civil war, launched by militant blue-collar Afrikaners, if he pushes for one-man, one-vote. One can only hope that an increasing number of white moderates continue to become involved outside the parliamentary system, as they have recently in such groups as Let South Africa Speak, Women for Peace and Jews for Justice. As I wrote earlier, it seems inconceivable that the white South African hasn't learned something from the lessons of African history. If the whites and nonwhites in South Africa can form a partnership before it is too late, there is every reason to believe the republic can escape many of the pitfalls that have befallen other countries on the continent.

Just as economic necessity has forced black African governments to start charting new courses, so must South Africa seek meaningful change if it is to survive as a republic. In both cases, the West can and should provide the needed technical, financial and moral support, but the impetus for change and the implementation of new policies can only come from Africa itself.

Africa still needs time, for the continent remains young in terms of independence. But the era is now past when Africa can blame all its problems on injustices rooted in history. Too much needs to be done. Africa must start looking forward—as I believe it has begun to do—and, with the help of the United States and Europe, undertake a rehabilitation program of post-wartime magnitude. The Africans really have no choice, because there is no alternative. The world needs a stable, self-sufficient Africa governed by the majority. And the Africans themselves surely need to be given hope that the worst is now behind them.

A Statistical Profile

Country	Capital	Last Colonial Power	Independence	Population (in millions)	Annual Per Capita Income	$$$ Earner	People per Sq Mile
Algeria	Algiers	France	1962	18.0	$1,260	oil	20
Angola	Luanda	Portugal	1975	7.0	300	oil	14
Benin	Cotonou	France	1960	3.3	230	cotton	78
Botswana	Gaborone	Britain	1966	0.75	620	diamonds	3
Burkina Faso	Ouagadougou	France	1960	5.5	160	exported labor	62
Burundi	Bujumbura	Belgium	1962	4.3	140	coffee	372
Cameroon	Yaoundé	France, Britain	1960	8.0	460	cocoa	44
Cape Verde	Praia	Portugal	1975	0.35	160	sugar cane	199
Central African Republic	Bangui	France	1960	2.0	250	diamonds	11
Chad	N'Djamena	France	1960	4.3	140	livestock	9
Comoros	Moroni	France	1975	0.4	180	copra	577
Congo	Brazzaville	France	1960	1.5	780	oil	11
Djibouti	Djibouti	France	1977	0.32	450	foreign aid	12
Egypt	Cairo	Britain	1922	40.0	400	cotton	109
Equatorial Guinea	Malabo	Spain	1968	0.35	100	cocoa	32
Ethiopia	Addis Ababa	—	—	31.0	120	coffee	65
Gabon	Libreville	France	1960	0.6	3,600	oil	5
Gambia, The	Banjul	Britain	1965	0.6	230	groundnuts	142
Ghana	Accra	Britain	1957	11.0	400	cocoa	119
Guinea	Conakry	France	1958	5.2	210	bauxite	50
Guinea-Bissau	Bissau	Portugal	1974	0.8	200	groundnuts	39
Ivory Coast	Abidjan	France	1960	8.0	1,000	cocoa	61
Kenya	Nairobi	Britain	1963	16.0	320	coffee	66
Lesotho	Maseru	Britain	1966	1.3	280	exported labor	109
Liberia	Monrovia	—	1847	1.8	460	rubber	40
Libya	Tripoli	Italy	1951	2.8	7,000	oil	4
Madagascar	Tananarive	France	1960	9.0	250	coffee	37
Malawi	Lilongwe	Britain	1964	6.0	180	tobacco	124
Mali	Bamako	France	1960	6.5	120	livestock	14
Mauritania	Nouakchott	France	1960	1.6	270	livestock	4
Mauritius	Port Louis	Britain	1968	1.0	830	sugar cane	1,169
Morocco	Rabat	France	1956	19.0	670	phosphate	110
Mozambique	Maputo	Portugal	1975	10.0	140	cashew nuts	33
Namibia	Windhoek	South Africa	—	0.95	1,080	diamonds	3
Niger	Niamey	France	1960	5.0	220	groundnuts	10
Nigeria	Lagos	Britain	1960	80.0	560	oil	202
Rwanda	Kigali	Belgium	1962	4.5	180	coffee	444
São Tomé and Príncipe	São Tomé	Portugal	1975	0.09	490	cocoa	215
Senegal	Dakar	France	1960	5.4	340	peanuts	71
Seychelles	Victoria	Britain	1976	0.06	1,060	tourism	351
Sierra Leone	Freetown	Britain	1961	3.3	210	diamonds	118
Somalia	Mogadishu	Italy, Britain	1960	4.0	130	livestock	14
South Africa	Pretoria	—	1910	28.5	1,480	gold	59
Sudan	Khartoum	Britain, Egypt	1956	18.0	320	cotton	18
Swaziland	Mbabane	Britain	1968	0.55	590	sugar cane	81
Tanzania	Dar es Salaam	Britain	1961	17.0	230	coffee	46

Country	Capital	Last Colonial Power	Independence	Population (in millions)	Annual Per Capita Income	$$$ Earner	People per Sq Mile
Togo	Lomé	France	1960	2.5	320	phosphate	110
Tunisia	Tunis	France	1956	6.0	950	oil	96
Uganda	Kampala	Britain	1962	13.0	200	coffee	140
Western Sahara	El Aaíún	Spain	—	0.075	200	phosphate	0.7
Zaire	Kinshasa	Belgium	1960	26.0	210	copper	31
Zambia	Lusaka	Britain	1964	5.3	480	copper	19
Zimbabwe	Harare	Britain	1980	7.0	480	chrome	46

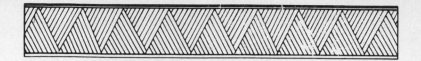

ACKNOWLEDGMENTS

▲

There is not room to thank the hundreds of people all across Africa who made this book possible by sharing their lives, confidences and knowledge with me. Many of them are mentioned in the preceding pages. I will single out only a few more here, but all have my lasting gratitude: The people who found me shelter in strange cities and towns where there was not an empty bed to be had; the teachers and doctors and government officials, the presidents and pesants wh ⸺e hospitality I shall never forget; the American and European diplomats, particularly Chris Crabbie of the British High Commission in Nairobi, who became friends and confidants; the fellow journalists with whom I shared good times and bad. To all, I say thank you.

This book reflects as much of my wife, Sandy Northrop, as it does of me, for if ever a foreign assignment was a team effort, ours was. Sandy traveled with me through more than twenty countries, and her photographs appeared in the *Los Angeles Times,* her fluency in Swahili and French saved me much stumbling, her instincts for sensing what was happening in Africa were frequently sharper than my own. She helped shape many of my newspaper articles, and her sharp eye and red pencil worked miracles on the first draft of my book. "Why not try it this way?" she would ask, and she was invariably right. But the greatest reward of all was Sandy's companionship. It was her love and spirit that got me the extra mile.

I also want to extend my deep appreciation to John D. Panitza, senior editor of *Reader's Digest* in Paris, who first suggested that I write this book; to my agent Carl D. Brandt, who offered much encouragement during the year that I spent six and seven days a week at my typewriter; to my editor at Random House, Robert Cowley, who showed me that the era of talented and caring editors did not end with Max Perkins; to Ambassador John Blane, an African expert at the U.S. State Department, who checked my manuscript for accuracy and who made suggestions that were incorporated into the text; to my editors at the *Times*, who gave me the opportunity to live in Africa, who worked with my stories while I was there and who later granted me a leave of absence to accept a Nieman Fellowship at Harvard University: William F. Thomas, the editor; George Cotliar, managing editor; Robert W. Gibson, foreign editor; Nick Williams Jr. and Robert Trounson, deputy foreign editors. Three other colleagues on the *Times* deserve special mention: Jack Foisie, the Johannesburg bureau chief, whose excellent coverage of southern Africa helped focus many of my own thoughts on key issues; Stanley Meisler, former Nairobi bureau chief, whose African reportage remains a model—ten years after he left the continent—of perceptive, sensitive writing that Africanist scholars still value; and John Anguma, who managed our Nairobi office and whose knowledge of East African politics helped me greatly.

Most books represent far more than the moment in time the author is writing about. They reflect many past experiences and people and wanderings, and this one is no exception. Four people who influenced my professional life and to whom I am indebted are: Brooks Hamilton, professor of journalism at the University of Maine, who taught me that newspapering is an honorable profession and that nothing counts more than accuracy; Jim Leavy, who gave me my first newspaper job in 1965 when I pulled into Las Vegas, 2,500 miles from home, with an ailing car, $20 in my pocket and no work; Arthur Schiff, an American living in Australia, who taught me the difference between being a domestic reporter and a foreign correspondent; Paul and Cilla Miller of Boston, who showed me the wonders of moving beyond the confines of my own small world.

During our four years in Africa I collected 3,200 pages of notes and built a reference library containing more than 5,000 newspaper and magazine articles, several hundred books and scores of periodicals. This material represents the backbone of my research. But my primary source for the book is my own eyes and ears. The observations are my own, as, I might add, are any errors that have survived the close scrutiny the manuscript has undergone.

Statistics provided by African governments are notoriously unreliable, and I have, whenever possible, used figures provided by the World Bank in Washington, D.C., the United Nations and various

Western embassies and research organizations. For general reference I used the *Encyclopaedia Britannica,* the *World Almanac & Book of Facts (1981),* and *Statesman's Year Book (1980).* The best maps I found were printed by Michelin in Paris. There are also several useful periodicals, published annually in Europe, that provide statistical data and summaries of contemporary political and economic events. They are listed in the bibliography, which is by no means complete, representing as it does only a fraction of the publications I read before writing this book. But the list does, I think, provide an enlightened perspective on where Africa has been and where it is going.

BIBLIOGRAPHY

▲

Africa Problems and Prospects: A Bibliographic Survey. U.S. Department of the Army (December 1977).

Africa South of the Sahara, 1979–80, 9th ed. London, Europa Publications, 1979.

Allen, Philip M., and Segal, Aaron, *The Traveler's Africa.* New York, Hopkinson and Blake, 1973.

Amnesty International Report 1980. London, Amnesty International Publications, 1980.

Bender, Gerald J., *Angola Under the Portuguese.* Los Angeles, University of California Press, 1978.

Bohannan, Paul, and Curtin, Philip, *Africa & Africans.* Garden City, N.Y., Natural History Press, 1971.

Cabral, Amilcar, *Revolution in Guinea: Selected Texts.* New York, Monthly Review Press, 1969.

Carter, Gwendolen M., *Which Way Is South Africa Going?* Bloomington, Indiana University Press, 1980.

Cervenka, Zdenek, *The Organization of Black Unity and Its Charter.* New York, Praeger, 1969.

Churchill, Winston, *My African Journey.* London, 1908.

——, *A Roving Commission.* New York, Scribner's, 1944.

Cloete, Stuart, *The African Giant.* Boston, Houghton Mifflin, 1955.

Conrad, Joseph, *Heart of Darkness.* New York, Bantam Books, 1969. (First published in 1902.)

Davidson, Basil, *Africa: History of a Continent.* London, Spring Books, 1966.

Death Penalty, The. London, Amnesty International Publications, 1979.

Decalo, Samuel, *Coups and Army Rule in Africa.* New Haven, Yale University Press, 1976.

Dinesen, Isak [Karen Blixen], *Out of Africa.* New York, Putnam, 1937; Random House, Modern Library, 1952.

Dinesen, Isak, *Shadows on the Grass.* New York, Random House, 1961.

Douglas-Hamilton, Iain and Oria, *Among the Elephants.* New York, Viking, 1975.

Fage, J. D., *A History of Africa.* New York, Knopf, 1978.

Gunther, John, *Inside Africa.* New York, Harper & Brothers, 1953.

Harris, Joseph E., *Africans and Their History.* New York, New American Library, 1972.

Haynes, George, E., *Africa: Continent of the Future.* New York, The Association Press, 1950.

Hemingway, Ernest, *Green Hills of Africa.* New York, Scribner's, 1935.

Henderson, Ian, with Goodhart, Philip, *Man Hunt in Kenya.* New York, Doubleday, 1958.

Huxley, Elspeth, *Four Guineas: A Journey Through West Africa.* London, Chatto & Windus, 1954.

Karimi, Joseph, and Ochieng, Philip, *The Kenyatta Succession.* Nairobi, Transafrica Books, 1980.

Kenyatta, Jomo, *Facing Mount Kenya.* London, Secker & Warburg, 1938; New York, Vintage, 1962.

————, *Harambee!* Nairobi, Oxford University Press, 1964.

Leakey, L. S. B., *Mau Mau and Kikuyu.* London, Methuen, 1952.

————, *Animals of East Africa.* Washington, D.C., National Geographic Society, 1969.

Legum, Colin; Zartmen, William I.; Langdon, Steven; and Mytelka, Lynn K., *Africa in the 1980s: A Continent in Crisis.* 1980s Project/ Council on Foreign Relations. New York, McGraw-Hill, 1979.

Livingstone, David, *A Popular Account of Dr. Livingstone's Expedition to the Zambesi and Its Tributaries.* London, John Murray, 1875.

Magary, Alan, and Magary, Kerstin Fraser, *East Africa: A Travel Guide.* New York, Harper & Row, 1975.

Marnham, Patrick, *Fantastic Invasion: Africa in the Nineteen Eighties.* New York, Harcourt, 1980.

Mazuri, Ali A., *Africa's International Relations.* London, Heinemann Educational Books, 1977.

Mboya Tom, *Freedom and After.* Boston, Little, Brown, 1963.

Meeker, Oden, *Report on Africa.* New York, Scribner's, 1954.

Military Balance, The. 1978–79 and 1979–80 eds. London, The International Institute for Strategic Studies.

Miller, Charles, *The Lunatic Express.* New York, Macmillan, 1971.

——, *Battle for the Bundu.* New York, Macmillan, 1974.

Moorehead, Alan, *The Blue Nile.* New York, Harper & Row, 1962.

Murray-Brown, Jeremy, *Kenyatta.* New York, Dutton, 1973.

Naipaul, Shiva, *North of South.* New York, Simon & Schuster, 1979.

Naipaul, V. S., *A Bend in the River.* New York, Knopf, 1979.

New African Yearbook 1980. London, IC Magazines.

New Africans, The: Reuters Guide to the Contemporary History of Emergent Africa and Its Leaders. London, Paul Hamlyn, 1967.

Nkrumah, Kwame, *Consciencism.* New York, Monthly Review Press, 1970.

Nyerere, Julius, *Freedom and Development: A Selection from Writings and Speeches 1968–73.* New York, Oxford University Press, 1974.

Paton, Alan, *Cry, the Beloved Country.* New York, Scribner's, 1948.

——, *Too Late the Phalarope.* New York, Scribner's, 1953.

Rosenblum, Mort, *Coups & Earthquakes.* New York, Harper & Row, 1979.

Rotberg, Robert I., *Suffer the Future: Policy Choices in Southern Africa.* Cambridge, Harvard University Press, 1980.

Ruark, Robert, *Something of Value.* New York, Doubleday, 1955.

——, *Uhuru.* New York, McGraw-Hill, 1962.

Snoxall, R. A., *A Concise English-Swahili Dictionary.* New York, Oxford University Press, 1958.

South Africa: Time Running Out. The Report of the Study Commission on U.S. Policy Toward Southern Africa. Los Angeles, University of California Press, 1981.

Sub-Saharan Africa and the United States. U.S. State Department, Washington, D.C., 1980.

Traveller's Guide to Africa 1980, 3rd ed. London, IC Magazines, 1979.

Trollope, Anthony, *South Africa.* London, Chapman & Hall, 1879.

Waugh, Evelyn, *Waugh in Abyssinia.* London, Longmans Green, 1936.

Willett, Frank, *African Art.* New York, Praeger, 1971.

World Bank Annual Report. 1980 ed. Washington, D.C., World Bank.

INDEX

ABOUT THE AUTHOR

DAVID LAMB has spent eight years roaming Africa for the *Los Angeles Times*. Before that he was their Australian bureau chief and was a battlefront reporter in Vietnam for United Press International (it was Lamb who named Hamburger Hill). He has reported for the *Times* from more than a hundred countries and on all seven continents. He has been an Alicia Patterson Fellow and a Nieman Fellow at Harvard, and has been nominated six times for the Pulitzer Prize. He is at present on the *Times*' national staff, based in Los Angeles. He is also the author of *The Arabs: Journeys Beyond the Mirage.*